ALSO BY H. L. MENCKEN

A SECOND
MENCKEN
CHRESTOMATHY

H. L. Mencken

A SECOND MENCKEN CHRESTOMATHY

Selected, Revised, and Annotated by the Author
Edited and with an Introduction by Terry Teachout

1995

ALFRED A. KNOPF
New York

THIS IS A BORZOI BOOK
PUBLISHED BY ALFRED A. KNOPF, INC.

Library of Congress Cataloging-in-Publication Data
Mencken, H. L. (Henry Louis), 1880–1956.
A second Mencken chrestomathy / by H. L. Mencken; selected,
revised, and annotated by the author; edited and with an
introduction by Terry Teachout. — 1st ed.
p.   cm.
ISBN 0-679-42829-1
I. Teachout, Terry. II. Title.
PS3525.E43A6 1994
818'.5209—dc20   94-12087
                                                      CIP

Manufactured in the United States of America
First Edition

Contents

Contents

VIII. *Man and Superman*

IX. *Men and Women*

X. *Progress*

Contents

XV. *European Novelists*

XVI. *American Novelists*

XVII. *Playwrights and Poets*

XVIII. *The Critic's Trade*

XXIV. Music

XXV. The Pursuit of Happiness

XXVI. Lesser Eminentoes

XXVII. Ironies

XXVIII. *Nietzsche*

XXIX. *Credos*

XXX. *Self-Portrait*

EDITOR'S INTRODUCTION

"I HAVE discovered something," Alfred Knopf said to H. L. Mencken one day in 1920. "It is that H. L. Mencken has become a good property." Knopf was talking about the unexpected popular success of *Prejudices: First Series*, the first of six collections of Mencken's essays, articles and reviews to appear under the Borzoi imprint between 1919 and 1927. In 1919 Mencken was still known outside Baltimore—his lifelong home and base of operations— mainly as coeditor of and book reviewer for the *Smart Set*, a shabby-looking magazine of modest circulation and raffish reputation. *Prejudices: First Series* was intended to bring his writing, and his personality, to the notice of a wider audience: "I made a deliberate effort to lay as many quacks as possible, and chose my targets, not only from the great names of the past, but also from the current company of favorites." The effort, like most of Mencken's exercises in self-promotion, paid off. *Prejudices: First Series* and its successors were all reviewed widely and, to the initial surprise of author and publisher alike, even sold well. It was through these neat little crown octavo volumes as much as through the *Smart Set* (and, later, the *American Mercury*) that American readers of the '20s came to know the man whom Walter Lippmann, writing in 1926, called "the most powerful personal influence on this whole generation of educated people."

In the '30s, Mencken fell from grace with Depression-era intellectuals, who found his literary tastes bourgeois and his politics neanderthal. ("Nearly all poverty is caused by idealism. The normal poor man is simply a semi-idiot whose dreams have run away with his capacities.") *Prejudices: First Series* sold only three-hundred-odd copies between 1931, when the plates were melted down, and 1942, when the last printing was exhausted. But he became a good property again with the publication in 1940 of *Happy*

Days, his best-selling childhood memoir, and it was doubtless no coincidence that around this time he began thinking of putting together a comprehensive anthology of his own writings. As early as 1943, Mencken discussed with Knopf the possibility of bringing out "a sort of Mencken Encyclopedia, made up of extracts from my writings over many years, arranged by subject and probably with additions." According to his diary, he went to work in earnest four years later: "Unable to do any writing, I have put in my time selecting and editing material for the 'Mencken Omnibus' that Knopf proposes to get out. . . . I am not reading all my old stuff, but I am trying to look through it."

The book that emerged from this lengthy period of gestation was a kind of super-*Prejudices*, a jumbo volume containing Mencken's thoughts on everything from the music of Johann Sebastian Bach (good) to the presidency of Franklin Delano Roosevelt (bad). Like the six *Prejudices*, it was assembled with loving care:

> I have got out a lot of stuff from the first four "Prejudices" books, and some from my early "Smart Set" book reviews. . . . I have also dug out a lot from magazine and newspaper files, never before printed in books. Some of it, not read for years, strikes me as pretty fair. . . . Most of it has needed a good deal of revision. It was full of references to the affairs of the time, some of them now almost unintelligible. But after cleaning them out, I find myself with [a] good deal of printable stuff. I shall pile it up without plan, and then make my selections. . . . Mrs. Lohrfinck [Rosalind Lohrfinck, Mencken's secretary] has already copied 300,000 or 400,000 words, and I'll probably have 1,000,000 before I settle down to make my selections.

By mid-September of 1948, Mencken had blue-penciled this mountain of typescript down to a 265,000-word draft. Knopf hated the proposed title, *A Mencken Chrestomathy* (according to Mencken, the word means "a collection of choice passages from an author or authors"), but Mencken insisted on it, going so far as to discreetly twit his old friend in the preface: "Nor do I see why

I should be deterred by the fact that, when this book was announced, a few newspaper smarties protested that the word would be unfamiliar to many readers, as it was to them. Thousands of excellent nouns, verbs and adjectives that have stood in every decent dictionary for years are still unfamiliar to such ignoramuses, and I do not solicit their patronage. Let them continue to recreate themselves with whodunits, and leave my vocabulary and me to my own customers, who have all been to school." Not surprisingly, the ever-practical Mencken was more responsive to Knopf's concerns about the length of the first draft: "I myself feel that there are things in the present text that had better come out, so we should be able to reach an agreement without difficulty. There is an excess of copied material about equal in bulk to the matter now in the book. Thus, if the 'Chrestomathy' has an encouraging sale I'll be ready to produce a second volume."

Mencken delivered a 185,000-word revised draft on September 24, 1948, and approved the copyedited manuscript on November 8. Fifteen days later, a massive stroke left him unable to read or write for the rest of his life. *A Mencken Chrestomathy* was published the following July, two months before Mencken's sixty-ninth birthday. It turned up on the *New York Times* best-seller list almost immediately, appearing alongside *Nineteen Eighty-Four, The Seven Storey Mountain, The Fountainhead, Cheaper by the Dozen,* John P. Marquand's *Point of No Return* and Nancy Mitford's *Love in a Cold Climate.* (They don't make best-seller lists like *that* anymore.) The *Chrestomathy* has sold slowly but steadily ever since: 27,000 copies in hardcover, 22,000 in paperback. Moreover, the book's influence has been completely out of proportion to its sales. With the exception of Malcolm Cowley's *Portable Faulkner,* no anthology of a modern American writer's work has done more to shape the reputation of its subject.

What makes this first *Mencken Chrestomathy* so compelling? To begin with, it is not a conventional anthology. Most single-author anthologies, including some very artful ones, are purely functional: they are meant to introduce the reader to an *oeuvre,* not to serve as ends in themselves. The *Chrestomathy* is different. Mencken claimed, somewhat disingenuously, that his purpose in editing the *Chrestomathy* was "simply to present a selection from my out-of-print writings, many of them now almost unobtainable." In fact, the text was the climax of a process of serial revision that in some cases lasted as long as three decades. Typically, Mencken took a Monday Article written for the Baltimore *Evening Sun*, recycled it into a *Smart Set* essay or an *American Mercury* editorial, polished that version for inclusion in one of the *Prejudices* and, finally, created a "definitive" version for the *Chrestomathy*.* This editorial process is of particular relevance because Mencken's output consisted mainly of essays; comparatively few of his books were, to coin a Menckenism, *durchkomponiert*. By selecting the best of these essays, revising them extensively and collecting them in one carefully arranged volume, he produced a book that is at once an anthology and a deliberate act of literary and intellectual self-definition. *A Mencken Chrestomathy* is not quite as comprehensive as it looks: much of Mencken's work was still in print in 1948 and is therefore not included. But despite the absence of any material from *A Book of Prefaces, Treatise on the Gods, Treatise on Right and Wrong* or the three *Days* books, it nonetheless contains a broadly representative cross section of his writings, one from which subsequent generations of readers have acquired a total sense of H. L. Mencken as man and artist.

That no sequel to *A Mencken Chrestomathy* has previously been attempted makes perfect sense. "Anthologies are, ideally, an essential species of criticism," Randall Jarrell has said. "Nothing expresses and exposes your taste so completely." This is especially true of self-anthologies like the *Chrestomathy*. No other editor, however skilled or sympathetic, could possibly assemble a collection of Mencken's writings equal in interest. The book you hold in your hands, however, is not a secondhand imitation of its celebrated predecessor but the real thing: a *Second Chrestomathy* based on manuscript material selected and edited by Mencken himself.

Mencken hinted at the existence of this material in a poststroke interview in which he spoke of his frustration at not being able to publish a sequel to the *Chrestomathy*: "I never got to read it in

---

*A longer discussion of Mencken's revisions can be found in Charles Fecher's *Mencken: A Study of His Thought* (New York: Alfred A. Knopf, 1978), pp. 320–48.

book form. I had enough material for maybe two more volumes like the *Chrestomathy*." His remark was more significant than anyone knew at the time, or for long afterward. By the time of his death in 1956, Mencken had transferred most of his private papers to the Enoch Pratt Free Library in Baltimore. Among them were five boxes of unsorted manuscript material intended for use in a second *Chrestomathy*. Much of it consisted of typescript passages edited by Mencken; some appear to have been part of the first draft of the original *Chrestomathy*, while the rest were presumably intended from the outset as a sequel. Mencken's diary entries imply that he revised the *Chrestomathy* passages as he selected them. This made it possible for him to assemble the first draft from edited typescript, at least some of which was re-edited before being cut from the final draft in September of 1948. (The introductory note to the reminiscence of the Baltimore *Sunpapers* included in this volume contains interlinear changes in Mencken's handwriting that could not have been made prior to the summer of 1948.) This explains why he had expected to be able to produce a second volume so easily: the hard work was already done.

In 1963 Betty Adler, then in charge of the Mencken Collection, proposed to Alfred Knopf that he publish a new anthology based partly on Mencken's notebooks and partly on the *Second Chrestomathy* material. It is not clear whether Knopf already knew that Mencken had culled enough material for a second full-length *Chrestomathy*. Whatever the case, he rejected Adler's proposal, and the five boxes of typescripts, carbons and newspaper clippings eventually found their way to the top shelf of the closet in the Pratt's Mencken Room, where they gathered dust for twenty-nine years. No one other than Betty Adler appears to have examined this material closely until the spring of 1992, when I looked through it in the course of my research for a forthcoming biography of Mencken and realized that he had done far more work on a sequel to the *Chrestomathy* than had previously been thought. Even though Mencken did not prepare a chapter outline or organize his material in any way, it was clear that it would be possible to shape the surviving manuscript material into a *Second Chrestomathy* that did justice to his intentions. This book is the result.

A *Second Mencken Chrestomathy*, like its companion volume,

is more than just a selection from Mencken's best-known work. Some 147 of the 238 passages reprinted here are, to the best of my knowledge, appearing in book form for the first time. Of the remaining passages, sixty-two come from books that are no longer in print. Another twenty-nine are currently in print in various Mencken anthologies; of these, twenty-one appear in previously unpublished versions prepared by Mencken specifically for the *Second Chrestomathy*. A case in point is "The Commonwealth of Morons," an abridged version of the essay "On Being an American," first published in *Prejudices: Third Series* and reprinted in two of the standard Mencken anthologies, James Farrell's *Prejudices: A Selection* (1958) and Huntingdon Cairns's *The American Scene* (1965). The *Second Chrestomathy* version comprises about one-third of the original essay, with a freshly written closing paragraph and dozens of other textual changes.

The uncollected material reprinted in this book says much about the breadth of Mencken's interests, as well as the essential unity of the philosophy underlying them. It includes excerpts from his vivid 1920 translation of Nietzsche's *Der Antichrist*, and from the "New Constitution for Maryland" he drew up in 1937 for the amusement and edification of readers of the Baltimore *Sun*: "No person shall be eligible [to serve in the state legislature] who is or has ever been a minister of the gospel, or who has ever been under guardianship as a lunatic." (It isn't hard to imagine the look on Mencken's face as he rapped out that sentence on his Underwood noiseless typewriter.) His formidable skills as a journeyman book reviewer are also on display, along with a witty apologia for the tastes of an omnivorous reader who chose to write—and did it well—not only about the novels of Theodore Dreiser and Sinclair Lewis but about such unlikely-sounding books as Nikolai Rimsky-Korsakov's *My Musical Life* and Apsley Cherry-Garrard's *The Worst Journey in the World*: "I do not review upon any systematic, symmetrical plan, with its roots in logic and the *jus gentium*, but haphazard and without a conscience, and so it may occur that a fourth-rate novel gets a page, or even two pages, while a work of high merit goes inequitably to my ash-barrel and is hauled away in the night, unwept, unhonored and unsung, along with my archaic lingerie and my vacant beer bottles." One might easily put together an extremely readable anthology out of Mencken's book reviews alone, which take up 105 pages of small print in Betty Adler's bibliography and of which the two *Chrestomathys* contain only a small sample.

"As I grow older," Mencken wrote in the preface to *Minority Report*, "I am unpleasantly impressed by the fact that giving each human being but one life is a bad scheme. He should have two at the lowest—one for observing and studying the world, and the other for formulating and settling down his conclusions about it. Forced, as he is by the present irrational arrangement, to undertake the second function before he has made any substantial progress with the first, he limps along like an athlete only half trained." Much of the interest of the *Chrestomathys* lies in the way they show how H. L. Mencken viewed his life's work from the vantage point of middle age (and, though he did not know it, at the very end of his career). These volumes contain the essays he most wanted to preserve, revised to his satisfaction; they are the closest thing to a literary testament he chose to leave behind. With the publication of *A Second Mencken Chrestomathy*, that testament is now available in its entirety.

A SECOND MENCKEN CHRESTOMATHY appears at a time when a great deal of journalistic attention has lately been devoted to H. L. Mencken. The opening of *My Life as Author and Editor* and *Thirty-Five Years of Newspaper Work*, the memoirs Mencken left to the Enoch Pratt Free Library on condition that they remain under seal for thirty-five years after his death, was treated not as a long-delayed footnote to his career but as a major news story in its own right. The publication of an abridged trade edition of the first of these memoirs—and, earlier, of Mencken's diary—triggered a flood of criticism and commentary, some of it as hostile as anything written during his lifetime.

That critics are still quarreling over Mencken would have astonished many of his contemporaries. Edgar Kemler, his first postwar biographer, claimed as early as 1950 that "except for *The American Language*, the *Days* books, and a few selections" from his other books, Mencken wrote "no works likely to endure." Mencken himself affected to believe that the shelf life of most of his work would be brief. "My happiest days," he said in the preface to the original

Chrestomathy, "have been spent in crowded press-stands, recording and belaboring events that were portentous in their day, but are now forgotten. . . . What the total of my published writings comes to I don't know precisely, but certainly it must run well beyond 5,000,000 words. A good deal of it, of course, was journalism pure and simple—dead almost before the ink which printed it was dry." Yet by 1948 Mencken must have suspected that he had already passed the test of time, and today there is no doubting it. He is the only American journalist of his generation whose work is still read—who is, indeed, a genuinely popular writer. The artificial respiration of tenure-hungry scholars has played no part in keeping his memory green; to the extent that he is remembered, it is because there is something about his writing that appeals to the common reader.

At first glance, the exact nature of this appeal is baffling. It's temptingly easy to treat Mencken as a period piece, a controversialist whose battles were won long ago and whose work has survived simply because it is so well written. But wonderful as his prose style is (and no finer prose has been written by an American), this explanation will not do. If good writing were enough to keep polemics alive, Mencken's Monday Articles on the ins and outs of Baltimore politics would be as widely read as "In Memoriam: W.J.B." or "The Sahara of the Bozart." In fact, Mencken's best journalism was concerned less with battles than with wars. At the heart of his critique of American life, for example, is his hatred of "the whole Puritan scheme of things, with its gross and nauseating hypocrisies, its idiotic theologies, its moral obsessions, its pervasive Philistinism," all of which he firmly believed to be intrinsic to the American national character. Theologies (and ideologies, their secular brethren) come and go, but the conceptions of human nature from which they spring are forever with us, and to leaf through the *Second Chrestomathy* is to be struck by how often Mencken, in the course of bashing away at long-forgotten manifestations of the "Puritan *Kultur*" of the '20s, says things scarcely less applicable to the very different America of today:

> In the United States there is a right way to think and a wrong way to think in everything—not only in theology, or politics,

or economics, but in the most trivial matters of everyday life. Thus, in the average American city the citizen who, in the face of an organized public clamor (usually fomented by parties with something to sell) for the erection of an equestrian statue of Susan B. Anthony in front of the chief railway station, or the purchase of a dozen leopards for the municipal zoo, or the dispatch of an invitation to the Structural Iron Workers' Union to hold its next annual convention in the town Symphony Hall—the citizen who, for any logical reason, opposes such a proposal—on the ground, say, that Miss Anthony never rode a horse in her life, or that a dozen leopards would be less useful than a gallows to hang the City Council, or that the Structural Iron Workers would spit all over the floor of Symphony Hall and knock down the busts of Bach, Beethoven and Brahms—this citizen is commonly denounced as an anarchist and a public enemy. It is not only erroneous to think thus; it has come to be immoral.

Much of what Mencken has to say is, of course, entirely predictable. He is the apostle of common sense, and of a realism so hard as to be hopelessly ill suited to the prevailing softness of our own Age of Sensitivity. Whatever the disorder in question, man's irremediable stupidity was Mencken's universal diagnosis, the horse-laugh his preferred antidote. Those who take offense easily are, now as ever, unlikely to find him anything other than offensive. This is particularly true of earnest believers in what he liked to call "the uplift." Anyone who spends his days grubbing for solutions to notoriously intractable social problems can have little in common with the cold-eyed skeptic who wrote in the first issue of the *American Mercury*: "The Editors have heard no Voice from the burning bush. They will not cry up and offer for sale any sovereign balm, whether political, economic or aesthetic, for all the sorrows of the world. . . . The world, as they see it, is down with at least a score of painful diseases, all of them chronic and incurable."

Even those who find Mencken's philosophy tonic are likely to shrink from some of its specific applications. His hardness too often shades into outright brutality; he is almost always simplistic, and very often demonstrably wrong on factual matters. Yet the substance of his opinions has surprisingly little to do with the pleasure we take in his way of expressing them. He once called poetry "a comforting piece of fiction set to more or less lascivious music," a sentiment echoed elsewhere in this volume. ("Walt Whitman was the greatest of American poets, and for a plain reason: he got furthest from the obvious facts. What he had to say was almost never true.") One might just as well speak of Mencken's own poetic quality. Writing in great unbroken arcs of gusto, he briskly sweeps the reader along from one outrageous assertion to the next:

> A dog is a standing proof that most so-called human rights, at bottom, are worth nothing. A dog is proverbially devoid of any such rights, and yet it lives well and is happy. For one dog that is starved and mistreated there are 10,000 that are coddled and overfed. . . . Yet a dog has none of the great rights that men esteem, glory in and die for. It cannot vote. It cannot get converted by Dr. Billy Sunday. It cannot go to jail for some great and lofty principle—say, equal suffrage or birth control. It is barred from the Elks, the Harvard Club and Congress. It cannot serve its country by dying of septicaemia or acute gastro-enteritis. It cannot read the *Nation*. It cannot subscribe to the Y.M.C.A. It cannot swear at waiters. It cannot eat in Pullman dining-cars. It cannot be a Presbyterian.

But to dismiss Mencken as a pure stylist, a Wodehouse-like juggler of shiny metaphors, is to ignore the fact that his attitude toward life is the point of his work. This attitude, as has often been remarked, is profoundly bleak: few American writers have had a stronger sense of the futility of man's earthly existence. Yet there is nothing lugubrious about Mencken's tragic sense of life. Perhaps the most revealing selection in *A Second Mencken Chrestomathy* is the Monday Article he wrote on the death of Albert Hildebrandt, one of his oldest friends: "The universe is run idiotically, and its only certain product is sorrow. But there are yet men who, by their generally pleasant spirits, by their extraordinary capacity for making and keeping friends, yet manage to cheat, in some measure, the common destiny of mankind, doomed like the beasts to perish." What was true of Hildebrandt was doubly true of his distinguished obituarist, whose habitual reply to the idiocies of the universe was a sardonic grin. "We live in a land of abounding quackeries," he once said, "and if we do not learn how to laugh we succumb to the melancholy disease which afflicts the race of viewers-with-alarm." This is the ultimate source of Mencken's abiding appeal: "He achieves his effect," Joseph Epstein has rightly and beautifully said, "through the magical transfer of *joie de vivre*." The man who can look into the abyss and laugh is rare enough; when he can also make his readers laugh along with him, it matters little whether he was right or wrong about capital punishment or the novels of Henry James.

In the end. H. L. Mencken's writing, like that of all the great essayists, is valuable not so much for what it has to say (undeniably compelling though that often is) as for what it tells us about the character of the man who said it. "The goods that a writer produces," he wrote in *My Life as Author and Editor*, "can never be impersonal; his character gets into them as certainly as it gets into the work of any other creative artist, and he must be prepared to endure investigation of it, and speculation upon it, and even gossip about it." Surely Mencken's own character got into every word he wrote, and it is writ large on every page of this book: witty and abrasive, self-confident and self-contradictory, sometimes maddening, often engaging, always inimitable.

A Second Mencken Chrestomathy is based on five letter files of manuscript material labeled "Material Collected by H.L.M. for a proposed second volume of A Mencken Chrestomathy" in the Mencken Collection of the Enoch Pratt Free Library. The first file contains approximately 250 edited typescripts (there are several duplicates and a few variant versions) of passages excerpted by Mencken from his uncollected newspaper and magazine articles and from ten of his books: *The American Credo, Damn! A Book of Calumny*, the revised version of *In Defense of Women*, *Notes on Democracy* and the six volumes of *Prejudices*. All of this material is in the typing of Mrs. Rosalind C. Lohrfinck, Mencken's secretary, with interlinear corrections by Mencken. The second and third files contain mounted clippings of columns from the Baltimore *Sunpapers* and unsorted carbons of various other published articles. The fourth and fifth files contain loose, unsorted clippings from newspapers and magazines, some dating as far back as the early 1900s.

This book contains 219 of the 250-odd typescript passages edited by Mencken, plus nineteen unrevised articles drawn from the second and third files.* The remaining passages either dealt with matters of little interest to modern-day readers, overlapped substantially with other passages or were too fragmentary to publish in their existing state. I have supplied sixty-seven passage titles, as well as all chapter titles. (In some cases Mencken failed to supply a title of his own; in others, he simply carried over the title of the original article from which the passage was drawn, often with misleading results.) I have supplied source notes where Mencken did not.

All introductory notes were written by Mencken especially for the *Second Chrestomathy*, with the following exceptions, adapted by me from other works by Mencken: The notes to "The Pushful American," "A Novel a Day," "A Novel of the First Rank" and "An American Novel" (and the footnote in "Marginal Note") are from *My Life as Author and Editor*. The note to "Interlude in the Socratic Manner" is from *Thirty-Five Years of Newspaper Work*. The note to "The Pulitzer Prize" is in part from *My Life as Author and Editor* and in part from *Thirty-Five Years of Newspaper Work*. The note to "The Metaphysic of Rotary" is from the prefaces to *Americana 1925* and *Americana 1926*. The note to "Notice to Neglected Geniuses" is from Mencken's Monday Article in the Baltimore *Evening Sun* for August 20, 1920. The note to "Criticism of Criticism of Criticism" is based on Mencken's handwritten notations in the *Second Chrestomathy* typescript.

The arrangement of this book, though modeled on the original *Chrestomathy*, is entirely my own doing. (Mencken left only a few sketchy marginal notes suggesting possible chapter titles.) I have

---

* A few passages from *A Second Mencken Chrestomathy* were subsequently included in the posthumous collection *Minority Report: H. L. Mencken's Notebooks*. Where the versions vary, I have followed the text of *Minority Report*, which Mencken edited in the '40s and revised for publication prior to his death in 1956.

done a limited amount of additional editing of the text, mostly to correct typographical errors and reconcile stylistic inconsistencies; I have retained Mencken's customary usages, including his idiosyncratic approach to capitalization and his period spelling. Following Mencken's example in the passages he revised most extensively, as well as in his editing of the original *Chrestomathy*, I have closed up line breaks and unnecessary paragraph breaks and excised superfluous exclamation points. I have also done a bit of topping and tailing on certain passages extracted from books or longer articles, and silently made a few cuts of my own in order to prune redundancies and now-obscure topical references. All ellipsis points are Mencken's and, as in the original *Chrestomathy*, are *not* intended to indicate cuts (except in "A New Constitution for Maryland" and "Nietzsche on Christianity"). All footnotes are Mencken's except for the one in "Robert Louis Stevenson," which is mine.

Needless to say, this book is a speculative reconstruction of the *Second Chrestomathy* Mencken would have prepared for publication had he not fallen ill in 1948. He would certainly have revised the text further, and his final choice of material, not to mention his arrangement of it, would just as certainly have differed from mine in many ways. But it is not misleading to say, as I have said on the title page, that *A Second Mencken Chrestomathy* was "selected, revised and annotated by the author," and I hope Mencken would have viewed my modest editorial contributions as a plausible substitute for the finishing touches he was unable to apply.

ALL SERIOUS students of the life and work of H. L. Mencken sooner or later make their way to the Mencken Room of the Enoch Pratt Free Library, where they are treated not as hostile intruders but as honored guests. It has been my pleasure to work with Averil Kadis, Neil Jordahl and their colleagues at the Pratt, without whom this volume would never have seen print. I am especially grateful to Vincent Fitzpatrick, assistant curator of the Mencken Collection and a scholar of limitless unselfishness. He probably knows more about the Mencken Room than anybody else in the world, and his aid and counsel were invaluable to me.

This is Mencken's book, but if it were mine, it would be dedicated to Vince.

I also want to thank my wife, Elizabeth, who took time from her own work to read, comment on and improve mine; Glen Hartley and Lynn Chu, my ever-vigilant agents; William F. Buckley, Jr., for his prompt and characteristic assistance; and Ashbel Green of Alfred A. Knopf, Inc., who had the wit to realize that his old boss missed a bet when he turned down Betty Adler's proposal of thirty years ago.

TERRY TEACHOUT

New York City
May 9, 1994

A SECOND
MENCKEN
CHRESTOMATHY

I. AMERICANA

The Commonwealth of Morons

From On Being an American,
Prejudices: Third Series, 1922, pp. 12–28, 59

In the United States the business of getting a living is enormously easier than it is in any other Christian land—so easy, in fact, that a forehanded man who fails at it must almost make deliberate efforts to that end. Here the general average of intelligence, of knowledge, of competence, of integrity, of self-respect, of honor is so low that any man who knows his trade, does not fear ghosts, has read fifty good books, and practices the common decencies stands out as brilliantly as a wart on a bald head. And here, more than anywhere else that I know of or have heard of, the daily panorama of human existence, of private and communal folly—the unending procession of governmental extortions and chicaneries, of commercial brigandages and throat-slittings, of theological buffooneries, of aesthetic ribaldries, of legal swindles and harlotries, of miscellaneous rogueries, villainies, imbecilities, grotesqueries, and extravagances—is so inordinately gross and preposterous, so perfectly brought up to the highest conceivable amperage, so steadily enriched with an almost fabulous daring and originality, that only the man who was born with a petrified diaphragm can fail to laugh himself to sleep every night.

A certain sough of rhetoric may be here, but fundamentally I am quite sincere. For example, in the matter of attaining to ease in Zion, of getting a fair share of the national swag. It seems to me, sunk in my Egyptian night, that the man who fails to do this in the United States today is a man who is hopelessly stupid— maybe not on the surface, but certainly deep down. Either he is

3

one who cripples himself unduly, say by setting up a family before he can care for it, or by making a fool's bargain for the sale of his wares, or by concerning himself too much about the affairs of other men; or he is one who endeavors fatuously to sell something that no normal American wants. Whenever I hear a professor of metaphysics complain that his wife has eloped with an ice-man who can at least feed and clothe her, my natural sympathy for the man is greatly corrupted by contempt for his lack of sense. Would it be regarded as sane and laudable for a man to travel the Soudan trying to sell fountain-pens, or Greenland offering to teach double-entry bookkeeping? Coming closer, would the judicious pity or laugh at a man who opened a shop for the sale of incunabula in Little Rock, Ark., or who demanded a living in McKeesport, Pa., on the ground that he could read Sumerian?

One seeking to make a living in a country must pay due regard to the needs and tastes of that country. Here in the United States we have no jobs for grand dukes, and none for palace eunuchs, and none for masters of the buckhounds—and very few for oboe-players, assyriologists, water-colorists, stylites and epic poets. There may come a time when the composer of string quartettes is paid as much as a railway conductor, but it is not yet. Then why prac-tise such trades—that is, as trades? The man of independent means may venture into them prudently; when he does so, he is seldom molested; it may even be argued that he performs a public service by adopting them. But the man who has a living to make is simply silly if he embraces them; he is like a soldier going over the top with a coffin strapped to his back. Let him abandon such puerile vanities, and take to the uplift instead, as, indeed, thou-sands of other victims of the industrial system have already done. Let him bear in mind that, whatever its neglect of the humanities and their monks, the Republic has never got half enough quack doctors, ward leaders, phrenologists, circus clowns, magicians, sol-diers, farmers, popular song writers, detectives, spies and *agents provocateurs*. The rules are set by Omnipotence; the discreet man observes them. Observing them, he is safe beneath the starry bed-tick, in fair weather or foul. *Boobus Americanus* is a bird that knows no closed season—and if he won't come down to Texas oil stock, or one-night cancer cures, or building lots in Swampshurst, he will always come down on Inspiration and Optimism, whether political, theological, pedagogical, literary or economic.

The doctrine that it is *infra dignitatem* for an educated man to take a hand in the snaring of this goose is one in which I see nothing convincing. It is a doctrine chiefly voiced, I believe, by those who have tried the business and failed. They take refuge behind the childish notion that there is something honorable about poverty *per se*, but this is nonsense. Poverty may be an unescapable misfortune, but that no more makes it honorable than a cocked eye is made honorable by the same cause. Do I advocate, then, the ceaseless, senseless hogging of money? I do not. All I advocate—and praise as virtuous—is the hogging of enough to provide security and ease. Despite all the romantic superstitions to the contrary, the artist cannot do his best work when he is oppressed by unsatisfied wants. Nor can the philosopher. Nor can the man of science. The clearest thinking of the world is done and the finest art is produced, not by men who are hungry, ragged and harassed, but by men who are well-fed, warm and easy in mind. It is the artist's first duty to his art to achieve that tranquillity for himself. Shakespeare tried to achieve it; so did Beethoven, Wagner, Brahms, Ibsen and Balzac. Goethe, Schopenhauer, Schumann and Mendelssohn were born to it. In the older countries, where competence is far more general and competition is thus more sharp, getting on in the world is often cruelly difficult, and sometimes almost impossible. But in the United States it is absurdly easy, given ordinary luck. Any man with a superior air, the intelligence of a stock-broker, and the resolution of a hat-check girl—in brief, any man who believes in himself enough, and with sufficient cause, to be called a journeyman at his trade—can cadge enough money, in this glorious commonwealth of morons, to make life soft for him.

And if a lining for the purse is thus facilely obtainable, given a reasonable prudence and resourcefulness, then balm for the ego is just as unlaboriously got, given ordinary dignity and decency. Simply to exist, indeed, on the plane of a civilized man is to attain, in the Republic, to a distinction that should be enough for all save the most vain. Nowhere else in the world is this more easily attained or more eagerly admitted. The chief business of the nation, as a nation, is the setting up of heroes, mainly bogus. Ten iron-molders meet in the backroom of a saloon, organize a lodge of the Noble and Mystic Order of American Rosicrucians, and elect a wheelwright Supreme Worthy Whimwham; a month later they send a notice to the local newspaper that they have been greatly honored by an official visit from that Whimwham, and that they plan to give him a jeweled fob for his watch-chain. The chief national eminentissimos cannot remain mere men. The mysticism of the medieval peasantry gets into the communal view of them, and they begin to sprout halos and wings. No intrinsic merit—at least, none commensurate with the mob estimate—is needed to come to such august dignities. Everything American is a bit amateurish and childish, even the national gods. The most conspicuous and re-spected American in nearly every field of endeavor, saving only the purely commercial, is a man who would attract little attention in any other country. The leading native musical director, if he went to Leipzig, would be put to polishing trombones and copying drum-parts. The chief living American military man of the 1914–18 crop—the national heir to Frederick, Marlborough, Wellington, Washington and Prince Eugene—was a member of the Elks, and proud of it. The leading American philosopher (now dead, with no successor known to the average pedagogue) spent a lifetime erect-ing an epistemological defense for the national aesthetic maxim: "I don't know nothing about music, but I know what I like."

All of which can be boiled down to this: that the United States is essentially a commonwealth of third-rate men—that distinction is easy here because the general level of culture, of information, of taste and judgment, of ordinary competence is so low. No sane man, employing an American plumber to repair a leaky drain, would expect him to do it at the first trial, and in precisely the same way no sane man, observing an American Secretary of State in negotiation, would expect him to come off better than second best. Third-rate men, of course, exist in all countries, but it is only here that they are in full control of the state, and with it of all the national standards. The land was peopled, not by the hardy adven-turers of legend, but simply by incompetents who could not get on at home, and the lavishness of nature that they found here, the vast ease with which they could get livings, confirmed and augmented their native incompetence. No American colonist, even in the worst days of the Indian wars, ever had to face such hardships as ground down the peasants of Central Europe during the Hundred Years War, nor even such hardships as oppressed the English lower classes during the century before the Reform Bill of 1832. In most of the colonies, indeed, he seldom saw any Indians at all: the one thing that made life difficult for him was his congenital dunderheadedness. The winning of the West, so rhetorically celebrated in American romance, cost the lives of fewer than 10,000 men, and the victory was much easier and surer.

The immigrants who have come in since those early days have been, if anything, of even lower grade than their forerunners. The old notion that the United States is peopled by the offspring of brave, idealistic and liberty-loving minorities, who revolted against injustice, bigotry and medievalism at home—this notion is fast succumbing to the alarmed study that has been given of late to the immigration of recent years. The truth is that the majority of non-Anglo-Saxon immigrants since the Revolution, like the majority of Anglo-Saxon immigrants before the Revolution, have been, not the superior men of their native lands, but the botched and unfit; Irishmen starving to death in Ireland, Germans unable to weather the *Sturm und Drang* of the post-Napoleonic reorganization, Italians weed-grown on exhausted soil, Scandinavians run to all bone and no brain, Jews too incompetent to swindle even the barbarous peasants of Russia, Poland and Roumania.

Nor is there much soundness in the common assumption, so beloved of professional idealists and wind-machines, that the people of America constitute "the youngest of the great peoples." That phrase turns up endlessly; the average newspaper editorial writer would be hamstrung if the Postoffice suddenly interdicted it. What gives it a certain specious plausibility is the fact that the American Republic, compared to a few other existing governments, is relatively young. But the American Republic is not necessarily identical with the American people; they might overturn it tomorrow and set up a monarchy, and still remain the same people. The truth is that, as a distinct nation, they go back fully three hundred years, and that even their government is older than that of most other nations. Moreover, it is absurd to say that there is anything properly describable as youthfulness in the American outlook. It is not that of young men, but that of old men. All the characteristics of senescence are in it: a great distrust of ideas, an habitual timorousness, a harsh fidelity to a few fixed beliefs, a touch of mysticism. The average American is a prude and a Methodist under his skin, and the fact is never more evident than when he is trying to disprove it. His vices are not those of a healthy boy, but that of an ancient paralytic escaped from the *Greisenheim*. His ways of thinking are the marks of the peasant and of his bastard offspring, the city wage-slave—more, of the peasant long ground down into the mud of his wallow, and determined at last to stay there—the peasant who has definitely renounced any lewd desire he may have ever had to gape at the stars.

The habits of mind of this dull, sempiternal *fellah*—the oldest man in Christendom—are, with a few modifications, the habits of mind of the American people. The peasant has a great practical cunning, but he is unable to see any further than the next farm. He likes money and struggles to amass property, but his cultural development is but little above that of the domestic animals. He is intensely and cocksurely moral, but his morality and his self-interest are crudely identical. He is emotional and easy to scare, but his imagination cannot grasp an abstraction. He is a violent nationalist and patriot, but he admires rogues in office and always beats the tax-collector if he can. He has immovable opinions about all the great affairs of state, but nine-tenths of them are sheer imbecilities. He is violently jealous of what he conceives to be his rights, but brutally disregardful of the other fellow's. He is religious, but his religion is wholly devoid of beauty and dignity. This man, whether city or country bred, is the normal Americano. He exists in all countries, but here alone he rules—here alone his anthropoid fears and rages are accepted gravely as logical ideas, and dissent from them is punished as a sort of public offense. Around every one of his principal delusions—of the sacredness of democracy, of the feasibility of sumptuary law, of the incurable sinfulness of all other peoples, of the menace of ideas, of the corruption lying in all the arts—there is thrown a barrier of taboos, and woe to the anarchist who seeks to break it down.

The multiplication of such taboos is obviously not characteristic of a culture that is moving from a lower plane to a higher—that is, of a culture still in the full glow of its youth. It is a sign, rather, of a culture that is slipping downhill—one that is reverting to the most primitive standards and ways of thought. The taboo is the trademark, not of the civilized man but of the savage, and wherever it exists it is a relentless and effective enemy of the enlightenment. The savage is the most meticulously moral of men; there is scarcely an act of his daily life that is not conditioned by unyielding prohibitions and obligations, most of them logically unintelligible. The mob-man, a savage set amid civilization, cherishes a code of the same draconian kind. He believes firmly that right and wrong are immovable things—that they have an actual and unchangeable existence, and that any challenge of them, by word or act, is a crime against society. And with the concept of wrongness, of course, he always confuses the concept of mere differentness—to him the two are indistinguishable. Anything strange is to be combatted; it is of the Devil. The mob-man cannot grasp ideas in their native nakedness. They must be dramatized and personalized for him, and provided with either white wings or forked tails. All discussion of them, to interest him, must take the form of a pursuit and scotching of demons. He cannot think of a heresy without thinking of a heretic to be caught, condemned and burned.

In all such phenomena I take unfeigned delight. They fill me with contentment, and hence make me a happier and better American.

The Pushful American

From the Preface to THE AMERICAN CREDO, by George Jean Nathan and H. L. Mencken, 1920, pp. 28–43. I wrote the whole of the preface, which filled more than half the volume and gave me a capital chance to plaster the super-patriots of the war years. But Nathan did a fair share of the work of editing, and we agreed to divide the proceeds fifty-fifty

What, then, is the character that actually marks the American — that is, in chief? If he is not the exalted monopolist of liberty that he thinks he is nor the noble altruist and idealist he slaps upon the chest when he is full of rhetoric, nor the degraded dollar-chaser of European legend, then what is he? We offer an answer in all humility, for the problem is complex and there is but little illumination of it in the literature; nevertheless, we offer it in the firm conviction, born of twenty years' incessant meditation, that it is substantially correct. It is, in brief, this: that the thing which sets off the American from all other men, and gives a peculiar color not only to the pattern of his daily life but also to the play of his inner ideas, is what, for want of a more exact term, may be called social aspiration. That is to say, his dominant passion is a passion to lift himself by at least a step or two in the society that he is a part of—a passion to improve his position, to break down some shadowy barrier of caste, to achieve the countenance of what, for all his talk of equality, he recognizes and accepts as his betters. The American is a pusher. His eyes are ever fixed upon some round of the ladder that is just beyond his reach, and all his secret ambition, all his extraordinary energies, group themselves about the yearning to grasp it. Here we have an explanation of the curious restlessness that educated foreigners, as opposed to mere immigrants, always make a note of in the country; it is half aspiration and half impatience, with overtones of dread and timorousness. The American is violently eager to get on, and thoroughly convinced that his merits entitle him to try and to succeed, but by the same token he is sickeningly fearful of slipping back, and out of the second fact, as we shall see, spring some of his most characteristic traits. He is a man vexed, at one and the same time, by delusions of grandeur and an inferiority complex; he is both egotistical and subservient, assertive and politic, blatant and shy. Most of the errors about him are made by seeing one side of him and being blind to the other.

Such a thing as a secure position is practically unknown among us. There is no American who cannot hope to lift himself another notch or two, if he is good; there is absolutely no hard and fast impediment to his progress. But neither is there any American who doesn't have to keep on fighting for whatever position he has; no wall of caste is there to protect him if he slips. One observes every day the movement of individuals, families, whole groups, in both

directions. All of our cities are full of brummagem aristocrats—
aristocrats, at all events, in the view of their neighbors—whose
grandfathers, or even fathers, were day-laborers; and working for
them, supported by them, heavily patronized by them, are clerks
whose grandfathers were lords of the soil. The older societies of
Europe, as every one knows, protect their caste lines a great deal
more resolutely. It is as impossible for a wealthy pork-packer or
company promoter to enter the true *noblesse*, even today, as it
would be for him to enter the boudoir of a queen; he is barred out
absolutely and even his grandchildren are under the ban. And in
precisely the same way it is as impossible for a count of the old
Holy Roman Empire to lose caste as it would be for the Dalai
Lama; he may sink to unutterable depths within his order, but he
cannot get himself out of it, nor can he lose the peculiar advantages that go with membership; he is still a *Graf*, and, as such,
above the herd. Once, in a Madrid café, the two of us encountered a Spanish marquis who wore celluloid cuffs, suffered from
pediculosis and had been drunk for sixteen years. Yet he remained
a marquis in good standing, and all lesser Spaniards, including
Socialists, envied him and deferred to him; none would have
dreamed of slapping him on the back. Knowing that he was quite
as safe within his ancient order as a dog among the *canidæ*, he
gave no thought to appearances. But in the same way he knew
that he had reached his limit—that no conceivable effort could lift
him higher. He was a grandee of Spain and that was all; above
glimmered royalty and the hierarchy of the saints, and both royalty
and the hierarchy of the saints were as much beyond him as
grandeeism was beyond the polite and well-educated head-waiter
who laved him with ice-water when he had *mania à potu*.

No American is ever so securely lodged. There is always something just ahead of him, beckoning him and tantalizing him, and
there is always something just behind him, menacing him and
causing him to sweat. Even when he attains to what may seem to
be security, that security is very fragile. The English soap-boiler,
brewer, shyster attorney or stock-jobber, once he has got into the
House of Lords, is reasonably safe, and his children after him; the
possession of a peerage connotes a definite rank, and it is as permanent as anything can be in this world. But in America there is

no such harbor; the ship is eternally at sea. Money vanishes, official dignity is forgotten, caste lines are as full of gaps as an ill-kept hedge. The grandfather of the Vanderbilts was a bounder; the last of the Washingtons is a petty employé in the Library of Congress.

It is this constant possibility of rising, this constant risk of falling, that gives a barbaric picturesqueness to the panorama of what is called fashionable society in America. The chief character of that society is to be found in its shameless self-assertion, its almost obscene display of its importance and of the shadowy privileges and acceptances on which that importance is based. It is assertive for the simple reason that, immediately it ceases to be assertive, it would cease to exist. Structurally, it is composed in every town of a nucleus of those who have laboriously arrived and a chaotic mass of those who are straining every effort to get on. The effort must be made against great odds. Those who have arrived are eager to keep down the competition of newcomers; on their exclusiveness, as the phrase is, rests the whole of their social advantage. Thus the candidate from below, before horning in at last, must put up with an infinity of rebuff and humiliation; he must sacrifice his self-respect today in order to gain the hope of destroying the self-respect of other aspirants tomorrow. The result is that the whole edifice is based upon fears and abasements, and that every device which promises to protect the individual against them is seized upon eagerly. Fashionable society in America therefore has no room for intelligence; within its fold an original idea is dangerous; it carries regimentation, in dress, in social customs and in political and even religious doctrines, to the last degree. In the American cities the fashionable man or woman must not only maintain the decorum seen among civilized folks everywhere; he or she must also be interested in precisely the right sports, theatrical shows and opera singers, show the right political credulities and indignations, and have some sort of connection with the right church. Nearly always, because of the apeing of English custom that prevails everywhere in America, it must be the so-called Protestant Episcopal Church, a sort of outhouse of the Church of England, with ecclesiastics who imitate the English sacerdotal manner much as small boys imitate the manner of eminent baseball players. Every fashionable Protestant Episcopal congregation in the land is full of ex-

Baptists and ex-Methodists who have shed Calvinism, total immersion and the hallelujah hymns on their way up the ladder. The same impulse leads the Jews, whenever the possibility of invading the citadel of the Christians begins to bemuse them (as happened during the late war, for example, when patriotism temporarily adjourned the usual taboos), to embrace Christian Science—as a sort of half-way station, so to speak, more medical than Christian, and hence secure against ordinary derisions. And it is an impulse but little different which lies at the bottom of the much-discussed title-hunt.

A title, however paltry, is of genuine social value, more especially in America; it represents a status that cannot be changed overnight by the rise of rivals, or by personal dereliction, or by mere accident. It is a policy of insurance against dangers that are not to be countered as effectively in any other manner. Miss G——, the daughter of an enormously wealthy scoundrel, may be accepted everywhere, but all the while she is insecure. Her father may lose his fortune tomorrow, or be jailed by newspaper outcry, or marry a prostitute and so commit social suicide himself and murder his daughter, or she herself may fall a victim to some rival's superior machinations, or stoop to fornication of some forbidden variety, or otherwise get herself under the ban. But once she is a duchess, she is safe. No catastrophe short of divorce can take away her coronet, and even divorce will leave the purple marks of it upon her brow. Most valuable boon of all, she is now free to be herself—a rare, rare experience for an American. She may, if she likes, go about in a Mother Hubbard, or join the Seventh Day Adventists, or declare for the Bolsheviki, or wash her own lingerie, or have her hair bobbed, and still she will remain a duchess, and, as a duchess, irremovably superior to the gaping herd of her political equals.

This social aspiration, of course, is most vividly violent and idiotic on its higher and more gaudy levels, but it is scarcely less earnest below. Every American, however obscure, has formulated within his secret recesses some concept of advancement, however meagre; if he doesn't aspire to be what is called fashionable, then he at least aspires to lift himself in some less gorgeous way. There is not a social organization in this land of innumerable associations that hasn't its waiting list of candidates who are eager to get in, but have not yet demonstrated their fitness for the honor. One can scarcely go low enough to find that pressure absent. Even the tin-pot fraternal orders, which are constantly cadging for members and seem to accept any one not a downright felon, are exclusive in their fantastic way, and no doubt there are hundreds of thousands of proud American freemen, the heirs of Washington and Jefferson, their liberty safeguarded by a million guns, who pine in secret because they are ineligible to membership in the Masons, the Odd Fellows or even the Knights of Pythias. On the distaff side, the thing is too obvious to need exposition. The patriotic societies among women are all machines for the resuscitation of lost superiorities. The plutocracy has shouldered out the old gentry from actual social leadership — that gentry, indeed, presents a prodigious clinical picture of the insecurity of social rank in America — but there remains at least the possibility of insisting upon a dignity which plutocrats cannot boast and may not even buy. Thus the county judge's wife in Smithville or the Methodist pastor's daughter in Jonestown consoles herself for the lack of an opera box with the thought (constantly asserted by badge and resolution) that she had a nobler grandfather, or, at all events, a decenter one, than the Astors, the Vanderbilts and the Goulds.

It seems to us that the genuine characters of the normal American, the characters which set him off most saliently from the men of other nations, are the fruits of all this risk of and capacity for change in status that we have described, and of the dreads and hesitations that go therewith. The American is marked, in fact, by precisely the habits of mind and act that one would look for in a man insatiably ambitious and yet incurably fearful, to wit, the habits, on the one hand, of unpleasant assertiveness, of somewhat boisterous braggardism, of incessant pushing, and, on the other hand, of conformity, caution and subservience. He is forever talking of his rights as if he stood ready to defend them with his last drop of blood, and forever yielding them up at the first demand. Under both the pretension and the fact is the common motive of fear — in brief, the common motion of the insecure and uncertain man, the *average* man, at all times and everywhere, but especially the motives of the average man in a social system so crude and unstable as ours.

"More than any other people," said Wendell Phillips one blue

day, "we Americans are afraid of one another." The saying seems
harsh. It goes counter to the national delusion of uncompromising
courage and limitless truculence. It wars upon the national vanity.
But all the same there is truth in it. Here, more than anywhere
else on earth, the status of an individual is determined by the general consent of the general body of his fellows; here, as we have
seen, there are no artificial barriers to protect him against their dis-
approval, or even against their envy. And here, more than anywhere else, the general consent of that general body of men is
colored by the ideas and prejudices of the inferior majority; here,
there is the nearest approach to genuine democracy, the most direct and accurate response to mob emotions. Facing that infinitely
powerful but inevitably ignorant and cruel corpus of opinion, the
individual must needs adopt caution and fall into timorousness.
The desire within him may be bold and forthright, but its satisfaction demands discretion, prudence, a politic and ingratiating habit.
The walls are not to be stormed; they must be wooed to a sort of
Jerichoan fall. Success thus takes the form of a series of waves of
protective coloration; failure is a succession of unmaskings. The
aspirant must first learn to imitate exactly the aspect and behavior
of the group he seeks to penetrate. There follows notice. There follows toleration. There follows acceptance.

Thus the hog-murderer's wife picks her way into the society of
Chicago, the proud aristocracy of the abattoir. And thus, no less,
the former whiskey drummer insinuates himself into the Elks, and
the rising retailer wins the *imprimatur* of wholesalers, and the rich
peasant becomes a planter and the father of doctors of philosophy,
and the servant girl enters the movies and acquires the status of a
princess of the blood, and the petty attorney becomes a legislator
and statesman, and Schmidt turns into Smith, and the newspaper
reporter becomes a *littérateur* on the staff of the *Saturday Evening
Post*, and all of us Yankees creep up, up, up. The business is never
to be accomplished by headlong assault. It must be done circum-
spectly, insidiously, a bit apologetically, *pianissimo*; there must be
no flaunting of unusual ideas, no bold prancing of an unaccustomed personality. Above all, it must be done without exciting fear,
lest the portcullis fall and the whole enterprise go to pot. Above
all, the manner of a Jenkins must be got into it.

The manner, of course, is not incompatible with a certain superficial boldness, nor even with an appearance of truculence. But what lies beneath the boldness is not really an independent spirit, but merely a talent for crying with the pack. When the American is most dashingly assertive it is a sure sign that he feels the pack behind him, and hears its comforting baying, and is well aware that his doctrine is approved. He is not a joiner for nothing. He joins something, whether it be a political party, a church, a fraternal order or one of the idiotic movements that incessantly ravage the land, because joining gives him a feeling of security, because it makes him a part of something larger and safer than he is himself, because it gives him a chance to work off steam without running any risk. The whole thinking of the country thus runs down the channel of mob emotion; there is no actual conflict of ideas, but only a succession of crazes. It is inconvenient to stand aloof from these crazes, and it is dangerous to oppose them. In no other country in the world is there so ferocious a short way with dissenters; in none other is it socially so costly to heed the inner voice and to be one's own man.

Thus encircled by taboos, the American shows an extraordinary timorousness in all his dealings with fundamentals, and the fact that many of these taboos are self-imposed only adds to their rigor. What every observant foreigner first notices, canvassing the intellectual life of the land, is the shy and gingery manner in which all the larger problems of existence are dealt with. We have, for example, positive laws which make it practically impossible to discuss the sex question with anything approaching honesty. The literature of the subject is enormous, and the general notion of its importance is thereby made manifest, but all save a very small part of that literature is produced by quacks and addressed to an audience that is afraid to hear the truth. So in politics. Almost alone among the civilized nations of the world, the United States pursues critics of the dominant political theory with medieval ferocity, condemning them to interminable periods in prison, proceeding against them by clamor and perjury, treating them worse than common blacklegs, and at times conniving at their actual murder by the police. And so, above all, in religion. This is the only country of Christendom in which there is no anti-clerical party, and hence no constant and effective criticism of clerical pretension and corruption. The result is that all of the churches reach out for tyranny among us, and that most of them that show any numerical strength already exercise it. In half a dozen of our largest cities the Catholic Church is actually a good deal more powerful than it is in Spain, or even in Austria. Its acts are wholly above public discussion; it makes and breaks public officials; it holds the newspapers in terror; it influences the police and the courts; it is strong enough to destroy and silence any man who objects to its polity.

The Metaphysic of Rotary

From the *American Mercury*, July, 1927, pp. 379–81. A review of ROTARY: A BUSINESS MAN'S INTERPRETATION, by Frank H. Lamb; Hoquiam (Washington), 1927. Americana, a monthly department of the *American Mercury*, consisted of press cuttings, drawn in part from newspapers of wide circulation and in larger part from little country papers, from broadsides and other such documents of purely local circulation, and from handbills and other advertisements observed along the streets. Its purpose was to make the enlightened minority of Americans familiar, by documentary evidence, with what was going on in the minds of the low-caste masses. Contributions were sent in by the thousands by readers

Mr. Lamb is a manufacturer of machinery in the rising town of Hoquiam, Wash., hard by the celebrated Centralia and not far from Tacoma. In 1920 he became a charter member of the Hoquiam Rotary Club and its first president. In 1922 he was advanced to the governorship of the First District, and a year later he became a director and third vice-president of Rotary International. His advancement has thus been rapid, and his book shows why; he is a man of philosophical mind, and has focused its powers upon the problems of the great order he serves and adorns. Those problems, it appears, are of a considerable complexity, for in Rotary, as in other human organizations, there are two parties, one of which dreams of great achievements and the other of which is content to improve the passing hour. As everyone knows, it is the former party that chiefly breaks into the newspapers. One hears of its spokesmen announcing that Moses, or Homer, or St. Francis, or Martin Luther, or George Washington was the first Rotarian, and arguing gravely that, when the next war threatens, only Rotary will be able to stop it. The members of this party wear the club emblem as proudly as if it were the Garter, and spend a great deal of their time worrying about such things as the crime wave, necking in the high-schools, the prevalence of adenoids, the doings of the League of Nations, and the conspiracy of the Bolsheviki to seize the United States and put every Cadillac owner to the sword. They have a taste for rhetoric, and like to listen to speeches by men with Messages. The boys of the other party are less concerned about such high matters. When there is nothing better afoot they go to the weekly luncheons, gnaw their way through the chicken patties and green peas, blow a few spitballs across the table, sing a few songs, and then, when the speech-making begins, retire to the washroom, talk a little business, and then prevail upon Fred or Charlie to tell the new one about Judd Gray and the chambermaid at Hornellsville, N.Y.

Mr. Lamb does not belong to this atheistic faction. Being a Rotarian is to him a serious business, and he believes that membership should be very strictly guarded. As is well known, the rules of the order provide that only one man of any given trade or profession may belong to any given club. This provision, it appears, is frequently the cause of difficulties and heart-burnings. Suppose, for example, that a club is confronted by "two leading banks doing practically a similar line of business, each with an executive that is fully capable of exemplifying Rotary." What to do? If the executive of one bank is elevated to membership, then the executive of the other will be full of shame and repining, and the fact, I daresay, will show itself the next time any member of the club asks him for accommodations. Many clubs have resolved such dilemmas by the arts of the sophist. They have put down one executive as a "commercial" banker and the other as a "savings" banker, and then elected both, yelling merrily the while, and bombarding the candidates with ham bones and asparagus. Mr. Lamb is against such subterfuges. He looks forward to what is bound to happen when two grocers try to horn in, or two electrical contractors, or two bootleggers—one, perhaps, disguised as a merchandise broker and the other as a wholesale druggist. The pressure from dubious men is naturally very great. They try to get into Rotary on account of the prestige and credit that membership gives, just as all the chiropractors in Washington try to get into the Cosmos Club, and all the social pushers everywhere in the Republic offer themselves for baptism in the Episcopal Church. If Rotary admitted them, it would soon descend to the level of the Shriners, the Moose, or the American Academy of Political and Social Science. But in small cities it is frequently hard to keep them out, for the only banker or newspaper editor or plumbing contractor available may be a palpably questionable fellow, with no taste whatever for Service. Thus the club is forced either to take him in despite his deficiencies, or to resign itself to staggering on without any representative of his important and puissant trade.

Such problems fever Mr. Lamb, who has a legal and moral cast of mind, and he gives over a large part of his book to a discussion of them. He believes that many of them would be solved if Rotary were confined strictly to the larger cities. The members of the clubs in such cities, going to a district or national convention, are often appalled on meeting their brethren from South Lockport and Boggsville. The former, as befits their high civic position, are commonly men of great austerity; the latter come to the meeting wearing flamboyant bands around their hats, carrying American flags and booster banners, and exhaling, perhaps, the fetor of rustic moonshine. It is hard for men of such disparate tastes and social habits to consider amicably, and to any ponderable public profit, the inordinately difficult and important questions with which Rotary deals. As well ask elephants and goats to gambol together. The big city clubs themselves face other problems, and some of them give great concern to the more thoughtful variety of Rotarians. There are those, as I have said, which flow out of the constitutional provision that but one member shall be admitted from each avocation. That rule frequently bars out men of the highest idealism, whose presence in the councils of Rotary would strengthen the organization and so benefit the Republic. The minute one wholesale grocer or patent medicine manufacturer is elevated to membership all the others in town are automatically barred, and among them, it appears, there are sometimes men of so large a passion for Service that they were plainly designed by Omnipotence to be Rotarians. Not a few classification committees, as I have hinted, stretch the rule to let such men in, but Mr. Lamb sees the danger of that sort of playing with fire, and sounds a solemn warning.

Another problem: what to do with active and useful members who change their occupation and so lose their classification? Suppose A, elected as a Ford dealer, abandons that great art and mystery for the knit underwear business? A representative of the knit underwear business, B by name, is already a member, and he naturally hangs on to the high privileges and prerogatives that go with the fact. Is A to be dropped, or is the rule against duplications to be once more invaded? Most Rotary clubs, according to Mr. Lamb, get around the difficulty by electing A to honorary membership, but as a purist he is against that device, for it simply begs the question. Moreover, it is unjust to A. If he is entitled to any membership at all, he is entitled to full membership, with the power to vote and hold office. The constitutional lawyers of Rotary have been wrestling with the problem for a long while, but so far they have failed to solve it. Mr. Lamb is naturally reluctant to discuss it in a doctrinaire manner, but I suspect that he is in favor of throwing A out altogether—a cruel scheme, certainly, but one that at least disposes of the difficulty. To permit A to hang around sucking his thumb while his successor radiates idealism is as indecorous as it would be for a lady married to her second husband to stable her first in the spare room. Raised to honorary membership, he becomes a sort of club eunuch. It would be kinder to strip him of his accoutrements and heave him out.

From all of this it is evident that the conscientious Rotarian is by no means the gay and happy fellow that he appears to be in the newspaper reports of his doings and in the columns of "Americana." All the while he is lavishing Service upon the rest of us his own heart is devoured by cares. The government of Rotary, like that of the United States, is one of law, not of men. The most stupendous Rotarian, in the eye of that law, is of no more importance than the humblest brother. Well, law hatches lawyers, and the minute lawyers appear there is trouble. Even the Elks have found that out. At their annual conventions they put in many weary hours trying constitutional cases. Outside the band is playing, but within the chamber of their deliberation they have to listen to long arguments, with a maddening gabble of precedents. An Elks' convention used to be a very lively affair, with the boys riding around in open barouches, covered with badges and throwing away money; now it is indistinguishable from a session of the Supreme Court of the United States. A Rotary convention becomes even worse, for Rotarians are more serious men than Elks. The idealism of the nation is in their keeping. If they took their responsibilities lightly there would be chaos.

The Yokel

From Four Moral Causes,
Prejudices: Fifth Series, 1926, p. 11

The yokel has scarcely any privacy at all. His neighbors know everything that is to be known about him, including what he eats and what he feeds his quadrupedal colleagues. His religious ideas are matters of public discussion; if he is recusant the village pastor prays for him by name. When his wife begins the biological process of giving him an heir, the news flies around. If he inherits $200 from an uncle in Idaho everyone knows it instantly. If he skins his shin, or buys a new plow, or sees a ghost, or takes a bath it is a public event. Thus living like a goldfish in a glass globe, he acquires a large tolerance of snoutery, for if he resisted it his neighbors would set him down as an enemy of their happiness, and probably burn his barn. It seems natural and inevitable to him that everyone outside his house should be interested in what goes on inside, and that this interest should be accompanied by definite notions as to what is nice and what is not nice, supported by pressure. So he submits to governmental tyranny as he submits to the village inquisition, and when he hears that city men resist, it only confirms his general feeling that they are scoundrels. They are scoundrels because they have a better time than he has—the sempiternal human reason.

Varieties of Envy

From the Baltimore *Evening Sun*, June 15, 1936

The central belief of every moron is that he is the victim of a mysterious conspiracy against his common rights and true deserts. He ascribes all his failure to get on in the world, all of his congenital incapacity and damfoolishness, to the machinations of werewolves assembled in Wall Street, or some other such den of infamy. If these villains could be put down, he holds, he would at once become rich, powerful and eminent. Nine politicians out of every ten, of whatever party, live and have their being by promising to perform this putting down. In brief, they are knaves who maintain themselves by preying on the idiotic vanities and pathetic hopes of half-wits.

What is thus promised, of course, always falls far short of fulfillment. The politicians devote themselves ardently enough to robbing A, who is an honest and useful man, eager only to pay his way, in order to bribe and flatter B, who is lazy, stupid and incompetent, and a very large part of the national income is dissipated in the process. But B still remains clearly inferior to A. He was inferior as a blastocyte, and he continues so as a nascent cadaver at a rally of Townsendites or New Dealers. He is therefore easy meat for the rascals who promise to give him, not merely a dole, but irresistible power. He dreams of becoming so mighty, *en masse*, if not on his own, that the nation will tremble at his tread, and Wall Street will entreat him for peace terms. In brief, he puts on a night-shirt and joins the Ku Klux Klan, the Black Legion, or some other such amalgamation of crooks and fools.

It seems to be little noticed that this yearning to dragoon and terrify all persons who happen to be lucky is at the bottom of the puerile radicalism now prevailing among us, just as it is at the bottom of Ku Kluxery. The average American radical today likes to think of himself as a profound and somber fellow, privy to arcana not open to the general; he is actually only a poor fish, with distinct overtones of the jackass. What ails him, first and last, is sim-

ply envy of his betters. Unable to make any progress against them
under the rules in vogue, he proposes to fetch them below the
belt by making the rules over. He is no more an altruist than
J. Pierpont Morgan is an altruist, or Jim Farley, or, indeed, Al
Capone.

Every such rescuer of the downtrodden entertains himself with
gaudy dreams of power, far beyond his natural fortunes and capacities. He sees himself at the head of an overwhelming legion of
morons, marching upon the fellows he envies and hates. He thinks
of himself in his private reflections (and gives it away every time
he makes a speech or prints an article) as a gorgeous amalgam of
Lenin, Mussolini and Genghis Khan, with the Republic under his
thumb, his check for any amount good at any bank, and ten million heels clicking every time he winks his eye. Not infrequently,
he throws in a private brewery or distillery, belching smoke in his
personal service, and a girl considerably more sightly than he can
scare up by his native magnetism. When such grotesque megalo-
mania reaches a certain virulence a black wagon dashes up, and
its two honest deckhands, Jack and Emil, haul off another nut to
the psychopathic hoosegow. But not many of the patients go that
far. They retain all their ordinary faculties. They can eat, drink,
talk, sweat, walk, dance and hope. They read the *New Masses*, sing
"The Internationale," and lecture on "Das Kapital" without having
read it. A vision enchants them, and perhaps one should allow
that, considering their natural gifts, it is as beautiful as any they are
capable of. But it will come to nothing. Like the dupes of the
Black Legion, they are doomed to be fooled.

The Immigration Problem

From the Baltimore *Evening Sun*, March 24, 1924

Congress is sure to make the new immigration law, whenever
it is passed, very strict, and once it is in force there will be a considerable decrease in immigration from Southern and Eastern
Europe. The result, in the long run, must be a complete reorgan-

ization of American industry, and to some extent, of American ag-
riculture. Both have been based, at least for a century past, upon
a free flow of immigrants. These immigrants have done all the
dirty work of the nation, and so left the native whites free to pursue higher enterprises. They have built the railroads of the country, paved the city streets, mined most of the coal and other
minerals, done the heavy labor of a large proportion of the farms,
and performed countless other varieties of menial and drudging
work. For three generations native white servants have been almost
unknown in America, and native whites have done very little shov-
eling in ditches. For years the word *laborer* was synonymous
among us with Irishman, just as it has been synonymous with Italian for the past two decades. The workers in the sweatshops have
never been Americans, but always Jews.

What will happen when this supply of drudges is cut off? Who
will go into the ditch with a shovel and pick when the laborious
Sicilian climbs out? Will it be his son, born in America? I doubt
it: the son of an immigrant almost invariably makes his way to a
level above his father's: the exceptions are rare and almost miraculous. Will it be, then, the Negro? Again I doubt it: there are not
enough Negroes to go 'round as it is, and they are not likely to increase either relatively or absolutely, for the death-rate among
them, as they come North and enter industry, grows enormous.
Who, then, will handle the pick? My belief is that it will be handled, soon or late, by the Anglo-Saxon—that he will slide down to
it inevitably—that he is already, along his lower margin, beginning
to descend—that, in brief, the net result of restricting immigration,
ostensibly in his interest, will be to enslave and degrade him.

I do not argue, of course, that the superior varieties of Anglo-
Saxons will take to the ditch: what I argue is simply that the lower
varieties, when the struggle to keep out of it comes on in earnest,
will prove to be inferior to the children of immigrants, and even
to the better sort of surviving Negroes, and that they will thus find
themselves forced down to the bottom. That these lower varieties
are already going downhill must be apparent to any observer. Even
as a whole, the strain is obviously not holding its old leadership. In
the arts, in the sciences, and even in the more complex sorts of
business the children of the later immigrants are running away

from the descendants of the original settlers. To call a list of Americans eminent in almost any field above that of mere money-grubbing is to call a list of strange and often outlandish names; even the roll of Congress presents an almost startling example. In areas when the competition between the new and the old strains is most sharp and clearcut, say in New York, in Massachusetts and in the agricultural States of the upper Middle West, the defeat of the Anglo-Saxon is overwhelming and unmistakable. Once his predominance everywhere was actual and undisputed; today, even where he remains heavily superior numerically, it is largely only sentimental.

On his lower levels his situation is even worse. He is not only not moving ahead at the same pace as his co-nationals of other stocks: he is rapidly degenerating, mentally, spiritually and even physically. Civilization is at its lowest ebb in the United States precisely in those areas where the Anglo-Saxon still rules unchallenged. He runs the whole South—and in the whole South there are not as many first-rate men as in many a single city of the mongrel North. Wherever he is dominant, there Ku Kluxery flourishes, along with Fundamentalism, and lynching, and Prohibition, and free silver, and all the other recurrent crazes of the Chandala. It is not in the big cities, with their mixed population, that the death-rate is highest, and politics is most corrupt, and religion is nearest to voodooism, and every decent human aspiration is suspect, but in the areas that immigration has not penetrated, where "the purest Anglo-Saxon blood in the world" still flows.

So far this lower variety of Anglo-Saxon has been able to profit by his historical advantages. White, broken to the national harness and at ease in the national language, he has evaded direct competition with both the Negroes and the invading hordes of non-Anglo-Saxon immigrants. But his present plight in the cotton areas of the South shows how illusory his immunity really is—how easy it is to deprive him of it. For years and years, in the South, the inferior whites lived by preying upon the Negroes. A correspondent in South Carolina, highly learned in such matters, tells me that most of them did no work whatever. They forced the darkey to work in the fields, and then robbed him of his earnings. For the rest, they sent their children into the cotton mills. Then, of a sudden, the darkey began to escape to the North. What to do? At first, characteristically, they tried to hold him by force. But he continued to escape, and presently they faced the dreadful necessity of going to work themselves. With what result? With the result that the Negroes who have remained, farming their own land, are now clearly their superiors. The poor white trash are at work at last—but the Negroes are better workmen. I incline to think that the same thing will happen in industry, once the lack of labor begins to be felt acutely. There will be a desperate competition for the better jobs. They will go to those workmen who are most diligent and most competent—in other words, to those who can best discharge their duties. The low-grade Anglo-Saxon is neither diligent nor competent. He tends to gravitate downward, even now, to puerile jobs; he is less and less the boss and more and more the clerk. When the abyss yawns at the bottom, I believe that he will fall into it.

Utopia in Little

From the *American Mercury*, May, 1922, pp. 123–26.
A review of ARCTIC VILLAGE, by Robert Marshall;
New York, 1933

In the Summer of 1929, having some idle time on his hands, Mr. Marshall took a map of Alaska from his shelf and searched it for blank spaces. He found that only two of any size were left— one in the vicinity of Mt. McKinley and the other at the headwaters of the Koyukuk river, north of the Arctic Circle. The latter, for various reasons, attracted him more than the former, so he set out for it by way of Fairbanks, and after a journey of 2,000 miles by rail, boat and air, found himself in the little town of Wiseman. He quickly made friends with its seventy-six white inhabitants, forty-four Eskimos, six Indians and one mulatto, and came to like them so much in a two-months' stay that he decided to return in 1930. He got back in August of that year, and remained more than a year. All the while he kept diligent notes of what he saw and heard, and now he offers his observations in the form of a somewhat elaborate study of the Wiseman *Kultur*. It is a sort of miniature "Middletown" and it makes a very interesting and valuable book.

The people of Wiseman, of course, are not really cut off from what is called civilization, despite the fact that they are snowed in from the middle of September to the middle of May, and surrounded by oceans of mud for two other months of every year. They get their groceries and a part of their clothing from the Outside, they have a wireless station to give them news, and at a pinch they can call an airplane from Fairbanks and be walking on paved streets in a couple of hours—that is, if the weather permits, which it often doesn't. A United States marshal lives among them, to police them if necessary, and there is also a United States commissioner, to order them to jail in Fairbanks in case they attempt counterfeiting, the manufacture of bootleg oleomargarine, the robbery of the mails, or piracy upon the high seas. But beyond that they are sufficient unto themselves, and Mr. Marshall shows at length how peacefully they live together, how easily they escape most of the evils that go with life Outside, and how content they are to remain in their remote isolation.

The seventy-seven white inhabitants (I include the colored brother among them, as Mr. Marshall does, for he is very light) offer a very fair cross-section of the people of the United States. Forty-five of them are native-born, and thirty-two are foreign-born, and among the latter are five Germans, five Scandinavians, three Herzogovinans, two Englishmen, two Austrians, and single representatives of Finland, Wales, Poland, Lithuania, Dalmatia, Serbia, Montenegro, Greece and the Shetland Islands. Fifty of the seventy-seven are country-bred, and all save two are the masters of useful trades, ranging from that of the farmer to those of the carpenter, blacksmith, electrician, baker, lumberman and butcher. Most of them have been in the Arctic a long while, and so their average age is somewhat above that of the American at home. Seven enjoy the honor of being female, and of these ladies one is a trained nurse, one is a schoolma'am, and two on their arrival from Outside long ago were prostitutes, though they have long since reformed.

The amazing thing about these people is how amicably they dwell together, and how little their apparent hardships oppress them. There is absolutely no color line among them. The lonely colored brother has every right, whether legal or social, that any other citizen has, and the Eskimos have precisely the same. When there is a communal dance, which is very often, every man, woman and child in the settlement is invited, regardless of race, color or wealth. A few of the inhabitants are pretty well heeled, but the great majority are poor, and there is no division along the line of money. If a given citizen falls into difficulties, and runs short of provender or other supplies, they are furnished instantly and without condescension by those who can spare them. If some one becomes ill and must be sent to Fairbanks or Seattle for treatment, the bills of the airplane man, the doctors and the hospital are shared by all, with each contributing according to his means. There is, of course, nothing approaching real communism. Every man's property is his own, and his right to it is respected by everyone. But in times of stress everything finds its way into a common pot, and so there is never any destitution. During the Hoover Depression the people of Wiseman heard of it as they heard of the battles in Manchuria—as of something remote from their concerns, and a bit fantastic. They noticed that they got less than usual for their furs, but that was all they knew of it by direct evidence.

In this far-flung and frostbitten Arcady the ordinary moral machinery of an American village is completely lacking. There is no church, and save for the inconspicuous devotions of a retired female missionary and a couple of pious Eskimos there is no regular practise of any religion. Most of the white males are skeptics, and so are most of the Eskimos, both male and female. In the palmy days of Prohibition no one paid any heed to it. The sexual behavior of adults is thought to be their own business, and no one presumes to harbor unfavorable views of it. Some of the Eskimo ladies are amiable, and now and then one of them falls in love with a white gentleman to the tune of a more or less public uproar, including the composition of amorous doggerel. But it is not considered seemly to denounce her disposition of her person, and hence there is no scandal, though people may remark her doings in a quietly satirical manner.

Crime is almost unknown in the Koyukuk country. At the height of the Alaska gold-rush it had a great many more inhabitants than it has now, but in its whole history there have been but three murders, one committed by a crazy man and the other two by a prospector in defense of his claim. There have been some fights but not many, and none of a serious nature; sentiment in the community is strongly opposed to quarrelling. Thefts are very rare, and the largest on record involved but $150. The wealth of most of the people is in the form of gold-dust, which is easily purloined, but they do not fear robbers, and never lock their doors when they leave home. Rape is regarded as a heinous crime and if there were ever a case of it the offender would be roughly handled, but there has never been a case. Adultery is unknown as either crime or sin, for public opinion in Wiseman holds that it is nobody's business save that of the contracting parties, and even the aggrieved spouse is expected to take it in a placid and philosophical manner.

Mr. Marshall gave the Binet-Simon test to forty-five of the adults of the settlement, and to most of the children. He found an extraordinarily large proportion of high IQ's. The Wisemannites, in fact, turned out to be on the general mental level of Harvard professors, members of the General Staff of the Army, and the superior minority of bootleggers, investment bankers and magazine editors. Only fourteen per cent fell below the American average, whereas forty-six per cent ranked above it. This fact, I believe, offers a plausible explanation of their felicity. They are naturally intelligent, and there is no agency among them to war upon their intelligence, and make it dangerous. They have no newspapers. They have no politicians. Their police force is rudimentary and impotent. Above all, they are not cursed with theologians. Thus they are free to be intelligent, and what is more, to be decent.

Bring On the Clowns

From THE BUTTE BASHKIRTSEFF,
PREJUDICES: FIRST SERIES, 1919, pp. 127–28

A mongrel and inferior people, incapable of any spiritual aspiration above that of second-rate English colonials, we seek refuge inevitably in the one sort of superiority that the lower castes of men can authentically boast, to wit, superiority in docility, in credulity, in resignation, in morals. We are the most moral race in the world; there is not another that we do not look down upon in that department; our confessed aim and destiny as a nation is to inoculate them all with our incomparable rectitude. In the last analysis, all ideas are judged among us by moral standards; moral values are our only permanent tests of worth, whether in the arts, in politics, in philosophy or in life itself. Even the instincts of man, so intrinsically immoral, so innocent, are fitted with moral false-faces. That bedevilment by sex ideas which punishes continence, so abhorrent to nature, is converted into a moral frenzy, pathological in the end. The impulse to cavort and kick up one's legs, so healthy, so universal, is hedged in by incomprehensible taboos; it becomes stealthy, dirty, degrading. The desire to create and linger over beauty, the sign and touchstone of man's rise above the brute, is held down by doubts and hesitations; when it breaks through it must be so by orgy and explosion, half ludicrous and half pathetic. Our function, we like to believe, is to teach and inspire the world. We are wrong. Our function is to amuse the world. We are the Bryan, the Henry Ford, among the nations.

II. POLITICS

The Politician Under Democracy

From NOTES ON DEMOCRACY, 1926, pp. 104–08

HE IS A man who has lied and dissembled, and a man who has crawled. He knows the taste of the boot-polish. He has suffered kicks in the tonneau of his pantaloons. He has taken orders from his superiors in knavery and he has wooed and flattered his inferiors in sense. His public life is an endless series of evasions and false pretenses. He is willing to embrace any issue, however idiotic, that will get him votes, and he is willing to sacrifice any principle, however sound, that will lose them for him. I do not describe the democratic politician at his inordinate worst; I describe him as he is encountered in the full sunshine of normalcy. He may be, on the one hand, a cross-roads idler striving to get into the State Legislature by grace of the local mortgage-sharks and evangelical clergy, or he may be, on the other, the President of the United States. It is almost an axiom that no man may make a career in politics in the Republic without stooping to such ignobility: it is as necessary as a loud voice. Now and then, to be sure, a man of sounder self-respect may make a beginning, but he seldom gets very far. Those who survive are nearly all tarred, soon or late, with the same stick. They are men who, at some time or other, have compromised with their honor, either by swallowing their convictions or by whooping for what they believe to be untrue. They are in the position of the chorus-girl who, in order to get her humble job, has had to admit the manager to her person. And the old birds among them, like chorus-girls of long experience, come to regard the business resignedly and even complacently. It is the price that a man who loves the clapper-clawing of the vulgar must pay for it under the democratic system. He becomes a coward and a trimmer *ex officio*. Where his dignity was in the days of his innocence there is now only a vacuum in the wastes of his subconscious. Vanity remains to him, but not pride.

Thus the ideal of democracy is reached at last: it has become a psychic impossibility for a gentleman to hold office under the Federal Union, save by a combination of miracles that must tax the resourcefulness even of God. But despite that grim dilemma there are still idealists, chiefly professional Liberals, who argue that it is the duty of a gentleman to go into politics—that there is a way out of the quagmire in that direction. The remedy, it seems to me, is quite as absurd as all the other sure cures that Liberals advocate. When they argue for it, they simply argue, in words but little changed, that the remedy for prostitution is to fill the bawdy-houses with virgins. The same alternatives confront the political aspirant who is what is regarded in America as a gentleman—that is, who is one not susceptible to open bribery in cash. The moment his leg goes over the political fence, he finds the mob confronting him, and if he would stay within he must adapt himself to its tastes and prejudices. In other words, he must learn all the tricks of the regular mountebanks. When the mob pricks up its ears and begins to whinny, he must soothe it with balderdash. He must allay its resentment of the fact that he is washed behind the ears. He must anticipate its crazes, and join in them vociferously. He must regard its sensitiveness on points of morals, and get what advantage he can out of his anæsthesia on points of honor. More, he must make terms with the mob-masters already performing upon its spines, chiefly agents of prehensile minorities. If he neglects these devices he is swiftly heaved over the fence, and his career in statecraft is at an end.

The Joboisie

From the Baltimore *Evening Sun*, Feb. 19, 1923

Practically all the elective offices in the United States, indeed, up to and including that of President, are filled by men who are just as much professional job-holders as the most forlorn clerk in the office of the chief clerk to the assistant secretary to the Fifth Assistant

Postmaster-General. They had other jobs before they got their present jobs, and they will seek yet other jobs the moment their terms expire. It is almost impossible to think of an exception. Even Woodrow Wilson, who had but one public office before he became President—even Dr. Wilson, at the end of his second term, was simultaneously a candidate for a third term, for the presidency of the League of Nations, and for the first vacancy in the Trinity.

The Men Who Rule Us

1
Grant

From the Baltimore *Evening Sun*, Sept. 30, 1931

Intelligence has been commoner among American Presidents than high character, but Grant ran against the stream by having a sort of character without any visible intelligence whatever. He was almost the perfect military man—dogged, devoted and dumb. In the White House he displayed an almost inconceivable stupidity. Whatever was palpably untrue convinced him instantly, and whatever was crooked seemed to him to be noble. If the American people could have kept him out of the presidency by prolonging the Civil War until 1877, it would have been an excellent investment. A more honest man never lived, but West Point and bad whiskey had transformed his cortex into a sort of soup.

2
Harding

From the Baltimore *Evening Sun*, July 19, 1923

No one on this earth has ever heard the Hon. Mr. Harding say anything intelligent. No one has ever heard him repeat an intelligent saying of anyone else without making complete nonsense of it. In the coining and dissemination of words that are absolutely devoid of sensible meaning, in the wholesale emission of sonorous and deafening bilge—in brief, in the manufacture and utterance of precisely the stuff that the plain people admire and venerate—he has no peer under Heaven.

3
Coolidge

From the Baltimore *Evening Sun*, Feb. 9, 1925

The man's merits, in the Babbitt view, are immense and incomparable. He seems, indeed, scarcely like a man at all, but more like some miraculous visitation or act of God. He is the ideal made visible, if not audible—perfection put into a cutaway coat and trotted up and down like a mannequin in a cloak and suit atelier. Nor was there any long stress of training him—no season of doubt and misgiving. Nature heaved him forth full-blown, like a new star shot into the heavens. In him the capitalistic philosophy comes to its perfect and transcendental form. Thrift, to him, is the queen of all the virtues. He respects money in each and every one of its beautiful forms—pennies, nickels, dimes, dollars, five-dollar bills, and so on *ad infinitum*. He venerates those who have it. He believes that they have wisdom. He craves the loan and use of that wisdom. He invites them to breakfast, and listens to them. The things they revere, he reveres. The things they long for, he longs to give them.

4
Mussolini

From the Baltimore *Evening Sun*, Aug. 3, 1931

One hears murmurs against Mussolini on the ground that he is a desperado: the real objection to him is that he is a politician. Indeed, he is probably the most perfect specimen of the genus politician on view in the world today. His career has been impeccably classical. Beginning life as a ranting Socialist of the worst type, he abjured Socialism the moment he saw better opportunities for himself on the other side, and ever since then he has devoted himself gaudily to clapping Socialists in jail, filling them with castor oil, sending blacklegs to burn down their houses, and otherwise roughing them. Modern politics has produced no more adept practitioner. He is its Shakespeare, its Michelangelo, its Bach.

Liberty and Democracy

From the Baltimore *Evening Sun*, April 13, 1925

Liberty and democracy are eternal enemies, and every one knows it who has ever given any sober reflection to the matter. A democratic state may profess to venerate the name, and even pass laws making it officially sacred, but it simply cannot tolerate the thing. In order to keep any coherence in the governmental process, to prevent the wildest anarchy in thought and act, the government must put limits upon the free play of opinion. In part, it can reach that end by mere propaganda, by the bald force of its authority—that is, by making certain doctrines officially infamous. But in part it must resort to force, *i.e.*, to law. One of the main purposes of laws in a democratic society is to put burdens upon intelligence and reduce it to impotence. Ostensibly, their aim is to penalize anti-social acts; actually, their aim is to penalize heretical opinions. At least ninety-five Americans out of every 100 believe that this process is honest and even laudable; it is practically impossible to convince them that there is anything evil in it. In other words, they cannot grasp the concept of liberty. Always they condition it with the doctrine that the state, *i.e.*, the majority, has a sort of right of eminent domain in acts, and even in ideas—that it is perfectly free, whenever it is so disposed, to forbid a man to say what he honestly believes. Whenever his notions show signs of becoming "dangerous," *i.e.*, of being heard and attended to, it exercises that prerogative. And the overwhelming majority of citizens believe in supporting it in the outrage.

Including especially the Liberals, who pretend—and often quite honestly believe—that they are hot for liberty. They never really are. Deep down in their hearts they know, as good democrats, that liberty would be fatal to democracy—that a government based upon shifting and irrational opinion must keep it within bounds or run a constant risk of disaster. They themselves, as a practical matter, advocate only certain narrow kinds of liberty—liberty, that is, for the persons they happen to favor. The rights of other persons do not seem to interest them. If a law were passed tomorrow taking away the property of a large group of presumably well-to-do persons—say, the bond-holders of the railroads—without compensation and even without colorable reason, they would not oppose it; they would be in favor of it. The liberty to have and hold property is not one that they recognize. They believe only in the liberty to envy, hate and loot the man who has it.

Leaves from a Note-book

1

From the Baltimore *Evening Sun*, Feb. 12, 1923

The fact that amateurs, at least transiently, so often defeat the professional politicians is due simply to the fact that an amateur, when he becomes a candidate, is nearly always brought into the combat by indignation—that he seeks office because he is violently against something. But it is just as hard to hold an amateur status in politics as it is in sports. The moment an amateur gets into office his indignation is diluted by solicitude, to wit, solicitude for his own job. He then begins to slide down the chute navigated by the late Bonaparte.

2

From the same

It is often urged, as a remedy for the obvious evils of democracy, that the citizens who now eschew politics should spit on their hands and horn in. But would this remedy really afford a cure? I can scarcely imagine anyone believing that it would. The moment the present outsiders became public-spirited they would begin to seek public office, and the moment they began to seek public office they would face the necessity of exposing themselves to the mob, and of trying to dance to its taste. In brief, the moment they become public-spirited they would become precisely the same flatterers and mountebanks that the existing politicians are.

3

From the same

To advocate free speech is quite useless: the thing itself would be fatal to democracy. But in advocating it one at least enjoys the satisfaction of exposing the hypocrisy and swinishness of those who oppose it.

4

From the Baltimore *Evening Sun*, Nov. 18, 1929

The danger in free speech does not lie in the menace of ideas, but in the menace of emotions. If words were merely logical devices no one would fear them. But when they impinge upon a moron they set off his hormones, and so they are justifiably feared. Complete free speech, under democracy, is possible only in a foreign language. Perhaps that is what we shall come to in the end.

Anyone will be free to say what he pleases in Latin, but everything in English will be censored by prudent job-holders.

5

From the Baltimore Evening Sun, March 5, 1923

The seasick passenger on an ocean liner detests the "good sailor" who stalks past him on deck 100 times a day, ostentatiously smoking a large, greasy, ammoniacal cigar. In precisely the same way the good democrat hates the man who is having a better time in the world. This is the origin of democracy—the long and short of democracy. It is also the long and short of Puritanism.

The True Immortal

From the Smart Set, Oct., 1919, pp. 84–85

If, in the course of long years, the great masses of the plain people gradually lose their old faiths, it is only to fill the gaps with new faiths that restate the old ones in new terms. Nothing, in fact, could be more commonplace than the observation that the crazes which periodically ravage the proletariat are, in the main, no more than distorted echoes of delusions cherished centuries ago. The fundamental religious ideas of the lower orders of Christendom have not changed materially in 2,000 years, and they were old when they were first borrowed from the heathen of Asia Minor and Northern Africa. The Iowa Methodist of today, imagining him able to understand them at all, would be able to accept the tenets of Augustine without changing more than a few accents and punctuation marks. Every Sunday his raucous ecclesiastics batter his ears with diluted and debased filches from "De Civitate Dei," and almost every article of his practical ethics may be found clearly stated in the eminent bishop's Ninety-third Epistle. And so in politics. The Bolsheviki of today not only poll-parrot the balderdash of the French demagogues of 1789; they also mouth what was gospel to every *bête blonde* in the Teutonic forests of the Fifth Century. Truth shifts and changes like a cataract of diamonds; its aspect is never precisely the same at two successive instants. But error flows down the channel of history like some great stream of lava or infinitely lethargic glacier. It is the one relatively fixed thing in a world of chaos. It is, perhaps, the one thing that gives human society the stability needed to save it from the wreck that ever menaces. Without their dreams men would have fallen upon and devoured one another long ago—and yet every dream is an illusion, and every illusion is a falsehood.

The Same Old Gang

From the *Smart Set*, July, 1923, pp. 142–44.
A review of THE DECAY OF CAPITALIST CIVILIZATION,
by Sidney and Beatrice Webb; New York, 1923

This is a book that is far too optimistically named—that is, considering that the authors are Socialists, and go to bed every night hoping that the millennium will come before dawn. What they describe as the "decay" of the "civilization" which now surrounds and kisses us, and whose speedy destruction they pray for, is nothing but a catalogue of imperfections, none of them fatal, nor even very painful. The worst, perhaps, are the ferocity with which war is waged under capitalism and the facility with which the more elemental varieties of producers, such as farmers and workingmen, are robbed and exploited by their masters. But it must be obvious to every calm man that neither has gone far enough to be unendurable.

The horrors of war, as I have often argued, are always greatly exaggerated by sentimentalists. Even in the actual trenches, as everyone who has been there knows, they are intermittent, and life in the intervals, to most of the men living it, is relatively easy and even amusing. After all, every conscript who is forced to go there is not killed, nor is every one wounded, nor is every one who is wounded hurt in any very forbidding manner. The killed simply anticipate the inevitable arrival of cancer, diabetes, pneumonia or syphilis, and in a swift and relatively painless fashion; the wounded, save for a small minority, are not seriously damaged, and have something to boast about all the rest of their lives. If the service were really as terrifying as stay-at-home romanticists say it is, then nine-tenths of the morons who face it would go crazy. Nor is war one-half as awful to non-combatants as it is made out to be, even in invaded nations. Think of the oceans of tears shed over the Belgians during the German invasion. And then recall the fact that the actual death-rate among them was less than the average death-rate in such paradises of peace as Lawrence, Mass., and Shamokin, Pa., and that large numbers of them got rich preying upon their oppressors, and that those who filtered out of the country, after a year or so of slavery, turned out to be so badly damaged by their lives of ease that they were quite unfit for regular industry. I do not indulge in paradox here; there are British government reports upon the subject. As for the effects of war upon persons further removed from the front, we had a good chance to study them in the United States between 1917 and 1919. For the vast majority of such persons, war is not a hardship at all, but a lark.

The fact that capitalistic government facilitates the exploitation of the inferior masses is no argument against capitalism; it is simply an argument against all civilized government, which, as Prof. Dr. Franz Oppenheimer has amply demonstrated, is always and inevitably no more than a vast machine for furthering such exploitation. Oppenheimer, true enough, dreams of a time when the exploiters will shut up shop, but that is only a dream, and of a piece with the one of Mr. and Mrs. Webb. We are living among realities, and one of the most salient of them is the fact that the inferior masses appear to have a congenital incapacity for self-government. They must be bossed in order to survive at all, and if kings do not boss them then they are bossed by priests, and if priests are kicked out then they submit to oligarchies of demagogues and capitalists, as now. It would not do them much good to get rid of either half of this combination, or of both halves.

What Mr. and Mrs. Webb seem to visualize for the future is a sort of superior bureaucracy of experts, like the bureaucracy that has long run the American railroad. But what reason is there for believing that it would refrain from exploiting its vast mob of incompetent and ignorant employers? I can see none whatever. The railroad bureaucracy of today, facing a relatively small group of employers, always including a number of highly-trained specialists in the safeguarding of money, nevertheless manages to butter its own parsnips very neatly. Railroad presidents and other such high officials, of course, receive large salaries, but it is rare for one to die without devising to his heirs a sum greatly in excess of his whole professional income since puberty; the rest is the *lagniappe* that goes with his office. There is absolutely no indication that such experts would throw off their intelligent self-interest if they ceased working for their stockholders and began working for the great masses of the plain people. There is still less indication that the labor leaders who now live by petty graft and blackmail would suddenly become honest if turned into Senators, Ambassadors and Cabinet ministers; on the contrary, it is extremely likely that they would become worse sharks than they are today, and that it would be much harder to keep them within bounds.

I am surely no fanatical advocate of the capitalistic system, which has defects so patent that they must be visible even to the most abject worshippers of money. When the control of Christendom passed from kings and priests and nobles to pawnbrokers and note-shavers it was a step downward, if only because kings and priests and nobles cherished concepts of professional honor, which are always as incomprehensible to pawnbrokers and note-shavers, *i.e.*, to the bankers who now rule us, as they would be to pickpockets and policemen. There were things that a king would not do, even to shake down the faithful for a good collection; there were things that a noble would not do, even to save his life. But there is absolutely nothing that a banker will not do to augment his products, short of going to jail. It is only fear of the law that restrains him. In other words, the thing that keeps him relatively in order is the thing that keeps a streetwalker relatively in order, and not at all the thing that keeps a gentleman in order. But what of the Socialist "expert" nominated to follow him on the throne? Is this candidate, then, a man of honor? To ask the question is to answer it.

However, we need not even ask it, for there is absolutely no sign in the world today that capitalism is on its deathbed, as Mr. and

Mrs. Webb hope, and, hoping, think. The example of Russia proves nothing. Capitalism went broke in Russia, and is now in the hands of the Jews, but it is by no means dead; once the country begins to accumulate new wealth, it will come out of hiding and begin to exploit the Russian masses once more; already, indeed, it ventures upon a few discreet experiments. France, Italy, Germany, the various component parts of Austria-Hungary, and all of the new republics save one or two are solidly capitalistic, despite occasional flares of communistic red fire. In England one hears doleful prognostications that the next government will be dominated by Labor, but that is but one more proof of the sad way in which words supplant realities in the thinking of man. Labor, in England, is now as tame as a tabby cat; capitalism has adopted it and put it out at nurse, as it has adopted Liberalism in the United States. The Labor party, if it ever gets into power, will be run by the same old gang of millionaires and professional politicians which now runs the Liberal party and the Tory party. There will be a change in the label, but none at all in the substance; Englishmen will continue to be exploited as they have been exploited ever since the first Norman hoof-print appeared on an English beach.

But it is in the United States that capitalism really enters into Heaven. Here alone does belief in it take on the virulence of a state religion; here alone are men jailed, beaten and done to death for merely meditating against it, as they used to be burned for "imagining the king's death." I doubt that in the whole country there are 50,000 native-born citizens who have so much as permitted their minds to dwell upon the theoretical possibility of ever supplanting it. That form of fancy, so instinctively abhorrent to the right-thinking Americano, is confined almost exclusively to foreigners—and, as every one knows, a foreigner has no rights, even of cogitation *in camera*, by American law, and whatever he is in favor of is *ipso facto* felonious, immoral and against God. Nay, capitalism is planted as firmly in These States as the belief in democracy. It will never be shaken down while you and I breathe and hope and sweat and pray. Long before it feels the first shooting pains down the legs there will be nothing left of us save the glorious immortality of heroes.

For these reasons, though I have read the work of Mr. and Mrs.

Webb with unflagging attention and great interest, I beg to suggest
again that their title is unduly optimistic.

Reflections on Government

From the Chicago *Tribune*, Sept. 18, 1927

Those earnest, and, in the main, quite honest ladies and gentlemen who were lately deafening the world with their uproar about
the Sacco and Vanzetti case fell into an ancient error: they assumed that the gross unfairness which showed itself in the prosecution was peculiar to the capitalistic system of government, and
that under some other system it would have been avoided. This I
presume to doubt. No government is ever fair in its dealings with
men suspected of enmity to it. One of the principal functions of
all government, indeed, is to put down such men, and it is one of
the few governmental functions that are always performed diligently and *con amore*. If Sacco and Vanzetti had been oil millionaires, or coal magnates, or archbishops, or men of any similar
training and prejudice, and if the scene of their trial had been
Moscow instead of Boston, they would have been sent to bliss eternal quite as enthusiastically, and to the tune of precisely the same
whoops and gloats.

I incline to think that in this business a capitalistic democracy
is apt to be rather slacker than either a strong monarchy or a communistic state. The reason is not far to seek. It lies in the fact that
under democracy the reigning plutocracy must execute its mandates through juries, which is to say, through the small bourgeoi-
sie. The judges are easy to control, but the juries are sometimes
very recalcitrant. Is it so soon forgotten that at least half of the men
the American Department of Justice tried to send to prison during
the late war for political heresies were acquitted by juries? The
case of poor Debs is remembered, as the case of Sacco and Vanzetti will be remembered, but no one seems to recall the scores of
imaginary "communists," "anarchists," "German spies" and other
hell-cats who, despite the best efforts of professional witnesses in

the employ of the government, *i.e.*, of the plutocracy, were turned loose. The fact is that it is dangerous for the plutocracy and its agents to push juries too far. The men in the box must be handled discreetly, else they will run amok. If Judge Webster Thayer had denounced Sacco and Vanzetti to the jury in the terms he is said to have used in private, enough of the twelve would have revolted to make a mistrial. For the natural sympathy of humble men is with other humble men, and they sometimes show it unexpectedly and very resolutely. The moment it becomes possible for them to imagine themselves in the prisoner's place—that moment they become skittish, and are no longer to be relied upon to serve God and country with due docility.

In the Sacco and Vanzetti case it was naturally hard for the jury to do any such imagining, for the two men were brought into court in a steel cage, and for weeks the local newspapers had been depicting them as dangerous anarchists, with a bomb in one hand and a stiletto in the other. They were, of course, nothing of the sort, but "philosophical" anarchists of the uplifting and sentimental variety—in brief, dreamers whose Utopia was scarcely to be distinguished from that of the Quakers. However, I am not so sure that the truth would have done them much good with the jury. For plain men dislike uplifters almost as much as they dislike bomb-throwers, and at the time of the trial there was a revulsion against the uplift throughout the United States. Thus, barring accident, it was pretty certain that Sacco and Vanzetti would be convicted, regardless of the actual evidence against them. They were, according to the ideas then prevailing, unpleasant and subversive men, and any stick was good enough to beat them with. They must tarry in Gehennah a long while before they get their revenge, but get it they will. At some time or other in the future there will be a Socialist government in one of the American States, and it will engage in the usual gaudy efforts to put down its enemies. Then the world will see a pair of stock-brokers go on trial for burning down a Labor Lyceum, and presently it will be horrified by their execution, and mobs of bank cashiers, butlers, newspaper editorial writers, clergymen, lawyers and other friends of the plutocracy will stone the American consulates at Barcelona, Lille and Montevideo.

Such are the ways of governments at all times and everywhere. I am surely no admirer of democracy, and so it pains me to have to say it, but I remain convinced that a democratic-capitalistic state is apt to be more humane in this department than any other kind of state. The cause of its relative mildness lies in its dual nature, which makes for weakness. Whenever a state is strong it is intolerant of dissent; when it is strong enough it puts down dissent with relentless violence. Here one state is as bad as another, or, at all events, potentially as bad. The Puritan theocracy of early New England hanged dissenters as gaily as they are now being hanged by the atheistic Union of Soviet Republics; the Prussian, Russian, Austrian, French and English monarchies were as alert against heresy as the militaristic-capitalistic *bloc* which now runs Italy or the plutocracy which runs Pennsylvania, California and Massachusetts.

The only way to make a government tolerant, and hence genuinely free, is to keep it weak. The Liberals of the United States, after years of bitter experience, are beginning to grasp that elemental fact, and so one finds them abandoning their old demands for more and more laws, and greater and greater hordes of jobholders. But they learn slowly, as is the habit of earnest and indignant men at all times and everywhere. In the face of the obscenity of Law Enforcement they have ceased to believe in Prohibition, but most of them, blind to the fact that the Postoffice is already one of the most sinister agents of oppression in the United States, still talk sentimentally of government ownership. Some day some realist on their General Staff, suddenly barred from the mails for violating the delicate pruderies of a tender bureaucrat, will begin to figure out what he would do for telephone service if the telephones were controlled by a docile political hack from Indiana, and how he would get from Chicago to New York if another of the same sort had the power to refuse tickets to "Reds."

Thomas Jefferson, the greatest of all American political philosophers, saw this clearly, and so he was in favor of keeping the government as weak as possible. He believed that in any dispute between a citizen and an official the citizen ought to have the benefit of every doubt. But Jefferson was too intelligent a man to believe that the sweet could be obtained without also taking in a certain amount of the bitter. He knew that a weak government was very likely to be an unstable one—that its very mildness would be no more than a symptom of sickness. He swallowed the fact bravely, and even went to the length of arguing in favor of frequent revolutions. But not many men of today would go with him so far.

Most men incline in the other direction. They like a strong government because, so long as they do not offend it, it gives them protection and security; they are quite willing to give up some of their liberty, and even a great deal of it, in return for those boons. This, I take it, is the position of most respectable Americans today. They are not precisely in favor of rushing innocent men to the electric-chair, as Sacco and Vanzetti were rushed; they are simply in favor of letting the government frame any definition of public enemies, so long as it takes and scotches those public enemies who are actually and palpably dangerous to the peaceable citizen. Their view of it is thus much like their view of the policeman. Not wanting to be clubbed by him, they are polite to him. But they do not protest very violently when they see him clubbing some one else, for they assume that he knows his business.

It is easy to deride this attitude, but not easy to formulate a better one. In the department of government, as in all other departments, the plain man is confronted by harsh alternatives. When political wizards offer to show him a way out, it almost always becomes plain in short order that their way is quite as bad as the old ones, and maybe worse. So he sticks to his rough guesses and approximations. He would welcome, no doubt, a perfect government, but his instinct teaches him that it is as unimaginable as a perfect wife.

The End of an Era

From the Baltimore *Evening Sun*, Sept. 14, 1931

On September 4, 476, a gang of ruffians commanded by Odoacer the barbarian seized young Romulus Augustulus, the last Roman Emperor, and clapped him into a dungeon. This was at 10:40 in the forenoon. At the same instant the Roman Empire blew up with a bang, and the Middle Ages began. The curious thing is that no one knew it. People went about their business as if nothing had happened. They complained that the times were hard, but that was all. Not even the learned were aware that a great epoch in history had come to a close, and another begun.

We of today may be just as blind. It may be that the so-called Modern Period is falling into chaos around our heads—that an entirely new epoch is beginning for mankind. It may be that the capitalistic system is blowing up, as the Roman system blew up. It may be that the new era is beginning in Russia, or somewhere else, or even here at home. If so, I can only say that I regret it extremely. The capitalistic system suits me precisely. I am aware of its defects, but on the whole it agrees with my prejudices and interests. If Communism is on the way I hope to be stuffed and on exhibition in the Smithsonian before it hits Maryland.

But all this is beside the point. The simple question is, can capitalism survive its present appalling attack of boils? Will it prevail against Bolshevism, or will it succumb? The question is by no means easy to answer. Capitalism is plainly wobbling, but is Bolshevism really any stronger? If it were as hard hit, wouldn't it wobble too? Only time can tell, and time tells slowly, even in a frantic age. Meanwhile, let us ponder two facts. The first is that in England the greatest trading corporation in history, the very pearl and model of the capitalistic system, is plainly bankrupt. The other is that in the United States, where capitalism has been elevated to the august estate of a national religion with fifty Popes and 10,000 gaudy Cardinals, the whole pack of these inspired brethren, though the God of Rotary is in hourly communication with them, face a similar bankruptcy with blank faces, and haven't the slightest notion what to do.

The Suicide of Democracy

From the Baltimore *Evening Sun*, May 12, 1940

No one can deny what is spread upon the minutes so copiously. The New Deal, only too plainly, is extending democracy to very remote places of decimals. Reaching out constantly for fresh fields and pastures new, it gradually takes over the entire business of living, including birth and death. It undertakes not only to carry on all the customary enterprises of government, with constant embellishment; it also horns into such highly non-political matters as the planting and harvesting of crops, the pulling of teeth, and the propagation of the species. In particular, it undertakes to succor every one who feels that he is suffering from injustice, whether at the hands of his fellowmen or of his own chromosomes. If there is something you want but can't get, it will get that something for you. And, contrariwise, if there is something you want and have got, it will take it away.

It would be hard to imagine a simpler system, or, in its first stages, a more successful one. Nearly all of us, in some particular or other, are have-nots, and here is an invitation to every have-not to step up to the bar and give it a name. The response is naturally large, and not only large but vociferous. The rejoicing of the beneficiaries is so loud that the groans of those who are mulcted can hardly be heard. The Hon. Mr. Roosevelt, the impresario of the riot, becomes the most popular politico ever known. So long as the money holds out, he can have not only a third term, but also a fourth, fifth and nth. The only question before the house is whether he will condescend to accept.

Meanwhile, theory keeps step with practise, and the career mendicant is supported and encouraged by the official metaphysician. It is the natural and bounden duty of democracy, we are told, to take care of its customers in all situations, at all times, and everywhere. If one of them lacks a job, then democracy must find it for him, and if the yield thereof is less than satisfactory to him, then democracy must adjust it to his desires. If he goes into business— say, farming—and makes a botch of it, his losses must be made good. If he craves a house beyond his means, then money to pay for it must be provided. If he has too many children, the supernumeraries must be lifted off his hands, and his energies released for the generation of more.

As I have said, the system is simple, and for a while it works well enough. The shrill gloats and exultations of A, who has got something for nothing, drown out the repining of B, who has lost something that he earned. B, in fact, becomes officially disreputable, and the more he complains the more he is denounced and detested. He is moved, it appears, by a kind of selfishness which is incompatible with true democracy. He actually believes that his property is his own, to remain in his keeping until he chooses to part with it. He is told at once that his information on the point is inaccurate, and his morals more than dubious. In an ideal democracy, he learns, property is at the disposal, not of its owners, but of politicians, and the chief business of politicians is to collar it by fair means or foul, and redistribute it to those whose votes have put them in office.

The Fathers of the Republic, who seem to have been men of suspicious minds, apparently foresaw that the theory of democracy might develop along such lines, and they went to some trouble to prevent it. Their chief device to that end was the scheme of limited powers. Rejecting the old concept of government as a kind of primal entity, ordained of God and beyond human control, they tried to make it a mere creature of the people. So far it could go, but no further. Within its proper province it had all the prerogatives that were necessary to its existence, but beyond that province it had none at all. It could do what it was specifically authorized to do, but nothing else. The Constitution was simply a record specifying its bounds. The Fathers, taught by their own long debates, knew that efforts would be made, from time to time, to change the Constitution as they had framed it, so they made the process as difficult as possible, and hoped that they had prevented frequent resort to it. Unhappily, they did not foresee the possibility of making changes, not by formal act, but by mere political intimidation—not by recasting its terms, but by distorting their meaning. If they were alive today, they would be painfully aware of their oversight. The formal revisions of the Constitution have been relatively few, but at this moment it is completely at the mercy of a gang of demagogues consecrated to reading into it governmental powers that are not only wholly foreign to its spirit, but categorically repugnant to its terms.

Such is the net effect of the Hon. Mr. Roosevelt's court-packing scheme—a failure in law but a dizzy success in fact. On matters which do not impinge upon the New Deal programme, his sardines of the Supreme Court still stick, more or less, to the Constitution as written, but when questions of policy come up they go with the politicians who made them, leaving the Constitution to lick its wounds. In brief, they reject the fundamental theory that governmental powers are strictly limited, and align themselves with the doctrine that the mountebanks who happen, at any moment, to be in office are quite free, within very wide limits, to attempt any experiment and inflict any injustice that will get them votes and safeguard their jobs.

A good many thoughtful men, I suppose, have been asking themselves of late a natural question: how are we to get rid of this nefarious imbecility? By what means are we to restore government to its constitutional functions, and put an end to its crazy and costly invasions of forbidden fields? I must say that I have no answer to offer. The Fathers, though they were well aware of the infamy of politicians, devised no really effective way to curb them. By resigning matters, in the last analysis, to a count of noses, they opened the door to demagogues, and after a century and a half of ardent practise those demagogues have attained to a magnificent virtuosity, and all of us are now under their hooves.

Whether or not they can be curbed by constitutional means remains to be seen. As for me, I begin to doubt it. There is obviously no way to get rid of Roosevelt and company so long as they are free to buy votes out of the public treasury, and there is no apparent way to prevent that buying of votes so long as they and their client-judges remain in office. Thus democracy turns upon and devours itself. Universal suffrage, in theory the palladium of our liberties, becomes the assurance of our slavery. And that slavery will grow more and more abject and ignoble as the differential birth rate, the deliberate encouragement of mendicancy and the failure of popular education produce a larger and larger mass of prehensile half-wits, and so make the demagogues more and more secure.

The alternatives all look unpleasant enough, God knows. No rational man can fail to see that the totalitarianisms so far invented abroad, if translated here, would be even worse, in many important ways, than Rooseveltian democracy, swinish though it may be. Perhaps we'll gradually work out something better than either. Or it may come by catastrophe. But, however it comes, come it must, for a series of Roosevelts stretching over fifty years, or even over twenty-five years, would plainly reduce the country to chaos, with the Chandala in the saddle and all decent people in the status of *ferae naturae*. Democracy may not be actually dying here, as it only too plainly is in Europe, but it is certainly very sick.

The Last Ditch

From the Baltimore *Evening Sun*, April 2, 1923

It seems to me that monarchy, even of the most absolute and intransigent kind, is appreciably superior to democracy here. A monarch elected and inaugurated by God, having no need to play the clown to the mob, can devote himself whole-heartedly to the business of his office, and no matter how stupid he may be he is at least in a better position to give effective service than a President who is likely to be quite as stupid as he is, and certain to be ten times as dishonest. It is not to the monarch's self-interest to be dishonest; he is more comfortable, like any other man, when he does what he genuinely wants to do. Moreover, the subordinate officers of the state, working under him, share his advantages. They do not have to grimace and cavort before the mob in order to get and hold their offices; the only person they have to please is the monarch himself, who is, at all events, a relatively educated man, with some notion of family honor and tradition in him, and uncorrupted by the habit of abasement.

Liberalism

A hitherto unpublished note

A Liberal is one who is willing to believe anything twice.

III. WAR

The War Against War

From the Chicago *Tribune*, July 24, 1927

OF ALL the varieties of uplifters who now sob and moan through the land, the most idiotic, I begin to suspect, are the pacifists. Not even the sex hygienists, the movie censors, or the reconcilers of science and religion show a more romantic and fantoddish spirit. At least half the devices they propose for ending war appear to have been borrowed from the gaseous armamentarium of the New Thought, that pink and spongy nonsense. Worse, they seem to have an unpleasant capacity for corrupting the logic and scattering the wits of otherwise sensible men. Here, for example, is Ambassador Houghton, our eminent agent at London, arguing solemnly that the way to end war is to resort to the referendum—that is, to put it to a vote every time it threatens. What could be more nonsensical? Call the scheme a scheme to make war certain, and you have very accurately described it. For it must be plain that a referendum would take time, and it must be equally plain that during that time the warlocks would have everything their own way. Imagine their gaudy tales about the prospective enemy's preparations. Imagine their pious, inflammatory talk about protecting the home from his hordes. And then try to imagine a referendum going for peace.

I am surely no admirer of politicians. Least of all do I admire the puerile, paltry shysters who constitute the majority of Congress. But I confess frankly that these shysters, whatever their defects, are at least appreciably superior to the mob. They are restrained in their excesses, if for no other reason, because they fear the sober second thought of the mob. But the mob itself is in

52

no terror of its own second thought. Once it is on the loose, it slashes around like a wild animal. It cannot be stopped until it is exhausted.

Next to the referendumeers, the most absurd of the pacifists now in practice among us are those who propose to put an end to war by setting up ironclad agreements between the principal predatory nations. To this lodge belongs another American ambassador, Monsieur Herrick, though it is somewhat difficult to determine, in the present negotiations, whether he represents the United States or France. His plan is for the two countries to agree to keep the peace forever hereafter, whatever the temptation to go to war. As I understand him, he is willing to go the whole hog. Even in the event that the French *gendarmerie* round up all the American drunks in Paris and chop off their heads, the United States is to refrain from doing anything beyond writing a sharp note.

To state this scheme is to provide a sufficient answer to it. No man who has read history can have any confidence in such grandiose agreements. They last until there is a good excuse for war, and then they blow up. In the late World War every participating nation, absolutely without exception, broke some treaty or other; most of them broke dozens. Even the United States, which, as every one knows, is extremely virtuous, engaged in this time-honored sport. It had a treaty with the Germans, honored by more than a century of life, which protected the merchant shipping of the two high contracting parties in case of war between them. It repudiated that treaty in order to grab the German ships interned in American harbors. No agreement with France would be worth a depreciated franc if that country and the United States ever came to a serious clash of interests. If the United States didn't repudiate it, then the French would repudiate it. Naturally enough, the party doing the repudiating would swathe the business in a great deal of moral rhetoric. All the blame would be unloaded on the other fellow. But it would be a repudiation nonetheless, and it would be followed by a grand attempt, in the ancient Christian manner, to let the other fellow's blood and grab his goods.

But must we have wars forever? I greatly fear so. Nevertheless, it should be possible to diminish their number, and even abate some of their ferocity. How? By a device that is as simple as mud, and has been tried often in the past, and with excellent success. In brief, by the device of the *Pax Romana*. Let the United States, which is now richer and stronger than any other nation, and perhaps richer and stronger than all of them put together, prepare such vast and horrible armaments that they are irresistible. Then let it launch them against France, or some other chronic trouble-maker, and proceed to give the victim a sound beating. And then let it announce quietly that war is adjourned, and that the next nation which prepares for it will get another and worse dose of the same medicine.

This scheme would more nearly approximate the course of justice within civilized states than any of the world courts, leagues of nations, and other such phantasms that now entertain sentimentalists—many of them with something to sell. The courts are obeyed among us, not because there is any solemn pact among litigants to respect their fiats, but simply and solely because they have force behind them. No individual—save he be, of course, a Prohibition agent or a heavy contributor to the funds of the Republican National Committee—is strong enough to defy them. If he loses he has no recourse: he must submit. Let him refuse and he is instantly laid by the heels and punished with great barbarity.

It seems to me that there can be no permanent peace among nations until some such system is set up among them. Of what avail are the mandates of a world court unable to enforce them—a world court that must seek help, when help is needed, among the body of litigants standing before it? Many of these litigants will inevitably sympathize with the worsted party; others will see no profit in tackling him. The effects of that lack of adequate police power, if a world court were actually in operation, would simply be to make the whole process of international justice ridiculous. Every powerful litigant would be free to defy the court, and so would every weak litigant with powerful friends.

I believe that the United States could put an end to this unpleasant situation and at no great cost or risk. If it started tomorrow to arm in earnest, no other nation could hope to keep up with it: they'd all be bankrupt in two years if they tried to hold the pace. This fact became obvious at the close of the world war, when even England, the richest of the contestants and the one that had profited most by the war, saw clearly that she could not keep up with Uncle Sam on the seas. So she had her agents in Washington root hard for the disarmament conference that silly American pacifists had already proposed, and the result was that the United States agreed to keep the American fleet down to the level of the English fleet. This was a great folly. It left England still able to dream of tackling and butchering the accursed Yankee, and so opened the way for more wars. If the United States had built twenty or thirty battleships and then employed them to sink all the English and Japanese battleships there would be peace in the world today, and it would be genuine. True enough, the English would have yelled blue murder and called upon God to witness that they were being undone by an international criminal, but they'd have got over it quickly, and by this time they'd have become used to keeping the peace. As it is, they remain free to start another war whenever they please, and it seems very likely that, unless France undergoes a transformation little short of miraculous, they will do so very soon. The United States will be drawn into it and will have to pay for it.

My scheme, to be sure, would exact force and put the whole world at the mercy of the United States. But that would be nothing new. The world is at the mercy of force today, and it is exerted by powers that, in the main, are even less reputable than the United States. Our own stealings are in Latin America, where no one ventures to oppose us. The others scramble for the loot elsewhere and constantly threaten war. The way to make them stop is not to get them to sign a vast mass of puerile and meaningless agreements, but to sharpen a terrible swift sword and let them feel its edge.

Summary Judgment

From the Baltimore *Evening Sun*, June 12, 1922

My conclusions about the late war remain as follows: (*a*) that the American pretense of neutrality down to 1917 was dishonest and dishonorable, (*b*) that the interests of the United States were actually on the side of Germany, and against both England and France, (*c*) that the propagation of the notion to the contrary was a very deft and amusing piece of swindling, and (*d*) that the American share of the war, after 1917, was carried on in an extremely cowardly manner. Every day I meet some man who was hot for the bogus Wilsonian idealism in 1916 and 1917, and is now disillusioned and full of bile. Such men I do not respect.

The Next Round

From the Baltimore *Evening Sun*, July 18, 1921

The surest way to bring on a war, it would seem, is to prove that it would be in violation of the great ethico-cosmic laws which produce sunsets, the laughter of little children, and all the lovely varieties of roses and sarcomata, and hence cannot conceivably take place. This benign process now works magnificently toward a clash between the two great empires of promoters and usurers, Japan and the United States. The same American Association for International Conciliation which demonstrated conclusively, in the Spring of 1914, that all Europe was bathed in good-will, is now marshaling its unanswerable proofs that we and the Japs must not and shall not fight. And to the benign business a vast multitude of lesser uplifters, vision-seers, Shakers, Muggletonians, human service-bringers, snatchers, chautauquans, message-bringers and civilization-embalmers also address themselves. I doubt that there is an editorial-writer in the Republic who has not written at least one leading article on the subject, and I doubt that a single such article has failed to describe the coming rough-house as unthinkable. Nevertheless, my agents in the Far East, hitherto very reliable, report that disbelief in the impossibility of the thing increases by geometrical ratio as one approaches the probable scene of the carnage. Here on the Atlantic seaboard practically every right-thinking man regards the whole alarm as no more than a bugaboo manufactured by Hearst. On the Pacific Coast men discuss it seriously. In Hawaii they discuss it fearfully. In Australia they dream horrible dreams about it. In Japan, so I hear, the grindstones work day and night, and every two-handed sword takes on a razor edge.

The Art of Selling War

From the Baltimore *Sun*, May 9, 1939

The fact that all the polls run heavily against American participation in the threatening European war is not to be taken seriously. A secret poll taken in any of the countries principally concerned would show the same result precisely. The overwhelming majority of Englishmen don't want war, and hope that it will never come again, and the same thing is true of the majority of Frenchmen, Germans, Italians, Poles, Russians, Roumanians and Serbs. It was true of the same people down to August 2, 1914 and of Americans down to April 6, 1917.

But wars are not made by common folk, scratching for livings in the heat of the day; they are made by demagogues infesting palaces. It is not necessary for these demagogues to complete the sale of a war before they send the goods home, as a storekeeper must complete the sale of, say, a suit of clothes. They send the goods home first, and then convince the customer that he wants them. History teaches that this is always very easy, for a number of reasons. One is that the very unpopularity of war makes people ready to believe, when they suddenly confront it, that it has been thrust upon them. They can't imagine wanting it themselves; *ergo*, it must have been willed by the other fellow. But why don't they blame their own demagogues? Because their own demagogues have been pretending, all the while, to be trying to prevent it. This attempt is now being made, and in a large and heroic way, by MM. Hitler, Mussolini and Chamberlain. It is also being made by the Hon. Mr. Roosevelt. Thus, when it fails, the other fellow is manifestly to blame.

Another reason why peaceful people are so easily fetched by war is that they fear to be thought cowards. Their very peacefulness is a suspicious fact, even in their own minds, and when they are challenged they try to get rid of it by playing brave. This accounts for the extraordinary bloodthirstiness, once war has begun, of pacifists, including especially the rev. clergy. They still dislike war, but they don't want anyone to think that they dislike it because they are afraid of it; so they set up a howl for force without stint, and preach that he who dallies is a dastard and he who doubts is damned.

But the main reason why it is easy to sell war to peaceful people is that the demagogues who act as salesmen quickly acquire a monopoly of both public information and public instruction. They pass laws penalizing anyone who ventures to call them to book, and in a little while no one does it any more. This happened at the time the United States entered the last World War, and it will happen again if the Hon. Mr. Roosevelt manages to whoop up another one. On the day war is declared the Espionage Act will come into effect, and all free discussion will cease. No one will have access to the radio who is not approved by the White House, and no newspaper will be able to dissent without grave risk of denunciation and ruin. Any argument against the war itself, and any criticism of the persons appointed to carry it on, will become aid and comfort to the enemy. The war will not only become moral all over; it will become the touchstone and standard of morality. This impeccability will extend at once to all acts and utterances of the Administration. It will become treason to observe that the Hon. Mr. Wallace has failed to save the farmers, and treason tinged with heresy to argue that the Hon. Mr. Ickes is a jackass.

A few weeks of that razzle-dazzle will suffice to convert most people to the war and to intimidate and silence the stray recalcitrants who hold out. All of us rationalize our necessities in this world, and one of the pressing necessities of war-time is to go along, or, at all events, not to fall back. It becomes harder and harder to resist, both socially and psychologically. The dissenter is not only suspected by all his neighbors; he also begins to suspect himself.

Thus the job of demagogy is completed, and a brave and united nation confronts a craven and ignominious foe. It is not until long afterward that anyone ventures to inquire into the matter more particularly, and it is then too late to do anything about it. The dead are still dead, the fellows who lost legs still lack them, war widows go on suffering the orneriness of their second husbands, and taxpayers continue to pay, pay, pay. In the schools children are taught that the war was fought for freedom, the home and God.

Onward, Christian Soldiers!

From the Baltimore *Evening Sun*, May 19, 1940

The Hon. Mr. Roosevelt's heroic attempt to rescue England from the law of natural selection has got off to a good start, and may be expected to develop with undiminishing radiancy. As everyone knows, it has been long in preparation, and it would have been launched months ago if the hazards of the third-term campaign had not counseled caution. But with the Hon. John N. Garner lying dead upon the field and nearly all the other erstwhile Fifth Column men leaping for cover, the way is now open to panic the booboisie in the grand manner, and this, no doubt, will be promptly undertaken and achieved. In a few weeks it will be a primary article of American dogma that it is an act of lunacy, and not only an act of lunacy but also immoral and against God, to change barrels going over Niagara. The impediment lying in the proletarian disinclination to be butchered must be considered, of course, but it is not likely to last long. The plain people having abandoned the barber-shop, the village grocery and the dream-book for the radio, are now wholly dependent upon it for information and ideology, and in very short order they will be getting a horse-doctor's dose of both. Six successive nights of White House crooning will make them pant for Hitler's poisonous blood; indeed, it would take only seven or eight to make them pant for Churchill's. That crooning will be on us anon, beginning for the same at middle C and running up gloriously to A above the clef.

War Without Art

From the *Smart Set*, April, 1918, pp. 142–43.
A review of THE STORY OF A COMMON SOLDIER
OF ARMY LIFE IN THE CIVIL WAR,
by Leander Stillwell; Kansas City, 1917

Judge Stillwell is a resident of Erie, Kansas, a remote outpost in the saleratus and hog cholera belt. After great difficulties my agents in Kansas City located the town, waited upon the judge, and procured a copy of the work. I have since read it with the utmost pleasure. It is a modest and excellent composition, a chronicle of war without any of the customary strutting and bawling in it. Judge Stillwell served in the Union Army for four years, and saw some of the most savage fighting of the Civil War, but he nowhere hints that the event of Appomattox was due to his personal butcheries, nor does he expose the strategical imbecilities of the generals he fought under, nor does he describe or discuss any battle at which he was not present, nor does he pile on the rhetoric in describing the battles he actually saw. In brief, a war book of a quite unusual sort, and an effective antidote to the gorgeous tomes which now burden the book-counters. More, it is done in plain, straightforward American, naked and unashamed.

The learned jurist, now a hearty ancient of seventy-three, went into the war a boy of eighteen. His home was in the jungle of southwestern Illinois and his whole service was seen as a member of Company D, 61st Illinois Infantry, a regiment raised by countrymen, and officered and manned by countrymen from first to last. Stillwell enlisted as a private, was made a corporal at the end of his training, and a good while later, after bearing himself creditably in the field, was promoted to sergeant. He remained a sergeant until near the end. Then, with the Confederacy in collapse and the war practically over, some of the officers of the regiment retired and he was made a second lieutenant and finally a first lieutenant. This was the full extent of his promotions. He came home with a sword over his shoulder, but he had never drawn it in battle. All his fighting had been done with a musket and in the ranks.

The 61st Illinois was at Shiloh and fought through the first day, but was held in reserve thereafter. Stillwell describes what he saw, and then shuts down; the battle, as he depicts it, was merely a small affair in the woods. But what a thrill he sets into that brief scene with his arctic, almost biblical phrases! One sees the row of plow-boys in their first, dismayed surprise; one hears the appalling slambang of it; one feels them stagger and fall back; one almost smells them in their swift, sweaty retreat. And then the retirement to the river, and the long wait by the water while Buell's divisions landed from the steamboats and clawed their way into the woods, and forty bands played "The Girl I Left Behind Me." The picture jumps and jiggers like a moving picture film. It is full of brilliant flashes, little episodes that stick in the mind. No better writing could be imagined.

The 61st was before Vicksburg, but never near enough to look down into the city. The judge does not lie about it; he doesn't pretend that he was nearer than he was; he doesn't tell how his eagle eye laid a 42-centimetre gun and shot off the campanile of the First Methodist Church; he mentions no wading in blood. What one actually gets from him is a dramatic vision of vast tumults on the horizon, of a gigantic battle sensed from afar. Occasionally a shell came near—but no one paid much attention to shells. The main business was to find something to eat, and especially something better than the salt-horse and Yankee beans of the Army. One fairly tastes those beans toward the close. They are mentioned on every page—perhaps 200 times. General Grant is mentioned but twice.

Another capital chapter describes an obscure and petty battle on the railroad below Murfreesboro, Tenn.—a battle so small that the history books probably do not mention it at all. But for Sergeant Stillwell it was the wildest combat of the whole war, and so he goes into it in detail, and makes it extraordinarily vivid. The 61st had been told off to guard a supply train, and the Confederates ambushed train and regiment in the woods. There followed a brisk fight in the night, and following the fight a disorderly retreat along the railroad tracks. The men floundered through thickets and country streams, lost and calling to one another. Their officers took to the woods, were driven out, fell wounded in the ditch along the track. The fat colonel, winded by his colossal sprinting, rolled over like an ox and was pounced upon by the yelling rebels. Altogether, a shocking and lamentable affair—and here set down superbly.

So to the end. One gets a constant feeling of reality; no mere artfulness could contrive it. Nor is all the good writing in the battle scenes. The last scene of all, the war done, is one of the best managed in the book. Here we see the return of the veteran of twenty-two, now proudly embellished with the shoulder-straps of an officer. Discharged at Springfield, after a long wait for his money, he makes his way to the little village nearest his home, his coat off, his sword shouldered like a musket. His expectations are not concealed; he has gallantly served his country; he glances about for signs of welcome. But no such signs appear. A yokel in the village store gapes at him idly but does not hail him; a house-dog barks as he passes on; that is all. "Discharged soldiers were now numerous and common, and no longer a novelty." Two hours later he is helping his father to cut and shock the corn.

I commend this little volume to your kind attention.

Memorials of Dishonor

From the *American Mercury*, Nov., 1929, pp. 381–82.
A review of THE TRAGIC ERA:
THE REVOLUTION AFTER LINCOLN,
by Claude G. Bowers; Boston, 1929

Mr. Bowers's book is a long one and in parts it is painfully dull; nevertheless, I'd be glad to second a motion to compel every Federal judge in America, every member of the W.C.T.U. and the D.A.R., every Rotarian and Kiwanian, and every self-confessed hero of the late war to memorize it on penalty of the bastinado. For it is a magnificent antidote to the whole rumble-bumble of Law Enforcement, with side swipes at all the other varieties of pious nonsense which now delude the American people. It deals with a period when "idealism" was loose upon the land as never before or since, and the tale it has to tell is one of almost unmitigated oppression, corruption and false pretenses. Then, as now, politicians, theologians and stock-jobbers combined to bring in the Millennium, and then, as now, the fruits were only extortion and excess. It is difficult, reading the record, to believe it. It seems a sheer impossibility that such things could have happened in a country pretending to be civilized. Yet happen they did, and not all the scouring and polishing of prostitute historians can ever erase the damning facts.

The period, of course, was that of the two Grant administrations. Ignorant, stupid, plebeian and uncouth, with the tastes of a village drunkard and the pathetic credulity of a yokel at a county fair, Grant staggered through his eight years of disgrace and dishonor. He had an instinct for trusting scoundrels which almost amounted to genius. So long as Lincoln lived the influence of that vast and mystical personage held him in leash, and in his final dealings with Lee the orders that came from above even got him some reputation as a humane and sensible man. But once old Abe was in the boneyard, his native imbecility developed rapidly and brilliantly. By 1866 he was already lined up with the harpies and fanatics who sought to destroy Andrew Johnson, and thereafter, until his second term ended in a blast of horrible stenches, he was the stalking-horse of every infamy. There is no record, after the first year or two, that he ever so much as suspected that most of his friends were scoundrels. In the midst of it all he believed that they were virtuous, and marvelled that their patriotic inspirations could be challenged. Today, appropriately enough, the largest American city does honor to his *manes*. It is sad, but it is fitting.

Mr. Bowers's eye is cast mainly below the Potomac. In his discussions of the sordid abominations of Reconstruction he piles up documents with relentless industry, but when it comes to what went on simultaneously in the North he is not so copious. Such half-fabulous frauds as Henry Ward Beecher get only a few tart words, and there is next to nothing about the thieveries and oppressions which begat the industrialism of today. The South, in the long run, will probably suffer as unpleasantly under that industrialism as it ever suffered under Reconstruction: the signs of that effect are already numerous and striking. But Mr. Bowers has no time or steam for the subject: he is concerned primarily with the robbery and debauchery which went on in the conquered States immediately after the war. There are few parallels to the story in the history of civilized man. The ancients, butchering their defeated foes out of hand, were relatively humane. It remained for 100% Americans to invent the scheme of first disarming them and then starving and looting them, of setting savages upon them, of cruelly and deliberately reducing them to desperation and despair. It was American soldiers in uniform who carried out that chivalrous business, and it was the most glorious of American captains who bossed the job. Let the fact be remembered by exuberant patriots whenever the flag goes by.

Mr. Bowers unearths some curious and sardonic details. When, at the height of the saturnalia, certain tender-minded Northerners protested against it on grounds of humanity, the Northern Methodist bishops demanded that the whip be laid on with unabated ferocity. From the learned jurists of the Federal judiciary came support no less hearty: they were always ready with decisions justifying the suspension of the writ of *habeas corpus*, the confiscation of private property, the stealing of elections, the waste of the public funds. History repeats itself in our own day, but the denizens of the New South are too stupid to read its lessons. Mr. Bowers makes no vain pretense to judicial impartiality. He is frankly against the Sumners, Thaddeus Stevenses and other such appalling sadists of the era, and apparently hopes that they are now in Hell. The ground he covers has been covered before, but his documentation is largely new. He makes heavy use of the files of the New York *World*, the paper he now serves as an editorial writer. He also dredges a lot of interesting stuff out of contemporary manuscripts, notably the unpublished diary of George W. Julian of Indiana, a follower of Stevens who gagged at what went on, and ended his career as a Democrat. The book, as I have said, has some dullness; Mr. Bowers is not a brisk writer. But the tale he has to tell is one that every American should study on his knees.

IV. CRIMINOLOGY

The Nature of Liberty

From PREJUDICES: THIRD SERIES, 1922, pp. 193–200.
First printed in *Issues of Today*, March 11, 1922

LET US suppose that you are a peaceful citizen on your way home from your place of employment. A police sergeant, detecting you in the crowd, approaches you, lays his hand on your collar, and informs you that you are under arrest for killing a trolley conductor in Altoona, Pa. Amazed by the accusation, you decide hastily that the officer has lost his wits, and take to your heels. He pursues you. You continue to run. He draws his revolver and fires at you. He misses you. He fires again and fetches you in the leg. You fall and he is upon you. You prepare to resist his apparently maniacal assault. He beats you into insensibility with his espantoon, and drags you to the patrol box.

Arrived at the watch house you are locked in a room with five detectives, and for six hours they question you with subtle art. You grow angry—perhaps robbed of your customary politeness by the throbbing in your head and leg—and answer tartly. They knock you down. Having failed to wring a confession from you, they lock you in a cell, and leave you there all night. The next day you are taken to police headquarters, your photograph is made for the Rogues' Gallery, and a print is duly deposited in the section labeled "Murderers." You are then carted to jail and locked up again. There you remain until the trolley conductor's wife comes down from Altoona to identify you. She astonishes the police by saying that you are not the man. The actual murderer, it appears, was an Italian. After holding you a day or two longer, to audit your income tax returns and investigate the pre-marital chastity of your wife, they let you go.

You are naturally somewhat irritated by your experience and perhaps your wife urges you to seek redress. Well, what are your remedies? If you are a firebrand, you reach out absurdly for those of a preposterous nature: the instant jailing of the sergeant, the dismissal of the police Commissioner. But if you are a 100% American and respect the laws and institutions of your country, you send for your solicitor—and at once he shows you just how far your rights go, and where they end. You cannot cause the arrest of the sergeant, for you resisted him when he attempted to arrest you, and when you resisted him he acquired an instant right to take you by force. You cannot proceed against him for accusing you falsely, for he has a right to make summary arrests for felony, and the courts have many times decided that a public officer, so long as he cannot be charged with corruption or malice, is not liable for errors of judgment made in the execution of his sworn duty. You cannot get the detectives on the mat, for when they questioned you you were a prisoner accused of murder, and it was their duty and their right to do so. You cannot sue the turnkey at the watch house or the warden at the jail for locking you up, for they received your body, as the law says, in a lawful and regular manner, and would have been liable to penalty if they had turned you loose.

But have you no redress whatever, no rights at all? Certainly you have a right, and the courts have jealously guarded it. You have a clear right, guaranteed to you under the Constitution, to go into a court of equity and apply for a mandamus requiring the police to cease forthwith to expose your portrait in the Rogues' Gallery among the murderers. This is your inalienable right, and no man or men on earth can take it away from you. You cannot prevent them cherishing your portrait in their secret files, but you can get an order commanding them to refrain forever from exposing it to the gaze of idle visitors, and if you can introduce yourself unseen into their studio and prove that they disregard that order, you can have them hailed into court for contempt and fined by the learned judge.

Thus the law, statute, common and case, protects the free American against injustice.

The Beloved Turnkey

From the Baltimore *Evening Sun*, Feb. 12, 1923

Whenever the liberties of the average citizen are grossly invaded and made a mock of, as happened, for example, in the United States during the late war, there are always observers who marvel that he bears the outrage with so little murmuring. There is, however, no real reason for wondering at it. The fact is that the average man's love of liberty is nine-tenths imaginary, exactly like his love of sense, justice and truth. He is not actually happy when free; he is uncomfortable, a bit alarmed, and intolerably lonely. Liberty is not a thing for the great masses of men. It is the exclusive possession of a small and disreputable minority, like knowledge, courage and honor. It takes a special sort of man to understand and enjoy liberty—and he is usually an outlaw in democratic societies. It is, indeed, only the exceptional man who can even stand it. The average man doesn't want to be free. He simply wants to be safe. . . . Nietzsche achieved something when he changed Schopenhauer's will-to-live into a will-to-power. But he didn't go far enough—or maybe he went *too* far, and in the wrong direction. He should have made it will-to-peace. What the average man wants in this world is the simplest and most ignominious sort of peace—the peace of a trusty in a humane penitentiary, of a hog in a comfortable sty. That is why he has such a superstitious regard for policemen. A policeman is one who protects him (*a*) from his superiors, (*b*) from his equals, and (*c*) from himself. This last service is the most esteemed of them all; theoretically, it keeps ice-wagon drivers, Y.M.C.A. secretaries, insurance collectors and other such morons from smoking opium, ruining themselves at champagne orgies, and travelling all over the country with Follies girls. It is a democratic invention.

Cops and Their Art

From the *American Mercury*, Feb., 1931, pp. 162–63

The basic trouble with the American *Polizei*, it seems to me, is that they are badly chosen for their work, and even worse trained for it. The rule almost everywhere in the country is that a recruit for the force must start at the bottom, and spend years pounding a beat before he is eligible to aspire to the higher ranks. This is a good way, perhaps, to train competent night watchmen and traffic regulators, but certainly it is an idiotic way to train detectives. The young man with intelligence enough to be a good detective simply refuses to waste the best years of his youth tagging automobiles parked in the wrong place, and stealing peanuts. He declines to take orders from a sergeant who, in nine cases out of ten, is an illiterate ignoramus, fit only for clubbing Communists and boozing in speakeasies. He is revolted by the thought of associating for years with men who, whatever their natural charm and virtue, are at best only a gang of truck-drivers and trolley motormen outfitted with shields, revolvers and shillelaghs. So he never goes upon the force at all, and his perhaps highly useful services are lost to law and order, and the subtle and difficult art of catching criminals falls to men who are truck-drivers and trolley motormen still, though every bootlegger bows to them and they are hymned by the newspapers, when a murderer accidentally walks into their hands, as the peers of Sherlock Holmes.

Imagine a Sherlock Holmes in real life, and at the beginning of his career. Naturally enough, he is aware of his gifts, and eager to display them, so he applies for a post on the constabulary. First he is examined by doctors to make sure that he is as strong as an ox, and then he is examined by other quacks to determine whether he can read and write. Having passed both tests, he becomes a probationer and is sent out with an older cop to learn the secrets of the profession. The first is a way of standing first on one foot and then on the other, so that mounting guard while a five-hour parade passes laboriously along the street will not result in varicose veins.

The second is a method of guessing under oath how long a given automobile has been parked at a given spot, without actually timing it. The third is a way of stealing three naps a night in a garage without getting caught by the roundsman. The fourth is a scheme of oral deodorization whereby an hour's earnest guzzling in a speakeasy will not arouse the suspicions of the captain. And so on, and so on. Sherlock stands it for a couple of weeks, and then turns in his equipment—to enter, perhaps, the investment securities business, to take holy orders, or to turn criminal himself. Hundreds and thousands of youngsters are thus lost to the police every year, and many of them belong to the most intelligent five per cent of recruits.

It is exactly as if every officer in the Army had to be a graduate from the ranks—as if every admiral in the Navy had to be a former coal-passer or mess attendant—as if every surgeon had to have years of service as a hospital orderly or dissecting-room *Diener* behind him. Now and then, to be sure, the scheme lets a really good man survive. I have known detectives, come up from pounding beats, who were extremely competent, just as I once knew a surgeon who actually began as an embalmer. But it must be plain that such things are miracles, and that the probabilities run cruelly against them. The average detective is simply an ex-paperhanger or bartender thrown into a job demanding five times the information and intelligence of a Harvard professor. He is pitted against men who, at their best, are shrewder than Morgan partners and more daring than deep-sea divers. Is it any wonder that they so often beat him? And is it any wonder that, conscious of his incompetence and revolting against it, he resorts to such brutalities as the third degree to conceal it?

Therapeutics is surely not my *Fach*, but in this case I venture upon a modest suggestion. It is that the corps of cops be divided into two halves, as the Army is divided. Let the rank and file be recruited from out-of-work grocery clerks, plumbers, bricklayers and farm-hands, as now, but let entrance into the higher posts be restricted to men of superior education and intelligence. I see no reason why an extraordinarily bright young man, if he survives pavement pounding, should not pass from the one category to the other, just as enlisted men in the Army are sometimes given commissions, but I can imagine no reason why *every* recruit should be forced to start at the bottom, with years of dull and stupid work amid depressing associations. If the good ones, after due examination, could begin as detectives, the whole force would be vastly improved, and it would be measurably less easy than it is now for criminals to escape detection and punishment. There is no real secret about detective work; it simply requires a good head. But under the present system it is open to men with good legs.

Jack Ketch as Eugenist

From PREJUDICES: FIFTH SERIES, 1926, pp. 284–85.
First printed in the *American Mercury*, July, 1925, p. 353

Has any historian ever noticed the salubrious effect, on the English character, of the frenzy for hanging that went on in England during the Eighteenth Century? When I say salubrious, of course, I mean in the purely social sense. At the end of the Seventeenth Century the Englishman was still one of the most turbulent and lawless of civilized men; at the beginning of the Nineteenth he was the most law-abiding. What worked the change in him? I believe that it was worked by the rope of Jack Ketch. During the Eighteenth Century the lawless strain was simply choked out of the race. Perhaps a third of those in whose veins it ran were actually hanged; the rest were chased out of the British Isles, never to return. Some fled to Ireland, and revivified the decaying Irish race; in practically all the Irish rebels of the past century there have been plain traces of English blood. Others went to the Dominions. Yet others came to the United States, and after helping to conquer the Western wilderness, begat the yeggmen, Prohibition agents, footpads, highjackers and other assassins of today.

The murder rate is very low in England, perhaps the lowest in the world. It is low because nearly all the potential ancestors of murderers were hanged or exiled in the Eighteenth Century. Why is it so high in the United States? Because the potential ancestors of murderers, in the late Eighteenth and early Nineteenth Centuries, were *not* hanged. And why did they escape? For two plain reasons. First, the existing government was too weak to track them down and execute them, especially in the West. Second, the qualities of daring and enterprise that went with their murderousness were so valuable that it was socially profitable to overlook their homicides. In other words, the job of occupying and organizing the vast domain of the new Republic was one that demanded the aid of men who, among other things, occasionally butchered their fellow men. The butchering had to be winked at in order to get their help. Thus the murder rate, on the frontier, rose to unprecedented heights, while the execution rate remained very low. Probably 100,000 men altogether were murdered in the territory west of the Ohio between 1776 and 1865; probably not 100 murderers were formally executed. When they were punished at all, it was by other murderers—and this left the strain unimpaired.

The Humanitarian Fallacy

From the Baltimore *Evening Sun*, Jan. 28, 1924

What brings penology so constantly to grief is the modern craze for reducing all punishment to a few simple, standardized penalties, thought erroneously to be humane. This craze was unknown before the Eighteenth Century. It originated in England toward the end of that century as a phase of a general humanitarian movement which, among other fruits, has succeeded so brilliantly in debasing the so-called Anglo-Saxon stock that the descendants of English peasants who, in the year 1700, were hearty, red-faced, tall and healthy animals are today a race of almost pathological men, small in stature, frail in body, without teeth, and wholly devoid of intelligence. In the field of penology the movement obliterated all the protean and often highly ingenious and effective penalties known to classical English jurisprudence and substituted fines and imprisonment, with hanging reserved for murder only. That is to say, all criminals regardless of the nature of their crimes and of the end sought to be achieved by punishing them at all, were thrown into prisons and there punished exactly alike. Thus, the penalty for getting drunk and falling off an omnibus became precisely the same, save for its duration, as the penalty for counterfeiting, highway robbery and bigamy. A boy taken in the act of stealing an apple from a grocer's barrel, voluptuously displayed to catch his eye, was sent to the same prison which sheltered men convicted of robbing widows and orphans, blowing safes, buying and selling prostitutes, and burning down churches.

Obviously, this scheme was quite insane. It not only failed to dissuade and reform the major criminals; it made major criminals of all the minor ones. A youth got into prison for breaking a window, and came out an accomplished and ambitious burglar. In the course of time even the imbeciles in charge of such high matters began to realize that there was something wrong, and the history of penology since that time has been a history of efforts to ameliorate and improve the prison system. Reformatories have been opened for young offenders, a parole system has been developed to sort out chance criminals from the professionals, and a hundred and one other devices have been proposed and tried to correct the plain defects of the underlying scheme. But in the United States, at least, all such devices, in the larger sense, have failed. Crime continues to increase among us, especially in its more violent and hence more dangerous anti-social forms. As our penal system has grown in humaneness toward the lesser varieties of criminals, and in the effectiveness, or, at all events, in the elaborateness of its artifices for reclaiming them and making docile drudges of them, it has steadily lost capacity to discourage or diminish the really serious crime. In order to avoid punishing the petty criminal too much, and so driving him in despair into genuine crime, we have had to reduce the punishment of the major criminal so greatly that, in many cases, it is now scarcely any punishment at all. A Jack Hart, robbing and murdering peaceable citizens in broad daylight while the *Polizei* snore in the adjacent garages, is sent to exactly the same prison which houses men whose only crime is that they have sold, perhaps, a drink of bay rum to a Prohibition officer disguised as a Christian down with cramps, and once Hart gets there he is treated exactly as they are.

He must, true enough, stay longer, at least in theory, but that is a detail. The main thing is that Jack's punishment is grossly inadequate to his crime, as that of many, and maybe most of his fellow-prisoners, is grossly excessive. It is not dreadful enough to make him reform, and it is not dreadful enough to dissuade other men of his peculiar nature. Worse still, it bears no sort of intelligible causal relation to his offense; it does not inflict upon him anything even remotely resembling what he inflicted on his victim. To elect a man to the Sweezey Club for robbery and murder is fundamentally as idiotic as to elect him to the Maryland Club for piracy on the high seas, and a great deal more humane. His inclination toward robbery and murder is not obliterated thereby, and his capacity for it is only temporarily suspended. Soon or late he will get out, either by a jail delivery or by due process of law, and resume his practice. Reduced to its elementals the transaction is simply this: that society bribes him, by paying the heavy cost of his upkeep, for transiently suspending his operations, and then turns him loose to renew them.

The English embraced penology before we did, and are getting rid of it sooner. They never elect a man to a club for robbery and murder, and pay his dues and his checks; they hang him. After the war they faced the same crime wave which now disturbs the United States, with crimes of violence constantly increasing. They formed no Sweezey Clubs and summoned no expert penologists. Instead they revived the whipping-post, abandoned in the Eighteenth Century, and now every hold-up man convicted is given a series of barbarous lashings, continued until he is all in. With what result? With the result that the Recorder of London, in his charge to his Grand Jury in May, 1920, pointed with satisfaction to the fact that there was but one charge of robbery with violence on his docket. The walls of our prisons are bulging; we are constantly paying out millions for new ones. In England—but let me quote the Committee on Law Enforcement of the American Bar Association: "The great English prison at Reading has been closed. Other prisons have been turned into Borstal Institutions [*i.e.*, reformatories for young offenders]. Prisons which formerly were crowded are now half-empty."

But would the cat-o'-nine-tails suffice to dispose of such fellows as Dr. Hart? Would it punish him enough? Perhaps not. But the cat-o'-nine-tails is not the only instrument of correction that might be rescued profitably from the great reservoir of the old English law. I am no uplifter and hence make no specific recommendation. But I confess that I often wonder that the ancient punishment of outlawry is not revived; it is still in force in England, though it has not been inflicted since 1859. Certainly it is simple enough in its workings. A man who deliberately chooses the career of an outlaw is made one officially. From that moment he has no rights whatever. Any citizen may beat him, wound him and even kill him without challenge. It is a misdemeanor knowingly to conceal him, or even to feed him. He is thrown into the exact position of the victim he assaults and robs, and is paid off in his own coin.

But is outlawry prohibited by Section Nine of the Constitution? I doubt it. That section prohibits bills of attainder, but attainder is certainly not outlawry, though it may be a part of it. In any case, why bother about the Constitution? Certainly the Federal courts have all forgotten it. The jails are now full of men who were railroaded there, without jury trials, in plain violation of the First Amendment. If it is moral to adjourn the Constitution in order to give the Anti-Saloon League a show, why shouldn't it be equally moral to adjourn it in order to protect decent citizens from robbery and assassination?

One Size Fits All

From the Baltimore *Evening Sun*, Sept. 24, 1928

It is hard for anyone who has not had personal experience of prisons to conjure up any image of their appalling reality. They are, even at their best, places of torture: at their worst they are so bad that only men of the lowest organization can endure them. It is not the loss of liberty that drives the men in them to frenzy: it is the intolerable rigidity, monotony and imbecility of their routine. Their arrangements, like those of the public schools, are made to meet the needs and character of inmates at the very bottom of the scale. No wonder prisoners of a higher caliber—and some of the most bold and incorrigible criminals are of a higher caliber—find life in them quite insupportable, and prefer death to a continuance of it.

Theoretically, these prisoners are wards of the law, which is supposed to be impersonal. But that supposition is as absurd in this case as it is in every other. The plain fact is that the men are the slaves of their keepers. It is these keepers who determine whether their imprisonment shall be tolerable or an endless agony, whether they shall be left with some common hope and spirit when they emerge or go out as complete wrecks. It is these keepers, under the maudlin parole system, who chiefly determine how long they shall be incarcerated. If you want to find out what sort of men hold such grave powers over their fellow human beings, go to any prison and palaver with the first keeper you meet. And if you have no access to prisons, then try to figure out what sort of men are likely to seek and cherish such jobs. Here I say nothing against the keepers as individuals. They do the best they can: many of them, I believe by sound evidence, are humane and even sentimental men. But it would be absurd to look for superior intelligence in them. They are, as every test made of them has shown, ignorant and simple-minded men, and not infrequently of a mentality below that of the average of their charges. They do the best they can—but what they are asked to do in the name of justice and righteousness would daunt a herd of Platos.

It is an ironical fact that all this penning of men in cages, all this frightful effort to hammer them into docility, all this cruel outraging of their primary instincts, is done in the name of humanity. The modern prison, in fact, is humanitarianism's masterpiece. It is a monument to its tears. There was a time when imprisonment was a rare punishment. Men were thrown into jails to await trial, but when they were tried at last they were commonly punished in other ways. Some were put to death. Others were deported. Others were flogged. Others lost certain civil rights. Yet others were mutilated.

But all these various and protean punishments were eventually outlawed by the humanitarians. They denounced capital punishment, though it at least got rid of the concrete criminal. They de-

nounced flogging, though offenders who had once tasted it wanted
no more of it. They denounced mutilation, though it robbed a
pickpocket of his chief tool. They denounced deportation, though
it turned many a felon into an honest and useful man. There remained only imprisonment. During the past century it has almost
completely supplanted all other modes of punishment. Hangings
grow rare, and flogging is seldom heard of. No one is mutilated
any more. No one is deported, at least in America. One and all,
large and small professionals and accidentals, men who run afoul
of the law are cast into cages, and there held at the disposal of
morons.

The astounding thing is that all this witless and shocking cruelty
is inflicted in the name of mercy—that Jack is bidden to believe
he was favored when he was delivered from the gallows. It is hard
to imagine anything more stupid. Would it have been more cruel
to hang him quickly than it is to torture him all the days of his
life? He is one, obviously, whose doings had to be stopped. He was
a professional murderer, and while he ran at large no man's life
was safe. Well, are the keepers' lives safe while he is in prison?
Will the rest of us be safe the next time he breaks out—with a maniacal lust for revenge on society reinforcing his natural villainy? It
is absurd to talk of reforming such men. The machinery for reforming them is crazily inadequate, even assuming that they are
reformable, which is not proved. The thing to do is to get rid of
them at the first chance, as quietly and humanely as possible. If
the poor simpletons told off to purge the world of them are un-
equal to the childish task, then let us get better ones. But let us
stop penning them in cages, and goading them to more crimes.

The majority of prisoners give their keepers no concern. They
are dull and unimaginative fellows, with little courage. Many of
them are as comfortable in prison as hogs in a wallow. But the
men of the minority—the bold, enterprising, pugnacious fellows—
keep every prison in an uproar. They begin to plan escape the moment they get in, and they never abandon the hope. They get the
worst of it every day because their keepers fear them. They make
fear the hallmark of the whole place. In order to hold them every
other prisoner, however harmless, must be tortured too. It must be
hell to guard such fellows, year after year. Now and then one kills

a keeper, escapes, sets the place into an uproar. He is caught, brought back, tortured some more. He tries to escape again. He kills a keeper. He is recaptured, brought back, hanged. The rules are made more drastic. Every prisoner suffers abominably. And the really bad ones go to dungeons. What a folly! What a cruelty! Prison is no more a place for these men than a Y.M.C.A. would be. It tortures them quite as irrationally, and almost as brutally. The thing to do with such professionals is to hang them at the first chance. The humanity of imprisonment is as false and fraudulent as the humanity of Prohibition.

But what of those culprits whose offenses do not justify doing them to death—whose continued existence is not a certain and ever-present danger to all of us? I see no difficulties in the problem. It needs only the most elemental ingenuity and common sense. Some time ago, as I recall it, a young man was sentenced in Baltimore to twenty years' imprisonment for a banal hold-up. He will get out, to be sure, in five or ten years, but meanwhile he will be brutalized and his life will be made useless. Wouldn't it have been better to give him a good lashing and then turn him out?

But the knout is degrading? It destroys self-respect? Well, what of sitting in a cage for twenty years?

More and Better Psychopaths

From the Baltimore *Evening Sun*, Dec. 3, 1934

The criminal career of the late Baby Face Nelson, LL.D., covered twelve years. During that time he is known to have a hand in the murder of three officers of the law, and in the intervals between these crimes he engaged in general practice as a thug and bully. The diligent cops first took him when he was only fourteen years old, but he was quickly rescued by the New Penology, which turned him loose on parole to perfect himself in his art. Taken again, he was paroled again, and thereafter he showed such rapid progress in technic that he was presently pushing Dr. John Dillinger and Dr. Pretty Boy Floyd for first honors. When they fell, he became undisputed cock of the walk.

The astounding thing about such scoundrels is that they survive so long. Nelson was a notorious thief and blackleg from 1922 to 1933, but he was behind the bars barely three years of that time. The cops arrested him over and over again, but always he managed to get out. Twice, as I have said, he was paroled, and once he managed to procure a pistol while in custody, and with it overcame a prison guard. How he escaped punishment the other times I don't know, but always he escaped. Finally, growing impatient with the cops who so constantly retook him, he decided to shoot them at sight, and during the last six months of his life he and his friends disposed of three of them.

Of such sort are the abysmal brutes that the New Penology tells us ought to be handled more tenderly. They are not responsible, it appears, for their wanton and incessant felonies; the blame lies upon society. And the way to deal with them is not to butcher them, nor even to jug them, but to turn them over to "trained experts," that they may be rehabilitated. Simply stating such imbecilities is sufficient refutation of them. Society is actually no more to blame for a gorilla of that kidney than it is for a mad dog, and the bogus "experts" can no more cure him than a madstone can cure the dog. There is only one way to deal with him, and that is to put him to death as soon as possible.

This the cops now do with great industry, to the applause of all sensible people. It is a hazardous business and the mortality is not all on one side, but there is plenty of courage in the constabulary camp, and it seems likely to suffice for the job. The cops, in fact, are the only agents of justice who show any competence and resolution. They almost always bring in their man, but once he is brought in he is in the hands of his friends, and if he doesn't escape by one trick he is pretty certain to escape by some other. Either he fools a jury or his lawyer fools a judge. And if both devices fail, then he buys a jail guard, or breaks out with firearms, or convinces a parole board that he deserves another chance.

An example of what all this amounts to was lately under our very eyes. Some time ago a professional criminal named Mais, wanted for various murders and robberies, went into hiding in Baltimore. The cops, getting his scent, tracked him down promptly, and took him into custody. He was heavily armed, and they risked their lives, but nevertheless they took him. Sent to Richmond to answer for a peculiarly brutal murder, he was convicted and sentenced to death. But in a few weeks he had broken out of jail, and on the way he had killed a policeman. Now he is at large again, and robbing and killing again, and other cops will have to risk death to take him again.

Dr. Mais' escape was a monument to the sentimentality with which such swine are now treated. Though he was known to be an incorrigible criminal, and all his friends were known to be of the same sort, he was permitted to receive visits from them in jail. Presently one of them slipped him a pistol, and the next day he was on his way, leaving one man dead and two wounded behind him. Suppose you were a cop, and met this Mais tomorrow? Would you approach him politely, tap him on the shoulder, and invite him to return to the death-house? Or would you shoot him at sight, at the same time giving thanks to God that he didn't see you first?

How many such men have been executed during the past year? I can recall but one—the Hon. John Pierpont, lately put to death in Indiana after two escapes. But the case of Dr. Pierpont was so exceptional that he must have been a victim of witchcraft rather than of justice. To his last moment he expected his lawyer to save him with some sort of preposterous writ or other, or his colleagues to break into the jail and deliver him by force. He went to the chair a much surprised and disappointed man, and well he should have been, for he was the first public enemy to face Jack Ketch since the memory of man runneth not to the contrary.

All sorts of lesser felons are hanged or electrocuted—women who poison bad husbands for the insurance, drunkards who shoot their mistresses, country Aframericans who run amok, and so on—, but it is almost unheard-of for a genuine professional to be dispatched in due form of law. Always he and his friends can raise money enough to hire a sharp lawyer, and always the lawyer is able to delay proceedings long enough for psychiatry and sentimentality to save him. Two years ago, in Missouri, such a scoundrel was convicted of kidnapping and promptly sentenced to death. But he is still very much alive, and very busy with writs, petitions and psychoanalysis, and he will still be alive long after most of us are no more.

But the real masterpiece of the New Penology is not to be found among such lowly brutes, but in the person of the Hon. Thomas H. Robinson, Jr., LL.D., who as I write is still being sought by the cops for the kidnapping and cruel bludgeoning of Mrs. Berry V. Stoll, of Louisville. The Hon. Mr. Robinson, if he is ever shot by Department of Justice agents or taken alive and hanged, should be stuffed by the psychiatrists and given the place of honor in their museum, for he is an alumnus of two of their plants for reconditioning the erring, and seems to have been a prize pupil.

Like all other such rogues, Dr. Robinson was a bad boy, and got into trouble early. His natural destination was the hoosegow, with the gallows to follow, but he was lucky enough to encounter a judge who was also a fool, and so he was turned over to "trained experts." Two separate gangs of them had at him. One (I quote from Dr. E. W. Cocke, State Commissioner of Institutions of Tennessee) diagnosed his malady as "dementia præcox (insanity)," and the other decided that he was a "psychopathic personality (not insane)." Between the two he wriggled out of custody, and was soon engaged in crime again, with literary endeavor as a sideline. His demand for ransom in the Stoll case was an eloquent argument for a literal carrying out of the New Deal.

If such deliberate and incorrigible criminals as Robinson are "psychopathic personalities," then what is a criminal? Obviously, the answer is that no such thing as a criminal exists, and that is the answer made by the more advanced wing of New Penologists. The felonious, they say, are simply sick, and the cause of their sickness is the faulty organization of society. Let wealth be better distributed, and the Robinsons will stop writing hold-up letters to the Stolls. And even though wealth continue to be distributed badly, the mysterious arcana of the "trained expert" can cure them.

How many sane people actually believe in this nonsense? Probably not many. Of one class I am pretty sure: the cops. I have never encountered or heard of one who thought of the Dillingers and Floyds, the Nelsons and Robinsons, as psychopaths, or as any other kind of paths. Nay, they think of these brethren as criminals, and when they go out to rope one of them they take their sidearms along. Certainly it is lucky for the rest of us that they do.

The Arbuckle Case

From the Baltimore *Evening Sun*, Oct. 10, 1921

This great moral cause, so obscenely wallowed in by the newspapers of late, offers an instructive indicator of the extent to which the "orderly process of the law" has been modified and improved in the United States. From its beginning it has been carried on like a circus, and without the slightest heed to the plain rights of the accused. Witnesses against Fatty Arbuckle, many of them of very dubious character, have been permitted to flood the press with preposterous attacks upon him. Volunteer committees of viragoes, knowing nothing of the evidence save what has come from such sources, have issued public proclamations against him, and sworn solemnly to see that he suffers the fullest penalties of the law. Finally, the prosecuting officer charged with the conduct of the case has ranted about it in the newspapers, apparently deliberately attempted to raise up prejudice against the prisoner in the dock, and undertaken over and over again to bring him to trial for a capital crime—all in the face of the fact that two juries, despite all this blather, have formally decided that his crime, if crime it was at all, was much less in degree and carries no capital punishment with it.

What is the matter with the bench of judges in San Francisco? The Mooney case, with its almost incredible perjuries, was enough to prove their lack of intelligence, but here there is no question of intelligence; it is simply a question of common decency. Why don't they give the prisoner before them the protection that the law is supposed to throw about every citizen accused of crime? Why don't they put an end to this revolting carnival of posturing and self-advertising—this open and undisguised attempt to get some profit out of a legal lynching? Why don't they hale the worst offenders before them—and especially some of the prosecuting staff—and send them to jail for contempt of court?

It is not my privilege to enjoy the honor of M. Arbuckle's acquaintance, and, since I never go to the movies, I have no prejudice in favor of him on aesthetic grounds. If it were proposed tomorrow to pass a law providing that every moving-picture actor in the country should be flogged at the cart's tail once a week, I'd probably be in favor of it, as I'd undoubtedly be in favor of a law providing for the same punishment for evangelists, tenors, members of Congress and golf-players. But no such law is on the books, or even proposed; a moving-picture actor is still theoretically a free citizen and possessed of all the rights that you or I possess. Is it giving him those rights to charge him absurdly, despite all the evidence and all the probabilities, with a capital offense, to permit a host of irresponsible zanies to flood the newspapers with filthy innuendoes against him, and to convert the inquiry into the matter into a clown-show, with a sworn officer of the law as chief mountebank?

Consider the circumstances. No one, not even the press-agent of the San Francisco prosecuting officer, alleges that Arbuckle deliberately murdered the late Mlle. Rappe. The worst argued against him is that he is constructively guilty of murder because he inflicted fatal injuries upon her while committing a lesser felony. What was that lesser felony? In brief, what the newspapers mellifluously call "criminal assault"—*Anglais:* rape. And how and where was that "assault" committed? In a hotel room—with the next room, separated by only a thin door, crowded with men and women, many of them intimate friends of the alleged victim. Try to think of something more ridiculous. Why didn't she call for help? Why didn't she denounce the accused immediately after the alleged crime? Why did the whole party, after her departure, continue in amicable conversation for an hour? Why did the physicians who attended her discover no evidence of the assault and bear no complaint about it from her, and make no report to the police? Finally, what sane man is going to believe that a woman who habitually frequented the low orgies of moving-picture actors—a familiar figure in their drunken and degraded society—who is going to believe that such a woman, entering the Arbuckle chamber publicly and willingly, would fight for her virtue so desperately as to sacrifice her life?

The whole case, indeed, reeks with nonsense. What must an intelligent foreigner, contemplating it, think of the administration of justice among us? Well, no matter how biliously he thinks about it, he will not be unjust himself. In many American jurisdictions, including especially California and New York, almost every case against a wealthy and prominent man is carried on in precisely the same way—the newspapers full of inflammatory tirades against him, the prosecuting officers eagerly grabbing all the publicity they can get out of it, a multitude of obscure scoundrels trying to horn into it as witnesses, and the learned judges observing the whole buffoonery with the utmost complacency, and even, on occasion—as during the war, for example—putting on the motley themselves, and leaping yelling into the ring. The question of Arbuckle's guilt or innocence does not enter into the matter. The important thing is that a poor and obscure man, standing in his boots, facing the evidence that he faces, would go to jail, perhaps, for sixty days, and then depart in peace. But Arbuckle, having plenty of money and being good for first-page stories every day, is actually brought into the shadow of the gallows—and if the State prosecuting officers, by some mischance, muff him, then their Federal brethren will take a hack at him for bootlegging and white slavery.

This last embellishment appears inevitably in every American *cause célèbre*. Let it begin to appear that a defendant of wealth and prominence, *i.e.*, a defendant who makes good hunting for prosecuting officers aspiring to higher office, is likely to be acquitted of the first charge brought against him, and at once he will be confronted by a series of other charges. Our insane laws, which prohibit thousands of acts that are committed by perfectly reputable persons every day, make it possible for almost any man, once he falls into the hands of the police, to be put on trial for some offense that may be severely punished. The Volstead Act is typical of this sort of dishonest legislation. It is violated by literally millions of Americans every day, and everyone knows that it is violated. It is violated as Fatty Arbuckle violated it—if he actually violated it at all—in every large American hotel every hour of the twenty-four. Not even so vast an ass as Volstead himself could imagine enforcing it equally against all men, as every law should be enforced.

But it is a nice thing to have in reserve. It gives an ambitious prosecuting officer a second crack at his victim. It is good for one more first-page story in the newspapers. It clothes the whole buffoonery with the solemn dignity of the national Government, which is to say, with the solemn dignity of the honorable corps of Prohibition officers, including those who are honest as well as those who are for sale.

As for the poor oaf, Arbuckle, to return to him, he is already ruined. The movie films showing his harmless clownings are barred from all the movie parlors, lest the persons who gobble the filth about him in the newspapers be contaminated by looking at them. His lawyers and investigators, I daresay, will fix their fees on the principle of the German indemnity. If he is found guilty of manslaughter, what will it show? That he actually committed manslaughter, or simply that the fulminations in the newspapers fetched enough jurors to convict him?

V. LAW AND LAWYERS

Stewards of Nonsense

From the *American Mercury*, Jan., 1928, pp. 35–37

THE SAD thing about lawyers is not that so many of them are stupid, but that so many of them are intelligent. The craft is a great devourer of good men; it sucks in and wastes almost as many as the monastic life consumed in the Middle Ages. There is something about it that is extraordinarily attractive to bright youngsters, at all events in the United States. It not only offers the chance of very substantial rewards in money; it also holds out the temptation of a sort of public dignity, with political preferment thrown in for good measure. Most of our politicians are lawyers, and hence most of our statesmen. They swarm in the Senate and have almost a monopoly of the White House. Nevertheless, it must be plain that the law, *as* the law, has few rewards for a man of genuine ambition, with a yearning to leave his mark upon his time. How many American lawyers are remembered, *as* lawyers? I can think of a few: John Marshall, Daniel Webster, Joseph H. Choate. But the list soon runs out. Even so powerful and successful an advocate as William M. Evarts is already forgotten. In his day he was in all the big cases, from the Beecher-Tilden business to the hearing of the *Alabama* claims, but if he is remembered today—that is, by the everyday well-informed man—it is only vaguely, and as a politician. For the rest he survives in a few stiff portraits on steel in the offices of old-fashioned lawyers, themselves doomed to the same swift oblivion that has swallowed him. His associates in the *Alabama* case were Caleb Cushing and Morrison R. Waite. Who remembers them today, even as names? Cushing, according to the New International Encyclopedia, was "a man of unusual erudition and

of rare ability, imposing in person and forcible in argument."
More, he was Attorney-General of the United States, Minister to
China and Spain, and a brigadier-general in the Civil War, and in
1873 he came very near being Chief Justice. But mainly he was a
lawyer, and as a lawyer his name was writ in water. Waite was actually Chief Justice, from 1874 to 1888. Today he lies forever forgotten among the innumerable John Smiths.

If lawyers were generally dull men, like the overwhelming majority of the rev. clergy, or simply glorified bookkeepers and shop-
keepers, like most bankers and business men, it would not be hard
to understand their humble station in history, but I don't think it
would be fair to put them into any of those categories. On the
contrary, it must be manifest that their daily work, however useless
it may be, demands intelligence of a high order, and that a numskull seldom if ever achieves any success at the bar, even of a police court. I speak, of course, of trial lawyers—of what the English
call barristers. It may take only the talents of a clerk in a lime and
cement warehouse to draw up mortgages and insert jokers into
leases, but once a cause in law or equity comes to bar it calls for
every resource of the human cerebrum. The lawyer standing there
is exposed to a singularly searching and bitter whirlwind. He must
know his facts, and he must think quickly and accurately. Those
facts, perhaps, are quite new to him; he has engulfed them so recently as last night. But he must have them in order and at his
command; he must be able to detect and make use of all the complicated relations between them; he must employ them as fluently
as if they were ancient friends. And he must fit them, furthermore,
into the complex meshes of the law itself—an inordinately intricate fabric of false assumptions and irrational deductions, most of
them having no sort of kinship with fact at all, and many of them
deliberately designed to flout it and get rid of it. This double job
of intellectual tight-rope walking the lawyer must undertake. More,
he must do it in the presence of an opponent who jogs and wiggles
the rope, and to the satisfaction of an audience that is bored, hostile, and, worse still, disunited. If, marshalling the facts adeptly, he
attempts a logical conquest of the jury, and if, while he is at-
tempting it, he manages to avoid offending the jurymen with a
voice that grates upon them, or a bald head that excites their ris-

ibilities, or a necktie that violates their *pudeurs*—if, by the lavish flogging of his cortex he accomplishes all this, then he is almost certain to grieve and antagonize the judge, to whom facts are loathsome and only the ultra-violet rays of the law are real. And if, wallowing in those rays, he arouses the professional interest and libido of the judge, then he is pretty sure to convince the jury that he is a sciolist and a scoundrel.

More than once, serving as a reporter for the press, I have lolled humbly in the bull-ring of jurisprudence, marvelling at the amazing dexterity and resilience of the embattled jurisconsults. What goes on there every day, year in and year out, far surpasses anything ever heard in any other arena. Compared to the jousting of lawyers, even of middling bad lawyers, the best that such theologians as the nation tolerates ever emit from their pulpits is as a crossword-puzzle to a problem in the differential calculus. Even in the halls of legislation nothing so apt, ingenious and persuasive is on tap, for though most legislators are lawyers they are all well aware that, as legislators, it would be fatal to them to talk sense. But in their strictly legal character, performing on the stage assigned to them, they let themselves go, and the result is often a series of intellectual exercises of the first chop. One may think of the courtroom of the Supreme Court of the United States as a theatre of dullness so heavy that the very catchpolls drowse, and of imbecility so vast that even Congress is shamed and made to hang its head; nevertheless, I have heard in my time, in that very chamber, arguments that stimulated me like the bouquet of a fine Moselle, or the smile of a princess of the blood, or an unexpected kick in the pantaloons.

Why, then, are lawyers, in essence, such obscure men? Why do their undoubted talents yield so poor a harvest in immortality? The answer, it seems to me, is not occult. Their first difficulty lies in the fact that at least nine-tenths of their intellectual steam is wasted upon causes and enterprises that live and perish with a day—that have, indeed, no genuine existence at all. And the second lies in the fact that when they engage in matters of more and permanent importance they almost invariably find themselves doomed to bring to them, not any actual illumination, but only the pale glow of a feeble and preposterous casuistry. Here they are on all fours with the theologians, and stand in the same shadows. It is their professional aim and function, not to get at the truth but simply to carry on combats under ancient and archaic rules. The best courtroom arguments that I have ever heard were not designed to unearth the truth; they were designed to conceal, maul and destroy the truth. More than once I have heard two such arguments opposed to each other, and both driving to the same depressing end. And at their conclusion I have heard the learned judge round up and heave out what remained of the truth in an exposition that surpassed both.

One reads many of the decisions of our higher courts, indeed, with a sort of wonder. It is truly astonishing that so much skill and cunning should be wasted upon such transparent folly. The thing becomes a mere crazy-quilt of platitude and balderdash—much of it, to be sure, immensely ingenious, but the whole of it of no more dignity, at bottom, than a speech by radio. It is as if eminent mathematicians should devote themselves for weeks running to determining the proper odds upon a dark horse at Tia Juana. It is as if a whole herd of gifted surgeons, summoned to cure a corn, should proceed solemnly to cut off the patient's leg at the hip. It is as if Aristotle, come back to earth, should get up at 5 A.M. to see a parade of the Mystic Shrine.

One admires the logician, but feels an unescapable repugnance to the man. And that feeling, I believe, is general in the world— nay, it increases steadily. In the formative days of the law the human race admired lawyers and judges, and even made heroes of them: the cases of Solon, C.J., Hammurabi, C.J., and John Marshall, C.J., will be recalled. But today the law has lost the blood of life and become a fossil, and its practitioners have petrified with it. Reduced to plain terms, what they engage in for a living is simply nonsense. It is their job, not to dispose of that nonsense, but to preserve it, pump it up, protect it against assault. So consecrated, they spend their lives in futility, and pass into oblivion unregretted and unsung.

Over the Side

From the Baltimore *Evening Sun*, Nov. 18, 1929

Of all the so-called learned professions, the law seems to be the least interesting to its practitioners. Relatively few of them are ever impelled to write anything about it, and nine-tenths of them seem eager to get out of it at the first chance—into politics, into business. This is surely not true of medicine. I know hundreds of medical men, but I can't think of one among them who really wants to abandon his trade. Now and then, of course, they talk against it gloomily, but this is only talk. At bottom, they like it, and for a plain reason: it is interesting and it is reasonably useful. Find a doctor who has political aspirations and five times out of six you have found a quack. But in the law even the best of them are always trying to get out.

The Judge

From the Baltimore *Evening Sun*, Aug. 26, 1929

Human beings spend a great deal of their time in laughing at one another. Every man seems absurd to his neighbor, not only in his diversions, but also in his sober labors. My own favorite object of mirth is one of the most austere and venerable figures in our society, to wit, the judge. If I frequent courtrooms very little, it is only because I have a high theoretical respect for his office, and so do not want to be tempted to laugh at him. That temptation, in his actual presence, is almost irresistible. There he sits for hour after hour, listening to brawling shysters, murkily dozing his way through obvious perjury, contemplating a roomful of smelly loafers, and sadly scratching himself as he wonders what his wife is going to have for dinner, all the while longing horribly for a drink. If he is not a comic figure, then there is none in this world.

Years ago, when I had literary ambitions, I blocked out a one-act play about a judge. Now that I am too old to write it I may as well give it away. The scene is a courtroom, and the learned judge is on the bench, gaping wearily at his customers. They are of the usual sort—witnesses trying to remember what the lawyers told them to say, policemen sweating in their padded uniforms, bailiffs on the lookout for pickpockets, newspaper readers and tobacco chewers, and long ranks of dirty and idiotic old men, come in to get warm. In front of the judge a witness is being examined by a lawyer. To one side twelve jurymen snooze quietly. The place smells like an all-night trolley-car on a Winter night.

The judge, unable to concentrate his attention upon the case at bar, groans wheezily. It is a dreadful life, and he knows it. Of a sudden the opposition lawyer objects to a question put to the witness, and the judge has to pull himself together. The point raised is new to him. In fact, it goes far beyond his law. He decides in loud, peremptory tones, notes the exception, and resumes his bitter meditations. What a life! What a finish for a man who was once a gay dog, with the thirst of an archbishop and an arm for every neck! What a reward for long years of toil and privation! A tear rolls down the judge's nose.

As he shakes it off his eyes sweep the courtroom, and a strange thrill runs through him. There, on the last seat, sandwiched between a police sergeant and a professional bondsman, is the loveliest cutie ever seen. There, in the midst of the muck, is romance ineffable. The judge shoots his cuffs out of his gown, twirls his moustache, permits a soapy, encouraging smirk to cover his judicial glower, and gives a genial cough. How thrilled the cutie will be when she sees that he notices her. What a day in a poor girl's life. What an episode to remember—the handsome and amiable judge, the soft exchange of glances. He coughs a bit louder.

The cutie, glancing up, sees him looking at her. Paralyzed with fright, she leaps out of her seat, climbs over the police sergeant, and flees the courtroom.

VI. FIRST THINGS

The Genesis of a Deity

From the *American Mercury*, Jan., 1933, pp. 121–22.
A review of THE MYTHOLOGY OF ALL RACES:
VOL. V, SEMITIC, by Stephen Herbert Langdon; Boston, 1931

IF THE standard reference works mention Yahweh at all, it is only to explain, with hollow erudition, that the original form of His name was YHWH, and that it was turned into Jehovah in the Eighth Century A.D. by giving YHWH the vowels of Adonai. But where Yahweh Himself came from they do not say. This lack is supplied by Dr. Langdon, who is Professor of Assyriology at Oxford and a man of great learning. His study of the evidence leads him to believe that the original god of the Jews and Christians was not Yahweh at all, but Ilani (later written Elohim), and that this Ilani was picked up from the Babylonians in the dark backward and abysm of time, long before the Jews settled in Palestine. In those days they were a wandering tribe of great pugnacity, and the Babylonians got rid of their raids and forays by making mercenary soldiers of them, and allowing them to engage in trade. They lived this life for five or six centuries at least, and gradually became more or less Babylonianized. For one thing, they adopted a large part of the Babylonian mythology, and through them it has come down to us—the story of the Flood, that of the Tower of Babel, that of the Fall of Man, and so on. And for another thing, they abandoned the primitive gods who had contented them in the desert, and adopted the Babylonian sun-god, who was widely popular among the peoples of Asia Minor and passed under various names. What the Jews called him at the start is unknown, but in the Fifteenth and Fourteenth Centuries B.C., when they began to move

westward toward the Mediterranean, they found that the Phoeni-
cians and Arameans called him El, and this name they presently
borrowed.

But El soon had a rival, for in the course of their wanderings in
search of land the Jews entered Canaan, and there they found another god, Yahweh. This Yahweh, compared to El, was a somewhat primitive deity. He was not a splendid sun-god but a simple
rain-god. El's province was the whole universe, but Yahweh confined Himself pretty strictly to Canaan. Nevertheless, there was
something powerfully attractive about Him, for Canaan was a dry
country, and a rain-god was of much more use in it than a sun-
god. So the Jews, like the other Semitic tribes who followed them
into Canaan, began to incline toward Him, and when they conquered the land and began their history as a settled people they
made Him their tribal god. He remains so to this day, and Christians and Moslems in their turn have borrowed Him, but no
reader of the Old Testament need be told that He never had it all
His own way, even in the palmy days of Israel. On the contrary,
He had to meet constant and serious competition from two sides.
On the one side were the primitive Baalim or village gods to
which the Jews of the remoter settlements were always returning,
to the rage and despair of the prophets in practise in Jerusalem.
And on the other side was the stately and elegant hierarchy of
Babylonian gods, headed by the gorgeous El, for which the so-
phisticates of the cities, especially in the cosmopolitan North, always had a nostalgic hankering.

In the end the Jewish priests had to make a sort of compromise
between Yahweh and El, and the two are amalgamated in the Old
Testament into a joint god who is spoken of first under one name
and then under the other. But the majority of Jews, at all events
in the southern part of Palestine, always leaned toward Yahweh.
He was a much more friendly and comfortable god, despite His
frequent rages, than El. El was all right in the over-refined cities
of the North, but down in the deserts of Judah the herdsmen and
shepherds preferred a god who was more approachable and had a
better understanding of the needs of simple men. In the Old Testament it is always Yahweh who appears in the most human and
charming situations—wrestling with Jacob, taking the air in the

Garden of Eden, suspicious and jealous of the builders of the Tower of Babel, gossiping with Moses, lunching with Abraham. There is nothing subtle about this Yahweh—nothing of the metaphysical elegance of El. He does not appear as the Word, but as a downright and even flat-footed old man—a sort of fatherly general superintendent of the Jews, very friendly when they obey His orders but cruel and vindictive when they try to fool Him.

The modern Jews, and the Christians and Moslems with them, have pretty well forgotten El. He survives only in a few refinements of ritual and in the books of learned divines. Yahweh has swallowed him—Yahweh, the honest old rain-god. He it is that the Jews have long trusted to restore them to the land of their fathers, and He that the Catholics hope will be kind enough to make their stay in Purgatory short, and He that the Methodists count upon joyously to burn all the rest of us in white-hot flames forever. He has been successful among gods largely because of His very crudity. No training in divinity is needed to understand Him. At times, as beseems a god, He may retreat into inscrutability, but in general He is quite comprehensible, and even transparent. His principles, indeed, are so simple that they are taught in the Sunday-schools to children of five or six. As in ancient Palestine, He increases in humanness as He gets away from the cities, and throws off the uncomfortable vestments of El. In the South of this great Republic He returns to the primitive estate of a rain-god, and when there is a drought His votaries turn out exactly as the desert Jews used to turn out in Southern Palestine, to demand confidently that He do something about it.

Christian Origins

From the *American Mercury*, Jan., 1932, pp. 125–27.
A review of THE MESSIAH JESUS AND JOHN THE BAPTIST,
by Robert Eisler; London, 1931

The problem Dr. Eisler here tackles is this: What actually happened in Jerusalem and thereabout in the first years of the Christian era? What were the origins of that Jesus of Nazareth who made such an uproar during the administration of the Roman Governor, Pontius Pilate, and what were the circumstances which made Him the founder of a new religion, the most widespread and powerful that the world has yet seen? The answers that we find in Christian literature are incomplete and unsatisfactory. The New Testament, as we have it, is full of obviously dubious history. It was written, in the main, by men who had not witnessed the events they describe, and hence it bristles with contradictions and absurdities. Worse, it shows plain signs of later tampering, so that the most we can say of it today is that it tells us, not what really happened, but simply what certain Christian theologians of the Third, Fourth, Fifth, and even later centuries, thought *may* have happened. Nor is any help to be found in non-Christian chronicles, for, as the great German scholar, Adolf Harnack, once said, all that they have to say might be printed on one quarto sheet of paper.

Dr. Eisler is convinced that it is a gross error to assume, as has been commonly done, that this paucity of records proves only that Jesus attracted little attention among the Romans—that His revolt was of no importance, and hence passed unnoticed. He shows, on the contrary, that they must have taken it very seriously, at all events, in its political aspect, and that it was their custom to keep elaborate official memoranda of such events, and that these memoranda were open to their historians. Why, then, have we so little about Jesus? In particular, why is there so little in the well-known history of Josephus, a Roman court historian, and why is that little so plainly unreliable? Why is the Jew Josephus made to say flatly that Jesus was a teacher of the Truth, that He arose from the dead, and that He was "the Christ"? Dr. Eisler's answer is simple. Josephus never said anything of the sort. The *Testimonium Josephi*, like so much of the New Testament, is an interpolation in the original text. What Josephus did say has been taken out, and what the Christians of Constantine's time wanted him to say has been put in. And what other historians said has been lost to us because, in those days, there was a vigorous and relentless censorship of anti-Christian documents, and every scrap of hostile writing was hunted down and destroyed—all save the few inconsiderable fragments mentioned by Harnack.

So far Dr. Eisler's case has little support in documentary facts. But he quickly produces an impressive body of such facts from Russia. In the libraries and monasteries of that country are a number of early MSS. of Josephus, mainly in Northern dialects of Old Slavic. They are translations from early Greek MSS. and though there are some traces in them of that Christian tampering which is found in all the Western MSS. of Josephus, many passages remain that have disappeared entirely in the West, and in them the acts and aims of Jesus are dealt with in a detailed and realistic manner. These passages, in not a few cases, are so phrased that they are apparently direct quotations from official records of the events preceding the Crucifixion, and so they are of high historical value. They coincide, broadly speaking, with the narrative in the Gospels, but in many important details they are at variance, for they tell the story from the Roman point of view. It would be going too far to call them impartial, but they are at least free from Christian coloring, and in consequence they answer many questions that the Gospel historians and the sophisticated Western Josephus evade, apparently deliberately.

In brief, Dr. Eisler concludes that Jesus was a member of a tribe of wandering craftsmen which still survives in the deserts of Palestine, and is now called the Sleb. Its members practise all the simple crafts that are in request among the nomads—carpentry, blacksmithing, and so on—and are noted for their gentle manners. They take no part whatever in the tribal feuds, accept only food and drink for their labor, and own no property. In times of trouble they are pacifists, preaching non-resistance and retiring to the desert when actual war breaks out. In the first years of the Christian era their influence was undoubtedly thrown against that spirit of revolt which was rising in Palestine, and was destined, in the year 70, to lead to a furious conflict with the Romans, fatal to the Jewish state. Jesus, like John the Baptist before Him, opposed this revolt, and proposed that His followers retire to the desert to escape it. But the little band was drawn, nevertheless, into the conspiracies of the Zealot faction, which was for an immediate attack on the Roman garrison, and Jesus, by virtue of His birth—He was, as a son of David, eligible to the Jewish throne—became willy-nilly a figure in the anti-Roman movement. In the end, cornered, He apparently abandoned conciliation for the sword, and when an attempt was made to seize the Temple He was a party to it. Its failure cost Him His life. And, as Luke tells us, "a superscription was written over Him in letters of Greek, and Latin, and Hebrew, THIS IS THE KING OF THE JEWS."

Dr. Eisler's reconstruction of Josephus's narrative throws a great deal of light upon some of the darkest places in the Synoptic Gospels. It explains the arming of the Disciples, otherwise so strangely at variance with the Sermon on the Mount. It makes understandable the great discrepancies between other parts of the early preaching, and the melodramatic events of the last few days. It gets rid of the Christian tradition, incredible on so many grounds, that the Romans had little if anything to do with the Crucifixion, but simply turned Jesus over to the Jews. It disposes of difficulties in a dozen other places, some of which have fevered theologians for many years. And incidentally, those parts of the Russian Josephus which deal with the person and personality of Jesus also give rational explanations of certain minor texts that have long been quite unintelligible, for example, the "Physician, heal thyself" of Luke iv, 23.

Altogether, Dr. Eisler has made an extraordinarily interesting book. If even so much as half of it be rejected, then enough remains to affect New Testament criticism very powerfully. The orthodox theologians, of course, will pass it over in silence, but more enlightened readers, whether clerical or lay, will find it well worth reading.

The Root of Religion

From DAMN! A BOOK OF CALUMNY, 1918, p. 90

The idea of liberal truth crept into religion relatively late: it is the invention of lawyers, priests and cheese-mongers. The idea of mystery long preceded it, and at the heart of that idea of mystery was an idea of beauty—that is, an idea that this or that view of the celestial and infernal process presented a satisfying picture of form, rhythm and organization. Once this view was adopted as satisfying, its professional interpreters and their dupes sought to reinforce it by declaring it true. The same flow of reasoning is familiar on lower planes. The average man does not get pleasure out of an idea because he thinks it is true; he thinks it is true because he gets pleasure out of it.

The Mask

From the same, p. 98

Ritual is to religion what the music of an opera is to the libretto: ostensibly a means of interpretation, but actually a means of concealment. The Calvinists made the mistake of keeping the doctrine of infant damnation in plain words. As enlightenment grew in the world, intelligence and prudery revolted against it, and so it had to be abandoned. Had it been set to music it would have survived—uncomprehended, unsuspected and unchallenged.

The Eternal Mob

From NOTES ON DEMOCRACY, 1926, pp. 66–68

Do I forget that democratic man, despite his general imbecility, has some shining virtues—specifically, that he is filled with humble piety, a touching fidelity to the faith? I forget nothing: I simply answer, what faith? Is it argued by any rational man that the debased Christianity cherished by the mob in all Christian countries today has any colorable likeness to the body of ideas preached by Christ? If so, then let us have a better teaching of the Bible in the public-schools. The plain fact is that this bogus Christianity has no more relation to the system of Christ than it has to the system of Aristotle. It is the invention of Paul and his attendant rabble-rousers—a body of men exactly comparable to the corps of evangelical pastors of today, which is to say, a body devoid of sense and lamentably indifferent to common honesty. The mob, having heard Christ, turned against Him, and applauded His crucifixion. His theological ideas were too logical and too plausible for it, and

His ethical ideas were enormously too austere. What it yearned for was the old comfortable balderdash under a new and gaudy name, and that is precisely what Paul offered it. He borrowed from all the wandering dervishes and soul-snatchers of Asia Minor, and flavored the stew with remnants of the Greek demonology. The result was a code of doctrines so discordant and so nonsensical that no two men since, examining it at length, have ever agreed upon its precise meaning. But Paul knew his mob: he had been a travelling labor leader. He knew that nonsense was its natural provender—that the unintelligible soothed it like sweet music. He was the *Stammvater* of all the Christian mob-masters of today, terrorizing and enchanting the mob with their insane damnations, passing the diligent plate, busy among the women.

Once the early church emerged from the Roman catacombs and began to yield to that reorganization of society which was forced upon the ancient world by the barbarian invasions, Paul was thrown overboard as Methodists throw Wesley overboard when they acquire the means and leisure for golf, and Peter was put in his place. Peter was a blackguard, but he was at least free from any taint of Little Bethel. The Roman Church, in the aristocratic feudal age, promoted him *post mortem* to the Papacy, and then raised him to the mystical dignity of Rock, a rank obviously quasi-celestial. But Paul remained the prophet of the sewers. He was to emerge centuries later in many incarnations—Luther, Calvin, Wesley, and so on. He remains today the archtheologian of the mob. His turgid and witless metaphysics make Christianity bearable to men who would be repelled by Christ's simple and magnificent reduction of the duties of man to the duties of a gentleman.

The IQ of Holy Church

From the *American Mercury*, Sept., 1930, pp. 33–34

There are some shrewd fellows among the Catholic clergy, and there are many more who are charming and amusing, but the church as a church, like any other ecclesiastical organization, is highly unintelligent. It is forever making thumping errors, both in psychology and in politics, and despite its occasional brilliant successes among sentimental pseudo-intellectuals, as in England, and among the *Chandala*, as in America, it seems likely to go downhill hereafter. Consider its position in the world today. After 1,800 years of uninterrupted propaganda, during 1,500 of which it was virtually unopposed in Christendom, scarcely a dozen really first-rate men subscribe to its ideas, and not a single first-rate nation.

Its poverty in this respect is well demonstrated by its almost comical excess of enthusiasm whenever a stray member of the *intelligentsia* succumbs. Reading the Catholic papers—I allude, of course, to the more intelligent of them, not to the dismal diocesan rags—an uninformed person might easily gather the impression that Hilaire Belloc was the greatest historian who ever lived, and G. K. Chesterton the most profound metaphysician. This gurgling over second-raters, it seems to me, is injudicious. A more moderate rejoicing would be far more convincing. And a more moderate reviling would probably do more damage to the church's chief current enemies—the birth controllers and the physical scientists. The war upon birth control, as it is commonly carried on by virgin bishops, is not only unfair, but also ridiculous, for it is based upon theological postulates that no educated man could conceivably accept. There is, I believe, a lot to be said against the birth controllers—for example, on the score of their false pretenses: they really know no more about preventing conception than any corner druggist. But their Catholic critics, so far as I know, have never said it. Instead, they ground their case upon a dogmatism that is offensive to every intellectual decency, and try to dispose of their opponents by denouncing them as mere voluptuaries. This last is sheer nonsense. The principal birth controllers are as serious as so many witch-burners, and the theory that they are voluptuaries is easily refuted by looking at one of them, preferably a female.

The war upon modern science is quite as silly. Its sole effect must be to make every enlightened Catholic blush. And in the long run, if he be of a reflective habit, it must make him wonder whether he really belongs in the Roman camp. Every Catholic of that sort, the world being what it is, has a hard enough time already to hold his faith: it is opposed not only by a multitude of objective evidences but also by the inner spirit of his day and generation. Certainly it does not help him to be told that Belloc is a great historian and that Gibbon was an ass, that Kilmer was a good poet and Hardy a bad one, and that Windle was superior to Einstein. Nor does it help him to be taught solemnly that the hatching of rachitic and syphilitic children is an act of merit, *ad maiorem Dei gloriam.*

Literary Theologians

1
G. K. Chesterton

From the *Smart Set*, Feb., 1909, pp. 154–55.
A review of ORTHODOXY, by G. K. Chesterton; New York, 1908

Gilbert Chesterton's "Orthodoxy," which pretends to describe the author's gradual conversion to Christianity, is the best argument for Christianity I have ever heard—and I have gone through, I suppose, fully a hundred. But after you lay it down you suddenly realize that Chesterton has been trying to prove, not only that Christianity is reasonable, but also that supernaturalism is truth. His argument, indeed, crossing the bounds of merely sectarian apologetics, passes on to the fundamental problem of philosophy: what is true? The materialists answer that anything man can prove is true. Chesterton answers that anything man can believe with comfort is true. Going further, he maintains that anything which gives disquiet is, *ipso facto*, false. Here we have pragmatism gone to seed, and here we have, too, a loud "No" to all human progress. As a matter of fact, the world gets ahead by losing its illusions, and not by fostering them. Nothing, perhaps, is more painful than disillusion, but all the same, nothing is more necessary. Because there were men willing to suffer painful doubts hundreds of years ago, we civilized white men of today were born without our ancestors' harassing belief in witches. Because a horde of impious critics hang upon the flanks of our dearest beliefs today, our children, 500 years hence, will be free from our present firm faith in political panaceas, unlucky days, dreams, hunches, and the influence of mind over matter. Disillusion is like quinine. Its taste is abominable—but it cures. Not even Chesterton, with all his skill at writing, and with all his general cleverness—and he is the cleverest man, I believe, in the world today, though also one of the most ignorant—can turn that truth into anything else.

2

Leo Tolstoy

From the *Smart Set*, May, 1920, pp. 142–43.
A review of THE PATHWAY OF LIFE, by Leo Tolstoy; New York, 1920

Leo Tolstoy's "The Pathway of Life" is precisely the sort of book that one might imagine the great Russian chautauquan keeping by his bedside, to be resorted to for solace whenever nightmares awakened him and the sorrows of the world gnawed his liver. That is to say, it is a huge compendium of ethical and theological mush, partly of Tolstoy himself and partly by other sages. The ideas running through it are those of the average Methodist evangelist of the Iowa backwoods. The one and only duty of man is to please God; all other duties are illusory and of the devil. So far, so good. But how is one to determine what is pleasing to God? Here the venerable bosh-monger is far from clear, but one may at least guess at his general answer. Whatever is unpleasant to man is pleasant to God. The test is the natural instinct of man. If there arises within one's dark recesses a hot desire to do this or that, then it is the paramount duty of a Christian to avoid doing this or that. And if, on the contrary, one cherishes an abhorrence of the business, then one must tackle it forthwith, all the time shouting "Hallelujah!" A simple enough religion, surely—simple, satisfying and idiotic. No wonder Tolstoy is the hero of Russian *muzhiks* and American Socialists.

The old rat-trap had a bold spirit: he never tried to evade the necessary implications of his doctrine. For example, consider the

matter of sex. Tolstoy believed and taught that passion was unqual-
ifiedly evil—that it was a sin against the Holy Ghost to cast a
friendly eye upon a pretty girl, or even upon one's lawful wife. His
disciples, poll-parroting this imbecile idea, quickly got into difficulties. What it inevitably led to was the advocacy of race suicide
upon a colossal scale. No passion, no *Stammhalter*. But Tolstoy
himself never bucked at this dilemma. Instead he boldly seized
both horns, took a long breath, and emerged with the doctrine that
the human race should be, must be, and of a right ought to be
exterminated. Here I had better leave him. His notions begin to
seduce me. . . .

3
Arthur Conan Doyle

From the *Smart Set*, Aug., 1918, pp. 141–42.
A review of THE NEW REVELATION,
by Sir Arthur Conan Doyle; New York, 1918

All that is yet known about life in Heaven is succinctly set forth
here by Sir Arthur Conan Doyle, author of "The Adventures of
Sherlock Holmes," "The Crime of the Congo," "The Hound of
the Baskervilles," and other favorite fancies. It is not, however,
fancy that he offers here, but, as he himself says, cold and indisputable fact. I have heard all the great ecclesiastics of the age
upon the geography, government and social organization of
Heaven, and they have unanimously left me unconvinced. All of
them are too subjective; one feels that subconscious yearnings, in
the Freudian manner, are corrupting their reports. Dr. Sunday describes the sort of Heaven that would undoubtedly please a senile
baseball player, but leaves out all accommodation for the nobility
and gentry. Dr. Henry Van Dyke simply pictures Princeton, N.J.,
during a Presbyterian *Sängerfest*. Dr. Newell Dwight Hillis shows
us Brooklyn purged of Tammany, the Rum Demon, Socialism,
Germans, atheism, automatic pianos and parturition. And the
Fifth avenue rectors, taking one with another, get little beyond
vague pictures of fashionable society, with overtones of quiet cock-

tails, Corona-Corona cigars and amorous intrigue. In these diligent projections of the unknown I find no comfort. Where is the
waiter, Emil? Where is the chamber-music? Where is the fellow
told off to shoot dogs, babies, Methodists, poets, owners of phonographs, issuers of dinner invitations, actors, hat-check girls, Bolsheviki? Where are the bouncers employed to keep out all women
under seventy-five?

Dr. Doyle, at his worst, is not guilty of any such self-centered
forgetfulness. He doesn't conjure up a Heaven to his own taste,
forgetting my taste and your taste; he confines himself to the few
details that are positively known. These come, not out of his private fancy, but from the reports of persons already in celestial
residence—in brief, from Raymond, Little Brighteyes, Wahwah
the Indian chief, and all the other tried and true communicants.
All he does is to collate and summarize their reports, introducing
nothing of his own invention. The facts that emerge are quite simple. At the moment of death a man "finds himself in a spirit body,"
which is the exact counterpart of his old one, save that all disease,
weakness, or deformity has passed from it. If he has been devoured by a wolf, he is nevertheless sound and undigested. If he
has died of drink, there is no *Katzenjammer*. This restored body "is
standing or floating beside the old body." The dead man, for the
moment, is not clearly aware that he is dead. Seeing the nurse still
in the room, powdering her nose against the arrival of the under-
taker, he attempts to speak to her. But in vain; she can't hear him.
Then he suddenly notices that there are others present, dead like
himself. With these conversation is easier. Some step up and shake
hands with him. Others kiss him. Finally, "some more radiant being," apparently a guide for newcomers, takes him in charge and
proceeds to show him the sights.

Before getting very far, however, the candidate begins to feel
drowsy, and presently he falls asleep. This sleep is long and profound; it may "extend for weeks or months." Then for his day in
court, and a rigid examination into his doings on earth. The details of celestial jurisprudence and penology are as yet somewhat
uncertain, for those who have been through the mill are naturally
rather reticent about telling of their punishment, but Dr. Doyle as-
sures us that a belief in Purgatory "is justified by the reports from

the other side." These same reports fix many other details of life there. The inhabitants, it appears, live in communities, like seeking like. No eating is done, but the arts are practised, including music. "Married couples do not necessarily reunite," but genuine love affairs are resumed, though "there is no sexuality in the grosser sense and no child-birth." The young gradually grow older and the old gradually grow younger, until all are about the same age. No one has any work to do. Clothes are still worn, "as one would expect, since there is no reason why modesty should disappear." Finally, everyone is "intensely happy."

I commend this clear and trustworthy description of life in Heaven to all who have been dismayed and disappointed by sacerdotal wind-music. Dr. Doyle has nothing to sell, nor is he trying to scare anyone into subscribing to any definite scheme of theology. All he pretends to do is to set down in a simplified form what has been communicated to gifted mediums by the more talkative folks beyond the rainbow. He is not a prophet, but merely a reporter. I believe that his little book will rid your mind of the doubts and horrors which now infest it, as it has rid mine.

The Believing Mind

From the *American Mercury*, June, 1932, pp. 251–52.
A review of HOUDINI AND CONAN DOYLE,
by Bernard M. L. Ernst and Hereward Carrington;
New York, 1932

Mr. Ernst is president of the parent assembly of the Society of American Magicians, and presumably represents Houdini in the combat here reported; Mr. Carrington, who is a well-known writer on table-tapping, slate-writing, thought-reading and other such ghostly marvels, is apparently in Doyle's corner. Just what hand each of them had in the book I do not know, but to me at least it seems to lean toward the transcendental side, despite a somewhat elaborate show of impartiality. Doyle, who was an indefatigable spook-chaser, gets nearly all the breaks. Even when his bovine credulity is exposed in the most patent and painful manner, and on evidence supplied fatuously by himself, he is yet represented to have been a sagacious and even scientific fellow, with no appetite save for the truth. By the same token poor Houdini is patronized rather heavily, and his weaknesses—for example, his vanity—surely get sufficient notice. Nevertheless, it is plain from the chronicle that he had all the better of Doyle, and that there can scarcely be two opinions as to which was the more intelligent.

The relation between the men was a curious one, and it is worth something to have this record of it. They began exchanging letters in 1920, and during the four years following met many times. Doyle, in those days, was busily whooping up spiritualism, and it was his obvious hope to convert Houdini, whose celebrity as a stage magician would have made his conversion a notable victory for the holy cause. But Houdini, though he was always willing and even eager to examine Doyle's "evidence," was never so much as flustered by it. Every time he came to close quarters with it he found that it was full of holes. Most of the tricks of Doyle's mediums he could do himself, and far better than they could; as for the remainder he saw every reason to believe that they would yield in the same way to a more careful approach. Doyle bombarded him with challenges and persuasions, but he never came into camp. When he died in 1926 he was fully convinced that spiritualism was buncombe. Few men ever had a better opportunity to judge it, or as much competence.

Though, as I have said, Doyle is treated very politely in this book, the fact that he was an almost fabulous ass cannot be concealed. It may sound incredible, but it is a simple fact that he passed to his brummagem Other World in 1930 thoroughly convinced that Houdini himself had been a medium. Houdini, while they were both alive, protested against this nonsense with great earnestness, and offered the most solemn assurance that all of his tricks—getting out of handcuffs, reading minds, staying under water for long periods, and so on—were tricks and nothing more, but Doyle kept on insisting idiotically that some "psychic" power was involved in them. I commend the fact to connoisseurs of human imbecility. It is, in its way, a superb measure of the intellectual dignity of the whole psychical research movement. Doyle was undoubtedly one of its great stars, and maybe it would not be too much to say that he was the greatest of them, yet he continued to believe that Houdini was infested by spooks in the face of the most direct and unanswerable evidence to the contrary. No wonder it was easy for professional mediums to fetch him. And no wonder he seemed a master mind to the dolts who sit trembling in dingy back parlors.

Once, at Atlantic City, he undertook to get a message from Houdini's dead mother, with Lady Doyle as the medium. The message turned out to be the usual maudlin stuff—"Oh, my darling, thank God, thank God, at last I'm through! . . . Why, of course, I want to talk to my boy—my own beloved boy," and so on. Houdini was polite, but it must have been hard for him to contain himself, for the whole message was in the ornate spiritualist dialect of English—and his mother, a Hungarian rabbi's widow, had only the most imperfect knowledge of the language, and never used it in speaking to him. When the seance was over he made some idle scratches on a sheet of paper, and presently wrote the name Powell. Thus Doyle described the episode in "Our American Adventure," printed a bit later on:

> Now, Dr. Ellis Powell, my first fighting partner in spiritualism, had just died in England—worn out, I expect [sic], by his own exertions, for he was a desperately hard worker in the cause. I was the man he was most likely to signal to, and here was his name coming through the hand of Houdini. "Truly, Saul is among the prophets," said I.

In brief, another "proof" that Houdini was a medium—and didn't know it. Unfortunately, Houdini himself also left a record of that sitting, and from it we learn that the Powell whose name occurred to him was not Dr. Ellis Powell at all, but one F. E. Powell, a fellow magician, at that moment stranded in Texas. Later on, Doyle protested against this and similar exposures of his fantastic credulity on the ground that he regarded spiritualism as a religion, and that his opponents ought to respect it as such.

The Road of Doubt

From DAMN! A BOOK OF CALUMNY, 1918, p. 87

The first effect of what used to be called natural philosophy is to fill its devotee with wonder at the marvels of God. This explains why the pursuit of science, so long as it remains superficial, is not incompatible with the most naïve sort of religious faith. But the moment the student of the sciences passes this stage of childlike amazement and begins to investigate the inner workings of natural phenomena, he sees how ineptly many of them are managed, and so he tends to pass from awe of the Creator to criticism of the Creator, and once he has crossed that bridge he has ceased to be a believer. One finds plenty of country doctors, amateur botanists, high-school physics teachers and other such quasi-scientists in the pews on Sunday, but one never sees a Huxley there, or a Darwin, or an Ehrlich.

Veritas Odium Parit

From PREJUDICES: FOURTH SERIES, 1924, pp. 198–99.
First published in the *American Mercury*, Jan., 1924, p. 78

Another old delusion is that one to the effect that truth has a mysterious medicinal power—that it makes the world better and man happier. The fact is that truth, in general, is extremely uncomfortable, and that the masses of men are thus wise to hold it in suspicion. The most rational religious ideas held in modern times are probably those of the Unitarians; the most nonsensical are those of the Christian Scientists. Yet it must be obvious to every observer that the average Unitarian, even when he is quite healthy, is a sour and discontented fellow, whereas the average Christian Scientist, even when he is down with gallstones, is full of an enviable peace. I have known, in my time, several eminent philosophers. The happiest of them, in his moments of greatest joy, used to entertain himself by drawing up wills leaving his body to a medical college.

VII. BRETHREN OF THE CLOTH

Playing with Fire

From the Baltimore *Evening Sun*, Dec. 17, 1927

THE TRUTH is that life without combat would be unbearable, and that men function freest and most gloriously under stress. Every effort to make humanity peaceable has failed, and I believe that all the efforts to come will fail. The colossal failure of Christianity must have been noticed, by this time, even by the clergy, a singularly naïve and deluded body of men. It came into the world to make an end of war; it has made more wars than avarice, or even than hunger. To this day, it is difficult for a Christian clergyman to arise in his pulpit without excoriating something, if that something be only war.

I surely do not complain of the fact, for on the whole the brethren of the cloth have contributed more to my mild and phosphorescent happiness in this life than any other class of men. There was a time when I had almost constant differences with them, and learnt to have a high respect for their dialectic talents. What makes them so formidable is their familiarity with weapons of a dreadful potency. They handle hell-fire as freely and easily as a barber handles his shears: it is their everyday arm. No other men are so formidably equipped. The most a lawyer ever demands of the victim before him is that he be hanged, but even the meekest clergyman is constantly proposing to doom his opponents to endless tortures in lakes of boiling brimstone.

This habit of playing daily with horrible weapons makes clergymen extraordinarily violent in controversy, and violence is what makes that great art charming. I can recall being tackled by them for trivial errors in political science—if, indeed, they were errors at all—in a manner almost suitable for flooring the appalling beasts described in the Book of Revelation. Once, when I argued that chasing poor harlots up and down the alleys of Baltimore would not make the town chaste, some of them accused me of having a proprietary interest in bawdy-houses. Another time, when I argued more or less calmly that Prohibition could never be enforced, they alleged that I was in the pay of the Whiskey Trust, and pledged to besot and ruin the youth of the Republic.

I don't recall ever having a controversy with a man of God that did not end in dreadful bawling. It is impossible to discuss them at all without getting an eye full of sulphur, though surely they are important men, and hence worth discussing. For years it was my high privilege to devote myself mainly to the follies of the Protestant pastors, and so many of them denounced me as an agent of the Pope. This got me friends in Catholic circles, and one of my constant visitors was a venerable monsignor who insisted very charmingly upon treating me as a servant of the True Faith. But of late, for uttering certain trifling platitudes about the American hierarchy, I have been violently denounced by Catholic clergymen, led by the Paulist Fathers. This makes me feel fair again. I am no longer biased.

The ecclesiastical habit of conducting all controversies *à outrance*—of assuming and insisting that every opponent is a scoundrel, and ought to be boiled and fried in Hell forever—this habit, as everyone knows, also marks those laymen whose convictions have a theological color—for example, Prohibitionists and anti-evolutionists. It has been my fortune to have many combats with such fellows: I can recall only one who ever showed any sign of good humor. That one was the Hon. William H. Anderson. He liked controversy for its own sake, and hence could carry it out without bile. The fact later undid him, for when the New York wets took him in some insignificant misdemeanor his brother drys deserted him, and he went to prison.

The rest of the drys all hit below the belt habitually, and as a matter of pious devotion. They saddled Prohibition upon the country, indeed, at a time when hitting below the belt was official, and any man who refused to do it got the attention of the *Polizei*. The anti-evolutionists are quite as bad. I know several of them who, in their private lives, are amiable enough, but when they mount the tub they get out all the weapons in the theological arsenal, and employ them with great gusto. I have been denounced in my time more than most, but never so violently as by anti-evolutionists.

Some time ago one of the most influential of them printed a long philippic damning me as a paretic, and alleging flatly that my sad state was due to transactions forbidden by Holy Writ. The charge, of course, was not new. It had been whispered here in Baltimore more than once, and by Christians of high tone, along with the hint that I was incessantly in my cups. But here the thing was plainly stated in print, and by a gentleman notorious for his solvency. It was a temptation indeed! The libel laws are very harsh in such matters. But, intrenched behind my lifelong principles, I somehow resisted, and soon afterward the gentleman was called to bliss eternal, and the tenements and hereditaments that I might have collared are now enjoyed by his heirs and assigns.

Shock Troops

From the *American Mercury*, Jan., 1928, pp. 123–25.
A Review of THE JESUIT ENIGMA, by E. Boyd Barrett;
New York, 1927

If this thoughtful and valuable book gets any notice at all from the literati of the Latin rite, it will probably be only abuse—the inevitable reply, from that quarter, to any man who proposes, however honestly and judiciously, to discuss the weaknesses of Holy Church. But that abuse cannot dispose of the manifest fact that Dr. Barrett knows what he is talking about, and deserves to be heard. For twenty years he was himself a Jesuit, and during that time his scholarship—he is a psychologist—shed credit upon the order, and he was in excellent repute both within and without its ranks. When he withdrew at last, it was not because of any apostasy to the faith. On the contrary, he apparently retained his belief in all the salient Catholic doctrines, and actually offered himself for service as an ordinary priest. What drove him out was simply his conviction that the Society of Jesus offered an impossible environment to a man of his intellectual curiosity and integrity. Its atmosphere of repression, of deliberate obscurantism, of petty intrigue, of childish spying and tale-bearing choked him, and so he departed.

He opens his book with a brief sketch of Jesuit history, proceeds to a somewhat elaborate description of Loyola's celebrated "Spiritual Exercises" and the Jesuit Constitutions, the two ruling documents of the order, and then launches into a long discussion of Jesuit practises. There is no tedious scandal-mongering in his story. He believes that the Jesuit rule regarding dealings with women is unworkable, and he shows that it is frequently evaded, but that evasion he pictures as due to necessity, not to looseness. For most Jesuits, as priests and as men, he apparently has high respect. But he is convinced that their education tends to make them narrow and bigoted, that the dreadful discipline under which they live breaks down their self-reliance and self-esteem and makes them mere cogs in an ecclesiastical machine, and that preferment among them, instead of going to the strongest men, only too often goes to the most complaisant. The Jesuit system of espionage, as he describes it, is really quite appalling. But it is not directed, as Ku Kluxers believe, against Methodist bishops, members of Congress and the Federal judiciary; it is directed solely against Jesuits. They live under a surveillance that would irk prisoners in a penitentiary. They literally have no privacy whatever, even of thought, and the method adopted for keeping watch over them offers obvious temptations to men with a talent for persecution. Accused, a Jesuit never knows his accusers. Punished, he is forbidden even to demand a trial.

Dr. Barrett offers many examples of the unpleasant workings of this system. It has the inevitable effect, he says, of shutting off the free play of ideas within the order, and it is responsible for the generally hackneyed and uninspiring character of Jesuit thinking. The members of the Society shine only in safe fields. They make capital astronomers, meteorologists, and so on, but where ideas are in conflict they are chained up by a medieval and inflexible philosophy. What that confinement amounts to was shown when

Dr. Barrett, on coming to America from Ireland, was invited to contribute some articles on the new psychology to the Jesuit weekly, *America*. His articles, it would seem, were harmless enough, and the editor at the time, Father Tierney, S.J., began printing them. But presently they were stopped by orders from above, and to this day Dr. Barrett has no explanation of that cavalier affront. Obviously, the new psychology, as banal as it is, was thought to be too heady for the customers of *America*. That the editors of the weekly (many of them able men) cannot do their work effectively under such conditions is plain enough; the fact sufficiently explains the failure of their magazine, which started out with high promise and no little uproar, to make any impression whatever upon American thought. A rival weekly, the *Commonweal*, edited by Catholic laymen, has got further in two or three years than *America* has got in twelve or fifteen. Yet it remains the best that the Jesuits have ever offered in this country. It measures them as fairly and as clearly as the *War-Cry* measures the Salvation Army.

Dr. Barrett's description of the Jesuit scheme of education is devastating. Himself a doctor of a secular university, he is in a singularly favorable position for judging it. It is in the main, he says, a witless ramming in of flyblown nonsense. Nothing is taught objectively; everything must be turned to the glory of the Church, and especially of the Jesuit order. The philosophy on tap is strictly Thomistic, and was abandoned by non-Catholic philosophers, save as an interesting curiosity, centuries ago. All the modern philosophers of any account, even including Kant and Hegel, are under the ban. The sciences are approached in a gingerly fashion; literature is simply Catholic literature. Worse, the pedagogical method is medieval and the teachers are often unprepared. Dr. Barrett himself, a psychologist, was put to teaching sociology at Georgetown University, despite his protests that he knew nothing of the subject. When he was relieved of that impossible duty at last, it was to be made professor of catechism. Finally, he was allowed "one short course of psychology toward the latter half of the school year." It was after this that he resigned from the order, and applied to Cardinal Hayes for assignment as a parish priest. In vain! The long arm of the Black Pope reached out from Rome. No ex-Jesuit may join any other order or serve as a secular priest. Shortly after Dr. Barrett resigned, a friend sent a letter to him at Georgetown. It was returned marked "Unknown."

His case is impressive, but it seems to me that he yet forgets something—that, in the last analysis, he seriously misunderstands the order he served for so many years. He appears to see it, ideally, as a sort of intellectual aristocracy within the Church, grounded in learning by a harsh, laborious and relentless process and devoted to widening learning's bounds. It is, I believe, nothing of the sort. Founded by a soldier, it remains essentially military, not scholarly. Its aim is not to find out what is true, but to defend and propagate what Holy Church says is true. All the ideas that it is officially aware of are fixed ideas: it knows of no machinery for changing them, and wants to hear of none. For a Jesuit to engage in free speculation would be as incongruous and as shocking as it would be for General Pershing to flout the ideals of the Elks. The black-robed and romantic brethren have a quite different opinion. It is to spread out fanwise where the Catholic ranks are thinnest, and there do battle for the Church—for God too, of course, but principally for the Church. They are at their best on the remotest frontiers. In Catholic countries they are suspect; more than once, indeed, they have been thrown out. But where the faithful are few and far between and the enemies of Peter rage and roar, there they yet use their ancient weapons effectively and are mighty soldiers of the Lord. As soldiers, they deserve a far easier testing than Dr. Barrett gives to them. A psychologist by trade, with a leaning toward psychoanalysis, he prods into their heads a bit too scientifically. Let him try to figure out what a competent Freudian would have made of St. Louis, or the Cid, or Washington, or even Robert E. Lee. The very hallmark of the military mind is repression. The moment soldiers begin to think, the war is over and there is Bolshevism. If Dr. Barrett had his way the Jesuits would be marching upon Rome (as they came near doing once before) and His Holiness, like his colleague of the Quirinal, would be a gilded prisoner in a very tight cage.

Story Without a Moral

From the *American Mercury*, Jan., 1924, p. 78

A number of years ago, in my newspaper days, I received a circular violently denouncing the Catholic Church. The circular stated that the Church was engaged in a hellish conspiracy to seize the government of the United States and put an agent of the Pope into the White House, and that the leaders of the plot were certain Jesuits, all of them foreigners and violent enemies of the American Constitution. Only one such Jesuit was actually named: a certain Walter Drum, S.J. He was denounced with great bitterness, and every true American was besought to be on the watch for him. Something inspired me to turn to "Who's Who in America"; it lists all the principal emissaries of Rome in the Republic, even when they are not Americans. This is what I found:

> Drum, Walter, S.J.; *b.* at Louisville, Ky., Sept. 21, 1870; *s.* Capt. John Drum, U.S.A., killed before Santiago.

I printed the circular of the Ur-Klansmen—and that eloquent sentence from "Who's Who." No more was heard against the foreigner Drum in that diocese. . . .

Eight or ten years later, having retired from journalism with a competence, I was the editor of a magazine. One day there reached me the manuscript of a short story by a young Princeton man, by name F. Scott Fitzgerald. It was a harmless and charming story about a young scholastic in a Jesuit seminary. A few months later it was printed in the magazine. Four days after the number was on the stands I received a letter from a Catholic priest, denouncing me as an enemy to the Church, belaboring the story as blasphemous and worse, and stating that the writer proposed to make a tour of all the Catholic women's clubs in the East, urging their members to blacklist and boycott the magazine. The name signed to the letter was Walter Drum, S.J.

Divine Virtuosity

From the *Smart Set*, Jan., 1923, p. 53

In no field does God work in a more mysterious and facile way, His wonders to perform, than in that of human plastic, or, as they say, physiognomy. I once knew a man who was, in head and face, the exact duplicate of the late Friedrich Wilhelm Nietzsche. He had precisely the same piercing eyes, the same Niagara of a moustache, the same watermelon brow, the same bellicose glare. He was the superintendent of a Methodist Sunday-school in a provincial town. . . . You think I lie? Unquestionably it seems probable. I therefore append his name and address. He was Thomas Gordon Hayes, and the scene of his theological endeavors was a house of worship on Edmondson avenue, Baltimore, opposite Harlem Square.

VIII. MAN AND SUPERMAN

The Great Illusion

From the *Smart Set*, April, 1919, p. 49

A DOG is a standing proof that most so-called human rights, at bottom, are worth nothing. A dog is proverbially devoid of any such rights, and yet it lives well and is happy. For one dog that is starved and mistreated there are 10,000 that are coddled and overfed. How many human beings, even under the perfect democracy which now exists in the United States, are so comfortable and contented? Perhaps a few actors—that is about all. . . . Moreover, it is idiotic to say that a dog's life is empty and bestial. A dog has highly fastidious tastes in food; it knows how to play and to be gay; it has a talent for amorous adventure; it acquires manners and prefers good society. In all those ways it is surely much superior to the average Methodist. Yet more, a dog is very religious and its religion is free from superstition. The god it believes in is its master, and that god actually exists, and is actually concerned about its welfare, and actually rewards it and punishes it, on a plan comprehensible to dogs and meeting with their approval, for its virtues and vices. Dogs need not waste any time over insoluble theological problems. Their god is plainly visible and wholly understandable—they have no need of clergy to guess for them, mislead them and get them into trouble. . . . Yet a dog has none of the great rights that men esteem, glory in and die for. It cannot vote. It cannot get converted by Dr. Billy Sunday. It cannot go to jail for some great and lofty principle—say, equal suffrage or birth control. It is barred from the Elks, the Harvard Club and Congress. It cannot serve its country by dying of septicaemia or acute gastro-enteritis. It cannot read the *Nation*. It cannot subscribe to the Y.M.C.A. It cannot swear at waiters. It cannot eat in Pullman dining-cars. It cannot be a Presbyterian.

Ethical Origins

From the *Smart Set*, July, 1919, p. 65

The concept of man as the moral animal *par excellence* is full of absurdity. The truth is that man is the least moral of all the mammals, and that what little native morality he possesses is an inheritance from his savage ancestors, and tends to vanish as he grows civilized. No race of men has ever punished violations of the moral code as severely as they are punished by the lower animals. Among tigers, lions, hyenas, jackals, elephants, leopards, cougars and wolves the punishment for adultery is death. This surely beats the Unitarians.

The Flesh Is Weak

From the Baltimore *Evening Sun*, June 12, 1922

Most religions lean heavily upon the fallacious assumption that there is a strong desire for virtue in human beings. But this desire, as a matter of fact, is very weak, and a great deal of effort is necessary to prevent the contrary desire for adventure from overpowering it. "Onward, Christian Soldiers!"—what else is this save an admission that virtue may be made tolerable only by transforming it into combat, *i.e.*, into rough-house. In the United States today, with Sunday-schools every few hundred yards, there are literally millions of women who hold their chastity so lightly that they will swap it for childish finery. And who ever heard of an American politician who wasn't ready to sacrifice his honor in order to get public office?

The Supreme Curse

From the *Smart Set*, June, 1920, p. 43

It is not materialism that is the chief curse of the world, but idealism. Men get into trouble by taking all their gaudy visions and hallucinations seriously. The lowly yokel, pausing in the furrow to mop his brow, dreams a dream of high achievement in the adjacent city. Ten years later there is a plow standing idle—and another victim of Wall Street is laboring as a bus-driver. Nearly all poverty is caused by idealism. The normal poor man is simply a semi-idiot whose dreams have run away with his capacities. Designed by nature to be a dish-washer in a lunch-room, he has endeavored to make himself a structural ironworker at $5 an hour— and so he has lost his leg, his means of existence, and his sacred honor. It is idealism that causes marriage. It is idealism that makes poets. Every poorhouse is full of idealists.

Thrift

From the Manchester (England) *Sunday Chronicle*, July 21, 1935

The human race detests thrift as it detests intelligence. The man who accumulates more than he needs and saves the surplus is disliked by all who either can't or won't follow his example, and that means the great majority of his fellow men. He makes them ashamed of themselves and they resent it.

The Genealogy of Etiquette

From PREJUDICES: FIRST SERIES, 1919, pp. 152–70. First printed in the *Smart Set*, Sept., 1915, pp. 304–10. Dr. Parsons was born in 1875 and died in 1941. She was educated at Barnard College and took her Ph.D.

in 1899. Her chief interest was in the American Indian, but her active mind also ranged widely into other fields. At the close of her life she was president of the American Anthropological Association

Why do the great majority of Presbyterians (and, for that matter, of Baptists, Episcopalians and Swedenborgians as well) regard it as unlucky to meet a black cat and lucky to find a pin? What are the logical steps behind the theory that it is indecent to eat peas with a knife? By what process does an otherwise sane man arrive at the conclusion that he will go to Hell unless he is baptized by total immersion? What causes men to be faithful to their wives: habit, fear, poverty, lack of imagination, lack of enterprise, stupidity, religion? What is the true nature of the vague pooling of desires that Rousseau called the social contract? Why does an American regard it as scandalous to wear dress clothes at a funeral, and a Frenchman regard it as equally scandalous *not* to wear them? Why is it that men trust one another so readily, and women trust one another so seldom? Why are we all so greatly affected by statements that we know are not true?—*e.g.*, in Lincoln's Gettysburg speech, the Declaration of Independence and the CIII Psalm. What is the origin of the so-called double standard of morality? Why do so many people dislike Jews? Why are women forbidden to take off their hats in church?

All these are questions of interest and importance to all of us, for their solution would materially improve the accuracy of our outlook upon the world, and with it our mastery of our environment, but the psychologists, busily engaged in chasing their tails, leave them unanswered, and, in most cases, even unasked. Thus the field lies open to the amateur, and not infrequently he enters it to good effect. The late Friedrich Wilhelm Nietzsche did it often, and the usufructs were many curious and daring guesses as to the genesis of this, that or the other common delusion of man—*e.g.*, the delusion that the law of the survival of the fittest may be repealed by an act of Congress. Into the same field several very interesting expeditions were made by Dr. Elsie Clews Parsons, a lady once celebrated by the newspapers for her invention of trial marriage—an invention, by the way, in which the Nietzsche aforesaid preceded her by at least a dozen years. The records of her researches are to be found in a brief series of books: "The Family" (1906), "The Old-Fashioned Woman" (1913), and "Fear and Conventionality" (1914). Apparently they have wrung relatively little esteem from the learned, and I seldom encounter a reference to them, and Dr. Parsons herself is not often recalled. Nevertheless, they are extremely instructive volumes, particularly "Fear and Conventionality." I know of no other work, indeed, which offers a better array of observations upon that powerful complex of assumptions, prejudices, instinctive reactions, racial emotions and unbreakable vices of mind which enters so massively into the daily thinking of all of us. The author does not concern herself, as so many psychologists fall into the habit of doing, with thinking as a purely laboratory phenomenon, a process *in vacuo*. What she deals with is thinking as it is done by men and women in the real world—thinking that is only half intellectual, the other half being as automatic and unintelligent as swallowing, blinking the eye, or falling in love.

The power of the complex that I have mentioned is usually very much underestimated, not only by psychologists, but also by all other persons who pretend to enlightenment. We take pride in the fact that we are thinking animals, and like to believe that our thoughts are free, but the truth is that nine-tenths of them are rigidly conditioned by the babbling that goes on around us from birth, and that the business of considering this babbling objectively, separating the true in it from the false, is an intellectual feat of such stupendous difficulty that very few men are ever able to achieve it. Not one of us is actually a free agent. Not one of us thinks for himself, or in any orderly and scientific manner. The pressure of environment, of mass ideas, of the socialized intelligence, improperly so called, is too enormous to be withstood. No genuine American, no matter how sharp his critical sense, can ever get away from the notion that democracy is, in some subtle and mysterious way, more conducive to human progress and more pleasing to a just God than any of the systems of government which stand opposed to it. In the privacy of his study he may observe very clearly that it exalts the facile and specious man above the really competent man, and from his reflections upon it he may draw the conclusion that its abandonment would be desirable, but once he emerges from his academic seclusion and resumes the rubbing of noses with his fellow men, he will begin to be tortured by a sneaking feeling that such ideas are heretical and unmanly, and the next time the band begins to play he will thrill with the best of them—or the worst.

It is the business of Dr. Parsons, in "Fear and Conventionality," to prod into certain of these ideas which thus pour into every man's mind from the circumambient air, sweeping away, like some huge cataract, the feeble resistance that his own powers of ratiocination can offer. In one direction they lay upon us the bonds of what we call etiquette, *i.e.*, the duty of considering the habits and feelings of those around us—and in another direction they throttle us with what we call morality, *i.e.*, the rules which protect the life and property of those around us. But, as Dr. Parsons shows, the boundary between etiquette and morality is very dimly drawn, and it is often impossible to say of a given action whether it is downright immoral or merely a breach of the punctilio. Even when the moral law is plainly running, considerations of mere amenity and politeness may still make themselves felt. Thus, as Dr. Parsons points out, there is even an etiquette of adultery. "The *ami de la famille* vows not to kiss his mistress in her husband's house"—not in fear, but "as an expression of conjugal consideration," as a sign that he has not forgotten the thoughtfulness expected of a gentleman. And in this delicate field, as might be expected, the differences in racial attitudes are almost diametrical. The Englishman, surprising his wife with a lover, sues the rogue for damages and has public opinion behind him, but for an American to do it would be for him to lose caste at once and forever. The plain and only duty of the American is to open upon the fellow with artillery, hitting him if the scene is south of the Potomac and missing him if it is above.

I confess to an endless interest in such puzzling niceties, and to much curiosity as to their origins and meaning. Why do we Americans take off our hats when we meet a female on the street, and yet stand covered before a male of the highest eminence? A Continental would regard this last as boorish to the last degree; in greeting any equal or superior, male or female, actual or merely conventional, he lifts his head-piece. Why does it strike us as ludicrous to see a man in dress clothes before 6 P.M.? The Continental puts them on whenever he has a solemn visit to make, whether the hour be six or noon. Why do we regard it as indecent to tuck the napkin between the waistcoat buttons—or into the neck—at meals? The Frenchman does it without thought of crime. So does the Italian. So does the German. All three are punctilious men— far more so, indeed, than we are. Why is it bad manners in Europe and America to ask a stranger his or her age, and a friendly attention in China? Why do we regard it as absurd to distinguish a woman by her husband's title—e.g., Mrs. Judge Jones, Mrs. Professor Smith? In Teutonic and Scandinavian Europe the omission of the title would be looked upon as an affront.

Such fine distinctions, so ardently supported, raise many interesting questions, but the attempt to answer them quickly gets one bogged. Several years ago I ventured to lift a sad voice against a custom in America: that of married men, in speaking of their wives, employing the full panoply of "Mrs. Brown." It was my contention—supported, I thought, by logical considerations of the loftiest order—that a husband, in speaking of his wife to his equals, should say "my wife"—that the more formal mode of designation should be reserved for inferiors and for strangers of undetermined position. This contention, somewhat to my surprise, was vigorously combated by various volunteer experts. At first they rested their case upon the mere authority of custom, forgetting that this custom was by no means universal. But finally one of them came forward with a more analytical and cogent defense— the defense, to wit, that "my wife" connoted proprietorship and was thus offensive to a wife's *amour propre*. But what of "my sister" and "my mother"? This discussion, alas, came to nothing. It was impossible to carry it on logically. The essence of all such inquiries lies in the discovery that there is a force within the liver and lights of man that is infinitely more potent than logic. His reflections, perhaps, may take on intellectually recognizable forms, but they seldom lead to intellectually recognizable conclusions.

Nevertheless, Dr. Parsons offers something in her book that may conceivably help to a better understanding of them, and that is the doctrine that the strange persistence of these rubber-stamp ideas, often unintelligible and sometimes plainly absurd, is due to fear, and that this fear is the product of a very real danger. The safety of human society lies in the assumption that every individual composing it, in a given situation, will act in a manner hitherto approved as seemly. That is to say, he is expected to react to his environment according to a fixed pattern, not necessarily because that pattern is the best imaginable, but simply because it is determined and understood. If he fails to do so, if he reacts in a novel manner—conducive, perhaps, to his better advantage or to what he thinks is his better advantage—then he disappoints the expectation of those around him, and forces them to meet the new situation he has created by the exercise of independent thought. Such independent thought, to a good many men, is quite impossible, and to the overwhelming majority of men, extremely painful. "To all of us," says Dr. Parsons, "to the animal, to the savage and to the civilized being, few demands are as uncomfortable, . . . disquieting or fearful, as the call to innovate. . . . Adaptations we all of us dislike or hate. We dodge or shirk them as best we may." And the man who compels us to make them against our wills we punish by withdrawing from him that understanding and friendliness which he, in turn, looks for and counts upon. In other words, we set him apart as one who is anti-social and not to be dealt with, and according as his rebellion has been small or great, we call him a boor or a criminal.

This distrust of the unknown, this fear of doing something unusual, is probably at the bottom of many ideas and institutions that are commonly credited to other motives. For example, monogamy. The orthodox explanation of monogamy is that it is a manifestation of the desire to have and to hold property—that the husband defends his solitary right to his wife, even at the cost of his own freedom, because she is the pearl among his chattels. But Dr. Parsons argues, and with a good deal of plausibility, that the real moving force, in both the husband and the wife, may be merely the force of habit, the antipathy to experiment and innovation. It is easier and more sanitary to stick to the one wife than to risk adventures with another wife—and the immense social pressure that I have just described is all on the side of sticking. Moreover, the indulgence of a habit automatically strengthens its bonds. What we have done once or thought once, we are more apt than we were

before to do and think again. Or, as William James put it, "the selection of a particular hole to live in, of a particular mate, . . . a
particular anything, in short, out of a possible multitude . . . carries
with it an insensibility to *other* opportunities and occasions—an insensibility which can only be described physiologically as an inhi-
bition of new impulses by the habit of old ones already formed.
The possession of homes and wives of our own makes us strangely
insensible to the charms of other people. . . . The original impulse
which got us homes, wives, . . . seems to exhaust itself in its first
achievements and to leave no surplus energy for reacting on new
cases." Thus the benedict looks no more on women (at least for a
while), and the post-honeymoon bride neglects the bedizenments
which got her her man.

In view of the popular or general character of most of the taboos
which put a brake upon personal liberty in thought and action—
that is to say, in view of their enforcement by people in the mass,
and not by definite specialists in conduct—it is quite natural to
find that they are of extra force in democratic societies, for it is the
distinguishing mark of democratic societies that they exalt the powers of the majority almost infinitely, and tend to deny the minority
any rights whatever. Under a society dominated by a small caste
the revolutionist in custom has a relatively easy time of it, for the
persons whose approval he seeks for his innovation are few in
number, and most of them are already habituated to more or less
intelligible and independent thinking. But under a democracy he
is opposed by a horde so vast that it is a practical impossibility for
him, without complex and expensive machinery, to reach and convince all its members, and even if he could reach them he would
find most of them quite incapable of rising out of their accus-
tomed grooves. They cannot understand innovations that are genuinely novel and they don't want to understand them; their one
desire is to put them down.

But how, then, explain the fact that the populace is constantly
ravished and set aflame by fresh brigades of moral, political and sociological prophets—that it is forever playing the eager victim to
new mountebanks? The explanation lies in the simple circumstance that these performers upon the public midriff are always
careful to ladle out nothing actually new, and hence nothing in-

comprehensible, alarming and accursed. What they offer is always the same old panacea with a new label—the tried and much-loved dose, the colic cure that Mother used to make. Superficially, the United States seems to suffer from an endless and astounding neophilism; actually all its thinking is done within the boundaries of a very small group of political, economic and religious ideas, most of them unsound. For example, there is the fundamental idea of democracy—the idea that all political power should remain in the hands of the populace, that its exercise by superior men is intrinsically immoral. Again, there is the doctrine that the possession of great wealth is a crime—a doctrine half a religious heritage and half the product of mere mob envy. Yet again, there is the peasant suspicion of the man who is having a better time in the world—a suspicion grounded, like the foregoing, partly upon undisguised envy and partly upon archaic and barbaric religious taboos. The whole history of the United States is a history of these three ideas. There has never been an issue before the people that could not be translated into one or another of them.

Here is a golden opportunity for other investigators: I often wonder that the field is so little explored. Why do otherwise sane men believe that they have immortal souls? What is the genesis of the American axiom that the fine arts are somehow unmanly? What is the precise machinery of the process called falling in love? Why do people believe newspapers?

At the Mercy of the Mob

From the *American Mercury*, Jan., 1929, pp. 123–24.
A review of CIVILIZATION, by Clive Bell; New York, 1928

Mr. Bell is, by trade, an art critic, and his chief interest lies in the moderns who have followed Cézanne. In consequence most of his writings are full of the vague and indignant rhetoric that the contemplation of green complexions and hexagonal heads seems to draw from even the best critical minds. But in "Civilization" he so far forgets his customary muttons that he writes smoothly, clearly and oftentimes brilliantly. He studies civilization by the case method: his exhibits are the civilizations that flourished in the Athens of Pericles, in the Florence of the Renaissance, and in the Paris of the Eighteenth Century, before the French Revolution. What had they in common? In particular, what had they in common that was indubitably civilized, and hence completely unimaginable under lower forms of culture? What did they show that we should strive for today, if, as is usually assumed, modern man really wants to be civilized?

Mr. Bell's answer is too long and complicated to be summarized in a paragraph, but parts of it may be given. It is one of the fundamental characteristics of a true civilization, he says, that it provides means for the ready exchange of ideas, and encourages the process. There must be sufficient people with time to hear them and the equipment to comprehend them, and they must be extremely tolerant of novelty. The concept of heresy, says Mr. Bell, is incompatible with civilization, and so is the concept of impropriety. But the civilized man yet has his pruderies. He cannot be impolite. He cannot be gross. He cannot be cheap and vulgar. He cannot be cocksure. Facing what he regards as error, he assaults it with all arms, but he never mistakes error for crime. He is free from deadly solemnity, and cultivates his senses as well as his mind. A society made up wholly of philosophers would not be civilized, nor one made up only of artists; there must also be charming women and good cooks. Creation is necessary; there must be an urge to progress; but appreciation is quite as needful. Perhaps the finest flower of civilization is not the creator at all, but the connoisseur. His existence presupposes economic security. It is as essential to civilization as enlightenment. A poor society cannot be wholly civilized.

Mr. Bell makes much of the difference between the civilized individual and a civilized society. The former may exist anywhere, and at any time. There may be men and women hidden in Oklahoma who would be worthy, if he were alive, to consort with Beethoven. It is not only possible; it is probable. But Oklahoma is still quite uncivilized, for such persons are extremely rare there, and give no color to the communal life. The typical Oklahoman is as barbarous as an Albanian or a man of Inner Mongolia. He is almost unaware of the ideas that engage the modern world; in so far as he has heard of them he is hostile to them. He lives and dies on a low plane, pursuing sordid and ridiculous objectives and taking his reward in hoggish ways. His political behavior is that of a barbarian, and his religious notions are almost savage. Of urbanity he has no more than a traffic cop. His virtues are primitive and his vices are disgusting.

It is not, of course, by examining the populace that civilizations are judged. The mob is always inferior, and even under high cultures it may be ignorant and degraded. But there can be no civilization so long as its ideas are accepted and have the force of custom. A minority must stand above it, sufficient in strength to resist its corruption. There must be freedom for the superior man — economic freedom primarily, but also personal freedom. He must be free to think what he pleases and to do what he pleases, and what he thinks and does must be the standard of the whole community, the accepted norm. The trouble in Oklahoma, as in the United States as a whole, is that the civilized minority is still at the mercy of the mob. It is not only disdained as heretical and unsafe; it is despised as immoral. One of the central aims of the laws is to curb it. It is to be lifted up to the moral level of the mob. Thus civilization has hard sledding among us. The free functioning of those capable of it is deliberately impeded. But it resists that hampering, and in the fact lies hope for the future. The big cities, at least, begin to move toward genuine civilization. They will attain to it if, when and as they throw off the yoke of the rustic Bible-preachers. Their own mobs are become disciplined and quiescent, but they still face danger from the dunghill Goths and Huns. The history of the United States during the next century will probably be a history of a successful revolt of the cities. They alone are capable of civilization. There has never been a civilized yokel.

The Goal

From Prejudices: Second Series, 1924, p. 204

The central aim of civilization, it must be plain, is simply to defy and correct the obvious intent of God, *e.g.*, that the issue of every love affair shall be a succession of little strangers, that cows shall devote themselves wholly to nursing their calves, that it shall take longer to convey a message from New York to Chicago than it takes to convey one from New York to Newark, that the wicked shall be miserable and the virtuous happy. Has civilization a motto? Then certainly it must be "Not *Thy* will, O Lord, but *ours*, be done!"

The Superman

From IN DEFENSE OF WOMEN, 1918; revised, 1922, pp. 106–07

Mediocrity, as every Mendelian knows, is a dominant character, and extraordinary ability is a recessive character. In a marriage between an able man and a commonplace woman, the chances that any given child will resemble the mother are, roughly speaking, three to one. The fact suggests the thought that nature is secretly against the superman, and seeks to prevent his birth. We have, indeed, no ground for assuming that the continued progress visualized by man is in actual accord with the great flow of the elemental forces. Devolution is quite as natural as evolution, and may be just as pleasing, or even a good deal more pleasing, to God. If the average man is made in God's image, then a man such as Beethoven or Aristotle is plainly superior to God, and so God may be jealous of him, and eager to see his superiority perish with his bodily frame. All animal breeders know how difficult it is to maintain a fine strain. The universe seems to be in a conspiracy to encourage the endless reproduction of lodge-joiners and Socialists, but a subtle and mysterious opposition stands eternally against the reproduction of philosophers.

Heredity

From the same, pp. 85–86

Despite a popular delusion that the sons of great men are always dolts, the fact is that intellectual superiority is inherited quite as commonly as bodily strength; and that fact has been established beyond cavil by the laborious inquiries of Galton, Pearson and the other anthropometricians of the English school. If such men as Spinoza, Kant, Schopenhauer, Spencer and Nietzsche had married and begotten sons, those sons, it is probable, would have contributed as much to philosophy as the sons and grandsons of Veit Bach contributed to music, or those of Erasmus Darwin to biology, or those of Hamilcar Barca to the art of war. Herbert Spencer's escape from marriage made English philosophy co-extensive with his life; since his death the whole body of metaphysical speculation produced in England has been of little more practical value to the world than a drove of hogs.

Even setting aside this direct influence of heredity, there is the equally potent influence of example and tuition—nurture as well as nature. It is a gigantic advantage to live on intimate terms with a first-rate man, and have his care. Hamilcar not only gave the Carthaginians a great general in his actual son; he also gave them a great general in his son-in-law, trained in his camp. But the tendency of the first-rate man to remain a bachelor is very strong, and Sidney Lee once showed that, of all the great writers of England since the Renaissance, more than half were either celibates or lived apart from their wives. Even the married ones revealed the tendency plainly. For example, consider Shakespeare. He was forced into marriage while still a minor by the brothers of Ann Hathaway, who was seven years his senior, and had debauched him and gave out that she was *enceinte* by him. He escaped from her abhorrent embraces as quickly as possible, and thereafter kept as far away from her as he could.

Happiness

From the *Smart Set*, Aug., 1923, p. 43

This great boon may be defined briefly as a state of mind occurring in an organism at a moment when it happens to pass through an environment exerting a minimum of irritation. It is thus most transitory in the highest and most sensitive organisms. A hog is therefore happier than a man, and a bacillus is happier than a hog. But when a man is drunk enough, he is sometimes almost as happy as a bacillus.

The Horns of the Dilemma

From the Baltimore *Evening Sun*, April 6, 1931

My conclusion at fifty is that men are wisest when they are cold sober, but happiest when they are a shade tight.

IX. MEN AND WOMEN

The Curse of Man

From IN DEFENSE OF WOMEN, 1918; revised, 1922, pp. 129–31

THE CURSE of man, and the cause of his worst woes, is his stupendous capacity for believing the incredible. He is forever embracing delusions, and each new one is more preposterous than all that have gone before. But where is the delusion that women cherish—I mean habitually, firmly, passionately? Who will draw up a list of propositions, held and maintained by them in sober earnest, that are obviously not true? As for me, I should not like to undertake such a list. I know of nothing, in fact, that properly belongs to it. Women, as a class, believe in none of the ludicrous rights, duties and pious obligations that men are forever gabbling about. Their superior intelligence is in no way more eloquently demonstrated than by their ironical view of all such phantasmagoria. Their habitual attitude toward men is one of aloof disdain, and their habitual attitude toward what men believe in, and get into sweats about, and bellow for, is substantially the same. It takes twice as long to convert a body of women to some new fallacy or charlatan as it takes to convert a body of men, and even then they halt, hesitate, and are full of mordant criticisms. Every normal woman believes, and quite accurately, that the average man is very much like her husband, John, and she knows very well that John is a weak, silly and knavish fellow, and that any effort to convert him into an archangel overnight is bound to come to grief. As for her view of the average creature of her own sex, it is marked by a cynicism so penetrating and so destructive that a clear statement of it would shock beyond endurance.

Le Vice Anglais

From the Baltimore *Evening Sun*, June 12, 1922

It is almost impossible for an Anglo-Saxon to write of sex without being dirty. Of the English writers now in practise, only George Moore does it decently—and Moore, of course, is not an Englishman at all, but an Irishman bred in France. This Anglo-Saxon dirtiness has its origin in a false assumption, to wit, that sex is a serious and even sombre matter. It is nothing of the kind: it is a variety of buffoonery. The French always treat it as such. The spectacle of a married woman eloping with an actor does not make them moan and roll their eyes; it makes them laugh. And why not? What, indeed, could be more ludicrous? Imagine a woman so idiotic that, after trying love and finding it a snare, she solemnly tries it again!

Sex on the Stage

From THE BLUSHFUL MYSTERY,
PREJUDICES: FIRST SERIES, 1919, pp. 201–07

The best and truest sex plays are not such overstrained shockers as "Le Mariage d'Olympe" and "The Second Mrs. Tanqueray," but such penetrating and excellent comedies as "Much Ado About Nothing" and "The Taming of the Shrew." In "Much Ado" we have an accurate and unforgettable picture of the way in which the normal male of the human species is brought to the altar— that is, by way of appealing to his hollow vanity, the way of capitalizing his native and ineradicable asininity. And in "The Taming of the Shrew" we have a picture of the way in which the average woman, having so snared him, is purged of her resultant vainglory and bombast, and thus reduced to decent discipline and decorum, that the marriage may go on in solid tranquillity.

The whole drama of sex, in real life as well as on the stage, revolves around these two enterprises. One-half of it consists of

pitting the native intelligence of women against the native sentimentality of men, and the other half consists of bringing women
into a reasonable order, that their superiority may not be too horribly obvious. To the first division belong the dramas of courtship,
and a good many of those are marital conflict. In each case the essential drama is not a tragedy but a comedy—nay, a farce. In each
case the conflict is not between imperishable verities but between
mere vanities and pretensions. This is the essence of the comic:
the unmasking of fraud, its destruction by worse fraud. Marriage,
as we know it in Christendom, though its utility is obvious and its
necessity is at least arguable, is just such a series of frauds. It begins with the fraud that the impulse to it is lofty, unearthly and disinterested. It proceeds to the fraud that both parties are equally
eager for it and equally benefited by it—which actually happens
only when two Mondays come together. And it rests thereafter
upon the fraud that what is once agreeable (or tolerable) remains
agreeable ever thereafter. This last assumption is so outrageous
that, on purely evidential and logical grounds, not even the most
sentimental person would support it. It thus becomes necessary to
reenforce it by attaching to it the concept of honor. That is to say,
it is held up, not on the ground that it is actually true, but on the
ground that a recognition of its truth is part of the bargain made
at the altar, and that a repudiation of this bargain would be dishonorable. Here we have honor, which is based upon a sense of
the deepest and most inviolable truth, brought in to support something admittedly not true. Here, in other words, we have a situation in comedy, almost exactly parallel to that in which a colored
bishop whoops the Apostles' Creed like a calliope in order to
drown out the crowing of the rooster concealed beneath his
chasuble.

   In all plays of the sort that are regarded as "strong" and "significant" by the newspaper critics connubial infidelity is the chief
theme. Smith, having a wife, Mrs. Smith, betrays her love and
trust by running off with Miss Rabinowitz, his stenographer. Or
Mrs. Brown, detecting her husband, Mr. Brown, in lamentable
proceedings with a neighbor, the grass widow Kraus, forgives him
and continues to be true to him in consideration of her children,
Fred, Pansy and Little Fern. The latter situation produces a great
deal of eye-rolling and snuffling, yet it contains not the slightest

touch of tragedy, and at bottom is not even honest. On the contrary, it is based upon an assumption that is unsound and ridiculous—the assumption, to wit, that the position of the injured wife is grounded upon the highest idealism—that the injury she suffers is directed at her lofty and impeccable spirit—that it leaves her standing in an heroic attitude. All this, soberly examined, is found to be untrue. The fact is that her moving impulse is simply a desire to cut a good figure before her world—in brief, that plain vanity is what animates her.

In frank comedy we see both situations more accurately dealt with and hence more honestly and more instructively. Instead of depicting one party as revolting against the assumption of eternal fidelity melodramatically and the other as facing the revolt heroically and tragically, we have both criticizing it by a good-humored flouting of it—not necessarily by act, but by attitude. This attitude is normal and sensible. It rests upon genuine human traits and tendencies. It is sound, natural and honest. It gives the comedy of the stage a high validity that the bombastic fustian of the stage can never show.

When I speak of infidelity, of course, I do not mean only the gross infidelity of the divorce courts, but that lighter infidelity which relieves and makes bearable the burdens of theoretical fidelity—in brief, the natural reaction of human nature against an artificial and preposterous assumption. The assumption is that a sexual choice, once made, is irrevocable—more, that all desire to revoke it, even transiently, disappears. The fact is that no human choice can ever be of that irrevocable character, and that the very existence of such an assumption is a constant provocation to challenge it and rebel against it. What we have in marriage actually— or in any other such contract—is a constant war between the impulse to give that rebellion objective reality and a social pressure which puts a premium on submission. The rebel, if he strikes out, at once collides with a solid wall, the bricks of which are made up of the social assumption of his docility, and the mortar of which is the frozen sentimentality of his own lost yesterday—his fatuous assumption that what was once agreeable to him would be always agreeable to him. Here we have the very essence of comedy—a situation almost exactly parallel to that of the pompous old gentleman who kicks a hat lying on the sidewalk, and stubs his toe against the brick within.

Under the whole of the conventional assumption reposes an assumption even more foolish, to wit, that sexual choice is regulated by some transcendental process, that a mysterious accuracy gets into it, that it is limited by impenetrable powers, that there is for every man one certain woman. This sentimentality not only underlies the theory of marriage, but is also the chief apology for divorce. The truth is that marriages in Christendom are determined, not by elective affinities, but by the most trivial accidents, and that the issue of those accidents is relatively unimportant. That is to say, a normal man could be happy with any one of at least two dozen women of his acquaintance, and a man specially fitted to accept the false assumptions of marriage could be happy with almost any presentable woman of his race, class and age. He is married to Marie instead of to Gladys because Marie definitely decided to marry him, whereas Gladys vacillated between him and some other. And Marie decided to marry him instead of some other, not because the impulse was irresistibly stronger, but simply because the thing seemed more feasible. In such choices, at least among women, there is often not even any self-delusion. They see the facts clearly, and even if, later on, they are swathed in sentimental trappings, the revelation is not entirely obliterated.

Here we have comedy double distilled—a combat of pretensions, on the one side, perhaps, risen to self-hallucination, but on the other side more or less uneasily conscious and deliberate. This is the true soul of high farce. This is something not to snuffle over but to roar at.

Women as Spectacles

From Appendix on a Tender Theme,
Prejudices: Second Series, 1920, pp. 238–39.
First printed in the *Smart Set*, Feb., 1920, pp. 48–49

Women, when it comes to snaring men through the eye, bait a great many hooks that fail to fluster the fish. Nine-tenths of their primping and decorating of their persons not only doesn't please men; it actually repels men. I often pass two days running without encountering a single woman who is charmingly dressed. Nearly all of them run to painful color schemes and absurd designs. One seldom observes a man who looks an absolute guy, whereas such women are very numerous; in the average theater audience they constitute a majority of at least nine-tenths. The reason is not far to seek. The clothes of men are plain in design and neutral in hue. The only touch of genuine color is in the florid blob of the face, the center of interest—exactly where it ought to be. If there is any other color at all, it is a faint suggestion in the cravat—adjacent to the face, and so leading the eye toward it. It is color that kills the clothes of the average woman. She runs to bright spots that take the eye away from her face and hair. She ceases to be woman clothed and becomes a mere piece of clothing womaned.

Even at the basic feminine art of pigmenting their faces very few women excel. The average woman seems to think that she is most lovely when her sophistication of her complexion is most adroitly concealed—when the *poudre de riz* is rubbed in so hard that it is almost invisible, and the penciling of eyes and lips is perfectly realistic. This is a false notion. Most men of appreciative eye have no objection to artificiality *per se* so long as it is intrinsically sightly. The marks made by a lipstick may be very beautiful; there are many lovely shades of scarlet, crimson and vermilion. A man with eyes in his head admires them for themselves; he doesn't have to be first convinced that they are non-existent, that what he sees is not the mark of a lipstick at all, but an authentic lip. So with the eyes. Nothing could be more charming than an eye properly reënforced; the naked organ is not to be compared to it; nature is an idiot when it comes to shadows. But it must be admired as a work of art, not as a miraculous and incredible eye.... Women, in this important and venerable art, stick too closely to crude representation. They forget that men do not admire the technic, but the result. What they should do is to forget realism for a while, and concentrate their attention upon composition, chiaroscuro and color.

Venus at the Domestic Hearth

From Prejudices: Fourth Series, 1924, pp. 108–10.
First printed in the *Smart Set*, Oct., 1921, p. 42

One inclines to the notion that women—and especially homely women—greatly overestimate the importance of physical beauty in their eternal conspiracy against the liberty of men. It is a powerful lure, to be sure, but it is certainly not the only one that fetches the game, nor even, perhaps, the most effective one. The satisfaction that a man gets out of conquering—which is to say, out of succumbing to—a woman of noticeable pulchritude is chiefly the rather banal one of parading her before other men. He likes to show her off as he likes to show his expensive automobile or his big door-knob factory. It is her apparent costliness that is her principal charm. Her beauty sets up the assumption that she was sought eagerly by other men, some of them wealthy, and that it thus took a lot of money or a lot of skill to obtain the monopoly of her.

But very few men are so idiotic that they are blind to the hollowness of such satisfactions. A husband, after all, spends relatively few hours of his life parading his wife, or even contemplating her beauty. What engages him far more often is the unromantic business of living with her—of listening to her conversation, of trying to fathom and satisfy her whims, or detecting and counteracting her plots against his ego, of facing with her the dull hazards and boredoms of everyday life. In the discharge of this business personal beauty is certainly not necessarily a help; on the contrary, it may be a downright hindrance, if only because it makes for the hollowest and least intelligent of all forms of vanity. Of infinitely more value is a quality that women too often neglect, to wit, the quality of simple amiability. The most steadily charming of all human beings, male or female, is the one who is tolerant, unprovocative, good-humored, kind. A man wants a show only intermittently, but he wants peace and comfort every day. And to get them, if he is sagacious, he is quite willing to sacrifice scenery.

Clubs

From DAMN! A BOOK OF CALUMNY, 1918, p. 49

Men's clubs have but one intelligible purpose: to afford asylum to fellows who haven't any girls. Hence their general gloom, their air of lost causes, their prevailing acrimony. No man would ever enter a club if he had an agreeable woman to talk to. This is particularly true of married men. Those of them that one finds in clubs answer to a general description: they have wives too unattractive to entertain them, and yet too watchful to allow them to seek entertainment elsewhere. The bachelors, in the main, belong to two classes: (*a*) those who have been unfortunate in amour, and are still too sore to show any new enterprise, and (*b*) those so lacking in sex appeal that no woman will pay any attention to them. Is it any wonder that the men one thus encounters in clubs are miserable creatures, and that they find their pleasure in such banal sports as playing cards, drinking highballs and talking politics? . . . The day a man's mistress is married one always finds him at his club.

Efficiency as Charm

From MINORITY REPORT, 1956, p. 224.
First printed in the *Smart Set*, July, 1919, p. 63

The most steadily attractive of all human qualities is competence. One invariably admires a man who is good at his trade, whatever it must be—who understands its technic thoroughly, and surmounts its difficulties with ease, and gets substantial rewards for his labors, and is envied by his rivals. And in precisely the same way one admires a woman who, in a business-like and sure-handed way, has gone out and got herself a good husband, and persuaded him to be grateful for her condescension, and so made herself secure.

Woman and the Artist

From Appendix on a Tender Theme,
Prejudices: Second Series, 1920, pp. 240–43.
First printed in the *Smart Set*, June, 1920, pp. 42–43

Much gabble is to be found in the literature of the world upon the function of woman as inspiration, stimulant and *agente provocateuse* to the creative artist. I incline to think that there is little if any basis of fact in the theory. Women not only do not inspire creative artists to high endeavor; they actually stand firmly against every high endeavor that a creative artist initiates spontaneously. What a man's women-folks almost invariably ask of him is that he be respectable—that he do something generally approved—that he avoid yielding to his aberrant fancies—in brief, that he sedulously eschew showing any sign of genuine genius. Their interest is not primarily in the self-expression of the individual, but in the well-being of the family, which means the safety of themselves. No sane woman would want to be the wife of such a man, say, as Nietzsche or Chopin. His mistress perhaps, yes—for a mistress can always move on when the weather gets too warm. But not a wife. I here speak by the book. Both Nietzsche and Chopin had plenty of mistresses, most of them hideous, but neither was ever able to get a wife.

Shakespeare and Ann Hathaway, Wagner and Minna Planer, Molière and Armande Béjart—one might multiply instances almost endlessly. Minna, at least in theory, knew something of music; she was thus what romance regards as an ideal wife for Wagner. But instead of helping him to manufacture his masterpieces, she was for twenty-five years the chief impediment of their manufacture. "Lohengrin" gave her the horrors; she begged Richard to give up his lunacies and return to the composition of respectable cornet music. In the end he had to get rid of her in sheer self-defense. Once free, with nothing worse on his hands than the illicit affection of Cosima Liszt von Bülow, he produced music drama after music drama in rapid succession. Then, married to Cosima, he descended to the anticlimax of "Parsifal," a truly tragic mixture of the stupendous and the banal, of work by genius and *sinfonia domestica*—a great man dying by inches, smothered by the smoke of French fried potatoes, deafened by the wailing of children, murdered in his own house by the holiest of passions.

Sentimentalists always bring up the case of Schumann and his Clara in rebuttal. But does it actually rebut? I doubt it. Clara, too, perpetrated her *attentat* against art. Her fair white arms, lifting from the keyboard to encircle Robert's neck, squeezed more out of him than mere fatuous smirks. He had the best head on him that music had seen since Beethoven's day; he was, on the cerebral side, a colossus; he might have written music of the very first order. Well, what he *did* write was piano music—some of it imperfectly arranged for orchestra. The sad eyes of Clara were always upon him. He kept within the limits of her intelligence, her prejudices, her wifely love. No grand experiments with the orchestra. No superb leapings and cavortings. No rubbing of sandpaper over critical ears. Robert lived and died a respectable musical *Hausvater*. He was a man of genuine genius—but he didn't leave ten lines that might not have been passed by old Prof. Jadassohn.

The truth is that, no matter how great the domestic concord and how lavish the sacrifices a man makes for his women-folk, they almost always regard him secretly as a silly and selfish fellow, and cherish the theory that it would be easily possible to improve him. This is because the essential interests of men and women are eternally antithetical. A man may yield over and over again, but in the long run he must occasionally look out for himself—and it is these occasions that his women-folk remember. The typical domestic situation shows a woman trying to induce a man to do something that he doesn't want to do, or to refrain from something that he does want to do. This is true in his bachelor days, when his mother or his sister is his antagonist. It is preëminently true just before his marriage, when the girl who has marked him down is hard at the colossal job of overcoming his reluctance. And after marriage it is so true that there is hardly need to state it. One of the things every man discovers to his disquiet is that his wife, after the first play-acting is over, regards him essentially as his mother used to regard him—that is, as a self-worshiper who needs to be policed and an idiot who needs to be protected. The notion that women *admire* their men-folks is pure moonshine. The most they ever achieve in that direction is to pity them.

Martyrs

From IN DEFENSE OF WOMEN, 1918; revised, 1922, pp. 155–56

The civilized woman is born half convinced that she is really as weak and heavily put upon as she later pretends to be, and the prevailing folklore offers her endless corroboration. One of the resultant phenomena is the delight in martyrdom that one so often finds in women, and particularly in the least alert and introspective of them. They take a heavy, unhealthy pleasure in suffering; they like to picture themselves as slaughtered saints. Thus they always find something to complain of, and the very conditions of domestic life give them a superabundance of clinical material. If, by any chance, such material shows a falling off, they are uneasy and unhappy. Let a woman have a husband whose conduct is not reasonably open to question, and she will invent mythical offences to make him bearable. And if her invention fails she will be plunged into utmost misery and humiliation. This fact probably explains many mysterious divorces: the husband was not too bad, but too good. For public opinion among women, remember, does not favor the woman who is full of a placid contentment and has no masculine torts to report; if she says that her husband is wholly satisfactory she is looked upon as a numskull even more dense than he is himself. A man, speaking of his wife to other men, always praises her extravagantly. Boasting about her soothes his vanity; he likes to stir up the envy of his fellows. But when two women talk of their husbands it is mainly atrocities that they describe. The most esteemed woman gossip is the one with the longest and most various repertoire of complaints.

Issue

1

From PREJUDICES: FOURTH SERIES, 1924, p. 112

It is still believed, apparently, that there is something mysteriously laudable about achieving viable offspring. I have searched the sacred and profane scriptures for many years, but have yet to find any ground for this notion. To have a child is no more creditable than to have rheumatism—and no more discreditable. Ethically, it is absolutely meaningless. And practically, it is mainly a matter of chance.

2

From IN THE ROLLING MILLS,
PREJUDICES: FOURTH SERIES, 1924, pp. 248–58.
First printed in the Baltimore *Evening Sun*, Nov. 5, 1923

One of the most amusing things in life to a bachelor is the horror that overcomes his married friends whenever one of their children turns out to be intelligent. They feel instinctively that the phenomenon offers a challenge to their parental dignity and authority, and when the child they suspect actually *is* intelligent it certainly does. For the first thing the youngster who has succumbed to the un-Christian vice of thinking attempts is a critical examination of its surroundings, and directly in the forefront of those surroundings stand the unfortunate composers of its being. The result, only too frequently, is turmoil and disaster at the domestic hearth. Even the most enlightened instruments of the Life Force are full of alarms when their progeny respond to Mendel's law: the very vigor and independence of judgment which they regard as their own most precious possession affrights them when it appears in their issue. I could tell some curious tales in point, but had better refrain. Suffice it to mention an old friend, extremely shrewd and realistic in all of his thinking, who was happily proud of his intelligent daughter until, at the age of sixteen, she threatened to get a job in a hat-shoppe if he sent her, as he promised, to a finishing-school. Then he collapsed in horror, despite the plain fact that her ultimatum was an excellent proof of the intelligence that he was proud of. As man, he admired her differentiation from the mass. But as father he was made uneasy by her sharp departure from normalcy.

The great majority of American fathers, of course, have a great deal less fundamental sense than this one, who quickly recovered from his instinctive reaction, and ended, indeed, by boasting that his daughter had spurned the finishing-school at his advice. To this majority education can only mean the inculcation, by intensive torture, of all the superstitions and prejudices that they cherish themselves. When little Felix comes home to his patriotic and Christian home with the news that the Fathers of 1776 were a gang of smugglers and profiteers, and when his sister Flora follows with the news that Moses did not write his own obituary and that the baby, Gustave, was but recently indistinguishable from a tadpole, and later on from a nascent gorilla—when such subversive and astounding doctrines are brought home from the groves of learning there ensues inevitably a ringing of fire-bells, with a posse on the march against some poor pedagogue.

The Burnt Child

From Appendix on a Tender Theme,
Prejudices: Second Series, 1920, p. 244.
First printed in the *Smart Set*, Sept., 1919, p. 43

Marriage shakes a man's confidence in himself, and so greatly diminishes his general competence and effectiveness. His habit of mind becomes that of a commander who has lost a decisive and calamitous battle. He never quite trusts himself thereafter.

On Connubial Bliss

From the Chicago *Tribune*, March 20, 1927

That something is wrong with the ancient estate of holy matrimony, so long in high esteem in the world, seems to be the unanimous view of all the self-constituted experts upon the subject, male and female, who now rage through the Republic. My mail is filled with the fulminations of these professors, many of whom appear to believe that, because I happen to be a bachelor by the grace of God, I am also a contemner of connubial bliss, and even an advocate of free love, that dreadful wickedness. The females among them, I observe without surprise, mainly argue that the American wife and mother of today is a slave, and ought to be set free. The males, going counter to this revelation, argue that the husband and father is a slave, and ought to be set free.

Most of these evangelists, naturally enough, back up their projects with concrete legislation, and not a little of it is already before the great and good men who make our so-called laws. The bills thus proposed by the more savage sort of suffragettes, if they are ever enacted, will reduce the ancient lord and master of the family to a rôle both onerous and ignominious. Whenever his lady, after consultation with her familiars (chiefly, I take it, spinsters) decides to favor posterity, he will be summoned. His duty done, he will be dismissed. Meanwhile, his whole earnings will be hers, to dispose of as she pleases, and the child or children issuing from her condescension will be completely under her control.

The partisans of the male are no less revolutionary. As things stand, they argue, an American husband is already so far gone in slavery that he has scarcely any rights at all. While his marriage endures his property, like his life, is at the mercy of his wife, and when she throws him out she is able, under our laws, to make off with nine-tenths of it in the form of alimony. They propose to get rid of this curse by abolishing alimony—or, at all events, by restricting its payment to ex-wives who are actually helpless and in need. The rest, they argue, can work, as their husbands must work.

If there are children, they can help to support them. No other scheme, it appears, is equitable.

Unluckily, I find myself out of sympathy with most of these reformers, and especially with those of the suffragette wing. Where they run aground is in mistaking the nature of marriage. They seem to believe that it is a purely contractual relation and that its terms, in consequence, may be changed like those of any other contractual relations—either by free bargaining, or by duress of law. It is, in fact, nothing of the sort. Marriage is not a contract; it is a way of life. Its essence, when it is sound, is a complete surrender of many of the natural rights of the individual. It is not comparable to buying an automobile or joining the Elks; it is comparable to entering a monastery or enlisting for war.

Most of the malaises that now afflict it among us are palpably due, it seems to me, to imprudent efforts to change its unescapable terms. Of such sort are all the dodges that sentimentality has put upon the law books of late years, each and every one of them designed to lighten the alleged burdens of the wife. Have they actually benefited wives? I doubt it. They have simply increased the number of rebellious and fugitive husbands. For they are all based upon the assumption that the husband dislikes his wife, and is trying to escape from her clutches. So long as that assumption is false they are supererogatory and insulting. And the moment it becomes true they are useless. Here, as in other fields, legislation is mainly nonsense. Its basic theory seems to be that when a man is uncomfortable and trying to rid himself of the things that make him so, the way to cure him is to make him more uncomfortable. Human nature, I fear, does not really work in that manner. So long as a man loves his wife and children, there is no need of laws to make him support and cherish them; he will do it at any cost to himself. Contrariwise, when he hates the one and is indifferent to the other, no conceivable law can wring out of him the full measure, nor even a tenth measure, of the devotion that he owes to them.

The trouble with the divorce laws in most American states, it seems to me, is not that they facilitate the breakup of marriages, but that they make it difficult, and often almost impossible, to break up marriages completely. The average decree, far from resolving the matter, is simply the beginning of even worse raids and forays than those that have gone before. The wife has a claim on her husband's property—not infrequently a very vexatious and burdensome claim—and the husband continues to have a vested interest in his wife's conduct. Each can annoy the other, and three times out of four they do so. The worst hatreds that I have ever encountered in this world issued out of just such post-connubial combats.

Are they unavoidable? I don't think so. They could be avoided by abandoning half measures for whole ones—that is, by making every divorce complete and absolute, with each party restored to the *status quo ante,* and neither, in consequence, with any claim on the other. But suppose the wife has no means of support? Then let her find one: women without husbands have to do it. If marriage has been simply her device for making a living, and nothing more, then let her marry again, just as a lady of joy, losing one client, seeks another. Certainly it is unfair to ask her husband to go on paying for services that he is no longer getting.

But the children? My belief is that their sufferings are far more poignant in moral statistics than they are in real life. In nine divorce cases out of ten, no children are heard of. When they exist, they have been grossly damaged already, and perhaps incurably. Their disposition should not be beyond the talents of a judge of reasonable sense. In cases wherein neither of their parents volunteers to care for them, prudence will suggest sending them to some comfortable orphan asylum or reformatory, where they will at least encounter decenter adults than they have been living with.

My point is that the law, like the social reformer, is quite unable to introduce conditions and precautions into so ancient and instinctive an institution as marriage. It is, perhaps, essentially a banality, but it is a banality of the most powerful authority. If it is not swallowed whole, it had better not be swallowed at all. Every effort to attach reservations to its complete submergence of interests and personalities is bound to lead to disaster. If it is a true marriage, those reservations are irrelevant and impertinent. And if it is not, they can do nothing to preserve it against the natural forces that seek its destruction.

In this department the reformers are even more unwise than the lawmakers. They are forever suggesting modifications of what they call the marriage contract, to the end that neither party may be put under any duress by the desires of the other. But that is simply trying to convert marriage into something that it is not. In anything rationally describable as a true marriage, it must be obvious that each party is not only willing, but eager to yield to the desires of the other. That, indeed, is the essential basis of the relationship. It is not a mere exchange of bribes and concessions. It is a mutual renunciation, with mutual happiness as its end. I am romantic enough to believe that this happiness is very often attained, though it is, at least in part, of such a character that it does not appeal very forcibly to my private tastes. But the happy wife is not that one who has driven a hard bargain with her husband, supported by laws that put him at her mercy; she is that one whose main desire is to be amiable and charming to him, and whose technic is sufficient to accomplish it. And the happy husband is not that one who has wrung from his wife a franchise to disport himself without regard to her peace and dignity, but that one whose devotion to her makes it impossible for him to imagine himself willingly wounding her.

Divorce

From the New York *World*, Jan. 26, 1930. This was a contribution to a symposium. The other contributors were H. G. Wells, Sinclair Lewis, Fannie Hurst, Floyd Dell and Bertrand Russell

I see no chance of dealing with the divorce question rationally until the discussion is purged of religious considerations. Certainly the world should have learned by this time that theologians make a mess of everything they touch, including even religion. Yet in the United States they are still allowed, against all reason and experience, to have their say in a great variety of important matters, and everywhere they go they leave their sempiternal trail of folly and confusion. Why those of the Christian species should be consulted about marriage and divorce is more than I can make out. It would be only a little less absurd to consult members of the W.C.T.U. about the mixing of drinks, for orthodox Christianity, as every one knows, views even the most decorous kind of marriage with lubricious suspicion, and countenances it only as a means of escape from something worse. In the whole New Testament there is but one message that speaks of it as an honorable estate, and that one is in the most dubious of the Epistles. Elsewhere it is always assumed to be something intrinsically and incurably vile. The really virtuous man avoids it as a plague; his ideal is complete chastity. If, tempted by Satan, he finds that chastity unbearable, he may take a wife to escape something worse, but that is only a poor compromise with his baser nature.

Modern theologians, of course, do not put the thing as coarsely as Paul did, but they still subscribe to his basic idea, however mellifluous and disarming their statement of it. A wife is primarily a sexual instrument, and as such must not flinch from her lowly duty. If she tries to avoid having children, then she is doomed to Hell again. As for a husband, he is bound in the same way and under the same penalties. Both would be better off if they were chaste, but as long as that is impossible they must be unchaste only with each other, and accept with resignation all the more painful consequences, whether biological or theological. Such notions, plainly stated, must needs seem barbaric to every civilized man; nevertheless, they continue to color the legislation of nearly all so-called Christian States. In New York, for example, the only general ground for divorce is adultery. A man may beat his wife all he pleases, but she cannot divorce him for it. In her turn she may waste his money, insult him in public and chase his friends out of the house, and he cannot get rid of her. So long as neither turns from the venal unchastity of marriage to the mortal unchastity outside they are indissolubly bound together, though their common life be intolerable to themselves and a scandal to every one else.

Obviously, it will be impossible to come to any sensible rearrangement of the relation between man and woman so long as such ancient imbecilities corrupt all thinking on the subject. The first thing necessary, then, is to get rid of the theologians. Let them be turned out politely but firmly; let us pay no further heed to their archaic nonsense. They will, to be sure, resist going, perhaps very stoutly, but their time has come and they must be on their way. What is needed is a purely realistic view of the whole question, uncontaminated by false assumptions and antediluvian traditions. That review must begin, not with remedies but with causes. Why, as a matter of actual practise, do men and women marry? And what are the factors that hold them together when marriage turns out to be endurable? Here there is a great gap in the assembled facts. The sociologists, like their brethren of medicine, have devoted themselves so ardently to the pathological that they have forgotten to study the normal. But no inquiry into the marriage that breaks up can be worth anything unless it is based upon a sound understanding of the marriage that lasts.

This fact explains the shallowness of many of the remedies currently whooped up—for example, companionate marriage. To propose that marriage be abandoned and half-marriage substituted is like advising a man with a sty to get a glass eye. He doesn't want a glass eye; he wants his own natural and perfect eye, with the sty plucked out. All such reformers forget that the real essence of marriage is not the nature of the relation but the performance of that relation. It is a device for time-binding, like every other basic human institution. Its one indomitable purpose is to endure. Plainly enough, divorce ought to be easy when the destruction of a marriage is an accomplished fact, but it would be folly to set up conditions tending to make that destruction more likely. Too much, indeed, has been done in that direction already. The way out for people who are incapable of the concessions and compromises that go with every contract is not to fill the contract with snakes but to avoid it altogether. There are, indeed, many men and women to whom marriage is a sheer psychic impossibility. But to the majority it is surely not. They find it quite bearable; they like it; they want it to endure. What they need is help in making it endurable.

My own programme I withhold, and for a sound reason—I have none. The problem is not going to be solved by prescribing a swift swallow out of this or that jug. It is going to be solved, if it is ever solved at all, by sitting down calmly and examining all the relevant facts, and by following out all their necessary and inevitable implications. In other words, it is going to be solved scientifically, not romantically or theologically. What marriage needs above all is hard, patient, impartial study. Before we may hope to cure even the slightest of its ills we must first find out precisely what it is, and how and why it works when it works at all.

Cast a Cold Eye

From PREJUDICES: FOURTH SERIES, 1924, p. 67

Love, in the romantic sense, is based upon a view of women that is impossible to any man who has had any extensive experience of them. Such a man may, to the end of his life, enjoy their society vastly, and even respect them and admire them, but, however much he respects and admires them, he nevertheless sees them more or less clearly, and seeing them clearly is fatal to the true romance. Find a man of forty who heaves and moans over a woman in the manner of a poet and you will behold either a man who ceased to develop intellectually at twenty-four or thereabout, or a fraud who has his eye on the lands, tenements and hereditaments (and perhaps also the clothes) of the lady's deceased first husband. Or upon her talents as nurse, cook, amanuensis and audience. This, no doubt, is what George Bernard Shaw meant when he said that every man over forty is a scoundrel.

X. PROGRESS

Aubade

From Prejudices: Sixth Series, 1927, pp. 281–89.
First printed in the *American Mercury*, Aug., 1927, pp. 411–13

THE NAME of the man who first made a slave of fire, like the name of the original Franklin Pierce man, is unknown to historians: burrow and sweat as they will, their efforts to unearth it are always baffled. And no wonder. For isn't it easy to imagine how infamous that name must have been while it was still remembered, and how diligent and impassioned the endeavor to erase it from the tablets of the race? One pictures the indignation of the clergy when so vast an improvement upon their immemorial magic confronted them, and their herculean and unanimous struggle, first to put it down as unlawful and against God, and then to collar it for themselves. Bonfires were surely not unknown in the morning of the Pleistocene, for there were lightnings then as now, but the first one kindled by mortal hands must have shocked humanity. One pictures the news flashing from cave to cave and from tribe to tribe—out of Central Asia and then across the grasslands, and then around the feet of the glaciers into the gloomy, spook-haunted wilderness that is now Western Europe, and so across into Africa. Something new and dreadful was upon the human race, and by the time the Ur-Mississippians of the Neander Valley heard of it, you may be sure, the discoverer had sprouted horns and was in the pay of the Devil.

His fate at home, though his name is unknown, presents no difficulties to adepts at public psychology. The bad boys of the neighborhood, one may safely assume, got to the scene first of all and were delighted by the show, but upon their heels came the local pastor, and in two minutes he was bawling for the police. The ensuing trial attracted such crowds that for weeks the sabre-toothed tiger (*Machærodus*) and the wooly rhinoceros (*R. antiquitatus*) roamed the wilds unmolested, feasting upon colporteurs and wandering flint pedlars. The fellow stood confronted by his unspeakable and unparalleled felony, and could only beg for mercy. Publicly and without shame, he had performed a feat never performed by man before: *ergo*, it was as plain as day that he had engaged, anteriorly, in commerce with the powers of the air. So much, indeed, was elemental logic: even a lawyer could grasp it. But *what* powers? There the clergy certainly had something to say, and what they said must have been instantly damning. They were themselves the daily familiars of all reputable powers of the air, great and small. They knew precisely what could be done and what could not be done. Their professional skill and knowledge were admitted everywhere and by all. What they could not do was thus clearly irregular and disreputable: it issued out of an unlawful transaction with fiends. Any other theory would be laughable, and in plain contempt of court. One pictures the learned judge summing up, and one pictures the headsman spitting on his hands. That night there was a head on a pole in front of the episcopal cave of the ordinary of the diocese, and more than one ambitious cave hyena (*H. spelaea*) wore himself out trying to shin up.

But the secret did not pass with the criminal. He was dead, his relatives to the third degree were sold into slavery to the Chellean heathen down the river, and it was a capital offense, with preliminary tortures, to so much as mention his name. But in his last hours, one must bear in mind, he had a spiritual adviser to hear his confession and give him absolution for his sorcery, and that spiritual adviser, it is reasonable to assume, had just as much natural curiosity as any other clergyman. So it is not hard to imagine that he wormed the trick out of the condemned, and later on, as in duty bound, conveyed it privately to his bishop. Nor is it hard to imagine its plans and specifications becoming generally known, *sotto voce*, to the adjacent clergy, nor some ingenious holy clerk presently discovering that they could be carried out without bringing any fiends into the business. The lawful and laudable powers of the air, already sworn to the service of Holy Church, were quite as potent: a hint from the bishop, then as now, was sufficient to set them to work. And so, if there is no flaw in my reasoning, the making of fire soon became one of the high privileges and prerogatives of the sacred office, forbidden to the laity upon penalty of the stone ax, and reserved in practise for high ceremonial uses and occasions. The ordination of a new rector, I suppose, was such an occasion. The consecration of a new cave was another. And among the uses were the laying of demons, the pursuit and scotching of dragons and other monsters, the abatement of floods and cyclones, the refutation of heresies, and the management of the sun, so that day always followed night and Spring came after Winter. I daresay fees were charged, for the clergy must live, but there was never any degradation of the new magic to sordid, secular uses. No one was allowed a fire to keep warm, and no one was allowed one to boil a bone.

It would be interesting to try to figure out, by the doctrine of probabilities, how long fire was thus reserved for sacramental purposes. The weather being, at this writing, too hot for mathematical exercises, I content myself with a guess, to wit, 10,000 years. It is probably over-moderate. The obvious usefulness of fire was certainly not enough to bring it into general use; it had to wait for the slow, tedious, extremely bloody growth of skepticism. No doubt there were heretics, even during the first two or three millennia, who set off piles of leaves far back in the woods, gingerly, cautiously and half expecting to be potted by thunderbolts. Perhaps there were even renegade clergymen who, unsettled in their faith by contemplation of *Pithecanthropus erectus*, the remote grandfather of the *P. biblicus* of our present Christian age, threw off the sacerdotal chemise, took to flight, and started forest fires. But the odds against such antinomians, for many centuries, must have been almost as heavy as the odds against an atheist in Dallas, Tex., today. They existed, but only as outlaws, with the ax waiting for them, and Hell beyond the ax. The unanimous sentiment of decent people was against them. It was plain to every one that a world in which they went unscotched would be a world resigned to sin and shame.

Nevertheless, they continued to exist, and what is worse, to increase gradually in numbers. Even when the regular force of police was augmented by bands of volunteer snouters, organized to search out unlawful fires in the deep woods and remote deserts, there were heretics who persisted in their contumacy, and even undertook to defend it with all the devices of sophistry. At intervals great crusades were launched against them, and they were rounded up and butchered by the hundred, and even by the thousand. The ordinary method of capital punishment prevailing in those times—to wit, decapitation with fifteen or twenty strokes of a stone ax—was found to be ineffective against such agents of the Devil, and so other and more rigorous methods were devised—chief among them, boiling to death in a huge pot set over a temple fire. More, the ordinary criminal procedure had to be changed to facilitate convictions, for the heretics were highly skilled at turning the safeguards of the law to their baleful uses. First, it was provided that a man accused of making fire should be tried, not before the judges who sat in common criminal cases, but before judges especially nominated for the purpose by the priests, or by the Anti-Fire League, an organization of citizens pledged to law and order. Then it was provided that no such prisoner should be permitted to consult counsel, or to enjoy the privilege of bail, or to call witnesses in his behalf. Finally, after all these half measures had failed, it was decided to abandon the whole sorry hocus-pocus of trial and judgment, and to hand the accused over to the public executioner at once, without any frivolous inquiry into the degree of his guilt.

This device seemed to work very well for a while. It worked very well, indeed, for perhaps 5,000 years. There were times during that long period when contraband fire-making seemed to be practically extinct in the world. Children grew up who had never seen a fire save in its proper place: a place of worship. Come to maturity, they begat children equally innocent, and so the thing went on for generations. But always, just as the fire heresy seemed about to disappear from human memory, some outlaw in the wilds revived it. These revivals sometimes spread as rapidly as their own flames. One year there would be complete peace everywhere and a spirit of obedience to the law; the next year bon-fires would suddenly sparkle in the hills, and blasphemous whispers would go 'round. The heretics, at such times, made great play at the young. They would lure boys into the groves along the river-bottoms and teach them how to roast chestnuts. They would send in spies disguised as Chellean serving-maids to show little girls how much easier it was to do the family washing with hot water than with cold. The constituted authorities answered such defiance with vigorous campaigns of law enforcement. Fireleggers were taken by the thousand, and put to death at great public ceremonials. But always some escaped.

In the end (or, at all events, so I work it out by the devices brought in by the new science of biometrics) enough escaped to make further proceedings against them dangerous and even impossible. No doubt it happened in what is now Southern France, in the region called the Dordogne. The fireleggers, taking to the hills, there organized a sort of outlaw state, and presently began passing laws of their own. The first of such laws, no doubt, converted fire-making from a crime into a patriotic act: it became the principal duty of every right-thinking citizen to keep a fire burning in front of his cave. Amendments soon followed. It became a felony to eat uncooked food, or to do the family washing in cold water. It became another to put out a fire, or to advocate putting it out, or to imagine putting it out.

Thus priests were barred from that outlaw state, and it became necessary to develop a new class of men skilled in public affairs, and privy to the desires of the gods. Nature responded with politicians. Anon these politicians became adept at all the arts that have distinguished them ever since. They invented new and more rigorous laws, they imposed taxes, they conscripted the fireleggers for military service. One day, having drilled a large army, they marched down into the plains, tackled the hosts of the orthodox, and overcame them. The next day the priests who had led these hosts were given a simple choice: either they could admit formally that fire-making for secular purposes was now lawful and even laudable, or they could submit to being burned alive upon their own sacramental pyres. Great numbers of them went heroically to the stake, firm in the hope of a glorious resurrection. The rest, retiring to their crypts and seeking divine guidance, emerged with the news that the gods were now in favor of universal fire-making. That night there was a cheerful blaze in front of every cave for

miles around, and the priests themselves sat down to a hearty banquet of roast megatherium (*M. cuvieri*). Eight thousand years later
a heretic who revived the primeval pagan habit of eating raw oysters was put to death for atheism.

Thomas Henry Huxley

From the Baltimore *Evening Sun*, May 4, 1925

On May 4, 1825, at Ealing, a third-rate London suburb, there
was born Thomas Henry Huxley, the son of a schoolmaster. I mention Huxley *père* in sheer humane politeness; having discharged
his august biological function, he passed into the obscurity
whence he had come. Young Thomas Henry, it appears, was
almost wholly the son of his mother. He had her piercing eyes,
he had her dark comeliness, and he had, above all, her sharp
wits. "Her most distinguishing characteristic . . . was rapidity of
thought." What her lineage was I don't know, but you may be sure
that there was good blood in it.

Huxley was educated in third-rate schools and studied what was
then regarded as medicine at Charing Cross Hospital. In 1846,
having no taste for medical practise, he joined the British Navy
as an assistant surgeon, and was presently assigned to the *Rattle-
snake* for a cruise in the South Seas. He was gone four years. He
came back laden with scientific material of the first importance,
but the Admiralty refused to publish it, and in 1854 he resigned
from the navy and took a professorship in the Royal School of
Mines. Thereafter, for forty years, he was incessantly active as
teacher, as writer and as lecturer. No single outstanding contribution to human knowledge is credited to him. He was not so much
a discoverer as an organizer. He found science a pretty intellectual
plaything, with overtones of the scandalous; he left it the chief serious concern of civilized man. The change aroused opposition,
some of it immensely formidable. Huxley met that opposition by
charging it, breaking it up, and routing it. He was one of the most
pertinacious fighters ever heard of in this world, and one of the

bravest. He attacked and defeated the natural imbecility of the human race. In his old age the English, having long sneered at him, decided to honor him. They made him a privy councillor, and gave him the right to put "The Right Hon." in front of his name and "P.C." after it. The same distinction was given at the same time to various shyster lawyers, wealthy soap manufacturers and worn-out politicians.

Huxley, I believe, was the greatest Englishman of the Nineteenth Century—perhaps the greatest Englishman of all time. When one thinks of him, one thinks of him inevitably in terms of such men as Goethe and Aristotle. For in him there was that rich, incomparable blend of intelligence and character, of colossal knowledge and high adventurousness, of instinctive honesty and indomitable courage which appears in mankind only once in a blue moon. There have been far greater scientists, even in England, but there has never been a scientist who was a greater man. A touch of the poet was in him, and another of the romantic, gallant knight. He was, in almost every way, the perfected flower of *Homo sapiens*, the superlatively admirable all-'round man.

Only too often on meeting scientific men, even those of genuine distinction, one finds that they are dull fellows and very stupid. They know one thing to excess; they know nothing else. Pursuing facts too doggedly and unimaginatively, they miss all the charming things that are not facts. Such scientists are responsible for the poor name which science so frequently carries among plain men. They radiate the impression that its service is dehumanizing—that too much learning, like too little learning, is an unpleasant and dangerous thing. Huxley was a sort of standing answer to that notion. His actual knowledge was probably wider than that of any other man of his time. By profession a biologist, he covered in fact the whole field of the exact sciences and then bulged through its four fences. Absolutely nothing was uninteresting to him. His curiosity ranged from music to theology and from philosophy to history. He didn't simply know something about everything; he knew a great deal about everything. But he was by no means merely learned; he was also immensely shrewd. I thumb his essays at random. Here is one on the Salvation Army—the most realistic and devastating treatise upon that maudlin imposture ever penned.

Here is one on capital and labor—a complete *reductio ad absurdum* of the Marxian balderdash in 3,000 words. And here is one on Berkeley's metaphysics—a perfect model of lucid exposition.

All of us owe a vast debt to Huxley, especially all of us of English speech, for it was he, more than any other man, who worked that great change in human thought which marked the Nineteenth Century. All his life long he flung himself upon authority—when it was stupid, ignorant and tyrannical. He attacked it with every weapon in his rich arsenal—wit, scorn, and above all, superior knowledge. To it he opposed a single thing: the truth as it could be discovered and established—the plain truth that sets men free.

It seems simple enough today, but it was not so simple when Huxley began. For years he was the target of assaults of almost unbelievable ferocity and malignancy. Every ecclesiastic in Christendom took a hack at him; he was denounced as the common enemy of God and man. Darwin, a mild fellow, threw "The Origin of Species" into the ring and then retired from the scene. It was Huxley who bore the brunt of the ensuing theological assault, and it was Huxley who finally beat it down, and forced the holy clerks to turn tail. It always amuses me today to read of intellectual clergymen championing what they call Modernism. Their predecessors of but two generations ago were unanimously engaged in trying to damn the first Modernist to Hell.

The row was over Darwinism, but before it ended Darwinism was almost forgotten. What Huxley fought for was something far greater: the right of civilized men to think freely and speak freely, without asking leave of authority, clerical or lay. How new that right is! And yet how firmly held! Today it would be hard to imagine living without it. No man of self-respect, when he has a thought to utter, pauses to wonder what the bishops will have to say about it. The views of bishops are simply ignored. Yet only sixty years ago they were still so powerful that they gave Huxley the battle of his life.

He beat them—beat them badly, and all their champions with them. His debate with Gladstone remains the greatest intellectual combat of modern times. Gladstone had at him with all the arts of the mob orator—and to them was added the passionate sincerity of a genuinely religious man. Huxley won hands down. Defeat became a rout. Gladstone retired from the field completely undone, with his cause ruined forever. You will find the debate, in full, in the two volumes, "Science and Hebrew Tradition" and "Science and Christian Tradition." Huxley's contribution to it constitutes one of the glories of the Nineteenth Century. Far more than forty wars, far more than all the politicians of the century, far more even than the work of Darwin, it liberated the mind of modern man.

Huxley was not only an intellectual colossus; he was also a great artist; he knew how to be charming. No man has ever written more nearly perfect English prose. There is a magnificent clarity in it; its meaning is never obscure for an instant. And it is adorned with a various and never-failing grace. It never struts like the prose of Macaulay; it never simpers like Pater's. It is simple, precise, unpretentious—and yet there is fine music in every line of it. The effects it achieves are truly overwhelming. One cannot read it without succumbing to it. Again I point to the two volumes of the debate with Gladstone. If they don't thrill you, then go back to the sporting page.

The Eternal Riddle

From the *American Mercury*, April, 1929, pp. 509–10.
A review of THE NATURE OF THE PHYSICAL WORLD,
by A. S. Eddington, New York, 1928; and MAN A MACHINE,
by Joseph Needham, New York, 1928

The historian of science, writing a century hence, will probably treat our present age of marvels with a considerable jocosity. It is marked by researches and discoveries hitherto unparalleled in the world, but it is also marked by a vast groping and uncertainty. The physicists, baffled by the wonders unfolded before them, wobble all over the lot, and the biologists perform scarcely less comically. The easy certainties of a Huxley are no more. Millikan, in physics, attempts a grotesque compromise with theology, and Driesch, in biology, concocts a metaphysics that even many theologians would balk at. The two authors here under review show the sad effects of this demoralization. Dr. Eddington, an astronomer, leaps so far into interstellar space that, at the end of his book, he is forced to admit gloomily that, even to himself, much of what he has written bears the aspect of "a well-meaning kind of nonsense." And Dr. Needham, who is a biochemist, closes a brilliant demonstration that the living organism is a machine, and responsive to natural laws like any other, with the amazing confession that the mechanistic theory, in the last analysis, is only "a methodological fiction."

What ails both of these learned men, and their brethren with them, is their constant assumption that what is known today is the sum total of possible knowledge. They protest endlessly that they assume nothing of the sort, but nevertheless they do so unconsciously, and the fact leads them into endless absurdities. For example, consider Dr. Eddington's dealing with the Planck quantum theory. Starting out by showing that it knocks out the laws of causality, as those laws have been understood in the past, he proceeds gaily to the postulate that they do not exist at all, and from that postulate he goes on to speculations which lead him, in the end, to the borders of supernaturalism. But why assume that the quantum theory disposes of causation? All that it actually does is to confront us with a variety of causation which, at the moment, we are unable to account for. But it may be accounted for very plausibly tomorrow or next day. Meanwhile, it is certainly just as rational to assume that it will be as to assume that it won't be. In the past man has solved far tougher problems. Why should it be set down as a fact that this one will forever baffle him?

Dr. Needham's error is of the same order. He proves conclusively that, from the biologist's standpoint, it is a sheer intellectual impossibility to think of the living organism as anything save a machine, and then he goes on to show that, from some other standpoint (say the theologian's) it must be thought of as something different. But why waste any time thinking of it in that way? Is there anything in the general thinking of theologians which makes their opinion on the point of any interest or value? What have they ever done in other fields to match the fact-finding of the biologists? I can find nothing in the record. Their processes of thought, taking one day with another, are so defective as to be preposterous. True enough, they are masters of logic, but they always start out from palpably false premises. I see no reason why anyone should bother about their nonsensical caveats. Whether or not man is a machine is a fact to be established by an examination of the evidence. If the answer turns out to be yes, then it will plainly be far from "a methodological fiction." And if it is no, then the theologians will still have to prove their case. For the virtue of A cannot be demonstrated by showing that B is a rogue.

There is a vast need, in the physical sciences, for a new Huxley. The discoveries of Einstein, Planck and company have brought in a reign of intellectual chaos. The Millikans, Eddingtons and Driesches, though they are worthy men otherwise, seem to be unable to grapple successfully with the unrolling facts. In their discussions of the huge problems confronting the scientific fraternity there is comfort for New Thoughters, university pedagogues and Methodist bishops, but not much for the rest of us. What is called for is a genius capable of grappling with the confusion now prevailing and getting some order into it. I herewith issue a summons for candidates. Whoever fills the bill is sure of great fame.

Two Benefactors of Mankind

From the New York *American*, Nov. 26, 1934

When I was a youngster, in the closing decades of the last century, two horrible plagues afflicted the American people. The first was the plague of flies and the second was that of corns. No one, in those days, knew how to get rid of either. We used to sleep under canopies of netting on Summer nights, but they were worse than useless, for on the one hand they kept out the air, and on the other they were no impediment to flies, which wriggled through their meshes and feasted on our carcasses within. By day these same flies gave their show on our dinner-tables, leaving us with cholera morbus or typhoid fever. On Sunday mornings they performed massively on clergy and laity; on weekdays they specialized in pedagogues and pupils. Save in the extreme North their season ran from Easter to Thanksgiving. While they raged, every American spent half his time dodging them, banging away at them, and damning them.

The curse of corns was almost as bad. Every man, woman and child in the country had them. There was no such thing as walking off in comfort in a new pair of shoes. The shoemakers shaped their lasts to rub and hurt, and rub and hurt they did. All through the '80s they grew narrower and narrower, until in the '90s the so-called toothpick toe came in, and the whole nation began to limp. Does it seem comic, looking back? Then believe me, friends, it was not comic to the sufferers. Every drug-store window was full of corn-cures, but none of them really worked. Corn-doctors practised in every American community, gouging, gashing and spreading streptococci. Desperate men cut off their own toes. Children at play stopped to hop around on one foot, holding the other and yelling.

No one seemed to be able to imagine release from either plague. The flies were looked upon as quite as natural and necessary as the sunshine, and the corns seemed to be as inevitable as death or taxes. Yet they were got rid of in the end, and very easily. In the first case it was the automobile that did the trick. When it drove out the horse, it shut down hundreds of thousands of stables, and with the stables went the flies that bred in them. Simultaneously, some one invented the copper-mesh window-screen, and the tale was told. There had been window-screens in my youth, but they were made of iron wire, and rusted quickly, and the flies got through them. When the plan was tried of painting them—mainly with florid Alpine scenes—, it did no good. But then came the copper-mesh screen, and the last fly, staggering in from the last livery-stable, gave up the ghost. Today, in any well-regulated American home or hotel, it would be as startling to see one as to see a buzzard.

Who invented the copper-mesh screen I don't know, but whoever he was, he deserves far better of his country than the inventor of the telephone, which is a boon but also a nuisance, or of the automobile, which is handy in its way but otherwise has taken the place of the sabre-toothed tiger and the wolf. The man who abolished corns remains almost as elusive, but nevertheless he may be tracked down and identified. He was a brigadier-general of the Army Medical Corps, by name Edward Lyman Munson.[1] In 1912 he designed a last that really followed the shape of the human foot, and during the World War it was used in making shoes for

---

[1] He lived, retired, until July 7, 1947.

the Army. After the war the secular shoemakers began imitating it, and corns began to disappear. A little while longer, and they will be as rare as smallpox. Any shoe-dealer who knows his business can now supply a shoe that makes them next to impossible.

These two inventors—General Munson and the unknown who hit on the copper flyscreen—deserve far more from their country than they have got. They furthered human progress immensely, and without any drawbacks. Every other great invention seems to carry an affliction with it, but not theirs. The automobile kills its thousands, the telephone and the radio drive their thousands frantic, and the electric light has not only made the country bright, but also hideous. But the disappearance of the fly is pure velvet, and so is that of the corn.

Elegy

From the *American Mercury*, Sept., 1931, p. 38

The steam locomotive, it appears, is doomed to follow the horse and buggy. It has disappeared from the N.Y., N.H. and H. up to New Haven, and it will presently disappear from the Pennsylvania down to Washington. Westward it will transform itself into an oil-burner, with no sparks on dark nights—or, worse, into a gasoline-burning flivver. A tragedy indeed, my masters! Something to moan and mourn about! For what other machine ever seen on earth is as stupendous as a locomotive thundering down a long stretch of track, with black smoke bursting from its stack and its mighty drivers pounding the rails? Where is there another such sight, at morning, noon or night? What other contrivance of human hands is so stately, so regal, so overpowering? A great ocean liner, at sea, is appallingly trivial looking; it thumps the imagination only when it is tied safe to a dock. A Zeppelin is a floating sausage. An airplane is not even a bird, but only a bug. An electric locomotive remains a toy, even though it weigh a hundred tons. But even a lowly yard engine, if there be steam in it, somehow fills and delights the eye. It belongs to the noble company of massive and gorgeous creatures—the elephants and whales, the mastodons and behemoths, the ceratopsia and sauropoda, monarchs of land and sea. There is something fearsome and prehistoric about it: it is nearer to the dinosaur than to any living animal. It breathes flame like a volcano, and it rumbles like an earthquake. When one stands by the trackside as it thunders by, belching its acrid smoke, every sense is arrested and excited—sight, hearing, touch, taste and smell. It stuns the mind, and coagulates the marrow of the bones. It is not a mere thing; it is a kind of cosmic event.

And now it is headed for the scrap-yard.

Sketch Maritime

From the *Smart Set*, March, 1920, pp. 48–49

The Pennsylvania Railroad this side of Wilmington. To the left the Delaware River. Somewhere below Chester there passes a British tramp-steamer—a hideous monster in the new style, with the engine and funnel directly over the propeller—a dirty drab in color—squat and waddling like a corn-stuffed hog—a clumsy machine manned by greasy men in overalls. This is the heir of the Viking ships, the caravels and galleons, the lordly four-masters, the windjammers, the clippers. This is the successor of Drake's *Golden Hind*—a tub full of union men. And think of her work in the world: to pile up money for the holders of first and second preferred stock, to haul cattle and baled hay, to ply endlessly between Cardiff and Philadelphia.

Penguin's Eggs

From the *American Mercury*, Sept., 1930, pp. 123–24. A review of THE WORST JOURNEY IN THE WORLD, by Apsley Cherry-Garrard; New York, 1930

The journey that Mr. Cherry-Garrard describes was made during the Antarctic Winter of 1912; it took but a month, covered but

100 miles, and was no more than a minor incident of Captain Robert F. Scott's successful (and fatal) dash to the South Pole. Nevertheless, it is probable that few travellers, ancient or modern, have ever met with greater difficulties or suffered greater agonies than Cherry-Garrard and his two companions, both of whom afterward perished with Scott.

The tale as he tells it—and he is a very candid and persuasive narrator—is really quite appalling. In a temperature that sometimes dropped to seventy-five degrees below zero, with dreadful hurricanes blowing, the three dragged their sleds across the glassy glaciers and tumultuous shore-ice of the Antarctic coast. To one side of them was the frozen sea: to the other loomed the sinister cone of Mt. Erebus, 13,350 feet high. They had no dogs or other transport animals. They had no shelter save a small tent. For thirty days and nights they struggled and suffered, shivered and shook. They fell into crevasses, were blinded by the whirling snow, and got lost in the trackless wastes. Horrible frost-bites tortured them. They went without food for days and saw their small supply of oil reduced to a few pints. But still they battled on, and at the end of their Dantesque month they were once more back at Scott's base—three shaking, speechless and dreadful caricatures of men. And to what end? For what purpose did they risk their lives so heroically? They did it because they wanted to get some eggs of the Emperor penguin. They came back with three.

Mr. Cherry-Gerrard, I suspect, is quite conscious of the futility of the adventure. More, there is reason to believe that he has his sly opinion about the whole enterprise of Polar exploration, though he himself is one of its shining ornaments and escaped sharing Scott's fate only by a hair. Certainly there is a plain touch of irony in his argument that such exploits as the one he describes so graphically are useful (and even necessary) to the progress of science. First he shows, on the authority of Professor Cossar Ewart of Edinburgh (whoever he may be: I can't find him in the reference-books) that the eggs of the Emperor penguin are enormously valuable—that they throw light upon the origin of all birds. And then he shows, on his own far safer testimony, that when he went to the Natural History Museum in South Kensington to get a receipt for those he had brought home at such cost he found that no one took any interest in them, and that he himself was regarded as a nuisance. Was the joke here on the English as scientists, or on Cherry-Garrard as hero? Perhaps it was on both.

These penguin eggs, however much the pundits at South Kensington may disdain them, were yet the most valuable scientific baggage brought home from the Antarctic by the Scott expedition. Scott himself, struggling back from the Pole and freezing to death within eleven miles of a secure and even comfortable camp, had nothing save thirty pounds of fossils, none of them very interesting. They were recovered when his body was found, and are probably at South Kensington today, keeping company with the eggs. The other members of the party took endless meteorological observations, but there is no evidence that they discovered anything save what was already palpable to their five senses, e.g., that it was very cold in such latitudes, that the Winter storms were most unpleasant, and that the glaciers kept on moving. Not all their observations were sufficient to save Scott and his four companions from death. They went to the Pole fully expecting, on the assurance of the expedition's scientific staff, to find mild Summer weather, and were undone by a tremendous blizzard. Moreover, their medical experts helped them no more than their meteorologists. At least one of them seems to have died, not of the blizzard, but of scurvy. Mr. Cherry-Garrard says, indeed, that he now believes the expedition's ration was grossly inadequate. Yet it had been planned very carefully, and was based upon Scott's experience on the Discovery expedition, upon more than a year of preparatory work, and upon the unanimous counsel of his medical men.

The truth is that the scientific value of Polar exploration is greatly exaggerated. The thing that takes men on such hazardous trips is really not any thirst for knowledge, but simply a yearning for adventure. But just as an American business man, having amassed a fortune, always tries to make it appear that he never had any desire for money, but only wanted to set up an orphan asylum or get time to study golf, so a Polar explorer always talks grandly of sacrificing his fingers and toes to science. It is an amiable pretension, but there is no need to take it seriously. Admiral Byrd actually took his armada South in order to be the first man to gape at the South Pole from an airship: the rest was no more than *la-*

gniappe. I am ready to venture that the whole scientific fruits of his enormously costly expedition were no greater than lowly zoölogists pluck every Summer at Wood's Hole. As for Lindbergh, another eminent servant of science, all he proved by his gaudy flight across the Atlantic was that God takes care of those who have been so fortunate as to come into the world foolish.

XI. MAKING A LIVING

The Professions

From the *Smart Set*, Jan., 1922, pp. 46–47

THE DIGNITY of the learned professions, always assumed in discussions of them, succumbs quickly to analysis. What, realistically described, is the function that a clergyman performs in the world? In brief, he gets a living by convincing idiots that he can save them from a mythical Hell. It is a business, at bottom, almost indistinguishable from that of selling Texas oil stocks. As for a lawyer, he is simply, under our cash-register civilization, one who teaches scoundrels how to commit their swindles without risk. As for a physician, he is one who spends his whole existence trying to prolong the lives of persons whose deaths, in nine cases out of ten, would be a public benefit. The case of the pedagogue is even worse. Consider him in his highest incarnation: the university professor. What is his function? Simply to pass on to fresh generations of numskulls a body of so-called knowledge that is fragmentary, unimportant and, for the most part, untrue. His whole professional activity is circumscribed by the prejudices, vanities and avarices of his university trustees, *i.e.*, a committee of soap-boilers, nail-manufacturers, bank-directors and politicians. The moment he offends these vermin he is undone. He cannot so much as think aloud without running a risk of having them fan his pantaloons.

There was a time when the profession of arms was honorable, but that is surely no longer true in America. The corps of officers of the United States Army seems to be fast sinking to the estate and dignity of a gang of longshoremen. One never picks up a newspaper without reading of the arrest of some officer or ex-officer for an offense involving dishonor. Not long ago one of them was hanged for murder. A few days later another one, in prison for the same crime, asked for a pardon on the ground that, in the region where he was brought up, murder was not regarded as criminal. Swindles, defalcations, rowdyism, drunkenness, extortions, cruelties—such offenses are so common that they pass almost unnoticed. Some time ago, I ventured the guess that the democratization of the officers' corps was to blame—that the introduction into it, by competitive examination, of youths unaccustomed to the amenities of civilization had destroyed the spirit left in it by Washington and Lee. But perhaps there is a more profound cause. Democracy, I daresay, is fundamentally opposed to that fine tradition of caste, that conscious superiority to ordinary temptations and ordinary aspirations, which makes the officer and gentleman. Warfare, as carried on by democracies, is inevitably polluted by the moral rages of inferior men. It converts itself into a sort of gang-fight, with bawling, yelling and biting in the clinches. Above all, it rejects the old ideal which prescribed an unimpassioned and chivalrous view of the enemy. Thus it grows less and less attractive to the old type of soldier. The general of tomorrow will be far more the evangelist and rabble-rouser than the gallant knight. And his officers, departing more and more from the type of Prince Eugene, will come closer and closer to the type of the Y.M.C.A. secretary.

Dazzling the Public

From the *Smart Set*, May, 1920, p. 35

The tendency of all men to magnify their trades by *escamoterie* is beautifully displayed in the case of the railway conductors. The work that a passenger conductor does is so simple and so trivial that any average eighteen-year-old boy could learn it in a week. Moreover, the notion that he carries an enormous responsibility, that the lives of his passengers depend upon his skill and diligence, is fully ninety-nine per cent. buncombe: all of the actual responsibility is upon the locomotive engineer. Nevertheless, the passenger conductors of the land, by parading before the public in florid uniforms and with heavy frowns upon their faces and by treating it in general as a German field-marshal must be expected to treat a mob of Socialist barbers, have so far convinced it of their importance that it consents readily to outrageous railway fares in order that they may be paid preposterous salaries, out of all reasonable proportion to their services. Of late the thing has gone even further. On many of the larger railways the conductor no longer deigns to collect tickets in person. Instead he stalks through the train with a so-called auditor, or adjutant, attending him, and this adjutant does all the actual work. And for this pompous parade the conductor is paid as much as a captain in the Army. In Europe the train conductor is paid probably one-fourth as much, and does ten times the work. He takes tips, but he earns them. A passenger who fees him may expect to get some service from him. He looks after windows, hears complaints politely, and even helps with the baggage. An American conductor would be staggered by any suggestion that he do such things. His sole duty is to enforce the notion of his stupendous dignity, to cow the boobery with his august and judicial mien, to keep up the grotesque farce that has made him what he is.

The Puppet's Pretension

From the *Smart Set*, Dec., 1912, pp. 157

Genius is altogether too fine a word to apply to stage players, just as it is too fine a word to apply to opera singers, fiddlers, piano thumpers, college professors, and other such retailers of better men's ideas. A first-rate actress, true enough, may be measurably better than a mere interpreter, a phonograph in skirts, a sentient marionette; she may actually add a valuable something to the thing created by the dramatist. But that something, after all, is no more than a good painter adds to a house. It is the architect and not the painter that creates the house, and in the same way it is the dramatist and not the actress that creates the character the actress plays. Creation is an act of the highest cerebral centers. It takes out of any man who attempts it the best that is in him. When it is essayed by a true genius it takes out of him the best that is in the human race. But interpretation is usually as much a physical as a psychic matter. An actress with only one eye would be in worse case than an actress with only one cerebral hemisphere; a Mischa Elman with defective hearing and clumsy thumbs would simply cease to exist as a Mischa Elman. And yet Lafcadio Hearn, with only one eye, created words of undoubted genius, and Ludwig van Beethoven, with defective hearing, and Richard Wagner, with clumsy thumbs, each revolutionized the art of music. The test of a genius is that he creates something great and different. The test of an interpreter is that he does not reduce that greatness to the commonplace and that differentness to rote. The one is greatest when he gives us most of himself; the other is greatest when he best effaces himself.

The Emancipated Housewife

From IN DEFENSE OF WOMEN, 1918; revised, 1922, pp. 120–22

The American housewife of an earlier day was famous for her unremitting diligence. She not only cooked, washed and ironed; she also made shift to master such more complex arts as spinning, baking and brewing. Her expertness, perhaps, never reached a high level, but at all events she made a gallant effort. But that was long, long ago, before the new enlightenment rescued her. Today, in her average incarnation, she is not only incompetent; she is also filled with the notion that a conscientious discharge of her few remaining duties is, in some vague way, discreditable and degrading.

To call her a good cook, I daresay, was never anything but flattery; the early American cuisine was probably a fearful thing, indeed. But today the flattery turns into a sort of libel, and she resents it, or, at all events, does not welcome it. I used to know an American literary man, educated on the Continent, who married a woman because she had exceptional gifts in this department.

Years later, at one of her excellent dinners, a friend of her husband tried to please her by mentioning the fact, to which he had always been privy. But instead of being complimented, as a man might have been if told that his wife had married him because he was a good lawyer, or surgeon, or blacksmith, this unusual housekeeper, suffering a renaissance of usualness, denounced the guest as a liar, spilled soup on his waistcoat, ordered him out of the house, and threatened to leave her husband.

This disdain of offices that, after all, are necessary, and might as well be faced with some show of cheerfulness, takes on the character of a cult in the United States, and the stray woman who attends to them faithfully is laughed at as a drudge and a fool, just as she is apt to be dismissed as a "brood sow" if she favors her lord with viable issue. One result is the notorious villainousness of American cookery—a villainousness so painful to a cultured uvula that a French hack-driver, if his wife set its masterpieces before him, would brain her with his linoleum hat. To encounter a decent meal in an American home of the middle class, simple, sensibly chosen and competently cooked, becomes almost as startling as to meet a Y.M.C.A. secretary in a bordello, and a good deal rarer. Such a thing, in most of the large cities of the Republic, scarcely has any existence. If the average American husband wants a sound dinner he must go to a restaurant to get it, just as if he wants to refresh himself with the society of charming and well-behaved children, he has to go to an orphan asylum. Only the recent immigrant can take his ease and invite his soul within his own house.

Honest Toil

From the *Smart Set*, April, 1922, pp. 47–49

As I grow older, old tastes and enthusiasms fade miserably into memories—yellowed leaves fluttering from the dying tree. An observation mellow with platitude, and yet every man, as he makes it for himself, must be filled with a Goethean melancholy, a kind of dismayed wonder. Am I actually the same mammal who, in the year 1894, was a baseball fan, and knew all the players without a score-card? It seems incredible—some outrageous fable out of history, like that about Washington and the cherry tree. I can imagine nothing more dismal today than a baseball game, or, for that matter, any sort of sport. The taste for it, the capacity for rising to its challenge, is as extinct in me as, say, the desire for immortality. I have absolutely no yearning to exist as a wraith for all eternity, and by the same token I have absolutely no yearning to play golf. Not long ago, when too much work at the desk—chained to a stool and a spittoon like a bookkeeper—brought me to a professor of internal medicine, and he prescribed more exercise, I turned to laying bricks to avoid the unbearable boredom of golf, tennis, and all the rest of it. In laying bricks there is at least some obvious intelligibility. One *makes* something, and it is there to look at and mull over after it is done. What is there after one has played a round of golf?

When I was a boy, bricklayers always fascinated me. No other mechanics wore such a lordly and distinguished air. Even in those days they got a great deal more money than other workingmen, and showed it in their manner. At noon, when the carpenters and tinners sat down in their slops to devour stale sandwiches out of tin cans, the bricklayers took off their white overalls, went to the Dutchman's at the corner, and there dined decently on *Linsensuppe* and *Sauerbraten*, with large horns of lager to flush their esophagi. Bricklayers were the only workmen who had recognized gangs of slaves to serve them, to wit, the hod-carriers. In those far-off times, in the city where I lived, all hod-carriers were colored men—usually great, shiny fellows with immense knots of muscles in their legs and arms. The Irish had already become lawyers, city detectives, saloonkeepers, gang bosses, and *Todsaufer* for breweries. These colored men, in Summer, liked to work with their chests bare. Swarming up the ladders in long files, each with his heavy hod on his shoulder, they made an exotic, Egyptian picture. One could fancy them descended in a direct line from the Nubians who carried the hod when Cheops built his pyramid. The bricklayers, forever cursing them fluently, but all the same palpably friendly to them, fitted into the fancy perfectly. The ma-son is the one workman who has resisted all change. He does his work today as he did it in Babylon, with deft hand and sharp eye. Compared with him, all the other mechanics of our time are upstarts: put him alongside the plumber, the structural iron worker, or the electrician. Moreover, what he does endures. The carpenter? A blower of soap bubbles, a maker of millinery! But the brick walls of Babylon stand to this day.

Laying bricks in my garden wall (to the great disquiet of my neighbor's dog) I learned a number of things worth knowing. One (discovered almost instantly) was this: that there is much more to a handicraft than the simple exercise of muscle. To lay bricks decently one must be careful, calculating, far-seeing, alert, a bit shrewd. Distances must be figured out very accurately, else there will presently appear a gap that no conceivable brick will fit. One deals in hard and immovable lines, precise distances, mathematical levels. A wall that leans, save when age has pushed it over, is a wall that must come down. There can be no easy compromises with the plumb-bob, no rough and ready evasions of the plan. A week or two of hard effort left me with a respect for bricklayers vastly transcending my old admiration. I knocked off a day and went out to watch a gang of them laying the front wall of a somewhat elaborate moving-picture theatre—a complex maze of arches, cornices, pilasters. I had, even by this time, some professional comprehension of their problems. I stood gaping in the hot sun as they solved them—quickly, ingeniously, perfectly. But that, after all, was an easy job. The hardest of all, I have been told, is to lay the wall of a sewer manhole. It is all curves—and they do not all run the same way. The men who tackle it do it wholly by the eye. It is as difficult, in its way, as playing Bach.

Another thing I learned was that it was quite as easy, and a good deal more pleasant, to lay bricks in a good design as it was to lay them in a bad design. Do bricklayers know it? Do they take any actual delight in their craft? I believe fully that the better ones do. An architect once told me that every effort he made to use bricks beautifully, no matter how vexatious the technical problems it involved, met a hearty response from them, and eager coöperation— that they delighted in matching the colors of the new tapestry bricks, and worked joyfully on a fine chimney. Unluckily, they seldom get the chance. Nine-tenths of the work they do for a living is shoddy—the uninspiring laying of bad bricks in inept and feeble designs. What could be more tiresome than running up a high blank wall? Or than encasing a skyscraper in its thin and puerile skin of clay? The only brickwork that can imaginably satisfy an honest bricklayer is honest brickwork—brickwork that stands upon its own bottom, and is precisely what it pretends to be. The main arch of that movie-parlor occupied four or five bricklayers for several days. It was a genuine arch, not a fake concealing concrete, and their delight in it was obvious. All day long their foreman hovered over them, watching every brick as it went into place, and buzzing all over the scaffolding with his blue-print and his level. I saw him regarding it from across the street when it was done, and the false work had been taken away. There was no mean satisfaction in his face, and it was no mean feat that satisfied him.

The Rewards of Virtue

From the Chicago *Tribune*, Oct. 10, 1926

The dream of the Socialists, if any survive, is now realized among us, and even exceeded: bricklayers and plasterers are getting better pay than college professors. I am certainly no Socialist myself, but somehow this consummation gives me agreeable sensations. Is it foul, preposterous, inequitable, and against God? If so, on what ground? I know, like most men of my trade and interests, something about college professors, but, rather unusually, I also know something about bricklayers. My belief is that the latter are far more useful than the former, and that, taking one with another, they are also far more amiable and amusing fellows.

The pedagogue, being excessively literate, has long poisoned the world with highfalutin tosh about his high dignity and consequence, and especially about his altruism. He is commonly regarded, even by those who ought to know better, as a hero who has made vast sacrifices for the good of the rising generation and the honor of learning. He is, in fact, seldom anything of the sort. He is simply a lazybones who has taken to the birch in order to escape implements of a greater laboriousness. The rising generation is not his pet, but simply his oyster. And he has no more respect for learning, in his average incarnation, than a congressman has for statecraft or a Prohibition agent or lawyer for law.

The world's stock of knowledge is seldom augmented by pedagogues; far more often they oppose its increase in a violent and implacable manner. Turn to physics or metaphysics, as you please. How many of the salient philosophers have been professors of philosophy? Probably not twenty per cent. And how much of the recent advance in the physical sciences is due to men professionally devoted to teaching them? So little that it is hard to detect it. During the last quarter of a century chemistry has been completely overhauled. The axioms that it was grounded on in 1900 are now all abandoned. But at least three-fourths of the chemistry teachers of America are still teaching the chemistry of 1900, as nine-tenths of the literature teachers are still teaching the literary principles and ideas of 1885.

The pedagogue, however, is not my theme; what I presume to argue is that the rewards that men get in this world, taking averages, run with their merit and value as members of society, and that those who are badly paid are usually paid very justly. The doctrine to the contrary is widespread, and upsetting it would probably be an impossibility, for it is supported vigorously by the thousands who are flattered by it. Nevertheless, it remains hollow and invalid, and a huge body of facts stands against it. Of late it was mouthed very affectingly by homilists at the bier of the deceased Valentino. It was, it appeared, a disgrace to humanity that Valentino got such vast rewards, and so many pious and laborious men such small ones. His daily income was fifty times that of a bishop, a hundred times that of a pedagogue, and perhaps a thousand times that of a poet. And what did he do to earn it? He postured absurdly in nonsensical movies. He filled hundreds of thousands of female morons with gaudy and often salacious dreams. He destroyed throughout America, and even throughout the world, the respect that should go to dull and industrious men, painfully earning livings for their families.

With all due respect, bosh! Valentino was actually one of the most useful men who ever lived in the federal union, and deserved every cent he took in. Into the life of a sordid, unimaginative and machine-bound people he brought a breath of romance. Thousands of poor girls doomed to marry book-keepers, garage-keepers and Kiwanians got out of his pulchritude a precious and lasting thrill. He lifted their eyes above the carpet sweeper and the slop pail. He made them, for a brief space, gloriously, royally, and even a bit sinfully happy. What bishop has ever done more for them, or at a lower rate per capita? And what pedagogue? And what poet?

The world has always rewarded its romance makers richly, and with sound reason. They are extremely valuable men. They take away the sting of life, and make it expansive and charming. They make the forlorn brigades of God's images forget the miseries that issue out of hard work, mounting debts, disintegrating kidneys, and the fear of Hell. And their value, socially, obviously runs in direct proportion to the number of people they can reach and tickle. A Greenwich Village advanced poet, writing unintelligible Freudian strophes, is worth only the $9 a week that he gets, for his work brings joy to very few people. But an Edgar A. Guest, though his compositions may gag the judicious, earns every dollar of his millions, for when he lifts up his customers he lifts them up at wholesale, and the belch of satisfaction that follows is stupendous.

Here I may seem to argue that the worse the artist the nobler the man. I actually argue nothing of the sort. I am speaking, not of imponderable rewards, but of rewards in cash. The genuine artist gets something that the Valentinos and Guests can never hope to get. It is the colossal inner glow that goes with difficult work competently done. Something else also comes to him: the respect and esteem of his peers. He gathers fame, and it tends to be lasting. He cherishes the rare and immensely satisfying certainty that he will be remembered after he has gone from these scenes—that he is definitely and permanently rescued from the depressing swarm of anonymous men. The Valentinos and Guests get no such reward. Guest is admired by Rotarians, and probably enjoys it, but he would enjoy it infinitely more if he were admired by men of taste. Poor Valentino was an even worse case. His customers, in the main, were idiots, and he was well aware of it. He would have willingly swapped all his money for an hour of the fame of Beethoven, for he was intelligent enough to see the adulation that surrounded him for what it was. But he was also intelligent enough to see that the fame of Beethoven was hopelessly beyond his reach, and so he raked in such rewards as actually came his way. It seems to me that he deserved them. He deserved them quite as much as any pedagogue in this glorious land deserves his $1,500 a year.

My experience of this worst of possible worlds convinces me that very few men are ever paid less than they are worth. Many are paid more, especially in America, where a great deal more money rolls in every year than the people of the country can earn, but not many are paid less. The cases that pop up almost always turn out, on inspection, to be extremely dubious. Some time ago, for example, the medical journals were full of sad articles on the meager earnings of the ordinary run of doctors—the modest fellows who confine themselves to neighborhood practise, and spend their days looking at tongues, dosing colds, and digging shoe buttons out of babies' ears and noses. But it was quickly apparent, as the discussion developed, that most of these worthies were getting, not less than they deserved, but a great deal more. The trouble with them was simply that they were incompetent at their trade. Most of them knew no more about modern medicine than so many chiropractors or ambulance drivers. Their practise constituted a swindle, and their customers, becoming aware of the fact, turned to specialists, *i.e.*, to men better equipped to do what they were paid to do. These same specialists were rolling in money, for in medicine, as in all other professions, even the most modest competence is relatively rare, and the man who has it is thus heavily rewarded.

The truth is that in the United States today men of all imaginable trades, including even that of poetry, are enormously well paid—provided only they have a reasonable skill at the thing they practise. The bellowing to the contrary comes from incompetents and frauds—doctors who are but little removed from Indian herb medicine men, lawyers who know no law, pedagogues who are jackasses, bootleggers who swindle their clients, authors with nothing to say, actors worse than clothing store dummies.

XII. PLACES TO LIVE

Totentanz

From PREJUDICES: FOURTH SERIES, 1924, pp. 145–57

I CAN think of no great city of this world (putting aside Rio de Janeiro, Sydney and San Francisco) that is set amid scenes of greater natural beauty than New York, by which I mean, of course, Manhattan. Recall Berlin on its dismal plain, Paris and London on their toy rivers, Madrid on its desert, Copenhagen on its swamp, Rome on its ancient sewer and its absurd little hills, and then glance at Manhattan on its narrow and rock-ribbed island, with deep rivers to either side and the wide bay before it. No wonder its early visitors, however much they denounced the Dutch, always paused to praise the scene! Before it grew up, indeed, New York must have been strangely beautiful. But it was the beauty of freshness and unsophistication—in brief, of youth—and now it is no more. The town today, I think, is quite the ugliest in the world— uglier, even, than Liverpool, Chicago or Berlin. If it were actually beautiful, as London, say, is beautiful, or Munich, or Charleston, or Florence, or even parts of Paris and Washington, then New Yorkers would not be so childishly appreciative of the few so-called beauty spots that it has—for example, Washington Square, Gramercy Park, Fifth avenue and Riverside drive. Washington Square, save for one short row of old houses on the North side, is actually very shabby and ugly—a blot rather than a beauty spot. The trees, year in and year out, have a mangy and sclerotic air; the grass is like stable litter; the tall tower on the South side is ungraceful and preposterous; the memorial arch is dirty and undignified; the whole place looks dingy, frowsy and forlorn. Compare it to Mt. Vernon Square in Baltimore: the difference is that between a char-

woman and a grand lady. As for Gramercy Park, it is celebrated
only because it is in New York; if it were in Washington or London it would not attract a glance. Fifth avenue, to me, seems to be
showy rather than beautiful. What gives it its distinction is simply
its spick and span appearance of wealth; it is the only New York
street that ever looks well-fed and clean. Riverside drive lacks even
so much; it is second-rate from end to end, and especially where
it is gaudiest. What absurd and hideous houses, with their brummagem Frenchiness, their pathetic effort to look aristocratic! What
bad landscaping! What grotesque monuments! From its heights
the rich look down upon the foul scars of the Palisades, as the rich
of Fifth avenue and Central Park West look down upon the ane-
mic grass, bare rocks and blowing newspapers of Central Park.
Alone among the great cities of the East, New York has never developed a domestic architecture of any charm, or, indeed, of any
character at all. There are neighborhoods in Boston, in Philadelphia, in Baltimore and in many lesser cities that have all the dignity and beauty of London, but in New York the brownstone
mania of the Nineteenth Century brought down the whole town
to one level of depressing ugliness, and since brownstone has gone
out there has been no development whatever of indigenous design,
but only a naïve copying of models—the skyscraper from Chicago
and the dwelling-house from Paris. Along Fifth avenue, from the
Fifty-ninth street corner to the upper end of Central Park, there is
not a single house that looks reposeful and habitable. Along Park
avenue—but Park avenue, for all its flash of creamy brick, is surely
one of the most hideous streets in all the world!

But the life of the city, it must be confessed, is as interesting as
its physical aspect is dull. It is, even more than London or Paris,
the modern Babylon, and since 1914 it has entered upon a period
of luxuriousness that far surpasses anything seen on earth since the
fall of the Eastern Empire. During many a single week, I daresay,
more money is spent in New York upon useless and evil things
than would suffice to run the kingdom of Denmark for a year. All
the colossal accumulated wealth of the United States, the greatest
robber nation in history, tends to force itself at least once a year
through the narrow neck of the Manhattan funnel. To that harsh
island come all the thieves of the Republic with their loot—

bankers from the fat lands of the Middle West, lumbermen from the Northwestern coasts, mine owners from the mountains, oil speculators from Texas and Oklahoma, cotton-mill sweaters from the South, steel magnates and manufacturers from the Black Country, blacklegs and exploiters without end—all laden with cash, all eager to spend it, all easy marks for the town rogues and panders. The result is a social organization that ought to be far more attractive to novelists than it is—a society founded upon the prodigious wealth of Monte Cristo and upon the tastes of sailors home from a long voyage. At no time and place in modern times has harlotry reached so delicate and yet so effusive a development; it becomes, in one form or another, one of the leading industries of the town. New York, indeed, is the heaven of every variety of man with something useless and expensive to sell. There come the merchants with their bales of Persian prayer-rugs, of silk pajamas, of yellow girls, of strange jugs and carboys, of hand-painted oil-paintings, of old books, of gim-cracks and tinsel from all the four corners of the world, and there they find customers waiting in swarms, their checkbooks open and ready. What town in Christendom has ever supported so many houses of entertainment, so many mimes and mountebanks, so many sharpers and coney-catchers, so many bawds and pimps, so many hat-holders and door-openers, so many miscellaneous servants to idleness and debauchery? The bootlegging industry takes on proportions that are almost unbelievable; there are thousands of New Yorkers, resident and transient, who pay more for alcohol every year than they pay for anything else save women. I have heard of a single party at which the guests drank 100 cases of champagne in an evening—100 cases at $100 a case—and it was, as entertainments go in New York today, a quiet and decorous affair. It is astonishing that no Zola has arisen to describe this engrossing and incomparable dance of death. Upton Sinclair once attempted it, in "The Metropolis," but Sinclair, of course, was too indignant for the job. Moreover, the era he dealt with was mild and amateurish; today the pursuit of sensation has been brought to a far higher degree of perfection. One must go back to the oriental capitals of antiquity to find anything even remotely resembling it. Compared to the revels that go on in New York every night, the carnalities of the

West End of Berlin are trivial and childish, and those of Paris and the Côte d'Azur take on the harmless aspect of a Sunday-school picnic.

What will be the end of the carnival? If historical precedent counts for anything, it will go on to catastrophe. But what sort of catastrophe? I hesitate to venture upon a prophecy. Manhattan Island, with deep rivers all around it, seems an almost ideal scene for a great city revolution, but I doubt very much that there is any revolutionary spirit in its proletariat. Some mysterious enchantment holds its workers to their extraordinarily uncomfortable life; they apparently get a vague sort of delight out of the great spectacle that they are no part of. The New York workman patronizes fellow workmen from the provinces even more heavily than the Wall Street magnate patronizes country mortgage-sharks. He is excessively proud of his citizenship in the great metropolis, though all it brings him is an upper berth in a dog kennel. Riding along the elevated on the East Side and gaping into the windows of the so-called human habitations that stretch on either hand, I often wonder what process of reasoning impels, say, a bricklayer or a truckdriver to spend his days in such vile hutches. True enough, he is paid a few dollars more a week in New York than he would receive anywhere else, but he gets little more use out of them than an honest bank teller. In almost any other large American city he would have a much better house to live in, and better food; in the smaller towns his advantage would be very considerable. Moreover, his chance of lifting himself out of slavery to some measure of economic independence and autonomy would be greater anywhere else; if it is hard for the American workman everywhere to establish a business of his own, it is triply hard in New York, where rents are killingly high and so much capital is required to launch a business that only Jews can raise it. Nevertheless, the poor idiot hangs on to his coop, dazzled by the wealth and splendor on display all around him. His susceptibility to this lure makes me question his capacity for revolution. He is too stupid and poltroonish for it, and he has too much respect for money. It is this respect for money in the proletariat, in fact, that chiefly safeguards and buttresses capitalism in America. It is secure among us because Americans venerate it too much to attack it.

What will finish New York in the end, I suppose, will be an on-slaught from without, not from within. The city is the least defensible of great capitals. Give an enemy command of the sea, and he will be able to take it almost as easily as he could take Copenhagen. It has never been attacked in the past, indeed, without being taken. The strategists of the General Staff at Washington seem to be well aware of this fact, for their preparations to defend the city from a foe afloat have always been half-hearted and lacking in confidence. Captain Stuart Godfrey, U.S.A., who contributes the note on the fortifications of the port to Fremont Rider's "New York City: A Guide to Travelers," is at pains to warn his lay readers that the existing forts protect only the narrow spaces in front of them — that "they cannot be expected to prevent the enemy from landing elsewhere," *e.g.*, anywhere along the long reaches of the Long Island coast. Once such a landing were effected, the fact that the city stands upon an island, with deep water behind it, would be a handicap rather than a benefit. If it could not be taken and held, it could at least be battered to pieces, and so made untenable. The guns of its own forts, indeed, might be turned upon it, once those forts were open to attack from the rear. After that, the best the defenders could do would be to retire to the natural bombproofs in the cellars of the Union Hill, N.J., breweries, and there wait for God to deliver them. They might, of course, be able to throw down enough metal from the Jersey heights to prevent the enemy occupying the city and reopening its theatres and bordellos, but the more successful they were in this enterprise the more cruelly Manhattan would be used. Altogether, an assault from the sea promises to give the New Yorkers something to think about.

That it will be attempted before many years have come and gone seems to me to be very likely and I have a sneaking fear that it may succeed. As a veteran of five wars and a life-long student of homicidal science, I am often made uneasy, indeed, by the almost universal American assumption that no conceivable enemy could inflict serious wounds upon the Republic — that the Atlantic Ocean alone, not to mention the stupendous prowess of *Homo americanus*, makes it eternally safe from aggression. This notion has just enough truth in it to make it dangerous. That the *whole* country could not be conquered and occupied I grant you, but no intelligent enemy would think for a moment of trying to conquer it. All that would be necessary to bring even the most intransigent patriots to terms would be to take and hold a small part of it—say the part lying to the East and North of the general line of the Potomac river. Early in the late war, when efforts were under way to scare the American *booboisie* with the German bugaboo, one of the Allied propagandists printed a book setting forth plans alleged to have been made by the German General Staff to land an army at the Virginia capes, march on Pittsburgh, and so separate the head of the country from its liver, kidneys, gizzard, heart, spleen, bladder, lungs and other lights. The plan was persuasive, but I doubt that it originated in Potsdam; there was a smell of Whitehall upon it. One of the things most essential to its execution, in fact, was left out as it was set forth, to wit, a thrust southward from Canada to meet and support the thrust northwestward. But even this is not necessary. Any invader who emptied New York and took the line of the Hudson would have Uncle Sam by the tail, and could enter upon peace negotiations with every prospect of getting very polite attention. The American people, of course, could go on living without New York, but they could not go on living as a great and puissant nation. Steadily, year by year, they have made New York more and more essential to the orderly functioning of the American state. If it were cut off from the rest of the country the United States would be in the hopeless position of a man relieved of his medulla oblongata—that is to say, of a man without even enough equipment left to be a father, a patriot and a Christian.

Nevertheless, it is highly probable that the predestined enemy, when he comes at last, will direct his first and hardest efforts to cutting off New York, and then make some attempt to keep it detached afterward. This, in fact, is an essential part of the new higher strategy, which is based upon economic considerations, as the old strategy was based upon dynastic considerations. In the Middle Ages, the object of war was to capture and hamstring a king; at present it is to dismember a great state, and so make it impotent. The Germans, had they won, would have broken up the British Empire, and probably detached important territories from France, Italy and Russia, besides gobbling Belgium *in toto*. The French, tantalized by a precarious and incomplete victory, attempted to break up Germany, as they broke up Austria. The chances are that an enemy capable of taking and holding New York would never give it back wholly—that is, would never consent to its restoration to the Union on the old terms. What would be proposed, I venture, would be its conversion into a sort of free state—a new Danzig, perhaps functioning, as now, as the financial and commercial capital of the country, but nevertheless lying outside the bounds politically. This would solve the problem of the city's subsistence, and still enable the conqueror to keep his hold upon it. It is my belief that the New Yorkers, after the first blush of horror, would agree to the new arrangement and even welcome it. Their patriotism, as things stand, is next to nothing. I have never heard, indeed, of a single honest patriot in the whole town; every last man who even pretends to kiss the flag is simply a swindler with something to sell. This indifference to the great heart-throbs of the hinterland is not to be dismissed as mere criminality; it is founded upon the plain and harsh fact that New York is alien to the rest of the country, not only in blood and tastes, but also in fundamental interests—that the sort of life that New Yorkers lead differs radically from the sort of life that the rest of the American people lead, and that their deepest instincts vary with it. The city, in truth, already constitutes an independent free state in all save the name. The ordinary American law does not run there, save when it has been specifically ratified, and the ordinary American *mores* are quite unknown there. What passes as virtue in Kansas is regarded as intolerable vice in New York, and *vice versa*. The town is already powerful enough to swing the whole country when it wants to, as it did on the war issue in 1917, but the country is quite impotent to swing the town. Every great wave of popular passion that rolls up on the prairies is dashed to spray when it strikes the hard rocks of Manhattan.

As a free state, licensed to prey upon the hinterland but unharassed by its Crô-Magnon prejudices and delusions, New York would probably rise to heights of very genuine greatness, and perhaps become the most splendid city known to history. For one thing, it would be able, once it had cut the painter, to erect barriers and conditions around the privilege of citizenship, and so save itself from the double flood that now swamps it—first, of broken-down peasants from Europe, and secondly and more important, of fugitive rogues from all the land West and South of the Hudson. Citizenship in New York is now worth no more than citizenship in Arkansas, for it is open to any applicant from the marshes of Bessarabia, and, still worse, to any applicant from Arkansas. The great city-states of history have been far more fastidious. Venice, Antwerp, London, the Hansa towns, Carthage, Tyre, Cnossus, Alexandria—they were all very sniffish. Rome began to wobble when the Roman franchise was extended to immigrants from the Italian hill country, *i.e.*, the Arkansas of that time. The Hansa towns, under the democracy that has been forced upon them, are rapidly sinking to the level of Chicago and Philadelphia. New York, free to put an end to this invasion, and to drive out thousands of the gorillas who now infest it—more, free from the eternal blackmail of laws made at Albany and the Methodist tyranny of laws made at Washington—could face the future with resolution and security, and in the course of a few generations it might conceivably become genuinely civilized. It would still stand as toll-taker on the chief highway of American commerce; it would still remain the premier banker and usurer of the Republic. But it would be loosed from the bonds which now tend so strenuously to drag it down to the level of the rest of the country. Free at last, it could cease to be the auction-room and bawdy-house that it is now, and so devote its brains and energy to the building up of a civilization.

Metropolis

From PREJUDICES: SIXTH SERIES, 1927, pp. 209–16

It is astonishing how little New York figures in American literature. Think of the best dozen American novels of the last generation. No matter which way your taste and prejudice carry you, you will find, I believe, that Manhattan Island is completely missing from at least ten of them, and that in the other two it is little more than a passing scene, unimportant to the main action. Perhaps the explanation is to be sought in the fact that very few authors of any capacity live in the town. It attracts all the young aspirants power-fully, and hundreds of them, lingering on, develop into very pro-ficient hacks and quacks, and eventually adorn the Authors' League and the National Institute of Arts and Letters. But not many remain who have anything worth hearing to say. They may keep quarters on the island, but they do their writing somewhere else.

Primarily, I suppose, it is too expensive for them: in order to live decently they must grind through so much hack work that there is no time left for their serious concerns. But there is also something else. The town is too full of distractions to be comfortable to art-ists; it is comfortable only to performers. Its machinery of dissipa-tion is so vastly developed that no man can escape it—not even an author laboring in his lonely room, the blinds down and chewing-gum plugging his ears. He hears the swish of skirts through the key-hole; down the area-way comes the clink of ice in tall glasses; some one sends him a pair of tickets to a show which whisper promises will be the dirtiest seen since the time of the Twelve Apostles. It is a sheer impossibility in New York to escape such ap-peals to the ductless glands. They are in the very air. The town is no longer a place of work; it is a place of pleasure. Even the up-State Christian must feel the pull of temptation, though he has been warned by his pastor. He wanders along Broadway to shiver dutifully before the Metropolitan Opera House, with its black rec-ord of lascivious music dramas and adulterous tenors, but before he knows what has struck him he is lured into a movie house even gaudier and wickeder, to sweat before a film of carnal love with lewd music dinning in his ears, or into a grind-shop auction house to buy an ormolu clock disgraceful to a Christian, or into an eating-house to debauch himself with such victuals as are seen in Herkimer county only on days of great ceremonial.

Such is the effect of organized badness, operating upon imper-fect man. But what is bad is also commonly amusing, so I con-tinue to marvel that the authors of the Republic, and especially the novelists, do not more often reduce it to words. Is there anything more charming and instructive in the scenes that actually engage them? I presume to doubt it. There are more frauds and scoundrels, more quacks and cony-catchers, more suckers and visionaries in New York than in all the country west of the Union Hill, N.J., breweries. In other words, there are more interesting people. They pour in from all four points of the compass, and on the hard rocks of Manhattan they do their incomparable stuff, day and night, year in and year out, ever hopeful and ever hot for more. Is it drama if Jens Jensen, out in Nebraska, pauses in his furrow to yearn heavily that he were a chiropractor? Then why isn't it drama if John Doe, prancing in a New York night club, pauses to wonder who the fellow was who just left in a taxi with Mrs. Doe? Is it tragedy that Nils Nilsen, in South Dakota, wastes his substance trying to horn into a mythical Heaven? Then why isn't it tragedy when J. Eustace Garfunkel, after years of effort, fails to make the steep grade of St. Bartholomew's Church?

New York is not all bricks and steel. There are hearts there too, and if they do not break, then they at least know how to leap. It is the place where all the aspirations of the Western world meet to form one vast master aspiration, as powerful as the suction of a steam dredge. It is the icing on the pie called Christian civilization. That it may have buildings higher than any other, and bawdry shows enough, and door-openers enough, and noise and confusion enough—that these imperial ends may be achieved, millions sweat and slave on all the forlorn farms of the earth, and in all the miserable slums, including its own. It pays more for a meal than a Slovak or a Pole pays for a wife, and the meal is better than the wife. It gets the best of everything, and especially of what, by all reputable ethical systems, is the worst. It has passed beyond all fear of Hell or hope of Heaven. The primary postulates of all the rest of the world are its familiar jokes. A city apart, it is breeding a race apart. Is that race American? Then so is a bashi-bazouk American. Is it decent? Then so is a street-walker decent. But I don't think that it may be reasonably denounced as dull.

What I marvel at is that the gorgeous, voluptuous color of this greatest of world capitals makes so little showing in the lovely letters of the United States. If only as spectacle, it is superb. It has a glitter like that of the Constantinople of the Comneni. It roars with life like the Bagdad of the Sassanians. These great capitals of antiquity, in fact, were squalid villages compared to it, as Rome was after their kind, and Paris and London are today. There is little in New York that does not spring from money. It is not a town of ideas; it is not even a town of causes. But what issues out of money is often extremely brilliant, and I believe that it is more brilliant in New York than it has ever been anywhere else. A truly overwhelming opulence envelops the whole place, even in hard times, even the slums. The slaves who keep it going may dwell in vile cubicles, but they are hauled to and from their work by machinery that costs hundreds of millions, and when they fare forth to recreate themselves for tomorrow's tasks they are felled and made dumb by a gaudiness that would have floored John Paleologus himself. Has any one ever figured out, in hard cash, the value of the objects of art stored upon Manhattan Island? I narrow it to paintings, and bar out all the good ones. What would it cost to replace the bad ones? Or all the statuary, bronzes, hangings, pottery and bogus antiques? Or the tons of bangles, chains of pearls, stomachers, necklaces and other baubles? Assemble all the diamonds into one colossal stone, and you will have a weapon to slay Behemoth. The crowds pour in daily, bringing the wealth wrung from iron and oil, hog and cow. Every dollar earned in Kansas or Montana finds its way, soon or late, to New York, and if there is a part of it that goes back, there is also a part of it that sticks.

What I contend is that this spectacle, lush and barbaric in its every detail, offers the material for a great imaginative literature. There is not only gaudiness in it; there is also a hint of strangeness; it has overtones of the fabulous and even of the diabolical. The thing simply cannot last. If it does not end by catastrophe, then it will end by becoming stale, which is to say, dull. But while it is in full blast it certainly holds out every sort of stimulation that the gifted literatus may plausibly demand. The shocking imbecility of Main Street is there and the macabre touch of Spoon River. But though Main Street and Spoon River have both found their poets, Manhattan is still to be adequately sung. How will the historian of the future get at it, imagining a future and assuming that it will have historians? The story is not written anywhere in official records. It is not in the files of the newspapers, which reflect only the surface, and not even all of that. It will not go into memoirs, for the actors in the melodramatic comedy have no taste for prose, and moreover they are all afraid to tell what they know. What it needs, obviously, is an imaginative artist. We have them in this bursting, stall-fed land—not many of them, perhaps—not as many as our supply of quacks—but nevertheless we have them. The trouble is that they either hate Manhattan too much to do its portrait, or are so bedazzled by it that their hands are palsied and their parts of speech demoralized. Thus we have dithyrambs of Manhattan—but no prose.

I hymn the town without loving it. It is immensely amusing, but I see nothing in it to inspire the fragile and shy thing called affection. I can imagine an Iowan loving the black, fecund stretches of his native State, or a New Englander loving the wreck of Boston, or even a Chicagoan loving Chicago, Loop, stockyards and all, but it is hard for me to fancy any rational human being loving New York. Does one love bartenders? Or interior decorators? Or elevator starters? Or the head-waiters of night clubs? No, one delights in such functionaries, and perhaps one respects them and even reveres them, but one does not love them. They are as palpably cold and artificial as the Cathedral of St. John the Divine. Like it, they are mere functions of solvency. When the sheriff comes in they flutter away. One invests affection in places where it will be safe when the winds blow.

But I am speaking now of spectacles, not of love affairs. The spectacle of New York remains—grand and gorgeous, stimulating like the best that comes out of goblets, and none the worse for its sinister smack. The town seizes upon all the more facile and agreeable emotions like band music. It is immensely trashy—but it remains immense. Is it a mere Utopia of rogues, a vast and complicated machine for rooking honest men? I don't think so. The honest man, going to its market, gets value for his money too. It offers him luxury of a kind never dreamed of in the world before—the luxury of being served by perfect and unobtrusive slaves, human and mechanical. It permits him to wallow regally— nay, almost celestially. The Heaven of the Moslems is open to any one who can pay the *couvert* charge and the honorarium of the hat-check girl—and there is a door, too, leading into the Heaven of the Christians, or, at all events, into every part of it save that devoted to praise and prayer. Nor is all this luxury purely physiological. There is entertainment also for the spirit, or for what passes for the spirit when men are happy. There were more orchestral concerts in New York last Winter than anywhere else on earth. The town, as I have said, is loaded with art to the gunwales, and steadily piling more on deck. Is it unfecund of ideas? Perhaps. But surely it is not hostile to them. There is far more to the show it offers than watching a pretty gal oscillate her hips; one may also hear some other gal, only a shade less sightly, babble the latest discoveries in antinomianism. All kinds, in brief, come in. There are parts for all in the *Totentanz*, even for moralists to call the figures. But there is, as yet, no recorder to put it on paper.

The Devil's Deal

From the Baltimore *Evening Sun*, Feb. 16, 1925

What makes New York so dreadful, I believe, is mainly the fact that the vast majority of its people have been forced to rid themselves of one of the oldest and most powerful of human instincts — the instinct to make a permanent home. Crowded, shoved about and exploited without mercy, they have lost the feeling that any part of the earth belongs to them, and so they simply camp out like hoboes, waiting for the constables to rush in and chase them away. I am not speaking here of the poor (God knows how they exist in New York at all!): I am speaking of the well-to-do, even of the rich. The very richest man, in New York, is never quite sure that the house he lives in now will be his next year — that he will be able to resist the constant pressure of business expansion and rising land values. I have known actual millionaires to be chased out of their homes in this way, and forced into apartments. Here in Baltimore, of course, the same pressure exists, but it is not oppressive, for the householder can meet it by yielding to it half-way. It may force him into the suburbs, even into the adjacent country, but he is still in direct contact with the city, sharing in its life, and wherever he lands he may make a stand. But on Manhattan Island he is quickly brought up by the rivers, and once he has crossed them he may as well move to Syracuse or Trenton.

Nine times out of ten he tries to avoid crossing them. That is, he moves into meaner quarters on the island itself, and pays more for them. His house gives way to a large flat—one offering the same room for his goods and chattels that his house offered. Next year he is in a smaller flat, and half of his goods and chattels have vanished. A few years more, and he is in three or four rooms. Finally, he lands in a hotel. At this point he ceases to exist as the head of a house. His quarters are precisely like the quarters of 50,000 other men. The front he presents to the world is simply an anonymous door on a gloomy corridor. Inside, he lives like a sardine in a can.

The Utopia of Tolerance

From the *Nation*, June 13, 1928, pp. 662–63

As a native and citizen of the Maryland Free State I am, of course, a subject of the United States—but that is about as far as it goes. For the Republic as a whole, I confess, I have very little affection: it amuses and delights me, but never touches me. If the Huns of Japan should launch themselves upon the Pacific Coast tomorrow and begin burning down the chiropractic hospitals and movie cathedrals of Los Angeles, the news would strike me as interesting but not poignant, for I have no investments in that appalling region, and few friends. (San Francisco, to be sure, is something else again, but the Japs are well aware of the fact: they would not burn it.) And if the Huns of the Motherland, assisted by the usual horde of chromatic allies, should take New York, or even Baltimore, it would not perturb me greatly, for the English scheme of things, when all is said and done, is far closer to the Maryland scheme than the American scheme. I was, no doubt, a patriot as a boy, just as I was a teetotaler; I remember glowing, or at all events yelling, when Dewey sank the tin fleet of the Spanish Huns in 1898. But since Good Friday of 1917 such thrills have missed me. It is difficult, indeed, for a man not born a Puritan to glow over the obscene, or even to yell. Moreover, the doctrine was promulgated in those gallant days that, as an American not of British blood and allegiance, I had lost certain of my constitutional rights. I let them go without repining, and sent a flock of duties after them.

Today, whenever my thoughts stray to such lofty and occult matters, I think of myself as a Marylander, not as an Americano. My forebears for three generations lie buried in the Free State, and I was born there myself, and have lived there all my life. I like to dwell upon the fact, and am proud of it. So far as I have been able to find out, no man has ever been jailed in Maryland for his opinions—that is, in my time. Even during the late struggle for human freedom, with the rest of the country handed over bodily to the blacklegs of the Department of Justice, a reasonable liberty survived there. It survives to this day, and even tends to increase. The present Governor of the State is an enlightened and civilized man, and as far from the Fullers as he is from the McCrays. There is no Webster Thayer on the State bench, and there never has been. The Mayor of Baltimore is an honest Moose, and favors fewer laws and lower taxes. Even the State Legislature, though it is ignorant and corrupt, is less ignorant and corrupt than any other State Legislature that I know of, and immensely less so than Congress. There is no State Volstead act in the *Såorstat*. There is no Comstock society. There is no Methodist Board of Morals. The Klan survives only in a few mountain counties, and even there its only recorded tar party landed its whole local membership, along with the wives thereof, in the House of Correction. In the entire United States there are but five great newspapers that are liberal, wet, sinful and intelligent; two of them are in Baltimore.

I could go on thus for columns; maybe even for acres. But the sad, alas, must go with the sweet. The Maryland Free State, by its own misguided generosity, lies adjacent to the District of Columbia, and in the District of Columbia is the city of Washington, and in the city of Washington are gigantic factories for making chains. These chains rattle, ever and anon, over the boundary. They are fastened upon the legs and arms of free Marylanders. Hordes of mercenaries wearing Government badges tote them; it is a facile matter to cross the imaginary line. But the free man, despite the chains, manages somehow to remain a free man. He hopes, and he resists. The two Federal courts in Baltimore spend more and more of their time rescuing Prohibition gunmen from the clutches of the State courts; on some blest tomorrow that benign evasion of the Fourteenth Amendment will break down, and there will be an old-time Maryland hanging, with fireworks in the cool of the evening. I must know thousands of Marylanders, old and young, rich and poor, virtuous and damned. I can recall but two who would honestly deplore that hanging. One is a bootlegger who is also a Quaker. The other is an elderly evangelist who professes to believe every word of the Bible, including the warning against witches, and who alleges that God once appeared to him personally, surrounded by glaring headlights.

The proximity of Washington, the citadel of scoundrels, only makes life in the Free State sweeter to the born and incurable Marylander. It throws up into tremendous relief the difference between the new *mores* of the United States and the traditional *mores* of Maryland. It makes him intensely conscious of his citizenship, and fills him with a vast satisfaction. He is an American legally, but not, thank God, by his own free act. Duties go with his predicament, and he discharges them, but where they end he stops. No heat of 100%. Americanism is in him. He harbors no great, brave urge to snout out, jail, and burn a Sacco and Vanzetti. He views the Klan and the I.W.W. with equal indifference, so long as they keep to rhetoric. There is no law in Maryland against red flags or red oratory. Birth-controllers are free of the air. Even during the war Socialists whooped from their soap-boxes, and went unscathed. Hearst reporters have been jailed in Baltimore for photographing, against his will, a gunman on trial for his life, but on the public street even Hearst reporters are safe, and the cops protect them in their ancient rights. I proceed to marvels: the American Legion, in the Free State, is polite, modest, intelligent, and soldierly. Its grand dragons are men who actually served in the war, and it has made but one attempt to blow up the Bill of Rights. That attempt ended in swift and ignominious disaster, and since then it has been tamer than a tabby cat.

In all this gabble of Maryland notions of the true and the good, of course, I allude to the notions entertained by those Marylanders whose IQ's run well above the middle line. The nether brethren exist there, too, but it is not the Maryland tradition to pay too much heed to them. If, assembled in the Legislature, they enact laws designed to convert Sunday into a day of woe and mourning, there is happily no disposition, save in a few remote and malarious counties, to enforce those laws. The city of Baltimore, as a body corporate, breaks them deliberately and officially, and the grand jury winks at the crime. The Rev. Dr. Billy Sunday was sent in to launch Prohibition, and the price of sound Scotch has been falling ever since. The town wowsers lead the dreary lives of town clowns. Evangelical pastors roar in tin tabernacles behind the railroad tracks, but there is not one of them whose public influence or dignity matches that of an imperial wizard of the Elks.

Do I limn Utopia? Well, why not? Utopia, like virtue, is a concept shot through with relativity. To men in jail, I daresay, the radio is a boon. To men doomed to be Americans the existence of such an asylum as the Free State ought to be comforting. How the more enlightened and self-respecting citizens of Massachusetts, Pennsylvania, Ohio, Mississippi and California can sleep at night is more than I can make out. I always feel vaguely uneasy when my literary apostolate takes me into their ghastly States, as I feel uneasy when I have to go to Washington, or to Paterson, New Jersey, or down in a coal mine. What would follow if the Ohio *Polizei* got a sniff of my baggage? How would it fare, in Mississippi, with one who has publicly argued that Aframericans accused of felony should be tried before being hanged? It is a solace, I assure you, to reflect that numerous swift and swell trains are still running, and that the tariff even from California is less than the cost of trephining a skull, broken by agents of what the heroic open-shoppers out there call the law.

When I cross the line I feel safer and happier. The low moan of Methodist divines comes from the swamps of the Chesapeake littoral, but it is only a moan, not a bark of "Attention!" Even coming from New York, that great city, I notice a change of air. The cops grow polite, and hold their cavalry charges for cases of foreign invasion. The Governor writes his own state papers, disdaining the aid of the reverend clergy. When a still blows up, no one is alarmed. The very Babbitts walk lightly, with eager eyes upon their betters. It could be better, to be sure—but remember what country it is in.

Closed Shop

From the Baltimore *Evening Sun*, Sept. 10, 1923

Why is it that architecture, the one art that none of us can escape, is so immune to public criticism? If an actor wholly without skill appears at one of the local theatres, even the dramatic critics revile him. If the Bentztown Bard rhymes *world* with *boiled*, his customers write in and call him a French spy. If the conductor of the Park Band gets drunk and beats four-four time for a waltz, his first cornetist takes his stick away from him and shoves him under the stand. But an architect is free to assault all of us with the most intolerable aesthetic obscenities without running any risk whatever. There are buildings in Baltimore, public and private, so abominably ugly that looking at them is as shocking as meeting a Tall Cedar of Lebanon in full armor. There are whole rows of houses, particularly in the jerry-built suburbs, that are affronts to every decent human feeling; to condemn poor people to live in them is as much a crime as to condemn them to wear stripes. Yet no one ever protests against such things. Even good architects are silent. Are good poets silent about bad poets? Are surgeons silent about the hawkers of cancer salves? Are honest men silent about burglars, child-stealers, Congressmen, lawyers, and Prohibition enforcement officers?

Washington

From ESSAY IN PEDAGOGY,
PREJUDICES: FIFTH SERIES, 1926, pp. 218–36

The novelists who write about Washington are partly recruited from the ranks of the Washington newspaper correspondents, perhaps the most naïve and unreflective body of literate men in Christendom, and for the rest from the ranks of those who read the dispatches of such correspondents, and take them seriously.

The result is a grossly distorted and absurd picture of life in the capital city. One carries off the notion that the essential Washington drama is based on a struggle between a powerful and corrupt Senator and a sterling young uplifter. The Senator is about to sell out the Republic to the Steel Trust or the Russians. The uplifter detects him, exposes him, drives him from public life, and inherits his job. The love interest is supplied by a fair stenographer who steals the damning papers from the Senator's safe, or by an Ambassador's wife who goes to the White House at 3 A.M., and, at the imminent peril of her virtue, arouses the President and tells him what is afoot. All this is poppycock. There are no Senators in Washington bold enough to carry on any such operations, and very few of them are corrupt: it is too easy to bamboozle them to go to the expense of buying them. The most formidable bribe that the average Senator receives from year's end to year's end is a case or two of very dubious Scotch, and that is just as likely to come from the agent of the South Central Watermelon Growers' Association as from the Money Devils. Nor are there any sterling young uplifters in the town. The last was chased out before the Mexican War. There are today only gentlemen looking for something for themselves—publicity, eminence, puissance, jobs—especially jobs. Some take one line and some another. Further than that the difference between them is no greater than the difference between tweedledum and tweedledee.

Ideas count for nothing in Washington, whether they be political, economic or moral. The question isn't what a man thinks, but what he has to give away that is worth having. Coolidge, while Harding was living, was an obscure and impotent fellow, viewed with contempt by everyone. The instant he mounted the throne he became a Master Mind. Harvey Fergusson got all of this into his "Capitol Hill," the only good Washington novel ever written. It is not the story of a combat between the True and the False in politics; it is the simple tale of a typical Washingtonian's struggle to the front—a tale that should be an inspiration to every larval Rotarian in the land. He begins as a petty job-holder in the Capitol itself, mailing congressional speeches to constituents on the steppes; he ends at the head of a glittering banquet table, with a Senator to one side of him and a member of the Cabinet to the other—a man who has somehow got power into his hands, and can dispense jobs, and is thus an indubitable somebody. Everybody in Washington who has jobs to dispense is somebody.

This eternal struggle is sordid, but, as Fergusson has shown, it is also extremely amusing. It brings out, as the moralists say, the worst that is in human nature, which is always the most charming. It reduces all men to one common level of ignominy, and so rids them of their customary false-faces. They take on a new humanity. Ceasing to be Guardians of the Constitution, Foes to the Interests, Apostles of Economy, Prophets of World Peace, Friends of Labor, and such-like banshees, they become ordinary men, like John Doe and Richard Roe. One beholds them sweating, not liquid idealism, but genuine sweat. I marvel that more American novelists have not gone to this lush and delightful material. The supply is endless and lies wide open. Six months in Washington should be enough to load an ambitious novelist for all eternity.

Interlude in the Socratic Manner

From Appendix from Moronia, Prejudices: Sixth Series, 1927, pp. 297–305. First printed in *Photoplay*, April, 1927, pp. 36–37, 118–20. In the Summer of 1926 I went on a grand tour of the South, to meet editors and look over the ground. At New Orleans I continued west to Los Angeles, where I put in a couple of weeks of pure holiday among the movie folk

Having completed your aesthetic researches at Hollywood, what is your view of the film art now?

I made no researches at Hollywood, and was within the corporate bounds of the town, in fact, only on a few occasions, and then for only few hours. I spent my time in Los Angeles, studying the Christian pathology of that great city. For the rest, I visited friends in the adjacent deserts, some of them employed in the pictures and some not. They treated me with immense politeness. With murderers as thick in the town as evangelists, nothing would have been easier than to have had me killed, but they let me go.

Did any of them introduce you to the wild night-life of the town?

The wildest night-life I encountered was at Sister Aimée Mc-Pherson's tabernacle. I saw no wildness among the movie-folk. They seemed to me, in the main, to be very serious and even gloomy people. And no wonder, for they are worked like Pullman porters or magazine editors. When they are engaged in posturing for a film and have finished their day's labor they are far too tired for any recreation requiring stamina. I encountered but two authentic souses in three weeks. One was a cowboy and the other was an author. I heard of a lady getting tight at a party, but I was not present. The news was a sensation in the town. Such are the sorrows of poor mummers: their most banal peccadilloes are magnified into horrors. Regard the unfortunate Chaplin. If he were a lime and cement dealer his latest divorce case would not have got two lines in the newspapers. But, as it was, he was placarded all over the front pages because he had had a banal disagreement with one of his wives.

So you caught no glimpses of immorality?

Immorality? Oh, my God! Hollywood, despite the smell of patchouli and rattle of revolver fire, seemed to me to be one of the most respectable towns in America. Even Baltimore can't beat it. The notion that actors are immoral fellows is a delusion that comes down to us from Puritan days, just as the delusion that rum is a viper will go down to posterity from our days. There is no truth in it. The typical actor, at least in America, is the most upright of men: he always marries the girl. How many actors are bachelors? Not one in a thousand. The divorce rate is high among them simply because the marriage rate is so high. An actor, encountering a worthy girl, leaps from the couch to the altar almost as fast as a Baptist leaps from the altar to the couch. It is his incurable sentimentality that fetches him: if he was not born a romantic he is not an actor. Worse, his profession supports his natural weakness. In plays and movies he always marries the girl in the end, and so it seems to him to be the decent thing to do it in his private life. Actors always copy the doings of the characters they impersonate: no Oscar was needed to point out that nature always imitates art. I heard, of course, a great deal of gossip in Los Angeles, but all save a trivial part of it was excessively romantic. Nearly every great female star, it appeared, was desperately in love, either with her husband or with some pretty and well-heeled fellow, usually not an actor. And every male star was mooning over some coy and lovely miss. I heard more sweet love stories in three weeks than I had heard in New York in the previous thirty years. The whole place stank of orange-blossoms. Is honest love conducive to vice? Then one may argue that it is conducive to delirium tremens to be a Presbyterian elder. One of the largest industries in Hollywood is that of the florists. Next comes that of the traffickers in wedding silver. One beautiful lady star told me that buying such presents cost her $11,000 last year.

But the tales go 'round. Is there no truth in them at all?

To the best of my knowledge and belief, none. They are believed because the great masses of the plain people, though they admire movie actors, also envy them, and hence hate them. It is the old human story. Why am I hated by theologians? It is because I am an almost unparalleled expert in all branches of theology. Whenever they tackle me, my superior knowledge and talent floor them. In precisely the same way I hate such fellows as the movie Salvini, Jack Gilbert. Gilbert is an amiable and tactful young man, and treats me with the politeness properly due to my years and learning. But I heard in Culver City that no less than 2,000 head of women, many of them rich, were mashed on him. Well, I can recall but fifteen or twenty women who have ever showed any sign of being flustered by me, and not one of them, at a forced sale, would have realized $200. Hence I hate Gilbert, and would rejoice unaffectedly to see him taken in some scandal that would stagger humanity. If he is accused of anything less than murdering his wife and eight children I shall be disappointed.

Then why do you speak for Mr. Chaplin?

Simply because he is not a handsome dog, as Gilbert is. The people who hate him do so because he is rich. It is the thought that his trouble will bust him that gives them delight. But I have no desire for money and so his prosperity does not offend me. I always have too much money; it is easy to get in New York, provided one is not a professing Christian. Gilbert, I suppose, is rich too; he wears very natty clothes. But it is not his wealth that bothers me: it is those 2,000 head of women.

So, failing researches, you continue ignorant of the film art?

Ignorant? What a question! How could any man remain ignorant of the movies after three weeks in Los Angeles? As well continue ignorant of laparotomy after three weeks in a hospital sun-parlor! No, I am full of information about them, some of it accurate, for I heard them talked day and night, and by people who actually knew something about them. There was but one refuge from that talk, and that was La McPherson's basilica. Moreover, I have hatched some ideas of my own.

As for example?

That the movie-folks, in so far as they are sentient at all, are on the hooks of a distressing dilemma. They have built their business upon a foundation of morons, and now they are paying for it. They seem to be unable to make a presentable picture without pouring out tons of money, and when they have made it they must either sell it to immense audiences of half-wits, or go broke. There seems to be very little ingenuity and resourcefulness in them. They are apparently quite unable, despite their melodramatic announcements of salary cuts, to solve the problem of making movies cheaply, and yet intelligently, so that civilized persons may visit the movie-parlors without pain. But soon or late some one will have to solve it. Soon or late the movies will have to split into two halves. There will be movies for the present mob, and there will be movies for the relatively enlightened minority. The former will continue idiotic; the latter, if competent men to make them are unearthed, will show sense and beauty.

Have you caught the scent of any such men?

Not yet. There are some respectable craftsmen in Hollywood. (I judged them by their talk: I have not seen many of their actual pictures.) They tackle the problems of their business in a more or less sensible manner. They have learned a lot from the Germans. But I think it would be stretching a point to say that there are any artists among them—as yet. They are adept, but not inspired. The movies need a first-rate artist—a man of genuine competence and originality. If he is in Hollywood today, he is probably bootlegging, running a pants pressing parlor, or grinding a camera crank. The movie magnates seek him in literary directions. They pin their faith to novelists and playwrights. I presume to believe that this is bad medicine. The fact that a man can write a competent novel is absolutely no reason for assuming that he can write a competent film. The two things are as unlike as Pilsner and Coca-Cola. Even a sound dramatist is not necessarily a competent scenario-writer. What the movies need is a school of authors who will forget all dialogue and description, and try to set forth their ideas in terms of pure motion. It can be done, and it will be done. The German, Dr. Murnau, showed the way in certain scenes of "The Last Laugh." But the American magnates continue to buy bad novels and worse plays, and then put over-worked hacks to the sorry job of translating them into movies. It is like hiring men to translate college yells into riddles. Æschylus himself would have been stumped by such a task.

When do you think the Shakespeare of the movies will appear? And where will he come from?

God knows. He may even be an American, as improbable as it may seem. One thing, only, I am sure of: he will not get much for his masterpieces. He will have to give them away, and the first manager who puts them on will lose money. The movies today are too rich to have any room for genuine artists. They produce a few passable craftsmen, but no artists. Can you imagine a Beethoven making $100,000 a year? If so, then you have a better imagination than Beethoven himself. No, the present movie-folk, I fear, will never quite solve the problem, save by some act of God. They are too much under the heel of the East Side gorillas who own them. They think too much about money. They have allowed it to become too important to them, and believe they couldn't get along without it. This is an unfortunate delusion. Money is important to mountebanks, but not to artists. The first really great movie, when it comes at last, will probably cost less than $5,000. A true artist is always a romantic. He doesn't ask what the job will pay; he asks if it will be interesting. In this way all the loveliest treasures of the human race have been fashioned—by careless and perhaps somewhat foolish men. The late Johann Sebastian Bach, compared to a movie star with nine automobiles, was simply a damned fool. But I cherish the feeling that a scientific inquiry would also develop other differences between them.

Are you against the star system?

I am neither for it nor against it. A star is simply a performer who pleases the generality of morons better than the average. Certainly I see no reason why such a performer should not be paid a larger salary than the average. The objection to swollen salaries should come from the stars themselves—that is, assuming them to be artists. The system diverts them from their proper business of trying to produce charming and amusing movies, and converts them into bogus society folk. What could be more ridiculous? And pathetic? I go further: it is tragic. As I have said in another place, nothing is more tragic in this world than for otherwise worthy people to meanly admire and imitate mean things. One may have some respect for the movie lady who buys books and sets up as an intellectual, for it is a creditable thing to want to be (or even simply to want to appear) well-informed and intelligent. But I can see nothing worthy in wanting to be mistaken for the president of a bank. Artists should sniff at such dull drudges, not imitate them. The movies will leap ahead the day some star in Hollywood organizes a string quartette and begins to study Mozart.

San Francisco: A Memory

From the Baltimore *Evening Sun*, July 21, 1920. San Francisco, of course, has gone downhill since this was written. The influx of Okies during the Depression, of Negroes during World War II, and of labor racketeers over the years has afflicted it sorely, and it has been even more sadly afflicted by the drag of the great congeries of morons gathered at Los Angeles. But it is still, I believe, fairer than any other American city. It is still *sui generis*

What is it that lifts San Francisco out of the common American wallow? I am not at all sure. It may be something intrinsic—specifically, something ethnological. The stock out there differs visibly from any Eastern stock I know. It is not that half of the people are actually foreigners, for that is also true of New York; it is that the native born belong to a distinct strain, mentally and physically—that the independence and virility of the Argonauts are still in them—that their blood is still running hot and clear. Above all, remember the recentness of this heritage. They are not the children of men who were bold and daring in the Seventeenth Century, but the children of men who were bold and daring in the mid-Nineteenth. There were very few pants-pressers and bookkeepers among their fathers. I met a man in the Bohemian Club who began to tell me casually of his grandmother. This lady, an Irishwoman of good birth, came to California from Ireland in 1849, by way of Panama. Imagine the journey: the long sea voyage, the infernal struggle across the Isthmus, the worse trip up the coast, the trek inland. Well, she brought a piano with her—got it aboard ship in Ireland, guarded it all the way to Panama, dragged it through the jungle, then shipped it again, and finally packed it to her home in the hills. I daresay many of us could find such grandmothers, going back far enough. But in 1849? The Baltimore grandmothers of 1849 were sitting snugly by the new Latrobe stoves, reading "Dombey and Son" and knitting tidies.

Mere geography helps, with a polite bow to meteorology. The climate, to an Easterner, is almost too invigorating. The heat of the Sacramento Valley sucks in such cold breezes through the Golden Gate that they over-stimulate like raw alcohol. An Arctic current comes down the coast, and the Pacific is so chilly that sea bathing is almost impossible, even in mid-Summer. Coming off this vast desert of ice water, the San Francisco winds tickle and sting. One arises in the morning with a gigantic sense of fitness—a feeling of superb well-being. Looking out at the clear yellow sunlight, one is almost tempted to crow like a rooster. It is a land of magnificent mornings. But of somewhat less magnificent nights, at least to one from the East. The thrill of it leads to over-estimates. One suffers from the optimism of a man full of champagne. Toward evening, perhaps, a clammy fog rolls in, and one begins to feel a sudden letting down. The San Franciscans have learned how to bear it. They are stupendously alive while they are in motion, but they knock off betimes. The town is rich in loafing places—restaurants, theatres, parks. No one seems to work very hard. The desperate, consuming industry of the East is quite unknown. One could hardly imagine a sweatshop in the town. Puffs of Oriental air come with the fog. There is nothing European about the way life is lived; the color is all Asiatic.

Now imagine the scene. A peninsula with the Pacific on one side of it and the huge bay on the other—a peninsula bumpy with bold, precipitous hills, some of them nearly 1,000 feet high. The San Franciscans work in the valleys and live on the hills. Cable cars haul them up in a few minutes, or they make the voyage in astonishing taxicabs—taxicabs that seem capable of running up a high roof. Coming down on foot, one hugs the houses. Going up on foot—but I had better confine myself to what I know.

The scene is more beautiful than any along the Grand Corniche; from the Twin Peaks San Francisco makes Monaco seem tawdry and trivial. Ahead is the wide sweep of the bay, with the two great shoulders of the Golden Gate running down. Behind is the long curtain of California mountains. And below is the town itself—great splashes of white, pink and yellow houses climbing the lesser hills—houses often sprawling and ramshackle, but nevertheless grouping themselves into lovely pictures, strange and charming. No other American town looks like that. It is a picture out of the East—dazzling, exotic and curiously romantic.

This foreign and half barbaric color gets into everything. One notices it at once without being able precisely to define it. There is the thing that no Atlantic town has ever been able to manage— gayety without grossness. The place is wide open, but not in the way that New York is wide open—vulgarly, garishly, hoggishly. The business is achieved with an air, almost a grand manner. It is good-humored, engaging, innocent. There is no heavy attitude of raising the Devil. One may guzzle as one will, but one may also drink decently and in order, and shake a leg in the style of Haydn, and lift an eye to a pretty girl without getting knocked in the head or having one's pocket picked. It is a friendly place, a spacious and tolerant place, a place heavy with strangeness and charm. It is no more American, in the sense that American has come to carry, than a wine festival in Spain or the carnival at Nice.

Boston

From the Baltimore *Evening Sun*, July 21, 1920

A potter's field; a dissecting-room.

Philadelphia

From the same

An intellectual slum.

XIII. THE WRITER IN AMERICA

The National Letters

From PREJUDICES: SECOND SERIES, 1920, pp. 87–90

WHAT AILS the beautiful letters of the Republic is what ails the general culture of the Republic—the lack of a body of sophisticated and civilized public opinion, independent of plutocratic or governmental control and superior to the infantile philosophies of the mob—a body of opinion showing the eager curiosity, the educated skepticism and the hospitality to ideas of a true aristocracy. This lack is felt by the American author, imagining him to have anything new to say, every day of his life. He can hope for no support, in ordinary cases, from the mob: it is too suspicious of all ideas. He can hope for no support from the spokesmen of the plutocracy: they are too diligently devoted to maintaining the intellectual *status quo*. He turns, then, to the *intelligentsia*—and what he finds is correctness. In his two prime functions, to represent the life about him accurately and to criticize it honestly, he sees that correctness arrayed against him. His representation is indecorous, unlovely, too harsh to be borne. His criticism is in contumacy to the ideals upon which the whole structure rests. So he is either attacked vigorously as an anti-patriot whose babblings ought to be put down by law, or enshrouded in a silence which commonly disposes of him even more effectively.

Soon or late, of course, a man of genuine force and originality is bound to prevail against that sort of stupidity. He will unearth an adherent here and another there; in the long run they may become numerous enough to force some recognition of him, even from the most immovable exponents of correctness. But the business is slow, uncertain, heart-breaking. It puts a burden upon the artist that ought not to be put upon him. It strains beyond reason his diligence and passion. A man who devotes his life to creating works of the imagination, a man who gives over all his strength and energy to struggling with problems that are essentially delicate and baffling and pregnant with doubt—such a man does not ask for recognition as a mere reward for his industry; he asks for it as a necessary *help* to his industry; he needs it as he needs decent subsistence and peace of mind. It is a grave damage to the artist and a grave loss to the literature when such a man as Poe has to seek consolation among his inferiors, and such a man as the Mark Twain of "What Is Man?" is forced to conceal his most profound beliefs. The notion that artists flourish upon adversity and misunderstanding, that they are able to function to the utmost in an atmosphere of indifference or hostility—this notion is nine-tenths nonsense. What the artist actually needs is comprehension of his aims and ideals by men he respects—not necessarily approval of his products, but simply an intelligent sympathy for him in the agony of creation. And that sympathy must be more than the mere fellow-feeling of other craftsmen; it must come, in large part, out of a connoisseurship that is beyond the bald trade interest; it must have its roots in the intellectual curiosity of an aristocracy of taste. Billroth, I believe, was more valuable to Brahms than even Schumann. His eager interest gave music-making a solid dignity. His championship offered the musician a visible proof that his labors had got for him a secure place in a civilized society, and that he would be judged by his peers, and safeguarded against the obtuse hostility of his inferiors.

No such security is thrown about an artist in America. The recurrent outbreaks of Comstockery are profoundly symbolical. What they show is the moral certainty of the mob in operation against something that is as incomprehensible to it as the theory of least squares, and what they show even more vividly is the distressing lack of any automatic corrective of that outrage—of any firm and secure body of educated opinion, eager to hear and test all intelligible ideas and sensitively jealous of the right to discuss them freely. When "The Genius" was attacked by the Comstocks, it fell to my lot to seek assistance for Dreiser among the *intelligentsia*. I found them almost unanimously disinclined to lend a hand. A small number permitted themselves to be induced, but the majority held back, and not a few actually offered more or less furtive aid to the Comstocks. I pressed the matter and began to unearth reasons. It was, it appeared, dangerous for a member of the *intelligentsia*, and particularly for a member of the academic *intelligentsia*, to array himself against the mob inflamed. If he came forward, he would have to come forward alone. There was no organized support behind him. No instinctive urge of class, no prompting of a great tradition, moved him to speak out.

The Emperor of Wowsers

From PREJUDICES: SECOND SERIES, 1920, pp. 87–90.
A review of ANTHONY COMSTOCK:
ROUNDSMAN OF THE LORD,
by Heywood Broun and Margaret Leech; New York, 1926.
First printed in the New York *Herald Tribune*, March 6, 1927

In an appendix to this amusing and instructive work, Mr. Broun states the case against Comstockery in a neat, realistic and unanswerable manner, but the book itself is by no means a philippic against old Anthony. On the contrary, it deals with him in a very humane and even ingratiating way. And why not? He was, in point of fact, a man of manifold virtues, and even his faults showed a rugged, Berserker quality that was sneakingly charming. It is quite impossible, at this distance, to doubt his *bona fides*, and almost as difficult, despite his notorious extravagances, to question his essential sanity. Like all the rest of us in our several ways, he was simply a damned fool. Starting out in life with an idea lying well within the bounds of what most men would call the rational, he gradually pumped it up until it bulged over all four borders. But he never departed from it altogether; he never let go his hold upon logic; he never abandoned reason for mere intuition. Once his premises were granted, the only way to escape his conclusions was to forsake Aristotle for Epicurus. Such logical impeccability, as all connoisseurs must know, is very common among theologians; they hold, indeed, almost a monopoly of it. The rest of us, finding that

our ratiocination is leading us into uncomfortable waters, give it
the slip and return to dry land. But not the theologians. They have
horribly literal minds; they are less men than intellectual machines. I defy any one to find a logical flaw in their proofs of the
existence of Hell. They demonstrate it magnificently and irrefut-
ably. Do multitudes of wise men nevertheless deny it? Then that
is only because very few wise men have any honest belief in the
reality of the thing that the theologians and other logicians call
truth.

Mr. Broun, in his appendix, tries to find holes in Anthony's
logic, but it turns out to be far from easy: what he arrives at, in the
end, is mainly only proof that a logician is an immensely unpleasant fellow. Turn, for example, to a typical and very familiar
Comstockian syllogism. First premiss: The effect of sexual images,
upon the young, is to induce auto-erotism. Second premiss: the effects of auto-erotism are idiocy, epilepsy and locomotor ataxia.
Ergo, now is the time for all good men to put down every book or
picture likely to evoke sexual images. What is wrong with all this?
Simply that Mr. Broun and you and I belong to a later generation
than Anthony's, and are thus skeptical of his premises. But let us
not forget that they were true for him. His first came out of the
hard, incontrovertible experience of a Puritan farm-boy, in executive session behind the barn. His second was supported, when he
was getting his education, by the almost unanimous medical opinion of Christendom. And so his conclusion was perfect. We have
made no progress in logic since his time; we have simply made
progress in skepticism. All his grand truths are now dubious, and
most of them are laughed at even by sucklings.

I think that he himself had a great deal to do with upsetting
them. The service that he performed, in his grandiose way, was no
more than a magnification of the service that is performed every
day by multitudes of humble Y.M.C.A. secretaries, evangelical
clergymen, and other such lowly fauna. It is their function in the
world to ruin their ideas by believing in them and living them.
Striving sincerely to be patterns to the young, they suffer the ironical fate of becoming horrible examples. I remember very well,
how, as a boy of ten, I was articled to the Y.M.C.A.: the aim was
to improve my taste for respectability, and so curb my apparently
natural flair for the art and mystery of the highwayman. But a few

months of contact with the official representatives of that great organization filled me with a vast loathing, not only for the men themselves, but also for all the ideas they stood for. Thus, at the age of eleven, I abandoned Christian Endeavor forevermore, and have been an antinomian ever since, contumacious to holy men and resigned to Hell. Old Anthony, I believe, accomplished much the same thing that the Y.M.C.A. achieved with me, but on an immeasurably larger scale. He did more than any other man to ruin Puritanism in the United States. When he began his long and brilliant career of unwitting sabotage, the essential principles of Comstockery were believed in by practically every reputable American. Half a century later, when he went upon the shelf, Comstockery enjoyed a degree of public esteem, at least in the big cities, halfway between that enjoyed by phrenology and that enjoyed by homosexuality. It was, at best, laughable. It was, at worst, revolting.

So much did one consecrated man achieve in the short span of his life. I believe that it was no mean accomplishment. Anthony managed it, not because there was any unusual ability in him, but simply because he had a congenital talent for giving shows. The fellow, in his way, was a sort of Barnum. A band naturally followed him, playing in time to his yells. He could not undertake even so banal a business as raiding a dealer in abortifacient pills without giving it the melodramatic air of a battle with a brontosaurus. So a crowd always followed him, and when he made a colossal ass of himself, which was very frequently, the fact was bruited about. Years of such gargantuan endeavor made him one of the national clowns—and his cause one of the national jokes. In precisely the same way, I believe, such gaudy zanies as the Rev. Dr. Billy Sunday are ruining the evangelical demonology in the Bible Belt. They make so much uproar that no one can fail to notice them. The young peasants, observing them, are gradually enlightened by them—unintentionally, but none the less surely. The men themselves are obviously charlatans; *ergo*, their ideas must be fraudulent too. What has been the net effect of the Scopes trial, with its solemn martyrdom of William Jennings Bryan? Its chief effect seems to be that societies of young atheists are now flourishing in all the Southern colleges. Has the study of Darwin been put down? Far from it. Darwin is now being read below the Potomac, and by the flower of Christian youth, as assiduously as "Only a

Boy" used to be read in New York in the great days of Anthony's
historic offensive against it.

Comstockery, of course, still lives, but it must be manifest that
its glories have greatly faded. There is, anon, a series of raids and
uproars, but they soon pass, and the work of the Devil goes on. It
would be hard to imagine Anthony taking orders from district attorneys, or going into amicable conference with his enemies (and
God's), or consenting to the appointment of joint committees
(mainly made up of obvious anti-Puritans) to discover and protect
the least dirty among the dirty plays of Broadway; he would have
raided them all, single-handed and alone. His heirs and assigns are
far milder men, and hence, I sometimes fear, more dangerous.
Their sweet reasonableness is disarming; it tends to conceal the
fact that they are nevertheless blue-noses at heart, and quite as
eager to harry and harass the rest of us as Anthony was. Those opponents who now parley with them had better remember the
warning against making truces with Adam-Zad. They may end by
restoring to Comstockery some of its old respectability, and so
throw us back to where we were during the Grant administration.
I sound the warning and pass on. It will take, at best, a long time,
and I'll be beyond all hope or caring before it is accomplished. For
Anthony's ghost still stalks the scenes of his old endeavors, to
plague and palsy his successors. His name has given a term of op-
probrium to the common tongue. Dead, and—as Mr. Broun and
Miss Leech so beautifully suggest, an angel with harp, wings and
muttonchops—he is yet as alive as Pecksniff, Chadband or Elmer
Gantry.

Well, here is his story, done fully, competently, and with excellent manners. There is much in it that you will not find in the
earlier biography by Charles Gallaudet Trumbull, for Trumbull
wrote for the Sunday-schools, and so had to do a lot of pious dodging and snuffling. The additional facts that Mr. Broun and Miss
Leech set forth are often very amusing, but I must add at once that
they are seldom discreditable. Old Anthony was preposterous, but
not dishonest. He believed in his idiotic postulates as devotedly as
a Tennessee Baptist believes that a horse-hair put into a bottle of
water will turn into a snake. His life, as he saw it, was one of sacrifice for righteousness. Born with a natural gift for the wholesale
drygoods trade, he might have wrung a fortune from its practice,

and so won an heroic equestrian statue in the Cathedral of St. John the Divine. Perhaps there were blue days when regret crept over him, shaking his Christian resolution. His muttonchop whiskers, the stigma and trademark of the merchant princes of his era, had a pathetic, Freudian smack. But I don't think he wobbled often. The Lord was always back of him, guiding and stimulating his fighting arm. So he was content to live in a drab suburb on the revenues of a second-rate lawyer, with his elderly, terrified wife and his half-witted foster-daughter. There was never any hint, in that humble home, of the gaudy connubial debaucheries that the modern sex hygienists describe so eloquently. Anthony had to go outside for his fun. Comstockery was his corner saloon.

I confess to a great liking for the old imbecile. He is one of my favorite characters in American history, along with Frances E. Willard, Daniel Drew and Brigham Young. He added a great deal to the joys of life in the Federal Republic. More than any other man, he liberated American letters from the blight of Puritanism.

Transcendentalism

From An Unheeded Law-Giver,
Prejudices: First Series, 1919, pp. 191–94.
First printed in the *Smart Set*, July, 1919, pp. 68–69

What one notices about Ralph Waldo Emerson chiefly is his profound lack of influence upon the main stream of American thought, such as it is. His cult, in America, has been an affectation from the start. Not many of the literary professors, vassarized old maids and other such bogus *intelligentsia* who devote themselves to it have any intelligible understanding of the Transcendentalism at the heart of it, and not one of them, so far as I can make out, has ever executed Emerson's command to "defer never to the popular cry." On the contrary, it is precisely within the circle of Emersonian adulation that one finds the greatest tendency to test all ideas by their respectability, to combat free thought as something intrinsically vicious, and to yield placidly to "some great decorum, some fetish of a government, some ephemeral trade, or war, or man." It is surely not unworthy of notice that the country of this prophet of Man Thinking is precisely the country in which every sort of dissent from the current pishposh is combated most ferociously, and in which there is the most vigorous existing tendency to suppress free speech altogether.

Thus Emerson, on the side of ideas, has left but faint tracks behind him. His quest was for "facts amidst appearances," and his whole metaphysic revolved around a doctrine of transcendental first causes, a conception of interior and immutable realities, distinct from and superior to mere transient phenomena. But the philosophy that actually prevails among his countrymen—a philosophy put into caressing terms by William James—teaches an almost exactly contrary doctrine: its central idea is that whatever satisfies the immediate need is substantially true, that appearance is the only form of fact worthy the consideration of a man with money in the bank, and the old flag floating over him, and hair on his chest. Nor has Emerson had any ponderable influence as a literary artist in the technical sense. There is no Emersonian school of American writers. Current American writing, with its cocksureness, its somewhat hard competence, its air of selling goods, is utterly at war with his loose, impressionistic method, his often mystifying groping for ideas, his relentless pursuit of phrases. In the same way, one searches the country in vain for any general reaction to the cultural ideal that he set up. What remains of him at home is no more than, on the one hand, a somewhat absurd affectation of intellectual fastidiousness, now almost extinct even in New England, and, on the other hand, a debased Transcendentalism rolled into pills for fat women with vague pains and inattentive husbands—in brief, imbecility.

The Man of Letters

From The National Letters,
Prejudices: Second Series, 1920, pp. 52–54

The man of letters, pure and simple, is a rarity in America. Almost always he is something else—and that something else commonly determines his public eminence. Mark Twain, with only his books to recommend him, would probably have passed into obscurity in middle age; it was in the character of a public entertainer that he wooed and won his country. The official criticism of the land denied him any solid literary virtue to the day of his death, and even today the campus critics and their journalistic valets stand aghast before "The Mysterious Stranger" and "What Is Man?" Emerson passed through almost the same experience. It was not as a man of letters that he was chiefly thought of in his time, but as the prophet of a new cult, half religious, half philosophical, and wholly unintelligible to nine-tenths of those who discussed it. So with Whitman and Poe—both hobgoblins far more than artists. So, even, with Howells: it was as the exponent of a dying culture that he was venerated, not as the practitioner of an art. Few actually read his books. His celebrity, of course, was real enough, but it somehow differed materially from that of a pure man of letters—say Conrad, Meredith, Hardy or Synge. That he was himself keenly aware of the national tendency to judge an artist in terms of the citizen was made plain at the time of the Gorky scandal, when he joined Clemens in an ignominious desertion of Gorky, scared out of his wits by the danger of being manhandled for a violation of the national pecksniffery.

They Also Serve

From the Baltimore *Evening Sun*, April 23, 1923

The Civil War in America ruined the South, and for two generations after Lee's surrender it was almost as inert artistically as Mexico or Asia Minor; even today it lags very far behind the North in letters, and still further behind in music, painting and architecture. But the Civil War, though it went on for four years, strained the resources of the North very little, either in men or in money, and so its conclusion found the North rich and cocky, and out of that cockiness came an impetus which, in a few decades, set up a new and extremely vigorous American literature, founded an

American school of painting, created an American architecture, and even laid the first courses of an American music. Mark Twain, Walt Whitman, Henry James and William Dean Howells, all of them draft-dodgers in the war itself, were in a very real sense products of the great outburst of energy that followed it, and all of them, including even James, were as thoroughly American as Jay Gould, P. T. Barnum or Jim Fiske. The stars of the national letters in the years before the war had been Americans only by geographical accident. About Emerson there hung a smell of Königsberg and Weimar; Irving was simply a New York Englishman; Poe was a citizen of No Man's Land; even Hawthorne and Cooper, despite their concern with American themes, showed not the slightest evidence of an American point of view. But Mark Twain, Howells and Whitman belonged to the Republic as palpably as Niagara Falls or Tammany Hall belonged to it, and so did James, though the thought horrified him and we must look at him through his brother William to get at the proof.

Once More, with Feeling

From the *Smart Set*, Aug., 1916, pp. 141–43

The history of American literature (and of English literature no less) is one long chronicle of publishers' imbecilities. The early books of Edgar Allan Poe, now run up in the auction rooms to hundreds and even thousands of dollars, were brought out, not by the leading publisher of Poe's time, nor, indeed, by any recognized publisher at all, but by what were really no more than neighborhood job printers. So with the books of Whitman; even to this day he is printed, not by the solemn booksellers who gabble about their high services to literature, but by smaller and more obscure fellows. Try to pick up the early books of Ambrose Bierce; you will find imprints you never heard of before. As for Mark Twain, he had to start a publishing house of his own to get a free hand. True enough, when this venture failed (through the fault of his partners) he went back to a regular publisher—but with what result?

With the result that it is quite impossible to buy a satisfactory edition of his collected works today. The only edition on the market contains many volumes that lack all, or a major part, of the original illustrations. Imagine "Huckleberry Finn" without Kemble's pictures—the best illustrations, it seems to me, that any book in English has ever had. Moreover, six years after his death his posthumous works remain unpublished, and among them, according to his biographer, are at least two books in his very best manner.

A glance at the first editions of Joseph Conrad (now selling for as much as $30 apiece, though the earliest goes back no further than 1895) shows what a hard time he had finding an appreciative publisher. The first eleven bear six different London imprints. His American editions tell an even stranger story: the first six of them were brought out by six different publishers. When a few years ago, the firm of Doubleday, Page & Co. conceived the plan of reprinting his books in a uniform edition, it was found impossible to bring together the widely dispersed rights to all of them, and the uniform edition is still full of gaps, and such important works as "Nostromo" and "An Outcast of the Islands" are not in it. I salute this firm for its enterprise—but do not forget that its chief claim to fame is that it suppressed Dreiser's "Sister Carrie." Today it makes amends by publishing Gerald Stanley Lee and Gene Stratton Porter—surely sweet companions for Conrad, who is bedizened for the department-store trade, by the way, in navy-blue limp leather and all the other gaudy trappings of Corn Belt *Kultur*. The Harpers, after an obscure publisher had shown the way, took over "Sister Carrie"—and then made their own bid for immortality by jumping from under "The Titan." The present publisher of the leading American novelist is the *English* firm of John Lane. . . .

Another mystery of publishing is to be found in the incomprehensible system by which review copies are distributed. I have been reviewing books for fifteen years past, and have had that system under my eye all the while, and yet I do no more understand it today than I understand liturgical Russian. Whenever I find an author who pleases me and take to praising him lavishly in these pages and calling upon all Christian men to buy him and read him, his publisher is sure to stop sending me his books. And if, on the contrary, I try some poor devil of a scribbler by the *lex talionis* and do execution upon him with Prussian frightfulness, his publisher invariably sends me all of his ensuing works, and favors me with idiotic circular letters testifying to their unquestioned merit. I get, almost every week, books that, under no imaginable circumstances, could be reviewed to any purpose in the *Smart Set*—for example, books for little girls, books upon economics and trade, and even scientific books. At least twice during the past year I have been at pains to explain that I do not review war books—that it is the policy of this magazine (copiously supported by the gratitude of its readers) to avoid any discussion of the war, even in fiction or poetry. Nevertheless, I continue to receive nearly all the war books that are published, including the current treatises on preparedness by college boys, old maids, newspaper reporters and job-seekers. More, this present note will not shut off the stream. During the month following its publication I shall receive at least thirty such tomes, despite three fair warnings that all of them will go into my hell-box unread. The Barabbasian skull seems to be of four-ply celluloid; it takes a fearful battering to penetrate it. Or can it be that publishers never read reviews? It is supported by the obvious fact that they never read the books they publish.

XIV. THE NOVEL

The Novel Defined

From the *Smart Set*, Jan., 1909, p. 153

Q. WHAT IS a novel?

A. A novel is an imaginative, artistic and undialectic composition in prose, not less than 20,000 nor more than 500,000 words in length, and divided into chapters, sections, books or other symmetrical parts, in which certain interesting, significant and probable (though fictitious) human transactions are described both in cause and effect, with particular reference to the influence exerted upon the ideals, opinions, morals, temperament and overt acts of some specified person or persons by the laws, institutions, superstitions of the human race, and the natural phenomena of such portions of the earth as may come under his, her or their observation or cognizance, and by the ideals, opinions, morals, temperament and overt acts of such person or persons as may come into contact, either momentarily or for longer periods, with him, her or them, either by actual, social or business intercourse, or through the medium of books, newspapers, the church, the theater or some other person or persons.

This definition represents the toil of several days and makes severe demands upon both eye and attention, but it is well worth the time spent upon it and the effort necessary to assimilate it, for it is entirely without loophole, blowhole or other blemish. It describes, with scientific accuracy, every real novel ever written, and by the same token, it bars out every last near-novel, pseudo-novel and quasi-novel, however colorable, and every romance, rhapsody, epic, saga, stuffed short story, tract and best-seller known to bibliographers.

Second Chorus

From the *Smart Set*, June, 1914, pp. 153–54

Discoursing in this place so long ago as the year 1909, I made a plain bid for the applause of the learned with a definition of the novel. This definition was a very fair specimen of lexicography—in 1909. But human knowledge has made great progress during the long years intervening, and so it is now possible to improve it, chiefly in the direction of making it more succinct. Bidding, as I say, for the applause of the learned, I stuffed it with sonorous but useless words, thus playing the sedulous ape to the learned themselves. Today I empty it, shrink it, chop off its excrescences. The result is this:

> A novel is a prose narrative of fictitious events, in which one or more normal persons are shown in reaction against a definite and probable series of external stimuli and a real state of civilization.

Here we have the novel in a nutshell, and yet no essential element is missing. The thing defined is not fiction in general, nor even prose fiction in general, but the novel in particular. All other forms of imaginative writing, however closely they may approximate it in this way or that, are excluded. The epic and the ballad, though grandparents of the novel, are barred out by the word "prose"; the drama, though its father and mother, by the word "narrative"; the moral fable, its feebleminded brother, by the word "probable." The romance, though it may deal, at least in part, with the passions and aspirations that move all of us, cannot get in: the state of civilization in Zenda is not "real" and heroes seven feet eight inches in height are not "normal." And the simple tale, the bald story, the plot in the altogether—we know it best as the detective story, the best-seller—this powerful stimulant of the liver and midriff is outlawed, too, for though it may enter into the making of a novel, its lack of attachment to a definite background prevents it being a novel itself.

It is the background, indeed, that chiefly marks the novel, and after the background, the normality of the people under observation. The aim in a genuine novel is not merely to describe a particular man, but to describe a typical man, and to show him in active conflict with a more or less permanent and recognizable environment—fighting it, taking color from it, succumbing to it. If that environment sinks into indistinctiveness or unimportance, if it might be changed, let us say, from the England of 1870 to the England of 1914 without materially modifying the whole character and experience of the man—or, as the ancient Greeks used to call him, the protagonist—then the story of his adventures is scarcely a novel at all, but merely a tale *in vacuo*, a disembodied legend, the dry bones of a novel. The better the novel, indeed, the more the man approaches Everyman, and the more the background overshadows him. In the average best-seller he is superb, irresistible and wholly autonomous. He is the easy master of every situation that his environment confronts him with; he is equally successful at killing cannibals, snaring burglars, operating airships, terrorizing the stock market or making love. He is not the product and plaything of fate, but its boss. The world is his oyster.

But as we ascend the scale of art and sense we find the protagonist gradually losing his superhuman efficiency. More and more he is swayed and conditioned by the civilization around him; the thing he does is not the forthright and magnificent thing that he would perhaps *like* to do, but the prudent and customary thing, that he *can* do; as the zoölogists say, he takes on protective coloration as he learns wisdom by experience. And when we get among masterpieces, we find that he tends to become no more than a function of his environment, a convenient symbol for representing and explaining that environment. The center of interest in "Lord Jim" is not so much he himself as the universal and overwhelming prejudice which drives him beyond the pale of the white man, and the vast, barbaric darkness which engulfs him. And in "Huckleberry Finn" it is not Huck as an individual that holds us, but the Eternal Boy within him and the Old South around him. And in "Henry Esmond" it is not Henry, nor even his Beatrice, but the London of Queen Anne. And in "Kim" it is the inscrutable East. And in "The Brothers Karamazov" it is brooding Russia.

On Realism

From the Chicago *Tribune*, Aug. 15, 1926

One of the strangest delusions of criticism is to be found in the notion that there is such a thing as realism—that is, realism grounded on objective fact in the same way that a scientific monograph, say, or the report of a law trial, is grounded upon objective fact. Nothing of the sort is imaginable. The arts do not and cannot deal with reality, for the moment they begin to do so they cease to be arts. Their function is something quite different, and even antagonistic. It is not to photograph the world, but to edit and improve the world. It is not to embrace the whole, but to select and exhibit the salient part. It is not to echo life, but to show a way of escape from life.

But perhaps I succumb to phrases. What I mean to say, in plain language, is that no genuine artist would paint a picture if he were completely satisfied with the thing he depicts. His dissatisfaction is precisely what makes him an artist: he is moved by a yearning to put in something or take out something, to make a comment, to frame a gloss upon the word of God—or, as it is usually put, to express himself. And the measure of his virtue as an artist lies in that contribution, not in what he takes bodily from nature. If what he has to say is novel and charming, then he is a good artist. If what he has to say is trite and dull, then he is a bad one. The first and last thing is what he has to say.

Certainly all this should be obvious, but for some reason or other it seems to be not so. I have read of late a long essay on James Joyce's "Ulysses," praising it in high, astounding terms as a complete and exact record of a day in the life of its people. It is, of course, nothing of the sort. At least nine-tenths of its materials came, not out of the Bloom family, but out of James Joyce. Even the celebrated unspoken monologue of Molly at the end is his, not hers. There are long sections of it that even the professional psychologists, who are singularly naïve, must detect as false—that is, false for Molly, false for a woman of her position, perhaps even false for any woman. But they are not false for Joyce.

Some years ago I enjoyed the somewhat laborious honor of reading, in manuscript, a new novel by a well-known American novelist, greatly esteemed for his fidelity to the metaphysical bug-aboo known as the truth. It was, in more than one way, a work of high merit, but it had a number of obvious defects. One was a painful superabundance of irrelevant detail. Another was an excess of detail of a sort likely to arouse the libido of the Comstocks, and so get the book a bad name. I called this last blemish to the atten-tion of the author, pointing especially to a scene depicting what has since come to be called a petting party. At once he rose to high dudgeon. "You are," he roared, "a — — — — — —. You are asking me to make my story false. It is like asking a woman to cut off the ears of her child. What you object to actually happened. It had to happen. It was inevitable. I defy you to describe a petting party without mentioning it."

I did not accept the challenge, but proceeded by a more indi-rect route. That is to say, I described the same petting party in dif-ferent terms. I included all the details that my eminent friend had included, but then went on to include some details of my own. The first brought him up. "But you can't—" he began, in some agitation.

"Did it happen?" I demanded. "Am I going outside the record?"

He retreated behind indignation, and I proceeded. My second canto drove him out of the room. But while I was in the midst of my fifth or sixth he returned and proposed peace. "You are quite right," he said. "It is impossible to tell it all. I thought I was doing it, but I see now that I really wasn't. Every passage you have ob-jected to comes out."

But this was going too far, and so I protested in turn. "Not at all," I said. "If they are true to you, then they stay in. It is your book, not mine. It doesn't represent objective reality; it represents your reaction to reality. Did those passages seem sound and inev-itable when you wrote them? Then they stay in."

So they stayed in, and the Comstocks duly raided the book.

Thus argument, as usual, led only to contradiction, enmity and disaster. On another such occasion the consequences were less de-plorable. I have another friend, a distinguished anatomical artist, whose drawings are celebrated for their precise and merciless fidel-ity to nature. He paints landscapes quite as well as livers and

lights, but in the same way. He is strongly against the new movement in painting, and believes that it is the artist's highest duty to
present the object depicted exactly as it stands. One day I told this
gentleman that I'd like to have a specimen of his work, and he presented me forthwith with a truly marvelous drawing. It represented, he told me, a kidney in the last stages of some dreadful
disease, and was to be reproduced in a forthcoming medical work.
Knowing nothing of kidneys, I could admire it as a work of art,
and as such it seemed to me to be magnificent. So greatly did I esteem it that I had it framed and hung in my office, that visiting
customers might share my pleasure in it.

The first visitor to see it was a critic of painting. He anchored
himself before it and gazed at it for ten minutes. "How do you like
it?" I asked at length.

"It is superb," he said. "Leonardo himself was not a better draftsman. You have a masterpiece. Where did you get it?"

"Do you know what it represents?" I asked.

"No," said the critic. "Who cares what it represents? It may be
whatever you choose to call it. All it represents to me is a first-rate
draftsman. The fellow can draw. And he has something to say."
Whereupon, in the manner of art critics, my friend proceeded to
a disquisition unintelligible to me. But one thing, at least, I understood: that this master realist had not fetched him by realism.

In so far as it has any meaning at all, indeed, realism simply
means the opposite of consciously false. Daisy Ashford's "The
Young Visiters" was brilliantly realistic, and in the best sense,
though it was full of palpable absurdities. But Daisy did not intend
them to be absurdities. She felt them as truths, and so she was a
realist. The world she depicted was authentically the world that
she saw. And what she added to it represented exactly her private
view of the way it might be made better and more charming. In
this sense—the only true sense—all novelists of any merit whatsoever are realists. Joseph Conrad was, though he dealt habitually
with strange people and unfamiliar situations, often near the border line of the fantastic. Anatole France was, though he more than
once crossed the line. Realism is simply intellectual honesty in the
artist. The realist yields nothing to what is manifestly not true,
however alluring. He makes no compromise with popular senti-

mentality and illusion. He avoids the false inference as well as the bogus fact. He respects his materials as he respects himself.

But all that certainly doesn't make him a photographer. In the world as he sees it there are facts that lie outside him and facts that lie within, and they are of equal importance. It is his contribution that converts a dead external reality into a living inner experience, and conveys his own emotion to the reader. If that emotion of his is common and shoddy, then what he writes will be common and shoddy, but if it has dignity in it, and some echo of the eternal tragedy of man, then he will produce a genuine work of art. What ails most of the so-called realists, particularly in this great Republic, is simply that they are inferior men. They see only what is visible to an ice-wagon driver. They bring to it only the emotional responses of a trolley conductor.

The Ultimate Realists

From PREJUDICES: THIRD SERIES, 1922, pp. 201–212.
First printed in the *Smart Set*, May, 1922, pp. 138–42.
With an addition from the same, April, 1921, p. 50

Much wind has been wasted upon a discussion of the differences between realistic novels and romantic novels. As a matter of fact, every authentic novel is realistic in its method, however fantastic may be its fable, and every realistic novel shows its sly touches of romance. Even the most gifted romantic holds himself in: his heroes may be seven feet in height, but no such fabulist has ever made them eight or ten. And even such a realist as Dreiser is full of discreet reservations: he tells us about the time his hero attempted a poor working girl, but he never tells us about the time he had cholera morbus, or picked up *pediculae* at a Baptist prayer-meeting, or found a Croton-bug in his soup. The one aim of the novel, at all times and everywhere, is to set forth, not what *might* be true about the human race, or what ought to be true, but what actually *is* true. This is obviously not the case with poetry. Poetry is the product of an effort to invent a world appreciably better than the one we live in; its essence is not the representation of the facts, but the deliberate concealment and denial of the facts. As for the drama, it vacillates, and if it touches the novel on one side it also touches the epic on the other. But the novel itself is concerned with human nature as it is practically revealed and with human experience as men actually know it. If it departs from that representational plausibility ever so slightly, it becomes to that extent a bad novel; if it departs violently it ceases to be a novel at all.

That women are still the chief readers of novels is known to every book clerk. What is less often noted is that women themselves, as they have gradually become fully literate, have forced their way to the front as makers of the stuff they feed on, and that they show signs of ousting the men, soon or late, from the business. Save in the department of lyrical verse, which demands no organization of ideas but only fluency of feeling, they have nowhere else done serious work in literature. There is no epic poem of any solid value by a woman, dead or alive; and no drama, whether comedy or tragedy; and no work of metaphysical speculation; and no history; and no basic document in any other realm of thought. In criticism, whether of works of art or of the ideas underlying them, few women have ever got beyond the *Schwarmerei* of Madame de Staël's "L'Allemagne." In the essay, the most competent woman barely surpasses the average Fleet Street *causerie* hack or Harvard professor. But in the novel the ladies have stood on a level with even the most accomplished men since the day of Jane Austen, and not only in Anglo-Saxondom, but also everywhere else—save perhaps in Russia.

It is my contention that women thus succeed in the novel—and that they will succeed even more strikingly as they gradually throw off the inhibitions that have hitherto cobwebbed their minds— simply because they are better fitted for realistic representation than men—because they see the facts of life more sharply, and are less distracted by mooney dreams. Women seldom have the pathological faculty vaguely called imagination. One doesn't often hear of them groaning over colossal bones in their sleep, as dogs do, or constructing heavenly hierarchies or political utopias, as men do. Their concern is always with things of more objective substance—roofs, meals, rent, clothes, the birth and upbringing of children. They are, I believe, generally happier than men, if only because the demands they make of life are more moderate and less romantic. The chief pain that a man normally suffers in his progress through this vale is that of disillusionment; the chief pain that a woman suffers is that of parturition. There is enormous significance in the difference. The first is artificial and self-inflicted; the second is natural and unescapable.

The psychological history of the differentiation I need not go into here; its springs lie obviously in the greater physical strength of man and his freedom from child-bearing, and in the larger mobility and capacity for adventure that go therewith. A man dreams of utopias simply because he feels himself free to construct them; a woman must keep house. In late years, to be sure, she has toyed with the idea of escaping that necessity, but I shall not bore you with arguments showing that she never will. So long as children are brought into the world and made ready for the trenches, the assembly-line and the gallows by the laborious method ordained of God she will never be quite as free to roam and dream as man is. It is only a small minority of her sex who cherish a contrary expectation, and this minority, though anatomically female, is spiritually male. Show me a woman who has visions comparable, say, to those of Swedenborg or Strindberg, and I'll show you a woman who is a very powerful anaphrodisiac.

Thus women, by their enforced preoccupation with the harsh facts of life, are extremely well fitted to write novels, which must deal with the facts or nothing. What they need for the practical business, in addition, falls under two heads. First, they need enough sense of social security to make them free to set down what they see. Secondly, they need the modest technical skill, the formal mastery of words and ideas, necessary to do it. The latter, I believe, they have had ever since they learned to read and write, say 300 years ago; it comes to them more readily than to men, and is exercised with greater ease. The former they are fast acquiring. In the days of Aphra Behn and Ann Radcliffe it was almost as scandalous for a woman to put her observations and notions into print as it was for her to show her legs; even in the days of Jane Austen and Charlotte Brontë the thing was regarded as decidedly unladylike. But now, within certain limits, she is free to print whatever she pleases, and many women novelists begin to do it.

I should like to read a "Main Street" by an articulate Carol Kennicott, or a "Titan" by one of Cowperwood's mistresses. It would be sweet stuff, indeed.... And it will come.

The Face Is Familiar

From Essay in Pedagogy,
Prejudices: Fifth Series, 1926, pp. 218–36

A first-rate novel is always a character sketch. It may be more than that, but at bottom it is always a character sketch, or, if the author is genuinely of the imperial line, a whole series of them. More, it is a character sketch of an individual not far removed from the norm of the race. He may have his flavor of oddity, but he is never fantastic; he never violates the common rules of human action; he never shows emotions that are impossible to the rest of us. If Thackeray had given Becky Sharp a bass voice, nine husbands and the rank of lieutenant-general in the British Army, she would have been forgotten long ago, along with all the rest of "Vanity Fair." And if Robinson Crusoe had been an Edison instead of a normal sailorman, he would have gone the same way.

The Hero Problem

From the *Smart Set*, Dec., 1912, pp. 156–57

It is seldom, indeed, that fiction can rise above second-rate men. The motives and impulses and processes of mind of the superman are too recondite for plausible analysis. It is easy enough to explain how John Smith courted and won his wife, and even how William Jones fought and died for his country, but it would be impossible to explain (or, at any rate, to convince by explaining) how Beethoven wrote the Fifth Symphony, or how Pasteur reasoned out the hydrophobia vaccine, or how Stonewall Jackson arrived at his miracles of strategy. The thing has been tried often, but it has always ended in failure. Those supermen of fiction who are not mere shadows and dummies are supermen reduced to saving ordinariness. Shakespeare made Hamlet a comprehensible and convincing man by diluting that half of him which was Shakespeare by a half which was a college sophomore. In the same way he saved Lear by making him, in large part, a silly and obscene old man—the blood brother of any average ancient of any average English taproom. Tackling Caesar, he was rescued from disaster by Brutus's knife. George Bernard Shaw, facing the same difficulty, resolved it by drawing a composite portrait of two or three London actor-managers and half a dozen English politicians.

New England Twilight

From THE NATIONAL LETTERS,
PREJUDICES: SECOND SERIES, 1920, pp. 19–20

One never remembers a character in the novels of those aloof and de-Americanized Americans of the New England decadence; one never encounters an idea in their essays; one never carries away a line out of their poetry. It is literature as an academic exercise for talented grammarians, almost as a genteel recreation for ladies and gentlemen of fashion—the exact equivalent, in the field of letters, of Eighteenth Century painting and German *Augenmusik*. What ails it, intrinsically, is a dearth of intellectual audacity and of aesthetic passion. Running through it, and characterizing the work of almost every man and woman producing it, there is an unescapable suggestion of the old Puritan suspicion of the fine arts as such—of the doctrine that they offer fit asylum for good citizens only when some ulterior and superior purpose is carried into them. This purpose, naturally enough, most commonly shows a moral tinge. The aim of poetry, it appears, is to fill the mind with lofty thoughts—not to give it joy, but to give it a grand and somewhat gaudy sense of virtue. The essay is a weapon against the degenerate tendencies of the age. The novel, properly conceived, is a means of uplifting the spirit; its aim is to inspire, not merely to satisfy the low curiosity of man in man. The Puritan, of course, is not entirely devoid of aesthetic feeling. He has a taste for good form; he responds to style; he is even capable of something approaching a purely aesthetic emotion. But he fears this aesthetic emotion as an insinuating distraction from his chief business in life: the sober consideration of the all-important problem of conduct. Art is a temptation, a seduction, a Lorelei, and the Good Man may safely have traffic with it only when it is broken to moral uses—in other words, when its innocence is pumped out of it, and it is purged of gusto.

XV. EUROPEAN NOVELISTS

Jane Austen

A hitherto unpublished note

IT WAS NOT until the Spring of 1945, when I was approaching 65, that I ever came to Jane Austen. My choice, naturally, was "Mansfield Park," for all the authorities seemed to agree that it was Jane's best. And what did I find? A dull novel about a stupid group of English country gentry, almost on the level of the sentimental serials that the *Ladies' Home Journal* used to publish in the '90s. The characters, to be sure, had a certain definition, and were thus better done than the cut-outs in the popular English novel of the generation immediately preceding, but it would surely be going too far to call them quite plausible. Their doings, at least half the time, seemed to me to be without logical motive, and in consequence the enrolling episodes were often pointless. Such poor sticks, no doubt, existed in the English hinterland of the period, but I could discern no reason, save the historical one, for being interested in them today. Most of the official critics praise La Austen lavishly for the naturalness of her dialogue, but I found nothing of the sort in it. On the contrary, it was extraordinarily stiff and clumsy, and even in moments of high passion the people of the tale had at one another with set speeches, many of them so ornate as to be almost unintelligible. I got as far as Chapter XXXIX and then had to give up, thus missing altogether the elopement of Crawford and Mrs. Rushworth. It was a somewhat painful experience, and I had to console myself with the reflection that novel-writing has made enormous progress since the first days of the Nineteenth Century. The veriest tyro of today creates characters who are far better observed, if not better imagined, and the worst dialogue perpetrated by an imitator of Ernest Hemingway is at least more natural than poor Jane's. Yet there have been literary historians, not palpably insane, who have ventured to argue that "Mansfield Park" is the greatest of English novels. If so, then Tom Robertson's "Caste" is the greatest of English plays.

Robert Louis Stevenson

From the *American Mercury*, Nov., 1924, pp. 378–80.
A review of THE LIFE OF ROBERT LOUIS STEVENSON,
by Rosaline Orme Masson, New York, 1924;
and AN INTIMATE PORTRAIT OF R.L.S., by Lloyd Osbourne;
New York, 1924

Dead thirty years, Robert Louis Stevenson still occupies a sort of receiving vault in the Valhalla of literary artists. The wake, meanwhile, goes on. No corpse, indeed, was ever surrounded by more enthusiastic mourners. There are far more Stevenson clubs than there are Whitman clubs, and no publishing season ever passes without making its contribution to Stevensoniana. But what is the net issue and sediment from all the uproar? Was Louis actually one of the first flight of English writers, a stylist in the grand manner? Or was he simply a clever fellow, enchanting to the defectively literate, but destined, in the end, to go below the salt? My impression is that the second guess, in the present state of human knowledge, is somewhat nearer to the truth than the first. The typical Stevensonian is bookish but not a bookman—in brief, a sort of gaper over the fence of beautiful letters. It is with the clan as it is with the fanatical Dickensians, who are mainly persons who have never read Thackeray, and with the Johnsonians, who are largely Babbitts who have never read anything, not even Johnson. I do not, of course, overlook such magnificoes as Henley, Henry James and Edmund Gosse—but Henley was Stevenson's friend, James was always amiable, and Gosse is in favor of everybody. I can detect no passion for Stevenson among the men and women who are actually making the literature of today. There are hot partisans among them for Joseph Conrad, for Hardy, for Meredith, for Flaubert, for Dostoievski and even for Dickens, but there are none, so far as I am aware, for good Louis. His customers, beginning with literary college professors, often female, fade into collectors of complete library sets. Himself always a boy of 17, he seems to hold best those readers whose delight in the wonders of the world is not too much contaminated by the cramps and questionings of maturity.

The two biographical volumes above listed make no effort to fix his place; they are wholly devoid of critical purpose. Miss Masson simply puts together all she can find out about his life, adds a few dozen pictures, and calls it a book. The thing is thorough, and, despite some pedaling here and there, very useful; in particular, it does justice to Stevenson's father, a strict Presbyterian but a gentleman. What miseries the old man must have suffered during Louis's early efforts to lead his own life! How the news that came home from Paris must have lacerated his Calvinistic pruderies, and then the later news from California! Moreover, all these antinomian monkeyshines cost him a great deal of hard money, and the money of a Scotsman flows in his very veins, along with the red corpuscles and the white. Nevertheless, he took it all like a man, and if the impression prevails that he starved and oppressēd a genius it is due far more to the sentimentality of the Stevensonians than to his own acts. He was actually fond, humane, long-suffering and excessively generous. Miss Masson, as I say, does him justice. In Mr. Osbourne's book there is only the scantest mention of him; he is simply an anonymous who gives Mrs. Stevenson a house and £500 on page 58 and slides gently from the scene on page 71. This Osbourne volume, otherwise, should be of immense interest to the Stevensonian. There are twelve short chapters, showing Louis at close range at various ages from 26 to 44. There is intimate knowledge of him in them, and fine feeling, and they are all capitally written. The pupil certainly does no discredit to the master. Stevenson himself seldom wrote anything better.

What is wanting is a full-length study of him, done objectively and by a realistic and scientific hand. There are models, each going about half of the way, in Van Wyck Brooks's autopsy of Mark Twain and Katharine Anthony's of Margaret Fuller.[1] It is a wonder,

---

[1] For a discussion of the latter, see p. 437.

indeed, that no Freudian has been tempted to the task, for Stevenson was surely one of the most beautiful masses of complexes ever encountered on this earth. His whole life was a series of flights from reality—first from Presbyterianism, then from the sordid mountebankery of the law, and then from the shackles of his own wrecked and tortured body. He fled in the spirit to the Paris of Charles VII as he fled in the flesh to the rustic Bohemia at Barbizon; later on he fled in both garbs to the South Seas. Doomed to spend half his life in bed, beset endlessly by pain, brought often to death's door by hemorrhages, and sometimes forbidden for days on end to work or even to speak, he found release and consolation in gaudy visions of gallant encounters, sinister crimes and heroic loves. He was the plow-boy dreaming in the hay-loft, the flapper tossing on her finishing-school bed. It was at once a grotesque tragedy and a pathetic farce, but it wrung out of him the best that was in him. What man ever paid more bitterly for the inestimable privilege of work? Stevenson, alas, wrote a great deal of third-rate stuff; even his most doting admirers must find it hard to read, for example, some of his essays. But out of his agony came also "Lodgings for the Night," "The Sire de Malétroit's Door," "Will o' the Mill," and "Treasure Island," and if they do not belong absolutely in the first rank, then certainly they go high in the second. Every one of them represents an attempt to escape the world of reality by launching into a world of compensatory fancy. In each of them the invalid buckles on an imaginary sword and challenges a very real enemy.

His weakness as an imaginative author lies in the fact that he never got beyond the simple revolt of boyhood—that his intellect never developed to match his imagination. The result is that an air of triviality hangs about all his work, and even at times, an air of trashiness. He is never very searching, never genuinely profound. More than any other man, perhaps, he was responsible for the revival of the romantic novel in the last years of the Nineteenth Century, and more than any other salient man of his time he was followed by shallow and shoddy disciples. These disciples, indeed, soon reduced his formula to absurdity. The appearance of Joseph Conrad, a year after his death, disposed of all his full-length romances save "Treasure Island," and that survived only as a story for boys. Put beside such things as "An Outcast of the Islands" and "Lord Jim," even the best of Stevenson began to appear superficial and obvious. It was diverting, and often it was highly artful, but it was hollow; there was nothing in it save the story. Once more Beethoven drove out Haydn. Or, perhaps more accurately, Wagner drove out Rossini. It is very difficult, after "Heart of Darkness," to get through "Dr. Jekyll and Mr. Hyde." The essays have gone the same way. They have a certain external elegance, as of a well-turned-out frock or charmingly decorated room, but the ideas in them are seldom notable either for vigor or for originality. When Stevenson wrote them he was trying to set up shop as a young literary exquisite in London. The breed, unluckily, is not yet extinct; its elaborate nothings still bedizen the English monthlies and weeklies. Stevenson was cured of that folly by his infirmities. They sent him headlong beyond the sky-rim. It was there he came to fame.

Stevenson Again

From the *American Mercury*, Jan., 1925, pp. 125–27.
A review of ROBERT LOUIS STEVENSON:
A CRITICAL BIOGRAPHY,
by John A. Steuart; Boston, 1924

In reviewing Miss Rosaline Masson's book on Stevenson, I bemoaned the lack of a critical biography of him, separating the facts about his life and work from the romantic gurgling of his admirers. Mr. Steuart's two large volumes make a gallant attempt in that direction. They depict the young Stevenson of the Edinburgh days very realistically: a grotesque young mountebank about town, dressed like a guy, boozing in the lowest pubs, and carrying on a long series of depressing love affairs with ladies of the town. One of them, a street-walker, he even proposed to marry. Whence came such aberrations in the son of the respectable Presbyterian? Mr. Steuart, with Scotch smugness and lack of humor, blames them all on a touch of French blood: on the Stevenson family tree, distaff side, there hung the glands of a certain Lizars, or Lisouris, who settled in Edinburgh about the year 1600. Perhaps the theory has something in it: for a pure Scot to become an artist, even a bad one, is surely rather unusual. But the long hair, the beer-bibbing and the wenching are sufficiently accounted for, it seems to me, in a simpler way. Louis came to adolescence in an era of rising doubt, with the name of Darwin on every Christian's lips and Huxley in full eruption. He was, furthermore, an only son, and greatly spoiled by a doting mamma. What more natural than for him to rebel violently against the parental Calvinism, and what more natural than for his revolt to take the form of gaudy waist-coats, disreputable hats, low companions, bad beer and loose women? One sees the same thing going on every day among the sons of the evangelical clergy; it is, indeed, almost an axiom that the first-born of a Methodist pastor is bound to be a hard egg. Is the case of Nietzsche so soon forgotten? Stevenson, I believe, took to the vine-leaves simply because the Westminster Catechism, to his generation, had become suddenly intolerable. He became an artist almost as a sort of afterthought. His first impulse was merely to get away from the hard-boiled, cast-iron, anthropophagous Yah-weh of the family home. It was not until he escaped to Paris that revolt turned into ambition, and he began to assault the magazines of the time with manuscripts. Greenwich Village is responsible for many transformations of precisely the same sort. The Baptist virgin from the Middle West arrives in Sheridan Square with no thought save to get rid of her flannel underwear and flood her recesses with Chianti. But in a few weeks she is making batiks, learning rhythmic dancing, writing a novel, or rehearsing for one of the plays of Harry Kemp.

Mr. Steuart shows how long it took Stevenson to learn his business—how, indeed, he never learned it at all until his last few years. His early work was all heavily imitative, and in some of it imitation went very close to plagiarism. Despite all the enthusiasm of his disciples, there is really very little that is sound and praise-worthy in his essays; most of them are ruined by transparent affec-tations. He wrote, in those days, as he dressed: like a popinjay. It was not until he came to "Treasure Island" that he acquired a style that was straightforward and clear—and "Treasure Island" was a deliberate imitation of the juvenile pot-boilers of a forgotten hack, one Alfred R. Phillips. Mr. Steuart recalls the curious fact that it was a complete failure when it was published serially in *Young Folks*, and hazards the opinion that it is not much read by boys, even today. I incline to agree with him. "Treasure Island," I believe, is mainly read by grown men, and in the same mood that takes them to detective stories—that is, the mood of deliberate relaxation. Men of the best taste, of course, do not often seek relaxation in that way. Detective stories are read by United States Senators and bank presidents, but not often, I believe, by artists. Stevenson never qualifies for the first table; in his best work there is always a strong flavor of the second-rate. Perhaps Mr. Steuart is right in arguing that he ought to be admitted, not for the genius that he probably lacked, but for the diligence and courage with which he tried to make the best use of the moderate talents he began with. His long and gallant struggle against ill health is surely not to be sniffed at. Beneath that motley of the mountebank there was a very real hero.

Mr. Steuart's work gets further than any of its predecessors, but it still leaves much to be said. Its materials are thrown together loosely and they are not sufficiently documented; moreover, the author intrudes his own personality too often, and it is uninteresting. When he essays to be critical in the grand manner, he sometimes becomes only sophomoric. What is still needed is a book on Stevenson by a first-rate critic—one sufficiently interested in him to treat him humanely, and yet sufficiently critical to examine him scientifically. Like many another—for example, Bronson Alcott, Thoreau, Björnson and Tolstoi—he was far more engaging as a man than as an artist. His flight to the South Seas gave a grand and gaudy realization to the dreams of every youth who rebels against the dreadful dullness of human existence under Christianity—the stupidity of his parents, the imbecility of his pastors, the sordid business of getting a living. The rest fret themselves into resignation, and one finds them, in the end, playing golf, or haranguing Kiwanis, or writing plays for Broadway. But now and then a Stevenson or a Conrad actually takes ship, and then there is a new hero in the world, and a glow of second-hand joy.

The Father of Them All

From the *American Mercury*, Dec., 1928, pp. 506–07.
A review of ZOLA AND HIS TIME, by Matthew Josephson;
New York, 1928

The eclipse of Zola is one of the strange phenomena of literary history. He is probably read less today than any other major novelist of his epoch, and in discussions of the current literary tides it is unusual to encounter any mention of his name. Yet it must be plain that, in certain important ways, he was the most influential novelist of the Nineteenth Century, not forgetting Scott, nor Balzac, nor Dickens, nor even Dostoievski, and that his mark is still distinctly visible upon all the considerable brethren of the craft. It was his function, deliberately assumed and triumphantly discharged, to relate his art to the new views of man and the world that came in with "The Origin of Species"—to pull it out of the cloister and bring it into the main stream of human thinking. He was at once a daring revolutionist and a brilliant and imaginative builder. Sweeping away at one colossal stroke the old subjective psychology that had sufficed novelists since the days of Job, he sought for the key to the external tragedy of man in the new science of biology. There the search goes on to this day. The modern novelist is only half an artist; the other half of him is a scientist—an incompetent one perhaps, but still a scientist.

Zola's own competence was surely not extraordinary: he was only too prone to accept the new scientific concepts of his time without critical examination, and even, indeed, without any examination whatever. Nevertheless, they took him in the right direction, for most of them, after all, were sound. Best of all, they implanted in him the habit of direct observation—they made him go for his material, not to his imagination, but to the facts. Such a novel as "La Terre" may have glaring defects as a work of art, but it is at least a tremendously accurate and moving human document. The people in it do not live as Hamlet and Ophelia live, in a pale mist of fancy; they live as a streptococcus lives, snared fast in a test-tube. It is no wonder that the book caused an uproar. We have, of late, heard the same uproar over "Elmer Gantry," and for the same reason. What stood against Zola, in the days of his greatest achievement, was that the readers compared his people, not to the real human beings he had studied, but to the imaginary human beings of other novelists. His enemy was Balzac, and he knew it. He was not simply another novelist; he was a novelist of quite a new kind.

His defect was that of all innovators and enthusiasts: he went so far with his formula that it became mechanical and inhuman. In his early works, even after he had taken the new line, there were sufficient concessions to the conventions of Nineteenth Century novel-writing to make them endurable, even to the sentimental customers of Daudet and company. But with "L'Assommoir" he abandoned the decorums of the boudoir for the harsh realism of the clinic, and by the time he came to "Germinal" and "La Terre" he was in the dissecting room. "Germinal" will probably survive as one of the great novels of all time, but the contemporary reviews of it were almost uniformly unfavorable and its huge contemporary sale was as pornography, not as work of art. People revolted from its appalling picture of human misery as they would from a meticulous report of a difficult labor or a true biography of Warren Gamaliel Harding. But it was true. And if the business of a novelist is to penetrate and reveal the agony of man in this world, it was a novel, and a great one.

After "La Terre," and especially after "La Débâcle," Zola began to weaken and wobble. Success enfeebled him, as it enfeebles all artists, not to say all scientists. He became a rich man, with a country house, servants, public engagements, investments, a conscience. He took a drastic cure to reduce his weight, and had his beard neatly clipped. Yearning for offspring and finding himself with a sterile wife who refused to be put away, he achieved a son and a daughter in collaboration with an amiable female neighbor. There was talk of putting him into the French Academy, an honor, like all French honors, comparable to being elected to the Elks. He was headed for the puerile melodrama of the Dreyfus affair, in which the rôle he played, observed calmly in retrospect, seems to have been little distinguishable from that of a movie star recommending Lucky Strikes. "Le Docteur Pascal" showed a new and "good" Zola—an optimist, a right-thinker. There followed the cities series, "Lourdes," "Rome" and "Paris." "Fécondité" found him at the bottom of the slide. Its last four or five chapters contain some of the most maudlin drivel ever penned by mortal man.

Zola had many defects as a man. He was vain, arrogant and intolerant. An Italian by ancestry, he naturally loved money, and there were times when his passion for it made a fool of him. He was an eager seeker for public notice, and maneuvered for it in a shameless manner. Afraid of his virago of a wife on the one hand, he grossly deceived and humiliated her on the other. His courage in the Dreyfus business has been greatly exaggerated in the telling, chiefly by English reporters eager to make propaganda against the French. He ran away at a critical moment, and frequently forgot Dreyfus in thinking of Zola. But he had many compensating virtues. He had a fine intelligence: he was eager for knowledge and able to grasp elusive facts. He was immensely diligent and took his trade seriously. The old-time novelist needed only pen, paper and a quiet room; Zola studied life at first hand, laboriously, conscientiously, thoroughly. Nothing that was human was uninteresting to him, and nothing that was human surprised or shocked him. His eye was made for the microscope; his hands were not cut out for the lute. For metaphysics he had a healthy contempt: what interested him was physiology. He had, in his best days, the vast impassivity of a Darwin, the true detachment of a born scientist. What men thought engaged only his passing attention; he devoted himself to observing what they did. He was, in a very real sense, the first behaviorist.

The good novels of his prime are now neglected, I suspect, mainly because he wrote so many bad ones in the days of his decline. He passed out of life somewhat ridiculous: a scientist turned uplifter. The messianic delusion has ruined many men, but few better ones. By his own single effort he reoriented the novel, and made every successor his debtor. There are romancers left who show no trace of his influence, but surely not many novelists. His marks are all over such men as Wells, Bennett, Mann, Sudermann and Proust. He has been vastly more influential than either Flaubert or Turgeniev. The novel that Dickens wrote survives today only as a conscious archaism; it seems idiotic after "Germinal" and "La Terre." Some day, I believe, these astounding works will be read again. Perhaps the tide is turning toward them already. For years they were obtainable in English only in mutilated versions, poorly printed. The Comstocks hunted them down relentlessly; in England their publisher, the elder Vizetelly, was thrown into jail, and died there. But now they begin to appear in better editions, with prefaces by various learned hands. Their day may be coming.

Freudian Autopsy upon a Genius

From the *American Mercury*, June, 1931, pp. 251–52.
A review of THE POLISH HERITAGE OF JOSEPH CONRAD,
By Gustaf Morf (Richard R. Smith); New York, 1931

Years ago, in the course of a review of one of the late Joseph Conrad's books, I permitted myself the observation that all of his characters, in the last analysis, were Poles. Sometimes he called them Germans, Frenchmen, Latin-Americans, Chinamen or Malays, and very often he called them Englishmen, but always they remained Poles like himself. This observation somewhat exercised Conrad, but his argument, when it reached me, convinced me only that a great artist is often a bad observer of his own psychological processes. This conviction is now heavily reënforced by Dr. Morf, for his book is devoted to proving, not only that practically all of the characters in the Conrad gallery are Poles, but also that the transactions in which they engage are largely echoes from Conrad's own life, or the lives of his relatives. The whole canon of his works, in fact, is moved over from English literature to Polish literature, and the circumstance that they are written in English becomes a trivial accident, like the circumstance that Frederick the Great's highly Prussian memoranda were written in French.

Whether or not Dr. Morf is a Pole himself I don't know, but he is quite at home in the Polish language, and so brings forward a great deal of material hitherto unknown to English critics. Part of it is to be found in the autobiography of Conrad's uncle and guardian, Tadeusz Bobrowski, part comes from the writings of Conrad's father, Apollo Korzeniowski, and part is in other family papers. Dr. Morf says that, both as boy and as man, Conrad was almost the archetypical Pole—full of grand projects, an incurable romantic, an ardent patriot, and, with it all, the victim of chronic repinings and despairs. He went to sea as a young man simply because he craved heroic adventure, and the Russians had the lid down so tightly in his part of Poland that there was no chance for it at home. Had the times been happier he would have taken to the field against the oppressor, as his forebears had done before him. But in the Poland of the early '70s a Polish patriot was as hopelessly hobbled as a biologist in Mississippi, and so young Józef Teodor Konrad Korzeniowski herbu Nalecz (thus Dr. Morf gives his name) had to content himself with dreams of the Congo and Cathay.

In his career as a sailor there was something touchingly ludicrous, though he himself seems to have been unaware of it. He was as ill-fitted for the sordid routine of a British merchant skipper as he would have been for the life of a ballet dancer. He was apparently resented as a foreigner and distrusted as a romantic. He took his ship too near to dangerous coasts, and proposed voyages that were far more glamorous than profitable. Finally, as every one knows, he abandoned deep water for the infernal Congo river trade, and there came near losing his life. Dr. Morf hints that he went to Africa less as a steamboat commander than as a sort of explorer—that he always liked to identify himself, not with the dull, respectable and often pious brethren of his mundane vocation, but with the glittering, and sometimes wicked adventurers of the past—Torres, Tasman, Cook, and so on. In this identification he sought an escape from his bafflement as a Polish patriot. If he could not slit the gullets of damned Muscovites he would at least prove that he was still a devil of a fellow, and not to be daunted by cannibals and mosquitoes.

Unfortunately, this escape mechanism, in the long run, failed to work. Conrad could never quite rid himself of his Polish conscience; he harbored to the end a disquieting feeling that he had deserted and betrayed Mother Polonia. Dr. Morf says that this feeling was responsible for "Lord Jim." He sees the whole story of Jim as a sardonic and shuddering projection, thrown up as by some ghastly magic lantern, of Conrad's own story. "It is," he says, "more than a novel; it is a confession. As a confession of a man tortured by doubts and nightmarish fears it must be understood, if it is to be understood at all." The central episode of the tale is almost too familiar to need recalling: Jim, a ship's mate, violates all the canons of his craft by deserting his ship in the face of disaster, and thereafter wanders forlorn and disconsolate in an Eastern jungle, a pariah beyond rehabilitation. The sinking ship, says Morf, is Poland, and Conrad is Jim. And the earnest of his desertion is his naturalization as a British subject. So long as he hesitated at that—and he hesitated a long while—there was some chance that fate would take him back to Poland, and restore him to the glorious enterprises of his ancestors. But once he had sworn to revere and cherish Queen Victoria he was lost forever.

I leave this theory to your prayerful consideration, but must add, in justice to Dr. Morf, that he supports it with a great deal of curious evidence. The parallel between Jim's career and Conrad's, indeed, is astonishingly close, and extends to many small details. They go to sea, for example, under the same circumstances, they suffer almost the same misadventures, and they are consoled by the same diversions. Both become known in their circles, not by their surnames, but by their given names. Both have noble titles. The name of Jim's ship is *Patna*, and Polska is the Polish name of Poland. Finally, the ship, after Jim deserts it, is towed to port by a French gunboat—an echo, says Morf, of the ancient Polish hope that the French would one day rescue them. "Lord Jim" was first published in 1900, the year that also saw the appearance of Freud's "Interpretation of Dreams." Conrad, says Morf, knew the Freud book, but disliked it intensely, and Freud with it. In that dislike there was something akin to his aversion to Dostoievski. Both were "too crude, too explicit." Like all of us, he "did not want to know the objective truth about his own work."

H. G. Wells

From THE LATE MR. WELLS, PREJUDICES: FIRST SERIES, 1919, pp. 22–35. Into this essay entered parts of reviews of Wells books that had appeared in the *Smart Set* between 1908 and 1919. In 1919 Wells still had The Outline of History (1920), The World of William Clissold (1926), The Science of Life (1929), The Work, Wealth and Happiness of Mankind (1932), The Shape of Things to Come (1933), and Experiment in Autobiography (1934) ahead of him, but his best work was done. The view of him that is set forth here was adopted by most of the more competent critics who attempted estimates of him after his death.

The high day of Wells lasted, say, from 1908 to 1912. It began with "Tono-Bungay" and ended amid the final scenes of "Marriage," as the well-made play of Scribe gave up the ghost in the last act of "A Doll's House." In "Marriage" were the first faint signs of something wrong. Invention succumbed to theories that somehow failed to hang together, and the story, after vast heavings, incontinently went to pieces. One had begun with an acute and highly diverting study of monogamy in modern London; one found one's self, toward the close, gaping over an unconvincing fable of marriage in the Stone Age. Coming directly after so vivid a personage as Remington in "The New Machiavelli," Dr. Richard Godwin Trafford simply refused to go down. And his Marjorie, following his example, stuck in the gullet of the imagination. One ceased to believe in them when they set out for Labrador, and after that it was impossible to revive interest in them. The more they were explained and vivisected and drenched with theories, the more unreal they became.

Into "The Passionate Friends" (1913) there crept the first downright dullness. By this time Wells's readers had become familiar with his machinery and his materials—his elbowing suffragettes, his tea-swilling London uplifters, his smattering of quasi-science, his intellectualized adulteries, his Thackerayan asides, his textbook paragraphs, his journalistic raciness—and all these things had thus begun to lose the blush of their first charm. To help them out

he now heaved in larger and larger doses of theory—often diverting enough, but in the long run a poor substitute for the proper in-
gredients of character, situation and human passion. Next came
"The Wife of Sir Isaac Harman" (1914), an attempt to rewrite "A
Doll's House" (with a fourth act) in terms of ante-bellum 1914.
The result was 500-odd pages of bosh, a flabby and tedious piece
of work, Wells for the first time in the rôle of unmistakable bore.
And then "Bealby" (1915), with its Palais Royal jocosity, its running
in and out of doors, its humor of physical collision, its reminis-
cences of "A Trip to Chinatown" and "Peck's Bad Boy." And then
"Boon" (1915), a heavy-witted satire, often incomprehensible, always incommoded by its disguise as a novel. And then "The Research Magnificent" (1915): a poor soup from the dry bones of
Nietzsche. And then "Mr. Britling Sees It Through" (1916). . . .

Here, for a happy moment, there seemed to be something
better—almost, in fact, a recrudescence of the Wells of 1910. But
that seeming was only seeming. What confused the judgment was
the enormous popular success of the book. Because it presented a
fifth-rate Englishman in an heroic aspect, because it sentimental-
ized the whole reaction of the English proletariat to the war, it offers a subtle sort of flattery to other fifth-rate Englishmen, and, *per
corollary*, to Americans of corresponding degree, to wit, the second. Thus it made a great pother, and was hymned as a masterpiece in such gazettes as the New York *Times*. But there was in the
book, in point of fact, a great hollowness, and that hollowness presently begat an implosion that disposed of the shell. I daresay many
a novel-reader returns, now and then, to "Tono-Bungay" (1909),
and even to "Ann Veronica" (1909), but surely only a reader with
absolutely nothing else to read would return to "Mr. Britling Sees
It Through." There followed—what? "The Soul of a Bishop"
(1917), perhaps the worst novel ever written by a serious novelist
since novel-writing began. And then—or perhaps a bit before, or
simultaneously—an idiotic religious tract—a tract so utterly feeble
and preposterous that even the Scotsman, William Archer, could
not stomach it. And then, to make an end, came "Joan and Peter"
(1918)—and the collapse of Wells was revealed at last in its true
proportions.

This "Joan and Peter," I confess, lingers in my memory as unpleasantly as a Summer cold, and so, in retrospect, I may perhaps exaggerate its intrinsic badness. I would not look into it again for gold and frankincense. I was at the job of reading it for days and days, endlessly daunted and halted by its laborious dullness, its flat-ulent fatuity, its almost fabulous inconsequentiality. It was, and is, nearly impossible to believe that the Wells of "Tono-Bungay" and "The History of Mr. Polly" wrote it, or that he was in the full pos-session of his faculties when he allowed it to be printed under his name. For in it there was the fault that the Wells of early days, al-most beyond any other fictioneer of the time, was incapable of— the fault of dismalness, of tediousness—the witless and contagious coma of the evangelist. Here, for nearly six hundred pages of fine type, he rolled on in an intellectual cloud, boring one abominably with uninteresting people, pointless situations, revelations that re-vealed nothing, arguments that had no appositeness, expositions that exposed naught save an insatiable and torturing garrulity. Where was the old fine address of the man? Where was his sharp eye for the salient and significant in character? Where was his in-stinct for form, his skill at putting a story together, his hand for making it unwind itself? These things were so far gone that it be-came hard to believe that they ever existed. There was not the slightest sign of them in "Joan and Peter." The book was a botch from end to end, and in that botch there was not even the palli-ation of an arduous enterprise gallantly attempted. No inherent difficulty was visible. The story was anything but complex, and surely anything but subtle. Its badness lay wholly in the fact that the author made a mess of the writing, that his quondam cunning, once so exhilarating, was gone when he began it.

Reviewing it at the time of its publication, I inclined momentar-ily to the notion that the war was to blame. No one could overes-timate the cost of that struggle to the English, not only in men and money, but also and more importantly in the things of the spirit. It developed national traits that were greatly at odds with the old ideal of Anglo-Saxon character—an extravagant hysteria, a tenden-cy to whimper under blows, political radicalism and credulity. It shook the old ruling caste of the land and gave the control of things to upstarts from the lowest classes—snuffling Methodists, shady Jews, prehensile commercial gents, disgusting demagogues, all sorts of self-seeking adventurers. Worst of all, the strain seemed to work havoc with the customary dignity and reticence, and even with the plain common sense of many Englishmen of a higher level, and in particular many English writers. The astounding bawling of Kipling and the no less astounding bombast of G. K. Chesterton were anything but isolated; there were, in fact, scores of other eminent authors in the same state of eruption, and a study of the resultant literature of objurgation will make a fascinating job for some sweating *Privat Dozent* of tomorrow. It occurred to me, as I say, that Wells might have become afflicted by this same demoralization, but reflection disposed of the notion. On the one hand, there was the plain fact that his actual writings on the war, while marked by the bitterness of the time, were anything but in-sane, and on the other hand there was the equally plain fact that his decay had been in progress a long while before the Germans made their fateful thrust at Liège.

The precise thing that ailed him I found at last on page 272 *et seq.* of the American edition of his book. There it was plainly de-scribed, albeit unwittingly, but if you will go back to the other nov-els after "Marriage" you will find traces of it in all of them, and even more vivid indications in the books of exposition and philos-ophizing that accompanied them. What slowly crippled him and perhaps disposed of him was his gradual acceptance of the theory, corrupting to the artist and scarcely less so to the man, that he was one of the Great Thinkers of his era, charged with a pregnant Message to the Younger Generations—that his ideas, rammed into enough skulls, would Save the Empire, not only from the satanic Nietzscheism of the public enemy, but also from all those inner Weaknesses that tainted and flabbergasted its vitals, as the tape-worm with nineteen heads devoured Atharippus of Macedon. In brief, he came down with a messianic delusion—and once a man begins to suffer from a messianic delusion his days as a serious art-ist are ended. He may yet serve the state with laudable devotion; he may yet enchant his millions; he may yet posture and gyrate be-fore the world as a man of mark. But not in the character of artist. Not as a creator of sound books. Not in the separate place of one who observes the eternal tragedy of man with full sympathy and understanding, and yet with a touch of god-like remoteness. Not as Homer saw it, smiting the while his blooming lyre.

I point, as I say, to page 272 of "Joan and Peter," whereon, im-

perfectly concealed by jocosity, you will find Wells's private view
of Wells. What it shows is the submergence of the artist in the tin-
pot reformer and professional wise man. A descent, indeed! The
man impinged upon us and made his first solid success, not as a
merchant of banal pedagogics, not as a hawker of sociological
liver-pills, but as a master of brilliant and life-like representation,
an evoker of unaccustomed but none the less deep-seated emotions, a dramatist of fine imagination and highly resourceful execution. It was the stupendous drama and spectacle of modern life,
and not its dubious and unintelligible lessons, that drew him from
his test-tubes and guinea-pigs and made an artist of him, and to
the business of that artist, once he had served his apprenticeship,
he brought a vision so keen, a point of view so fresh and sane and
a talent for exhibition so lively and original that he straightway
conquered all of us. Nothing could exceed the sheer radiance of
"Tono-Bungay." It is a work that glows with reality. It projects a
whole epoch with unforgettable effect. It is a moving-picture conceived and arranged, not by the usual ex-bartender or chorus man,
but by an extremely civilized and sophisticated observer, alert to
every detail of the surface and yet acutely aware of the internal
play of forces, the essential springs, the larger, deeper lines of it. In
brief, it is a work of art of the soundest merit, for it both represents
accurately and interprets convincingly, and under everything is a
current of feeling that coördinates and informs the whole.

But in the success of the book and of the two or three following
it there was a temptation, and in the temptation a peril. The audience was there, high in expectation, eagerly demanding more.
And in the ego of the man—a true proletarian, and hence born
with morals, faiths, certainties, vastly gaseous hopes—there was an
urge. That urge, it seems to me, began to torture him when he set
about "The Passionate Friends" (1913). In the presence of it, he
was dissuaded from the business of an artist,—made discontented
with the business of an artist. It was not enough to display the life
of his time with accuracy and understanding; it was not even
enough to criticize it with a penetrating humor and sagacity. From
the depths of his being, like some foul miasma, there arose the
old, fatuous yearning to change it, to improve it, to set it right
where it was wrong, to make it over according to some pattern su-

perior to the one followed by the Lord God Jehovah. With this sinister impulse, as aberrant in an artist as a taste for legs in an archbishop, the instinct that had created "Tono-Bungay" and "The New Machiavelli" gave battle, and for a while the issue was in doubt. But with "Marriage" (1912) its trend began to be apparent—and before long the evangelist was triumphant, and his bray battered the ear, and in the end there was a quite different Wells before us, and a Wells worth infinitely less than the one driven off. Today one must put him where he had begun to put himself—not among the literary artists of English, but among the brummagem prophets of England.

The prophesying business is like writing fugues; it is fatal to every one save the man of absolute genius. The lesser fellow—and Wells, for all his cleverness, was surely one of the lesser fellows—is bound to come to grief at it, and one of the first signs of his coming to grief is the drying up of his sense of humor. Compare "The Soul of a Bishop" or "Joan and Peter" to "Ann Veronica" or "The History of Mr. Polly" (1910). One notices instantly the disappearance of the comic spirit, the old searching irony. It was in "Boon" (1915), I believe, that this irony showed its last flare. There is a passage in that book which somehow lingers in the memory: a portrait of the United States as it arose in the mind of an Englishman reading the *Nation* of the pre-war years: "a vain, garrulous and prosperous female of uncertain age, and still more uncertain temper, with unfounded pretensions to intellectuality and an idea of refinement of the most negative description ... the Aunt Errant of Christendom." A capital whimsy—but blooming almost alone. A sense of humor, had it been able to survive the theology, would certainly have saved us from Lady Sunderbund, in "The Soul of a Bishop," and from Lady Charlotte Sydenham in "Joan and Peter." But it did not and could not survive. It always withers in the presence of the messianic delusion, like justice and the truth in front of patriotic passion. What takes its place is the oafish, witless buffoonishness of the radio—for example, the sort of thing that makes an intolerable bore of "Bealby."

Nor were Wells's ideas, as he so laboriously expounded them, worth the sacrifice of his old lively charm. They were, in fact, second-hand, and he often muddled them in the telling. In "First and Last Things" (1908) he preached a flabby Socialism, and then, toward the end, admitted frankly that it would not work. In "Boon" he erected a whole book upon an eighth-rate platitude, to wit, the platitude that English literature, in these latter times, is platitudinous—a three-cornered banality, indeed, for his own argument was a case in point, and so helped to prove what was already obvious. In "The Research Magnificent" he smouched an idea from Nietzsche, and then mauled it so badly that one began to wonder whether he was in favor of it or against it. In "The Undying Fire" (1919) he first stated the obvious, and then fled from it in alarm. In his war books he borrowed right and left—from Dr. Wilson, from the British Socialists, from Romain Rolland, even from such profound thinkers as James M. Beck, Lloyd George and the editor of the New York *Tribune*—and everything that he borrowed was flat. In "Joan and Peter" he first argued that England was going to pot because English education was too formal and archaic, and then that Germany was going to pot because German education was too realistic and opportunist. He seemed to respond to all the varying crazes and fallacies of the day; he swallowed them without digesting them; he tried to substitute mere timeliness for reflection and feeling. And under all the rumble-bumble of bad ideas lay the imbecile assumption of the jitney messiah at all times and everywhere: that human beings may be made over by changing the rules under which they live, that progress is a matter of intent and foresight, that an act of Parliament can cure the blunders and check the practical joking of God.

Such notions are surely no baggage for a serious novelist. A novelist, of course, must have a point of view, but it must be a point of view untroubled by the crazes of the moment, it must regard the internal workings and meanings of existence and not merely its superficial appearances. A novelist must view life from some secure rock, drawing it into a definite perspective, interpreting it upon an ordered plan. Even if he hold (like Conrad, Dreiser, Hardy and Anatole France) that it is essentially meaningless, he must at least display that meaninglessness with reasonable clarity and consistency. Wells showed no such solid and intelligible attitude. He was too facile, too enthusiastic, too eager to teach today what he had learned only yesterday.

What remains of him? There remains a little shelf of truly excellent books, beginning with "Tono-Bungay" and ending with "Marriage." It is a shelf flanked on the one side by a long row of extravagant romances in the manner of Jules Verne, and on the other side by an even longer row of puerile tracts. But let us not underestimate it because it is in such uninviting company. There is on it some of the liveliest, most original, most amusing, and withal most respectable fiction that England has produced in our time. In that fiction there is a sufficient memorial to a man who, between two debauches of claptrap, had his day as an artist.

Arnold Bennett

From Prejudices: First Series, 1919, pp. 36–51. My reviews of Bennett's books in the *Smart Set* began with one of Denry the Audacious (published in England as The Card) in May, 1911. The following essay, in large part, was first printed in the magazine for Sept., 1919, pp. 138–44. Bennett was born in 1867 and died in 1931

Of Bennett it is quite easy to conjure up a recognizable picture by imaging everything that Wells was not—that is, everything interior, everything having to do with attitudes and ideas, everything beyond the mere craft of arranging words in ingratiating sequences. As stylists, of course, they had many points of contact. Each wrote a journalese that was extraordinarily fluent and tuneful; each was apt to be carried away by the rush of his own smartness. But in their matter they stood at opposite poles. Wells had a believing mind, and could not resist the lascivious beckonings and eye-winkings of meretricious novelty; Bennett carried skepticism so far that it often took on the appearance of a mere peasant-like suspicion of ideas, bellicose and unintelligent. Wells was astonishingly intimate and confidential, and more than one of his novels reeked with a shameless sort of autobiography; Bennett, even when he made use of personal experience, contrived to get impersonality into it. Wells, finally, was a sentimentalist, and could not conceal his feelings; Bennett, of all the English novelists of his day, was the most steadily aloof and ironical.

This habit of irony, in truth, was the thing that gave him all his characteristic color, and was at the bottom of both his peculiar merit and his peculiar limitation. On the one hand it set him free from the besetting sin of the contemporary novelist: he never preached, he had no messianic delusion, he was above the puerile theories that have engulfed more romantic men. But on the other hand it left him empty of the passion that is, when all is said and done, the chief mark of the true novelist. The trouble with him was that he could not feel with his characters, that he never involved himself emotionally in their struggles against destiny, that the drama of their lives never thrilled or damaged him—and the result was that he was unable to arouse in the reader that penetrating sense of kinship, that profound and instinctive sympathy, which in its net effect is almost indistinguishable from the understanding born of experiences actually endured and emotions actually shared. Joseph Conrad, in a memorable piece of criticism, once put the thing clearly. "My task," he said, "is, by the power of the written word, to make you hear, to make you feel—it is, above all, to make you *see*." Here seeing, it must be obvious, is no more than feeling put into physical terms; it is not the outward aspect that is to be seen, but the inner truth—and the end to be sought by that apprehension of inner truth is responsive recognition, the sympathy of poor mortal for poor mortal, the tidal uprush of feeling that makes us all one. Bennett, it seems to me, could not evoke it. His characters, as they pass, have a deceptive brilliance of outline, but they soon fade; one never finds them haunting the memory as Lord Jim haunts it, or Carrie Meeber, or Huck Finn, or Tom Jones. The reason is not so far to seek. It lies in the plain fact that they appeared to their creator, not as men and women whose hopes and agonies were of poignant concern, not as tragic comedians in isolated and concentrated dramas, but as mean figures in an infinitely dispersed and unintelligible farce, as helpless nobodies in an epic struggle that transcended both their volition and their comprehension. In brief, he failed to humanize them completely, and so he failed to make their emotions contagious. They are, in their way, often vividly real; they are thoroughly accounted for; what there is of them is unfailingly life-like; they move and breathe in an environment that pulses and glows. But the attitude of the author toward them remains, in the end, the attitude of a biologist toward his laboratory animals. He does not *feel* with them—and neither does his reader.

Bennett's chief business, in fact, was not with individuals at all, even though he occasionally brought them up almost to life-size. What concerned him principally was the common life of large groups, the action and reaction of castes and classes, the struggle among societies. In particular, he was engrossed by the colossal and disorderly functioning of the English middle class—a category of mankind inordinately mixed in race, confused in ideals, and illogical in ideas. It is a group that has had interpreters aplenty, past and present; a full half of the literature of the Victorian era was devoted to it. But never, I believe, has it had an interpreter more resolutely detached and relentless—never has it had one less shaken by emotional involvement. Here the very lack that detracts so much from Bennett's stature as a novelist in the conventional sense is converted into a valuable possession. Better than any other man of his time he got upon paper the social anatomy and physiology of the masses of average, everyday, unimaginative Englishmen. One leaves the series of Five Towns books with a sense of having looked down the tube of a microscope upon a huge swarm of infinitely little but incessantly struggling organisms—creatures engaged furiously in the pursuit of grotesque and unintelligible ends—helpless participants in and victims of a struggle that takes on, to their eyes, a thousand lofty purposes, all of them puerile to the observer above its turmoil. Here, he seems to say, is the middle, the average, the typical Englishman. Here is the fellow as he appears to himself—virtuous, laborious, important, intelligent, made in God's image. And here he is in fact—swinish, ineffective, inconsequential, stupid, a feeble parody upon his maker. It is irony that penetrates and devastates, and it is unrelieved by any show of the pity that gets into the irony of Conrad, or of the tolerant claim of kinship that mitigates that of Fielding and Thackeray. It is harsh and cocksure. It has, at its moments, some flavor of actual bounderism: one instinctively shrinks from so smart-alecky a pulling off of underclothes and unveiling of warts.

It is easy to discern in it, indeed, a note of distinct hostility, and even of disgust. The long exile of the author is not without its sig-

nificance. He not only got in France something of the Frenchman's aloof and disdainful view of the English; he must have taken
a certain distaste for the national scene with him in the first place,
else he would not have gone at all. An Italian adventure, I daresay,
would have produced the same effect, or a Spanish, or Russian, or
German. But it happened to be French. But what such a Bennett
story as "The Pretty Lady" attempts to do is what every serious
Bennett story attempts to do: to exhibit dramatically the great gap
separating the substance from the appearance in the English character. It seems to me that its prudent and self-centered G. J. Hoape
is a vastly more real Englishman of his class, and, what is more, an
Englishman vastly more useful and creditable to England, than
any of the gaudy Bayards and Cids of romantic fiction. Here, indeed, the irony somehow fails. The man we are obviously expected to disdain converts himself, toward the end, into a man not
without his touches of the admirable. He is no hero, God knows,
and there is no more brilliance in him than you will find in an average country squire or Parliament man, but he has the rare virtue
of common sense, and that is probably the virtue that has served
the English better than all others. Curiously enough, the English
reading public recognized the irony but failed to observe its con-
futation, and so the book got Bennett into bad odor at home, and
into worse odor among the sedulous apes of English ideas and
emotions on this side of the water. But it is a sound work
nevertheless—a sound work with a large and unescapable defect.

That defect is visible in a good many of the other Bennett
books. It is the product of his emotional detachment and it commonly reveals itself as an inability to take his own story seriously.
Sometimes he poked open fun at it, as in "The Roll-Call"; more
often he simply abandoned it before it was done, as if weary of a
too tedious foolery. This last process is plainly visible in "The
Pretty Lady." The thing that gives form and direction to that story
is a simple enough problem in psychology, to wit: what will happen when a man of sound education and decent instincts, of sober
age and prudent habit, of common sense and even of certain mild
cleverness—what will happen, logically and naturally, when such
a normal, respectable, cautious fellow finds himself disquietingly
in love with a lady of no position at all—in brief, with a lady but

lately on the town? Bennett set the problem, and for a couple of hundred pages investigated it with the utmost ingenuity and address, exposing and discussing its sub-problems, tracing the gradual shifting of its terms, prodding with sharp insight into the psychological material entering into it. And then, as if suddenly tired of it—worse, as if suddenly convinced that the thing has gone on long enough, that he had given the public enough of a book for its money—he forthwith evaded the solution altogether, and brought down his curtain upon a palpably artificial dénouement. The device murdered the book. One is arrested at the start by a fascinating statement of the problem, one follows a discussion of it that shows Bennett at his brilliant best, fertile in detail, alert to every twist of motive, incisively ironical at every step—and then, at the end, one is incontinently turned out of the booth. The effect is that of being assaulted with an ice-pick by a hitherto amiable bartender, almost that of being bitten by a pretty girl in the midst of an amicable buss.

That painful affront is no stranger to the reader of the Bennett novels. One encounters it in many of them. There is a tremendous marshalling of meticulous and illuminating observation, the background throbs with color, the sardonic humor is never-failing, it is a capital show—but always one goes away from it with a sense of having missed the conclusion, always there is a final begging of the question. It is not hard to perceive the attitude of mind underlying this chronic evasion of issues. It is agnosticism carried to the last place of decimals. Life itself is meaningless; therefore, the discussion of life is meaningless; therefore, why try futilely to get a meaning into it? The reasoning, unluckily, has holes in it. It may be sound logically, but it is psychologically unworkable. One goes to novels, not for the bald scientific fact, but for some interpretation of it, and hence some amelioration of it. When they carry that amelioration to the point of uncritical certainty, when they are full of glib explanations that click and whirl like machines, then the mind revolts against the childish naïveté of the thing. But when there is no organization of the spectacle at all, when it is presented as a mere formless panorama, when to the sense of its unintelligibility is added the suggestion of inherent chaos, then the mind revolts no less. Art can never be simple representation. It cannot deal solely with precisely what is. It must, at the least, present the real in the light of some recognizable ideal; it must give to the eternal farce, if not some moral, then at all events some direction. For without that formulation there can be no clear-cut separation of the individual will from the general stew and turmoil of things, and without that separation there can be no coherent drama, and without that drama there can be no evocation of emotion, and without that emotion art is unimaginable. The field of the novel is very wide. There is room, on the one side, for a brilliant play of ideas and theories, provided only they do not stiffen the struggle of man with man, or of man with destiny, into a mere struggle of abstractions. There is room, on the other side, for the most complete agnosticism, provided only it be tempered by feeling. Conrad was quite as unshakable an agnostic as Bennett; he was a ten times more implacable ironist. But there was yet a place in his scheme for a sardonic sort of pity, and pity, however sardonic, is perhaps as good an emotion as another. The trouble with Bennett was that he essayed to sneer, not only at the futile aspiration of man, but also at the agony that goes with it. The result is an air of affectation, of superficiality, almost of stupidity. The manner, on the one hand, is that of a highly skillful and profoundly original artist, but on the other hand it is that of a sophomore just made aware of Huxley, Haeckel and Nietzsche.

Bennett's unmitigated skepticism explains two things that have constantly puzzled his critics, and that have been the cause of a great deal of idiotic writing about him—for him as well as against him. One of these things was his utter lack of anything properly describable as artistic conscience—his extreme readiness to play the star houri in the seraglio of the publishers; the other was his habit of translating platitudes into racy journalese and gravely offering them to the suburban trade as "pocket philosophies." Both crimes, it seems to me, had their rise in his congenital incapacity for taking ideas seriously, even including his own. "If this," he appeared to say, "is the tosh you want, then here is another dose of it. Personally, I have little interest in that sort of thing. Even good novels—the best I can do—are no more than compromises with a silly convention. I am not interested in stories; I am interested in the anatomy of human melancholy; I am a descriptive sociologist, with overtones of malice. But if you want stories, and can pay for them, I am willing to give them to you. And if you prefer bad stories, then here is a bad one. Don't assume you can shame me by deploring my willingness. Think of what your doctors do every day, and your lawyers, and your men of God, and your stockbrokers, and your traders and politicians. I am surely no worse than the average. In fact, I am probably a good deal superior to the average, for I am at least not deceived by my own mountebankery—I at least know my sound goods from my shoddy." Such, I daresay, was the process of thought behind such hollow tradegoods as "Buried Alive" and "The Lion's Share." One does not need the man's own amazing confidences to hear his snickers at his audience, at his work and at himself.

The books of boiled-mutton "philosophy" probably had much the same origin. What appears in them is less a weakness for ideas that are stale and obvious than a distrust of all ideas whatsoever. The public, with its mob yearning to be instructed, edified and pulled by the nose, demands certainties; it must be told definitely and a bit raucously that this is true and that is false. But there *are* no certainties. *Ergo,* one notion is as good as another, and if it happens to be utter flubdub, so much the better—for it is precisely flubdub that penetrates the popular skull with the greatest facility. The way is already made: the hole already gapes. An effort to approach the hidden and baffling truth would simply burden the enterprise with difficulty. Moreover, the effort is laborious and ungrateful. Yet more, there is probably no hidden truth to be uncovered. Thus, by the route of skepticism, Bennett apparently arrived at his sooth-saying. That he actually believed in it is inconceivable. He was far too intelligent a man to hold that any truths within the comprehension of the popular audience were sound enough to be worth preaching, or that it would do any good to preach them if they were.

So much for two of the salient symptoms of his underlying skepticism. Another is to be found in his incapacity to be, in the ordinary sense, ingratiating; it was simply beyond him to say the pleasant thing with any show of sincerity. Of all his books, probably the worst are his book on World War I and his book on the United States. The latter was obviously undertaken with some notion of paying off a debt. Bennett had been to the United States; the newspapers had hailed him in their side-show way; the women's clubs had pawed over him; he had, no doubt, come home a good deal richer. What he essayed to do was to write a volume on the Republic that should be at once colorably accurate and discreetly agreeable. The enterprise was quite beyond him. The book not only failed to please Americans; it offended them in a thousand subtle ways, and from its appearance dates the decline of the author's vogue among us. His war book missed fire in much the same way. It was workman-like, it was deliberately urbane, it was undoubtedly truthful—but it fell flat in England and it fell flat in America.

What all this amounts to may be very briefly put: in one of the requisite qualities of the first-rate novelist Bennett was almost completely lacking, and so it would be no juggling with paradox to argue that, at bottom, he was scarcely a novelist at all. His books, indeed—that is, his serious books, the books of his better canon—often failed utterly to achieve the effect that one associates with the true novel. One carried away from them, not the impression of a definite transaction, not the memory of an outstanding and appealing personality, not the after-taste of a profound emotion, but merely the sense of having witnessed a gorgeous but incomprehensible parade, coming out of nowhere and going to God knows where. They were magnificent as representation, they bristled with charming detail, they radiated the humors of an acute and extraordinary man, they were entertainment of the best sort—but there was seldom anything in them of that clear, well-aimed and solid effect which one associates with the novel as work of art. Most of these books, indeed, were no more than collections of essays defectively dramatized. What was salient in them was not their people, but their backgrounds—and their people were forever fading into their backgrounds. Is there a character in any of these books that shows any sign of living as Pendennis lives, and Barry Lyndon, and Emma Bovary, and David Copperfield? Who remembers much about Sophia Baines, save that she lived in the Five Towns, or even about Clayhanger? Young George Cannon, in "The Roll-Call," is no more than a chart for a lecture on modern marriage. Hilda Lessways-Cannon-Clayhanger is not only inscrutable; she is also dim. The man and woman of "Whom God Hath Joined," perhaps the best of all the Bennett novels, I have so far forgotten that I cannot remember their names. Even Denry the Audacious grows misty. One remembers that he was the center of the farce, but now he is long gone and the farce remains.

But though Bennett may not have played the game according to the rules, the game that he did play was nevertheless extraordinarily diverting and called for an incessant display of the finest sort of skill. No writer of his time looked into its life with sharper eyes, or set forth his findings with a greater charm and plausibility. Within his deliberately narrow limits he did precisely the thing that Balzac undertook to do, and Zola after him: he painted a full-length portrait of a whole society, accurately, brilliantly and, in certain areas, almost exhaustively. The middle Englishman—not the individual, but the type—is there displayed more vividly than he is displayed anywhere else that I know of. The thing is rigidly held to its aim; there is no episodic descent or ascent to other fields. But within that one field every resource of observation, of invention and of imagination has been brought to bear upon the business—every one save that deep feeling for man in his bitter tragedy which is the most important of them all. Thus Bennett, whatever his failing in his capital function of the artist, is certainly of the very highest consideration as craftsman. Scattered through his books, even his bad books, there are fragments of writing that are quite unsurpassed in the latter-day English novel—the shoe-shining episode in "The Pretty Lady," the adulterous interlude in "Whom God Hath Joined," the dinner party in "Paris Nights," the discussion of the Cannon-Ingram marriage in "The Roll-Call," the studio party in "The Lion's Share." Such writing is rare and exhilarating. It is to be respected. And the man who did it is not to be forgotten.

Somerset Maugham

From the *Smart Set*, Nov., 1919, pp. 138–40.
A review of THE MOON AND SIXPENCE,
by W. Somerset Maugham; New York, 1919

"The Moon and Sixpence" is an absurdly vague and vapid title for an extremely sound piece of work. This Maugham, half a dozen years ago, was well-known as a writer of bad comedies of the slighter, smarter variety, by Oscar Wilde out of the Tom Robertson tradition—the sort of thing that John Drew used to do—labored epigrams strung upon a thread of drawing-room adultery. In the intervals between them he wrote third-rate novels: "The Explorers," "The Magician" and others, all now forgotten. One day, entirely without warning, he gave London a surprise by publishing a story of a different kind, to wit, "Of Human Bondage," an interminably long, solemn and inchoate but nevertheless curiously sagacious and fascinating composition—very un-English in its general structure, almost Russian in some of its details. This book came to me for review, but when I observed its count of pages I quietly dropped it behind the piano. Two or three years later a woman of sound taste in fiction advised me to unearth it and read it, and I made a futile search for it. Another year passed and a second woman began talking it up. Having been long convinced that women are much better judges of novels than men—who ever heard of a woman who read detective stories?—I now got hold of the book and read it, an enterprise absorbing the leisure of a whole week. I left it very much impressed. The story was too garrulous; it often threatened to get beyond the author; it was, in more than one place, distressingly young; but all the same there was a fine earnestness in it, and a great deal of careful observation, and some passages of capital writing. The Maugham of the shallow comedies for West End theatres was nowhere visible. This Maugham was a man who was trying very hard to present his characters honestly, and to get beneath their skins, and to put behind them a living and recognizable background, and what is more, he was, in chapter after chapter, coming pleasantly close to success. In brief, a very unusual book—something worthy of being mentioned in the same breath with such things as Walpole's "The Gods and Mr. Perrin," George's "The Making of an Englishman," Bennett's "Whom God Hath Joined" and Wells' "Ann Veronica."

Now, in "The Moon and Sixpence," Maugham takes another leap forward. That leap is from the uncertainty of the neophyte to the sureness of the accomplished craftsman, from unsteady experimentation to fluent and easy technic. It is, indeed, an astonishing progress; I know of no other case that quite parallels it. The book, if it were hollow as a jug otherwise, would still be remarkable as a sheer piece of writing. It has good design; it moves and breathes; it has a fine manner; it is packed with artful and effective phrases. But better than all this, it is a book which tackles head-on one of the hardest problems that the practical novelist ever has to deal with, and which solves it in a way that is both sure-handed and brilliant. This is the problem of putting a man of genius into a story in such fashion that he will seem real—in such fashion that the miracle of him will not blow up the plausibility of him. Scores of novelists have tried to solve it, and failed. Every publishing season sees half a dozen new tales with Nietzsche, or Chopin, or Bonaparte, or Wagner for hero—and half a dozen creaking marionettes, no more real than your aunt's false teeth. But Maugham, with his painting genius, his Kensington Gauguin, somehow achieves the impossible. One gets the unmistakable feeling that the fellow is extraordinary—not merely odd, but of genuinely superior quality—and yet there is nothing operatic and fabulous about him; he remains an authentic man in the midst of all his gaudiest doings. It is a novelistic feat of a high order, and, as Woodrow says, I should be lacking in perfect frankness if I did not admit that I have been a good deal surprised by Maugham's performance of it. It is as if John Philip Sousa should suddenly spit on his hands and write a first-rate symphony. It is almost as if a Congressman should suddenly become honest, self-respecting, courageous and intelligent.

Naturally, the thing is done very simply. Maugham's success, in fact, lies a good deal less in what he positively does than in what he discreetly leaves undone. He gets the colors of life into his Charles Strickland, not by playing a powerful beam of light upon him, but by leaving him a bit out of focus—by constantly insisting, in the midst of every discussion of him, upon his pervasive mystery—in brief, by craftily making him appear, not as a commonplace, simple and completely understandable man, but as the half comprehended enigma that every genuine man of genius seems to all of us when we meet him in real life. The average novelist, grappling with such a hero, always makes the fatal error of trying to account for him wholly—of reducing him to a composite of fictional rubber-stamps. Thus he inevitably takes on commonness, and in proportion as he is clearly drawn he loses plausibility as a man of genius. Maugham falls into no such blunder. Of Strickland, the unit of human society—the Strickland who eats, sleeps, travels about, reads the newspapers, changes his shirt, has his shoes polished, dodges automobiles and goes to business every morning like the rest of us—we get a portrait that is careful, logical and meticulous—in brief, that is brilliantly life-like. But of the vaster, darker Strickland who is a man of genius—the Strickland who deserts his family to go to Paris to paint, and there plods his way to extraordinary achievement, and then throws away his life in the South Seas—of this Strickland we see only an image made up of sudden and brief points of light, like flashes of Summer lightning below the horizon. He is, in one aspect, made convincingly vivid; he is, in the other, left in the shadow of mystery. That is precisely how we all see a man of genius in real life; he is half plain John Smith and half inscrutable monster. It remained for Maugham to get the thing into a novel. If there were no other merit in his book, it would stand out from the general for that unusually deft and effective character sketch.

As for the machinery of the effect, part of it is borrowed from Joseph Conrad, to wit, the device of presenting the story through the medium of an onlooker, himself fascinated and daunted by the enigma of it. This device, of course, was not invented by Conrad, but it seems to me that he has employed it to better purpose than any other novelist writing in English. Consider, for example, how magnificently it is used in "Typhoon," in "Lord Jim," and in "Heart of Darkness." These stories, straightforwardly told, would still be stories of very high quality, but I believe that a good deal of their present strange flavor would be gone; they would cease to suggest the sinister and inexplicable. There appears to be a theory among novelists that the precisely contrary method is the more convincing—that the way to write a tale that will carry the air of reality is to do it in the autobiographical form. But that is surely not true. When he adopts the autobiographical form the novelist is compelled to account for his protagonist completely; he must attain to realism by pretending to omniscience. That pretension has brought many an otherwise sound novel to disaster. I am almost convinced that it would have brought even "Lord Jim" into difficulties. What holds our interest in Jim to the last, and leaves us with a memory of him that glows for long days, is the dark wonder of him. We learn enough about him to see him clearly, but we never quite penetrate his soul—we are never quite certain about the interplay of motives that brings him to his romantic catastrophe. Take away the droning Marlow, and he would come too close to the camera. Thus there lies, beyond the crude realism of white light, the finer, softer realism of delicately managed shadows. More than half the charm of Conrad, I daresay, is due to his superb capacity for managing them. At the end of every one of his incomparable tales there is a question-mark. He leaves us to answer as we will, each according to the light within. . . . I think that Maugham, borrowing that device, has employed it with noteworthy success. He is, God knows, no Conrad, but he has written a very excellent novel, and in it there is plenty of evidence that its quality is no mere accident, but the product of very deliberate and intelligent effort.

Scherzo for the Bassoon

From the *Smart Set*, May, 1922, pp. 142–43.
A review of CROME YELLOW, by Aldous Huxley; New York, 1922

Aldous Huxley's "Crome Yellow," if it be called a novel, violates all of the rules and regulations that I have laid down so smugly. But why call it a novel? I can see absolutely no reason for doing so, save that the publisher falls into the error in his slip-cover, press-matter and canned review. As a matter of fact, the book is simply an elaborate piece of spoofing, without form and without direction. It begins, goes on aimlessly, and then suddenly stops. But are only novels fit to read? Nay; try "Crome Yellow." If it does not make you yell with joy, then I throw off the prophetical robes forever. It is a piece of buffoonery that sweeps the whole range from the most delicate and suggestive tickling to the most violent thumping of the ribs. It has made me laugh as I have not laughed since I read the Inaugural Harangue of Dr. Harding.

This Huxley, in truth, is a fellow of the utmost shrewdness, in-

genuity, sophistication, impudence, waggishness and contumacy—
a literary atheist who is forever driving herds of sheep, hogs,
camels, calves and jackasses into the most sacred temples of his
people. He represents the extreme swing of the reaction against
everything that a respectable Englishman holds to be true and
holy. The attitude is no pose, as it would be among the fugitives
from the cow states in Greenwich Village; it comes to him legit-
imately from his grandfather, Thomas Henry Huxley, perhaps the
roughest and most devastating manhandler of gods ever heard of
in human history. Old Thomas Henry was a master of cultural
havoc and rapine simply because he never grew indignant. In the
midst of his most fearful crimes against divine revelation he maintained the aloof and courtly air of an executioner cutting off the
head of a beautiful queen. Did he disembowel the Pentateuch, to
the scandal of Christendom? Then it was surely done politely—
even with a certain easy geniality. Did he knock poor old Gladstone all over the lot, first standing him on his head and then
bouncing him upon his gluteus maximus? Then the business
somehow got the graceful character of a *Wienerwalz*. Aldous is obviously less learned than his eminent grandpa. I doubt that he is
privy to the morphology of *Astacus fluviatilis* or that he knows anything more about the Pleistocene or the Middle Devonian than is
common gossip among Oxford barmaids. But though he thus
shows a falling off in positive knowledge, he is far ahead of the *Ur*-
Huxley in worldly wisdom, and it is this worldly wisdom which
produces the charm of "Crome Yellow." Here, in brief, is a civilized man's *reductio ad absurdum* of his age—his contemptuous
kicking of its pantaloons. Here, in a short space, delicately, ingra-
tiatingly and irresistibly, whole categories and archipelagoes of
contemporary imbecilities are brought to the trial by wit. In some
dull review or other I have encountered the news that all the characters of the fable are real people and that the author himself is
Denis, the minor poet, who loses his girl by being too cerebral and
analytical to grab her. Nonsense! Huxley, if he is there at all, is
Scogan, the chorus to the whole drama, with his astounding common sense, his acidulous humor, and his incomparable heresies.

D. H. Lawrence

From the *Smart Set*, Feb., 1923, pp. 140–41

The case of Lawrence continues to baffle me. First I read the current encomiums of him as a man of genius, then I pray humbly to God, and then I read his books. They leave me hopelessly convinced, despite all the high testimony to the contrary, that what is in them is extremely hollow and trivial stuff—that they are full of false psychology, preposterous episodes, and stiff and artificial people. Of late I have been giving hard study to what is widely regarded as the author's masterpiece, to wit, "Women in Love." In brief, the story of two provincial English-women, sisters, who track down a pair of husbands. This business, it turns out, is not easy. The swains are coy, and one of them, at least, carries about with him a very violent anti-connubial complex. Nevertheless, the girls persist, and in the end they are successful, though both have to employ the desperate device of offering their favors before the parson cries "Go!" The dialogues which forward the benign business are set forth at extreme length, and to me, at all events, they appear magnificently nonsensical. If this is "psychology," as the Lawrence fanatics would have us believe, then it is unquestionably the psychology of maniacs. One of the swains, Birkin, actually runs amok more than once. I submit his conversation, as Lawrence reports it, to the judgment of a candid world. His most massive ideas are simply psychopathological. As for the girls, they are both fools. In brief, a book full of blowsy tosh.

But why, then, the vast esoteric vogue of Lawrence? He is highly esteemed, I am convinced, simply because he is rather bold in his dealing with sexual transactions. He is not content to stop with the usual eye-rolling and hard breathing; he proceeds to physiological phenomena of a far less seemly character. When Hermione, the fat girl, whacks her beau over the head, the effects upon her own central nervous system are those described in certain chapters of Krafft-Ebing. I do not say that these effects are improbable, and I certainly do not argue that Lawrence sets them forth with anything properly describable as indecency: the Comstockian attack upon his book, indeed, is characteristically imbecile. But what I do say is that his current celebrity rests very largely upon his obvious preoccupation with such things, and that all his antecedent "psychology," though it is mainly nonsensical, is taken on trust for the sake of them. Standing by itself, or leading to some less blushful goal, that "psychology" would simply bore his customers. It is, as I have said, extremely bizarre and unconvincing. People do not do things for the motives that he credits to them, nor do they explain their acts in the outlandish terms he uses. To argue, as some of his admirers do, that his work marks an advance in the inner structure and content of the English novel, and that he is teaching all other novelists something about their business that they never knew before he mounted the stump—to argue thus is to depart definitely from all sense and logic. There is nothing in his novels—and I have now read them all, and some of them twice—that properly deserves such astounding encomiums. They are, in spots, competently written, but those spots are few and wide apart. In the main, he is horribly dull.

XVI. AMERICAN NOVELISTS

The Puritan Abroad

From the *Smart Set*, Oct., 1915, p. 152

MARK TWAIN was a great artist, but his nationality hung around his neck like a millstone. So long as he confined himself to the sympathetic portrayal of American people and American scenes, laughing gently and caressing while he laughed—for example, in "Huckleberry Finn"—he produced work that will live long after the artificialities of the Boston Brahmins are forgotten. But the moment he came into conflict, as an American, with the ideas and ideals of other peoples, the moment he essayed to convert his humor into something sharp and destructive, that moment he became merely silly and the joke was on him. One plows through "The Innocents Abroad" and through parts of "A Tramp Abroad" with something akin to amazement. Is such coarse and ignorant clowning to be accepted as humor? Is it really the mark of a smart fellow to laugh at "Lohengrin"? Is Titian's chromo of Moses in the bulrushes really the best picture in Europe? Is there nothing in Catholicism save petty grafting, monastic scandals, and the worship of the knuckles and shin-bones of dubious saints? May not one, disbelieving in it, still be profoundly moved by its dazzling history, the lingering monuments of its old power, the charm of its prodigal and melancholy beauty? In the presence of the unaccustomed, Mark Twain the artist was obliterated by Mark Twain the American: all he could see in it was strangeness, and all he could see in strangeness was hostility. There are chapters in "Huckleberry Finn" in which he stands side by side with Cervantes and Molière; there are chapters in "The Innocents Abroad" in which he is indistinguishable from Mutt and Jeff. Had he been born in

France (the country of his chief abomination) instead of in a Puritan village of the United States, he would have conquered the world. But try as he would, being what he was, he could not get rid of the Puritan smugness, the Puritan distrust of ideas, the Puritan incapacity for seeing beauty as a thing in itself, entirely distinct from and beyond all mere morality.

George Ade

From PREJUDICES: FIRST SERIES, 1919, pp. 114–22.
First printed in part in the *Smart Set*, Feb., 1913,
pp. 154–55, and in part in the New York *Evening Mail*, July 7, 1917

George Ade was one of the few genuinely original literary craftsmen in practice among us in his time. He came nearer to making sound and living literature, when he had full steam up, than any save a scant half-dozen of the contemporary novelists, and the whole body of his work, both in books and for the stage, was as thoroughly American, in cut and color, in tang and savor, in structure and point of view, as the work of Mark Twain. No single American novel of the first years of the century showed more sense of nationality, a keener feeling for national prejudice and peculiarity, a sharper and more pervasive Americanism than such Adean fables as "The Good Fairy of the Eighth Ward and the Dollar Excursion of the Steam-Fitters," "The Mandolin Players and the Willing Performer," and "The Adult Girl Who Got Busy Before They Could Ring the Bell on Her." Here, under all the labored extravagance, there are brilliant flashlight pictures of the American people in the Roosevelt I era, and American ways of thinking, and the whole of American *Kultur*. Here the veritable Americano of the early 1900s stands forth, lacking not a waggery, a superstition, a snuffle or a wen.

Ade himself, for all his story-teller's pretense of remoteness, was as absolutely American as any of his prairie-town traders and pushers, Shylocks and Dogberries, beaux and belles. He fairly reeked with the national Philistinism, the national respect for respectability, the national distrust of ideas. He was a marcher, one fancies, in parades; he joined movements, and movements against movements; he knew no language save his own; he regarded Roosevelt I quite seriously and a Mozart or an Ibsen as a joke; one would not be surprised to hear that, until he went off to his fresh-water college, he slept in his underwear and read the *Epworth Herald*. But, like Dreiser, he was a peasant touched by the divine fire; somehow, a great instinctive artist got himself born out there in that lush Indiana countryside. He had the rare faculty of seeing accurately, even when the thing seen was directly under his nose, and he had the still rarer faculty of recording vividly, of making the thing seen move with life. One often doubts a character in a novel, even in a good novel, but who ever doubted Gus in "The Two Mandolin Players," or Mae in "Sister Mae," or, to pass from the fables, Payson in "Mr. Payson's Satirical Christmas"? Here, with strokes so crude and obvious that they seem to be laid on with a broom, Ade achieved what O. Henry, with all his sideshow-barker smartness, always failed to achieve; he filled his bizarre tales with human beings. There was never any artfulness on the surface. The tale itself was never novel, or complex; it never surprised; often it was downright banal. But underneath there was an artfulness infinitely well wrought, and that was the artfulness of a story-teller who dredged his story out of his people, swiftly and skillfully, and did not squeeze his people into his story, laboriously and unconvincingly.

Needless to say, a moralist stood behind the comedian, for he was 100% American. He would teach; he even grew indignant. Roaring like a yokel at a burlesque show over such wild and light-hearted jocosities as "Paducah's Favorite Comedians" and "Why 'Gondola' Was Put Away," one turns with something of a start to such things as "Little Lutie," "The Honest Money Maker," and "The Corporation Director and the Mislaid Ambition." Up to a certain point it is all laughter, but after that there is a flash of the knife, a show of teeth. Here a national limitation closed in upon the satirist. He could not quite separate the unaccustomed from the abominable; he was unable to avoid rattling his Philistine trappings a bit proudly; he must prove that he, too, was a right-thinking American, a solid citizen and a patriot, unshaken in his lofty rectitude by such poisons as aristocracy, adultery, *hors* d'oeuvres and the sonata form. But in other directions this thorough-going nationalism helped him rather than hindered him. It enabled him, for one thing, to see into sentimentality, and to comprehend it and project it accurately. I know of no book which displays the mooniness of youth with more feeling and sympathy than "Artie," save it be Frank Norris's forgotten "Blix." In such fields Ade achieved a success that is rare and indubitable. He made the thing charming and he made it plain.

But all these fables and other compositions of his are mere sketches, inconsiderable trifles, impromptus in bad English, easy to write and of no importance? Are they, indeed? Do not believe it for a moment. Back in 1905 or thereabout, when Ade was at the height of his celebrity as a newspaper Sganarelle, scores of hack comedians tried to imitate him—and all failed. I myself was of the number. I operated a so-called funny column in a daily newspaper, and like my colleagues near and far, I essayed to manufacture fables in slang. What miserable botches they were! How easy it was to imitate Ade's manner—and how impossible to imitate his matter. No; please don't get the notion that it is a simple thing to write such a fable as that of "The All-Night Seance and the Limit That Ceased to Be," or that of "The Preacher Who Flew His Kite, But Not Because He Wished to Do So," or that of "The Roystering Blades." Far from it, indeed. On the contrary, the only way you will ever accomplish the feat will be by first getting Ade's firm grasp upon American character, and his ability to think out a straightforward, simple, amusing story, and his alert feeling for contrast and climax, and his extraordinary talent for devising novel, vivid and unforgettable phrases. Those phrases of his sometimes wear the external vestments of a passing slang, but they are no more commonplace and vulgar at bottom than Gray's "mute, inglorious Milton" or the "somewheres East of Suez" of Kipling. They reduce an idea to a few pregnant syllables. They give the attention a fillip and light up a whole scene in a flash. They are the running evidences of an eye that saw clearly and of a mind that thought shrewdly. They give distinction to the work of a man who so well concealed a highly complex and efficient artistry that few ever noticed it.

James Branch Cabell

In part from the New York *Evening Mail*, July 3, 1918,
and in part from the New York *American*, Dec. 20, 1935

His name is alone sufficient to separate him sharply from the latter-day Southerner: to be a Cabell in Virginia is almost equivalent to being a Cecil in England. And in the whole bent of his mind there are belated evidences of that aristocratic tradition which came to its doom at Appomattox. He is remote, unperturbed, skeptical, leisurely, a man sensitive to elusive and delicate values. The thing that interests him is the inutile thing. He likes to toy with ideas, and is impatient of purposes. Reacting against the sordid and ignoble culture surrounding him, he seeks escape in bold and often extravagant projections of the fancy. In brief, a true artist, a civilized man—set down among oafish hawkers and peasants like a lone cocktail at a banquet of chautauqua orators.

What one finds, above all, in such books as "The Cream of the Jest," "The Eagle's Shadow," and "The Rivet in Grandfather's Neck" is style—a painter's feeling for form and color, a musician's feeling for rhythm. The thing said, though it is often excellent, is of secondary consideration: of chief importance is the way of saying it. And that way does not stop at the mere choice of words; it extends to the sentence as a whole, to the chapter as a whole: there is an adept search for the right measure, the right cadence. Reading Cabell, one gets a sense of a flow of harmonious sound. The inner ear responds to a movement that is subtly correct and satisfying. Such writing, of course, is very rare in America. When our novelists and essayists attempt it, the best they commonly achieve is a sort of idiotic sing-song—the sonorous gurgling of an evangelist exhorting sinners. But in Cabell's prose the trick is somehow managed. In Cabell there is vastly more than juicy three-four time, as there was vastly more in Synge, Wilde and Pater.

What lies under the style—and often the style is so charming that one doesn't look much beyond it—is the quality of irony, the somewhat disdainful detachment of a man who is beyond taking his fable seriously, but not beyond sensing every atom of its comedy. This quality, in our American writing, is almost as rare as sound prose. Our typical novelist is quite incapable of it. He not only believes that his tale is important; he also commonly believes that some great piece of moral philosophy (or theology) lies imbedded in it—that there is a message there for suffering humanity capable of curing our metaphysical chilblains if we will only heed it.

The peculiar charm of Cabell's romances of Poictesme does not lie in the fact that his heroes practise magic and slaughter dragons, for such things have been going on in fairy tales since time immemorial; it lies in the fact that they carry on their fantastic operations in the manner of honest American Rotarians, stopping anon to take lunch, to scratch themselves, and to slang their wives. It is, of course, not easy to manage the dichotomy. A bad author would make either the magic incredible or the heroes unreal. But Cabell, having great skill at such tricks, keeps both balls in the air very neatly, and the result, say in "The High Place," is an extremely amusing book, full of both gaudy nonsense and penetrating observation. One recognizes the people as real, and, having so recognized them, one is ready to follow them through wholly fabulous adventures.

In Cabell's so-called realistic stories—for example, "The Rivet in Grandfather's Neck"—the thing runs the other way. The people here are undoubtedly as real as the cop on the corner, but nevertheless they are deftly hoisted above the commonplace, and made to perform in a very romantic way. They do things that are plausibly natural, and yet very far from the usual; their thoughts are yours and mine, and yet they reach bizarre conclusions. In brief, they are real people treated romantically, just as the dragon-chasers of Poictesme are romantics treated realistically. The effect in both cases is much the same. One enjoys the solid pleasure of recognition, and yet one is taken on an exhilarating flight through empyrean.

Not in French

From the *Smart Set*, Jan., 1920, 138–40.
A review of JURGEN, by James Branch Cabell; New York, 1919

"Jurgen," estimated by current American standards, whether of the boobery or of the super-boobery, is everything that is abhorrent. On the negative side, it lacks all Inspiration, all Optimism, all tendency to whoop up the Finer Things; it moves toward no shining Goal; it even neglects to denounce Pessimism, Marital Infidelity, Bolshevism, the Alien Menace and German *Kultur*. And on the positive side it piles up sins unspeakable: it is full of racy and mirthful ideas, it is brilliantly written, it is novel and daring, it is ribald, it is heretical, it is blasphemous, it is Rabelaisian. Such a book simply refuses to fit into the decorous mid-Victorian pattern of American letters. It belongs to some outlandish literature, most probably the French. One might imagine it written by a member of the French Academy, say Anatole France. But could one imagine it written by a member of the American Academy of Arts and Letters, say Bliss Perry? The thought is not only fantastic; it is almost obscene.

Cabell came near sneaking into refined society, a few years ago, as a novelist. Several of his novels, like the earlier pieces of Hergesheimer, trembled on the verge of polite acceptance. Both writers were handicapped by having ears. They wrote English that was delicately musical and colorful—and hence incurably offensive to constant readers of Rex Beach, Thomas H. Dixon, and the New York *Times*. Hergesheimer finally atoned for his style by mastering the popular novelette formula; thereafter he was in the *Saturday Evening Post* and the old maids who review books for the newspapers began to praise him. A few weeks ago I received an invitation to hear him lecture before a Browning Society; in a year or two, if he continues to be good, he will be elected to membership in the National Institute of Arts and Letters, in full equality with Ernest Poole, Oliver Herford, Henry Sydnor Harrison and E. W. Townsend, author of "Chimmie Fadden." Cabell, I fear, must resign himself to doing without the accolade. "Beyond Life" spilled many a bean; beneath its rumblings one discerned more than one cackle of satanic laughter. "Jurgen" wrecks the whole beanery. It is a compendium of backwardlooking and wrong-thinking. It is a Devil's sonata, an infernal *Kindersinfonie* for slap-stick, seltzer-siphon and bladder-on-a-string. . . . And, too, for the caressing violin, the lovely and melancholy flute. How charmingly the fellow writes! What a hand for the slick and slippery phrase he has! How cunningly he winds up a sentence, and then flicks it out with a twist of the wrist—a shimmering, dazzling shower of nouns, verbs, adverbs, adjectives, pronouns and prepositions! It is curious how often the gift of irony is coupled with pedantry. Think of old François and his astounding citations from incredible authorities—almost like an article in a German medical journal. Or of Anatole France. Or of Swift. Cabell, in "Jurgen," borrows all the best hocus-pocus of the professors. He reconstructs an imaginary medi-eval legend with all the attention to detail of the pundits who pub-lish college editions of "Aucassin et Nicolette"; until, toward the end, his own exuberance intoxicates him a bit, he actually makes it seem a genuine translation. But his Jurgen, of course, is never a medieval man. No; Jurgen is horribly modern. Jurgen is the mod-ern man in reaction against a skepticism that explains everything away and yet leaves everything inexplicable. He is the modern man in doubt of all things, including especially his own doubts. So his quest is no heroic enterprise, though it takes him over half the earth and into all the gaudiest and most romantic kingdoms thereof, for the thing that he seeks is not a great hazard and an Homeric death but simply ease and contentment, and what he comes to in the end is the discovery that they are nowhere to be found, not even in the arms of a royal princess. Jurgen acquires the shirt of Nessus and the magical sword Caliburn; he becomes Duke of Logreus, Prince Consort in Cocaigne, King of Eubonia, and Emperor of Noumaria; he meets and loves the incomparable Guenevere in the moonlight on the eve of her marriage to King Arthur; he unveils the beauty of Helen of Troy; he is taught all the ineffable secrets of love by Queen Anaïtis; he becomes a great poet; he sees strange coasts; he roams the whole universe. But in the end, he returns sadly to a world "wherein the result of every human endeavor is transient and the end of all is death," and takes his old place behind the counter of his pawnshop, and resumes philosophically his interrupted feud with his faded wife, Dame Lisa.

In brief, a very simple tale, and as old in its fundamental dolorousness as arterio-sclerosis. What gives it its high quality is the richness of its detail—the prodigious gorgeousness of its imagery, the dramatic effectiveness of its shifting scenes, the whole glow and gusto of it. Here, at all events, it is medieval. Here Cabell evokes an atmosphere that is the very essence of charm. Nothing could be more delightfully done than some of the episodes—that of Jurgen's meeting with Guenevere in the Hall of Judgment; that of his dialogue with old King Gogyrvan Gawr, that of his adventure with the Hamadryad, that of the ceremony of the Breaking of the Veil, that of his invasion of the bed-chamber of Helen of Troy. The man who could imagine such scenes is a first-rate artist, and in the manner of their execution he proves the fact again. Time and again they seem to be dissolving, shaking a bit, going to pieces—but always he carries them off. And always neatly, delicately, with an air. The humor of them has its perils; to Puritans it must often seem shocking; it might easily become gross. But here it is no more gross than a rose-window. . . .

Toward the end, alack, the thing falls down. The transition from heathen Olympuses and Arcadies to the Christian Heaven and Hell works an inevitable debasement of the comedy. The satire here ceases to be light-fingered and becomes heavy-handed: "the religion of Hell is patriotism, and the government is an enlightened democracy." It is almost like making fun of a man with inflammatory rheumatism. Perhaps the essential thing is that the book is a trifle too long. By the time one comes to Calvinism, democracy, and the moral order of the world one has begun to feel surfeited. But where is there a work of art without a blemish? Even Beethoven occasionally misses fire. This "Jurgen," for all such ifs and buts, is a very fine thing. It is a great pity that it was not written in French. Done in English, and printed in These States, it somehow suggests Brahms scoring his Fourth Symphony for a jazz band and giving it at an annual convention of the Knights of Pythias.

Jack London

From PREJUDICES: FIRST SERIES, 1919, pp. 236–39.
London was born in 1876 and died in 1916

The quasi-science of genealogy, as it is practised in the United States, is directed almost exclusively toward establishing aristocratic descents for nobodies. That is to say, it records and glorifies decay. Its typical masterpiece is the discovery that the wife of some obscure county judge is the grandchild, infinitely removed, of Mary Queen of Scots, or that the blood of Geoffrey of Monmouth flows in the veins of a Philadelphia stock-broker. How much more profitably its professors might be employed in tracing the lineage of truly salient men. For example, Jack London. Where did he get his hot artistic passion, his delicate feeling for form and color, his extraordinary skill with words? The man, in truth, was an instinctive artist of a very respectable order, and if ignorance often corrupted his art, it only made the fact of his inborn skill the more remarkable. No other popular writer of his time did any better writing than you will find in "The Call of the Wild," or in parts of "John Barleycorn," or in such short stories as "The Sea Farmer" and "Samuel." Here, indeed, are all the elements of sound fiction: clear thinking, a sense of character, the dramatic instinct, and, above all, the adept putting together of words—words charming and slyly significant, words arranged, in a French phrase, for the respiration and the ear. You will never convince me that this aesthetic sensitiveness, so rare, so precious, so distinctively aristocratic, burst into abiogenetic flower on a San Francisco sand-lot. There must have been some intrusion of an alien and superior strain, some *pianissimo* fillip from above; there was obviously a great deal more to the thing than a routine hatching in low life.

But London the artist did not live *a cappella*. There was also London the Great Thinker, and the second often hamstrung the first. That great thinking of his, of course, took color from the misery of his early life; it was, in the main, a jejune Socialism, wholly uncriticised by humor. Some of his propagandist and expository

books are almost unbelievably nonsensical, and whenever he allowed any of his so-called ideas to sneak into an imaginative work
the intrusion promptly spoiled it. Socialism, in truth, is quite incompatible with art; its cook-tent materialism is fundamentally at
war with the first principle of the aesthetic gospel, which is that
one daffodil is worth ten shares of Bethlehem Steel. It is not by accident that there has never been a book on Socialism which was
also a work of art. Papa Marx's "Das Kapital" at once comes to
mind. It is as wholly devoid of graces as "The Origin of Species"
or "Science and Health"; one simply cannot conceive a reasonable
man reading it without aversion; it is as revolting as a barrel organ.
London, preaching Socialism, or quasi-Socialism, or whatever it
was that he preached, took over this offensive dullness. The mate-
rialistic conception of history was too heavy a load for him to
carry. When he would create beautiful books he had to throw it
overboard as Wagner threw overboard democracy, the superman
and free thought. A sort of temporary Christian created "Parsifal."
A sort of temporary aristocrat created "The Call of the Wild."

Also in another way London's early absorption of social and economic nostrums damaged him. It led him into the typical social-
istic exaltation of mere money; it put a touch of avarice into him.
Hence his too deadly industry, his relentless thousand words a day,
his steady emission of half-done books. The prophet of freedom, he
yet sold himself into slavery to the publishers, and paid off with his
soul for his ranch, his horses, his trappings of a wealthy cheese-
monger. His volumes rolled out almost as fast as those of E. Phillips Oppenheim; he simply could not make them all good at such
a gait. There are books on his list that are little more than garrulous notes for books. But even in the worst of them one comes
upon sudden splashes of brilliant color, stray proofs of the adept
penman, half-wistful reminders that London, at bottom, was really
an artist. There was in him a vast delicacy of perception, a high
feeling, a sensitiveness to beauty. And there was in him, too, under
all his blatancies, a poignant sense of the infinite romance and
mystery of human life.

Dreiser as Philosopher

From the *Smart Set*, May, 1920, pp. 138–40.
A review of HEY RUB-A-DUB-DUB,
by Theodore Dreiser; New York, 1920

It is easy enough to understand the impulse which prompted Dreiser to write "Hey Rub-a-Dub-Dub," his new book of essays and fulminations all compact. There comes times in every sentient man's life when he must simply unload his ideas, or bust like a star-shell in the highroad. If he is at that end of the scale which touches the rising ladder of the *Simiidae* he becomes a Socialist on a soap-box or joins the Salvation Army; if he is literate and has a soul he writes a book. Hence the great, whirring, infernal machines which chew up the forests of Canada, now and then salting the dose with the leg or arm of a Canuck. Hence the huge ink industry, consuming five million tons of bone-black a year. Hence democracy, Bolshevism, the moral order of the world. Hence sorrow. Hence literature.

In every line of "Hey Rub-a-Dub-Dub" there is evidence of the author's antecedent agony. One pictures him sitting up all night in his sinister studio down in Tenth street, wrestling horribly with the insoluble, trying his darndest to penetrate the unknowable. One o'clock strikes, and the fire sputters. Ghosts stalk in the room, fanning the yellow candle-light with their abominable breath—the spooks of all the men who have died for ideas since the world began—Socrates, Savonarola, Bruno (not Guido, but Giordano), Ravaillac, Sir Roger Casement, John Alexander Dowie, Dr. Crippen. Two o'clock. What, then, is the truth about marriage? Is it, as Grover Cleveland said, a grand sweet song, or is it, as the gals in the Village say, a hideous mockery and masquerade, invented by Capitalism to enslave the soul of woman—a legalized *Schweinerei*, worse than politics, almost as bad as the moving-pictures? Three o'clock. Was Marx right or wrong, a seer or a mere nose-puller? Was his name, in fact, actually Marx, or was it Marcus? From what ghetto did he escape, and cherishing what grudge complex: *cherchez le Juif!* (I confess at once: my great-grandpa, Moritz, was rector of the Oheb Shalon *Schul* in Grodno.) Three o'clock. . . .

Back to Pontius Pilate! *Quod est veritas?* Try to define it. Look into it. Break it into its component parts. What remains is a pale gray vapor, an impalpable emanation, the shadow of a shadow. Think of the brains that have gone to wreck struggling with the problem—cerebrums as large as cauliflowers, cerebellums as perfect as pomegranates. Think of the men jailed, clubbed, hanged, burned at the stake—not for embracing error, but for embracing the *wrong* error. Think of the innumerable caravan of Burlesons, Mitchell Palmers, Torquemadas, Cotton Mathers. . . . Four o'clock. The fire burns low in the grate. A gray fog without. Across the street two detectives rob a drunken man. Up at Tarrytown John D. Rockefeller snores in his damp Baptist bed, dreaming gaudily that he is young again and mashed on a girl named Marie. At Sing Sing forty head of Italians are waiting to be electrocuted. There is a memorial service for Charles Garvice in Westminster Abbey. The Comstocks raid the Elsie books. Ludendorff is elected Archbishop of Canterbury. A poor working-girl, betrayed by Moe, the boss's son, drowns herself in the Aquarium. It is late, ah me: nearly four thirty. . . . Who the deuce, then, is God? What is in all this talk of a future life, infant damnation, the Ouija board, Mortal Mind? Dr. Jacques Loeb is the father of a dozen bull-frogs. Is the news biological or theological? What became of the Albigenses? Are they in Heaven, in Purgatory or in Hell? . . . Five o'clock. Boys cry the *Evening Journal*. Is it today's or tomorrow's? The question of transubstantiation remains. There is, too, neo-transcendentalism. . . . In Munich they talk of *Expressionismus* . . . Poof! . . .

It is easy, as I say, to imagine a man beset by such reflections, and urged irresistibly to work them out on paper. Unluckily, the working out is not always as simple a business as it looks. Dreiser's first impulse as novelist, I daresay, was to do it in novels—to compose fictions full of ideas, saying something, teaching something, exposing something, destroying something. But the novelist also happens to be an artist, and at once the artist entered an effective caveat against that pollution. A work of art with ideas in it is as sorry a monster as a pretty girl full of Latin. The aim of a work of art is not to make one think painfully, but to make one feel beautifully. What is the idea in "Jennie Gerhardt"? Who knows but God? But in "Jennie Gerhardt" there is feeling—profound, tragic, exquisite. It is a thing of poignant and yet delicate emotions, like Brahms's Fourth Symphony. It lies in a sort of intellectual fourth dimension. It leaves a memory that is vivid and somehow caressing, and wholly free from doubts, questionings, head-scratchings. . . . So Dreiser decided to make a serious book of it, a book of unalloyed ratiocination, a book in the manner of Herbert Spencer. The result is "Hey Rub-a-Dub-Dub"—solemn stuff, with never a leer of beauty in it—in fact, almost furious. Once or twice it grows a bit lyrical; once or twice it rises to the imaginatively grotesque. But in the main it is plain exposition—a book of speculation and protest. He calls it himself "a book of the mystery and terror and wonder of life." I suspect that he lifted this subtitle from an old review of H.L.M. If so, then welcome! From him I have got more than is to be described in words and more than I can ever pay.

But what of the thing itself? Is it good stuff? My feeling is that it isn't. More, my feeling is that Dreiser is no more fitted to do a book of speculation than Joseph Conrad, say, is fitted to do a college yell. His talents simply do not lie in that direction. He lacks the mental agility, the insinuating suavity, the necessary capacity for romanticising a syllogism. Ideas themselves are such sober things that a sober man had better let them alone. What they need, to become bearable to a human race that hates them and is afraid of them, is the artful juggling of a William James, the insurance-agent persuasiveness of an Henri Bergson, the boob-bumping talents of a Martin Luther—best of all, the brilliant, almost Rabelaisian humor of a Nietzsche. Nietzsche went out into the swamp much further than any other explorer; he left such pall-bearers of the spirit as Spencer, Comte, Descartes and even Kant all shivering on the shore. And yet he never got bogged, and he never lost the attention of his audience. What saved him was the plain fact that he always gave a superb show—as good, almost, as a hanging. He converted the problem of evil into a melodrama with nine villains; he made of epistemology a sort of intellectual bed-room farce; he amalgamated Christianity and the music of Offenbach. . . . Well, Dreiser is quite devoid of that gift. Skepticism, in his hands, is never charming; it is simply despairing. His criticism of God lacks ingenuity and audacity. Earnestly pursuing the true, he too often unearths the merely obvious, which is something not true at all. One misses the jauntiness of the accomplished duellist; his manner is rather that of an honest householder repelling burglars with a table-leg. In brief, it is enormously serious and painstaking stuff, but seldom very interesting stuff, and never delightful stuff. The sorrows of the world become the sorrows of Dreiser himself, and then the sorrows of his reader. He remains, in the last analysis, the novelist rather than the philosopher. He is vastly less a Schopenhauer than a Werther.

Dreiser as Stylist

From the *American Mercury*, Feb., 1930, p. 254

Dreiser's writing continues to be painful to those who seek a voluptuous delight in words. It is not that he writes merely bald journalese, as certain professors have alleged, but that he wallows naïvely in a curiously banal kind of preciosity. He is, indeed, full of pretty phrases and arch turns of thought, but they seldom come off. The effect, at its worst, is that of a hangman's wink. He has been more or less impressed, apparently, by the familiar charge that his books are too long—that his chief sin is garrulousness. At all events, he shows a plain awareness of it: at one place he pauses in his narrative to say, "But hold! Do not despair. I am getting on." The point here, however, is not well taken. He is not actually garrulous; he always says something apposite, even though it may be obvious. What ails him is simply an incapacity to let anything go. Every detail of the human comedy interests him so immensely that he is bound to get it down. This makes, at times, for hard reading, but it has probably also made Dreiser. The thing that distinguishes him from other novelists is simply his astounding fidelity of observation. He sees every flicker of the eye, every tremor of the mouth, every change of color, every trivial gesture, every awkwardness, every wart. It is the warts, remember, that make the difference between a photograph and a human being.

Abraham Cahan

From the Jewish *Daily Forward*, April 21, 1940. This was a special issue in celebration of Cahan's eightieth birthday

"The Rise of David Levinsky" was one of the great literary events of the last dismal war to save democracy, and the book sticks in my mind to this day as one of the best American novels ever written. There were high hopes, at the time, that its distinguished success would draw Mr. Cahan away from the razzle-dazzle of daily journalism, and set him up as what might be called a career novelist, but he chose to go on giving his chief energies to his paper. Though I may regret that decision, I think I can at least understand it, for my own main interest, despite a number of ventures into books, has always been in the sort of writing that is printed today and forgotten tomorrow. It is quickly gone, but it is done while the mood is hot, and there is a kind of satisfaction in it that no work for the library can ever quite match. I like to think that even Shakespeare, when he pulled up to his desk, had the Bankside audience of next month, next week, or even next day in mind; not the cloistered scholars who, in some uncertain future, were to snuffle his texts. Mr. Cahan has given us no more "David Levinskys," but he has done hard service, day in and day out, upon busy and hazardous fronts, and at eighty he may look back, as few men can ever look back, upon a long series of genuinely valuable accomplishments. It is a fine feat to write a first-rate novel, but it is also a fine feat to steer a great newspaper from success to success in difficult times. He has done both, and so my congratulations on his birthday are double—first, those of journalist to journalist, and then those of critic to novelist. I add the felicitations of an old friend who laments the fact that, in these later years, I have had the happiness of seeing him only too seldom.

The merits of "The Rise of David Levinsky" do not dim as the

years pass. It remains a fascinating story, and a completely competent piece of writing. It is difficult, re-reading it, to believe that the
author, at the time it was under way, was doing most of his daily
writing in another language. As I said of it back in 1917, it is done
in English that is not only clear and honest, but also full of notable subtleties. The right word is always in the right place; there is
none of the dull obviousness that marks so much American fiction, even today. We have had in this country native novelists —
and good ones, too — with no more feeling for the language than
a cat. We have had novels that read as if they had been written in
Choctaw, and then clawed into English by translators having only
the most meagre grasp of either language. But Mr. Cahan wrote as
if English had been his tongue since childhood, and its writing his
chief occupation. There was a brilliant surface to the book, and it
was rich in happy and penetrating phrases. No critical acumen
was needed to see that it had not been thrown off in a hurry: it was
the mature and painstaking work of an artist with long experience
behind him, and an extraordinary talent. Thus it is remembered
today after nearly a quarter of a century, though most of the other
fiction of its year is now as forgotten as the contemporary fashion
in women's hats.

It was remarkable also as a social document, and holds its importance in that character. No better novel about the immigrant
has ever been written, or is likely to be written. The proletarian
authors of our own day have devoted themselves heavily to the
subject, and brought out a great many indignant and shocking
books, but none of them has ever come within miles of the philosophical insight of Mr. Cahan. His David Levinsky is not a mere
bugaboo in a political pamphlet; he is an authentic human being,
shrewdly observed and very adroitly carved and painted. A man
above the general, but still a man authentically of the general. The
old East Side swarms about him; he never steps out of the ranks
of his own people; they belong to his story as much as he himself
belongs to it. Thus he takes on, in the end, a kind of representative character, and becomes the archetype of a civilization now
greatly changed, and in most ways not for the better. If any more
vivid presentation of the immigrant's hopes and disappointments,
thoughts and feelings, virtues and vices has ever been got upon pa-

per, then it has surely escaped me. All other novels upon the same theme fall short, in one way or another, of this one.

Mrs. Wharton

1

From the *Smart Set*, Jan., 1909, pp. 157–58.
A review of THE HERMIT AND THE WILD WOMAN,
by Edith Wharton; New York, 1908

Mrs. Edith Wharton's new volume of short stories is one of those genteel and well-made books which seem to presuppose a high degree of culture and no little personal fastidiousness in the reader. I have read Conrad and Kipling on the deck of a smelly tramp steamer, with my attire confined to a simple suit of pajamas, and somehow, the time, the place and the garb seemed in no wise indecent; but after I had passed the first story in Mrs. Wharton's book, I began to long for a velvet smoking jacket and a genuine Havana substitute for my corncob pipe. That is to say, the main concern of this charming and excellent writer is with the doings and meditations of ultra-civilized folks. The mental processes of an artist losing faith in his work, of a statesman tortured by an indiscreet wife, of a social climber reaching higher and higher—these are the problems in psychology that engage her. Her Hermit and her Wild Woman, true enough, are savages, but after all, they are mere figures of speech, and one feels that she means them to typify far more complex persons. In all the other stories we are frankly above the level of those who sweat and swear. It is not especially fashionable persons that she draws, for she knows well enough that fashionable persons often have elemental minds. A fairly accurate notion of her field may be derived from the thought that her average hero would suffer acutely on hearing a ragged entrance of the wood wind, or on suddenly encountering, by some mischance, a portrait in crayon. Of such are the people of her stories, and it is needless to say that she pictures them with a sure and artistic hand.

2

From the *Smart Set*, Dec., 1911, p. 151.
A review of ETHAN FROME, by Edith Wharton; New York, 1911

The virtue of "Ethan Frome" is the somewhat uncommon virtue of dignity—of that dignity which belongs to sound, conscientious, thoughtful execution. In design the thing is far from impeccable. Mrs. Wharton, in truth, begins downright clumsily. The narrative proper is hidden behind a sort of prologue—a device unnecessary and fruitful of difficulties. But once she gets into that narrative, once the bad start is over, the rest of the tale is managed with such grace and skill, with such nice balance and care for detail, that one quickly forgets the artificiality of its beginning. We have here, in brief, an excellent piece of writing. Mrs. Wharton has seldom given better evidence of her craftsmanship. The dismal story of Ethan Frome, the lorn New England farmer; of his silent sacrifices for his insane mother, his hypochondriac wife; of his pitiful yearning for little Mattie Silver; of his endless, hopeless struggle with the unyielding soil; of the slow decay and death of his hopes, his ambitions, his lingering joy in life—this story, as it is set down, gathers the poignancy of true tragedy. One senses the unutterable desolation of those Northern valleys, the meaningless horror of life in those lonely farmhouses. A breath of chill Norwegian wind blows across the scene. There is in Ethan some hint of Alfred Allmers, of Hjalmar Ekdal. He is the archetype of an American we have been forgetting, in our eagerness to follow the doings of more pushful and spectacular fellows. He is the American whom life has passed over like the lightnings, leaving him hurt and mute by the roadside.

Disaster in Moronia

From the Baltimore *Sun*, May 28, 1939.
A review of THE GRAPES OF WRATH,
by John Steinbeck; New York, 1939

A shrill falsetto of enthusiasm for "The Grapes of Wrath" is passing through the pink weeklies and other such heralds of the New
Day. That enthusiasm, of course, is only formally literary, for in a
pink's starry eyes fidelity to the Moscow theology always comes
first, and aesthetic form and rational content only afterward.
Whether or not Mr. Steinbeck is a Marxian, I don't know, but I
suspect that he isn't. There are times, to be sure, when he seems
to incline that way, but there are also times when he hauls up suddenly and busts out with the plain truth.

The story he has to tell is quite simple. A family of share-
croppers in the Arkansas cotton belt, having afflicted the soil for
years and gone further and further into debt, is finally chased off
its so-called farm by the owner, who puts in tractor crews in an effort to get at least a part of his money back. At the moment this
foul scheme of Wall Street goes into effect the circular of a California labor agent falls into the hands of the head of the house.
Spelling it out, he discovers that it offers huge wages in the or-
chards and vineyards out there, with all the levantine domestic
comforts of Hollywood. So the poor idiot piles his family into a
rickety truck and the whole gang makes tracks for the new Utopia.

The result, it goes without saying, is something hard to distinguish from disillusion. After a hard trip over the deserts and mountains, the Joads find that California is really not Utopia at all. On
the contrary, it is an unfriendly land swarming with other poor idiots looking for the same easy and lucrative jobs—sometimes only
a dozen to each job, but more often a hundred. In consequence,
wages are down to the bare sustenance level, and in many case below it, and general living conditions approximate those of a badly
run hog-pen. The effects upon the Joads are naturally catastrophic.
When we leave them at last they are in an advanced stage of dis-

integration and apparently starving to death. Two of them have died and been buried along the road, a third is a fugitive from justice, two more have deserted, a sixth has gone crazy, a baby has been born and died, and another is on the way. Meanwhile, a fellow-traveler has been first jailed and then murdered. The survivors have run out of gas, food and hope.

It is not a pleasant story, but Mr. Steinbeck tells it with considerable skill. Though some of his personages are so grotesque that they often verge upon the ludicrous, he yet manages to keep them more or less real, and even to enlist the reader's sympathy for them. He makes them talk in a dialect that is authentically vulgar American, and save when the temptation besets him to unload his political and theological theorizings upon them, he holds them in character. In the mother of the flock, and its only even remotely intelligent member, he has produced a very plausible figure, and one that, moreover, is undeniably appealing. But it is one thing to draw a gallery of convincing men, women and children, and quite another thing to work out in a rational way the genesis of their destiny. This last is the business of any really first-rate novelist, but at it Mr. Steinbeck surely does not shine. The best he can suggest is that all the troubles of the Joads are due to the evil machinations of economic royalists. In brief, the ideational structure of his story is borrowed, lock, stock and barrel, from the dismal hooey that fills the pink weeklies every week. Most of his interludes of formal exposition and speculation—there is one between every two chapters—might have been lifted almost verbatim from the editorials in the *New Republic*, and whenever he attempts to give his narrative a flavor of *Tendenz* the result is indistinguishable from the sociological gurgling that goes on *ad nauseam* in the *Nation*.

In brief, he wrecks an interesting story, otherwise competently told, by trying to convert it into a puerile tract. As I have said, there are moments when his zest as a historian overcomes him, and he blurts out the truth—for example, in the episode of the one-eyed man, pp. 244 and 245. But in the main he sticks to his highly dubious thesis, and the result is that a tale intrinsically very interesting is reduced to the level of revival sermon. Almost the same tale was told three or four years ago by H. L. Davis, in "Honey in the Horn." The theme was the same, the people were the same, and the scene was not far removed. But Mr. Davis produced a wise and poignant story, free from banality and genuinely a work of art, whereas Mr. Steinbeck has produced only a sugar-teat for the intellectually under-privileged.

Its incidental merits remain, and they are not to be sniffed at. I have heard some complaint against it on the ground that it is full of naughty words, and must needs shock the tender. If so, then let the tender read "Pollyanna" and "Goodbye, Mr. Chips." As for me, I believe that Mr. Steinbeck solves his problem here with great skill, and a sufficient show of good taste. The loutish yearning to outrage the ladies' aid society which defaces so much of Hemingway is not in "The Grapes of Wrath." The author is dealing with people who are low-down in speech as in all things, and he must indicate that elemental fact, but he goes no further than is necessary. His dialogue is by no means as stenographically perfect as that of James T. Farrell, but nevertheless it is well observed and reported.

The pity is that a book of so many merits should be spoiled by so transparently silly a point of view. The job of interpreting and accounting for the morons who now swarm in the United States, consuming its substance and menacing its future, is not going to be done by college dunderheads, disguised as "trained experts," or by political mountebanks at Washington, or even by wizards writing in the reptile press; it is probably going to be done, if it is ever done at all, by novelists. It needs imagination as well as information; it calls for men who can distinguish clearly between what fools believe and what is really true; it demands a kind of wisdom that is not the common wisdom. Here Mr. Steinbeck fails miserably. He reduces an immense complex of hidden causes and baffling effects to a mere problem in kindergarten morals. He tries to account for the collapse of a culture—and even the simian society of Arkansas share-croppers was based on a kind of culture—by finding a villain miles away, and blaming him. This is the sort of blah one hears from many otherwise sane people in wartime; it is heard only from the excessively credulous in the days of presumable normalcy. It is the lollipop on which bogus Liberals, New Dealers, and members of the "I-am-not-a-Communist—but" Society feed.

What is needed is a full-length investigation of the share-cropper and his allied anthropoids by someone with a novelist's sharp eye for the apparently inconsequential but enormously significant fact, and a scientific freedom from childish prepossessions and flimsy theories. This year of prosperity sent its benefits to even the backwaters of the country, and encouraged the wholesale proliferation of marginal people. The years of scarcity are shoving more and more of them over the line, and they emerge from their wallows bellowing for succor.

But can any conceivable succor really restore them to self-sustaining? I begin to doubt it seriously. Life becomes tighter and more exigent than it was in the Golden Age, and it will probably go on growing tighter and more exigent for years to come. To nurse it back into people who are clearly unfit for it is simply to encourage the multiplication of their botched and hopeless kind. That idiotic process is now under way in the United States, and on an appalling scale. The problem before the house is to find some way to reverse it. A solution will never be reached by a resort to puerile sophistries, and sentimentalities by the New Deal out of the Uplift, with music by Karl Marx.

XVII. PLAYWRIGHTS AND POETS

George Bernard Shaw

From The Ulster Polonius, Prejudices:
First Series, 1919, pp. 181–90.
Partly reprinted from the *Smart Set*, Aug., 1916, pp. 138–40

A GOOD HALF of the humor of Mark Twain consisted of admitting shamelessly to vices and weaknesses that all of us have and few of us care to acknowledge. Practically the whole of the sagacity of George Bernard Shaw consisted of bellowing vociferously what every one knows. I think I am as well acquainted with his works, both hortatory and dramatic, as the next man. I wrote the first book ever devoted to a discussion of them, in any language or in any land,[1] and I read them steadily and eagerly for long years. Yet, so far as I can recall, I never found an original idea in them — never a single statement of fact or opinion that was not anteriorly familiar, and almost commonplace. Put the thesis of any of his plays into a plain proposition, and I doubt that you could find a literate man in Christendom who had not heard it before, or who would seriously dispute it. The roots of each one of them are in platitude; the roots of *every* effective stage-play are in platitude; that a dramatist is inevitably a platitudinarian is itself a platitude double damned. But Shaw clung to the obvious even when he was not hampered by the suffocating conventions of the stage. His Fabian and other tracts were veritable compendiums of the undeniable; what was seriously stated in them was quite beyond logical dispute. They excited a great deal of ire, they brought down upon him a great deal of amusing abuse, but I have yet to hear of any

---

[1] George Bernard Shaw: His Plays; Boston, 1905.

one actually controverting them. As well try to controvert the Copernican astronomy. They are as bullet-proof in essence as the multiplication table, and vastly more bullet-proof than the Ten Commandments or the Constitution of the United States.

Well, then, why did the old boy kick up such a pother? Why was he regarded as an arch-heretic almost comparable to Galileo, Nietzsche or Simon Magnus? For the simplest reasons. Because he practised with great zest and skill the fine art of exhibiting the manifest in unexpected and terrifying lights—because he was a master of the logical trick of so matching two apparently safe premises that they yield an incongruous and inconvenient conclusion—above all, because he was a fellow of the utmost charm and address, quick-witted, bold, limber-tongued, persuasive, humorous, iconoclastic, ingratiating—in brief, a Celt, and so the exact antithesis of the solemn Saxons who ordinarily instruct and exhort us.

Turn to his "Man and Superman," perhaps the greatest of all his plays, and you will see the whole Shaw machine at work. What he starts out with is the self-evident fact, disputed by no one not idiotic, that a woman has vastly more to gain by marriage, under Christian monogamy, than a man. That fact is as old as monogamy itself; it was, I daresay, the admitted basis of the palace revolution which brought monogamy into the world. But now comes Shaw with an implication that the sentimentality of the world chooses to conceal—with a deduction plainly resident in the original proposition, but kept in safe silence there by a preposterous and hypocritical taboo—to wit, the deduction that women are well aware of the profit that marriage yields for them, and that they are thus much more eager to marry than men are, and ever alert to take the lead in the business. This second fact, to any man who has passed through the terrible years between twenty-five and forty, is as plain as the first, but by a sort of general consent it is not openly stated. Violate that general consent and you are guilty of *scandalum magnatum*. Shaw was simply one who was guilty of *scandalum magnatum* habitually, a professional criminal in that department. It was his life work to announce the obvious in terms of the scandalous.

What lies under the common horror of such blabbing is the

deepest and most widespread of human weaknesses, which is to say, intellectual cowardice, the craven appetite for mental ease and security, the fear of thinking things out. All men are afflicted by it more or less; not even the most courageous and frank of men likes to admit, in specific terms, that his wife is fat, or that she decoyed him to the altar by a transparent trick, or that their joint progeny resemble her brother or mother, and are thus trash. A few extraordinary heroes of logic and evidence may do such things occasionally, but only occasionally. The average man never does them at all. He is eternally in fear of what he knows in his heart; his whole life is made up of efforts to dodge it and conceal it; he is always running away from what passes for his intelligence and taking refuge in what pass for his higher feelings, *i.e.*, his stupidities, his delusions, his sentimentalities. Shaw devoted himself brutally to the art of hauling this recreant fellow up. He was one who, for purposes of sensation, often for the mere joy of outraging the tenderminded, resolutely and mercilessly thought things out—sometimes with the utmost ingenuity and humor, but often, it must be said, in the same muddled way that the average right-thinker would do it if he ever got up the courage. Remember this formula, and all of the fellow's alleged originality becomes no more than a sort of bad-boy audacity, usually in bad taste. He dragged skeletons from their closet and made them dance obscenely—but every one, of course, knew that they were there all the while. He would have produced an excitement of exactly the same kind (though perhaps superior in intensity) if he had walked down the Strand bared to the waist, and so reminded the shocked Londoners of the unquestioned fact (though conventionally concealed and forgotten) that he was a mammal and had an umbilicus.

Turn to a typical play-and-preface of his hey-day, say "Androcles and the Lion." Here the complete Shaw formula is exposed. On the one hand there is a mass of platitudes; on the other hand there is the air of a peep-show. On the one hand he rehearses facts so stale that even suburban clergymen have probably heard of them; on the other hand he states them so scandalously that the pious get all of the thrills out of the business that would accompany a view of the rector in liquor in the pulpit. Here, for example, are some of his contentions:

(*a*) That the social and economic doctrines preached by Jesus were indistinguishable from what is now called Socialism.

(*b*) That the Pauline transcendentalism visible in the Acts and the Epistles differs enormously from the simple humanitarianism set forth in the Four Gospels.

(*c*) That the Christianity on tap today would be almost as abhorrent to Jesus, supposing Him returned to earth, as the theories of Nietzsche.

(*d*) That the rejection of the Biblical miracles, and even of the historical credibility of the Gospels, by no means disposes of Christ Himself.

(*e*) That the early Christians were persecuted, not because their theology was regarded as unsound, but because their public conduct constituted a nuisance.

It is unnecessary to go on. Could any one imagine a more abject surrender to the undeniable? Would it be possible to reduce the exegesis of a century and a half to a more depressing series of platitudes? But his discussion of the inconsistencies between the Four Gospels is even worse; you will find all of its points set forth in any elemental treatise upon New Testament criticism. He actually dishes up, with a heavy air of profundity, the news that there is a glaring conflict between the genealogy of Jesus in Matthew i, 1–17, and the direct claim of divine paternity in Matthew i, 18. More, he breaks out with the astounding discovery that Jesus was a good Jew, and that Paul's repudiation of circumcision (now a cardinal article of the so-called Christian faith) would have surprised Him and perhaps greatly shocked Him. The whole preface, running to 114 pages, is made up of just such shop-worn stuff. Searching it from end to end with eagle eye, I have failed to find a single fact or argument that was not as obvious as a wart.

Nevertheless, this preface makes bouncing reading—and therein lies the secret of the vogue of Shaw. He had a large and extremely uncommon capacity for provocative utterance; he knew how to get a touch of bellicosity into the most banal of doctrines; he was forever on tiptoe, forever challenging, forever *sforzando*. His matter might be from the public store, even from the public junk-shop, but his manner was always all his own. The tune was old, but the words were new. Consider, for example, his discussion of the personality of Jesus. The idea is simple and obvious: Jesus was not a long-faced prophet of evil, like John the Baptist, nor was He an ascetic, or a mystic. But here is the Shaw way of saying it: "He was ... what we call an artist and a Bohemian in His manner of life." The fact remains unchanged, but in the statement of it there is a shock for those who have been confusing the sour donkey they hear of a Sunday with the tolerant, likable Man they profess to worship—and perhaps there is even a genial snicker in it for their betters. So with his treatment of the Atonement. His objections to it are time-worn, but suddenly he gets the effect of novelty by pointing out the quite manifest fact that acceptance of it is apt to make for weakness, that the man who rejects it is thrown back upon his own courage and circumspection, and is hence stimulated to augment them. The first argument—that Jesus was of free and easy habits—is so commonplace that I have heard it voiced by a bishop. The second suggests itself so naturally that I myself once employed it against a chance Christian encountered in a Pullman smoking-room. This Christian was at first shocked as he might have been by reading Shaw, but in half an hour he was confessing that he had long ago thought of the objection himself, and put it away as immoral. I well remember his fascinated interest as I showed him how my inability to accept the doctrine put a heavy burden of moral responsibility upon me, and forced me to be more watchful of my conduct than the elect of God, and so robbed me of many pleasant advantages in finance, the dialectic and amour.

A double jest conceals itself in the Shaw legend. The first half of it I have already disclosed. The second half has to do with the fact that Shaw was not at all the wholesale agnostic his fascinated victims saw in him, but an orthodox Scotch Presbyterian of the most cocksure and bilious sort—in fact, almost the archetype of the blue-nose. In the theory that he was Irish I take little stock. His very name was as Scotch as haggis, and the part of Ireland from which he sprang is peopled very largely by Scots. The true Irishman is a romantic. He senses life as a mystery, a thing of wonder, an experience of passion and beauty. In politics he is not logical, but emotional. In religion his interest centers, not in the commandments, but in the sacraments. The Scot, on the contrary, is almost devoid of romanticism. He is a materialist, a logician, a utilitarian. Life to him is not a poem, but a series of police regulations. God is not an indulgent father, but a hanging judge. There are no saints, but only devils. Beauty is a lewdness, redeemable only in the service of morality. It is more important to get on in the world than to be brushed by angels' wings.

Here Shaw ran exactly true to type. Read his critical writings from end to end, and you will not find the slightest hint that objects of art were passing before him as he wrote. He founded, in England, the superstition that Ibsen was no more than a tin-pot evangelist—a sort of brother to General Booth, Mrs. Pankhurst and the syndics of the Sex Hygiene Society. He turned Shakespeare into a bird of evil, croaking dismally in a rain-barrel. He even injected a moral content (by dint of herculean straining) into the music dramas of Richard Wagner—surely the most colossal sacrifices of moral ideas ever made on the altar of beauty. Always the ethical obsession, the hall-mark of the Scotch Puritan, was visible in him. His politics was mere moral indignation. His aesthetic theory was cannibalism upon aesthetics. And in his general writing he was forever discovering an atrocity in what was hitherto passed as no more than a human weakness; he was forever inventing new sins, and demanding their punishment; he always saw his opponent, not only as wrong, but also as a scoundrel. I have called him a Presbyterian. Need I add that he flirted with predestination under the quasi-scientific *nom de guerre* of determinism—that he seemed to be convinced that, while men may not be responsible for their virtues, they are undoubtedly responsible for their offendings, and deserve to be clubbed therefor?. . . .

And this Shaw the revolutionist, the heretic! Next, perhaps, we shall be hearing of St. Ignatius, the atheist.

Ibsen the Trimmer

From the *Smart Set*, Oct., 1911, pp. 151–52

Ibsen, like his German disciples, never quite achieved the thing he set out to do. Always there was a compromise, and the practitioner vetoed the reformer. You will find in every one of the great

Norwegian's plays, from the beginning of the third act of "A Doll's House" onward, a palpable effort to shake off the old shackles — but you will also hear those old shackles rattling. In "Hedda Gabler" Sardoodledom actually triumphs, and the end is old-fashioned fifth-act gunplay. In "The Master Builder" and "Ghosts" logic and even common sense are sacrificed to idle tricks of the theater; in "The Wild Duck" and "Rosmersholm," as in "Hedda Gabler," there are melodramatic and somewhat incredible suicides; and in "John Gabriel Borkman," as Shaw wittily puts it, the hero dies of "acute stage tragedy without discoverable lesions." The trouble with the conventional catastrophes in these plays is not that they strain the imagination, for Ibsen was too skillful a craftsman to overlook any aid to plausibility, however slight, but that they strain the facts. They are not impossible, nor even improbable, but merely untypical. In real life, unfortunately, for the orthodox drama, problems are seldom solved with the bare bodkin, else few of us would survive the scandals of our third decade. The tragedy of the Oswald Alvings and Hedda Gablers and Halvard Solnesses we actually see about us is not that they die, but that they live. Instead of ending neatly and picturesquely, with a pistol shot, a dull thud and a sigh of relief, real tragedy staggers on. And it is precisely because Brieux is courageous enough to show it thus staggering on that Shaw places him in the highest place among contemporary dramatists, most of whom think that they have been very devilish when they have gone as far as Ibsen, who, as we have seen, always made a discreet surrender to the traditions — save perhaps, in "Little Eyolf" — before his audience began tearing up the chairs.

Edgar Lee Masters

From The New Poetry Movement, Prejudices:
First Series, 1919, pp. 88–89

There is some excellent stuff in "The Spoon River Anthology" and parts of it — for example, "Ann Rutledge" — seem likely to be remembered for a long while, but what made it a nine-days' wonder in 1915 was not chiefly any great show of novelty in it, nor any extraordinary poignancy, nor any grim truthfulness unparalleled, but simply the public notion that it was improper. It fell upon the country at the height of one of the recurrent sex waves, and it was read, not as work of art, but as document. Its large circulation was mainly among persons to whom poetry *qua* poetry was as sour a dose as symphonic music. To such persons, of course, it seemed not only pleasantly spicy, but something new under the sun. They were unacquainted with the verse of George Crabbe; they were quite innocent of E. A. Robinson and Robert Frost; they knew nothing of the *Ubi sunt* formula; they had never heard of the Greek Anthology. The roar of his popular success won Masters's case with the critics, at first very shy. His undoubted merits in detail—his half-wistful cynicism, his capacity for evoking simple emotions, his deft skill at managing the puny difficulties of *vers libre*—were thereupon pumped up to such an extent that his defects were lost sight of. Those defects, however, shine blindingly in his later books. Without the advantage of content that went with the anthology, they reveal themselves as volumes of empty doggerel, with now and then a brief moment of illumination. It would be difficult, indeed, to find poetry that is, in essence, less poetical. Most of the pieces are actually only tracts, and many of them are very bad tracts.

Dichtung und Wahrheit

From DAMN! A BOOK OF CALUMNY, 1918, p. 70

Deponent, being duly sworn, saith: My taste in poetry is for delicate and fragile things—to be honest, for artificial things. I like a frail but perfectly articulated stanza, a sonnet wrought like ivory, a song full of glowing nouns, verbs, adjectives, adverbs, pronouns, conjunctions, prepositions and participles, but without too much hard sense to it. Poetry, to me, has but two meanings. On the one hand, it is a magical escape from the sordidness of metabolism and the class war, and on the other hand it is a subtle, very difficult and hence very charming art, like writing fugues or mixing mayonnaise. I do not go to poets to be taught anything, or to be heated up to indignation, or to have my conscience blasted out of its torpor, but to be soothed and caressed, to be lulled with sweet sounds, to be wooed into forgetfulness, to be tickled under the metaphysical chin.

Walt Whitman

A hitherto unpublished note

Walt Whitman was the greatest of American poets, and for a plain reason: he got furthest from the obvious facts. What he had to say was almost never true.

XVIII. THE CRITIC'S TRADE

The Pursuit of Ideas

From the Introduction to the revised edition
of In Defense of Women, 1922, pp. vii–xii.
First printed in the *Smart Set*, Dec., 1921, pp. 26–27

As a professional critic of life and letters, my principal business in the world is that of manufacturing platitudes for tomorrow, which is to say, ideas so novel that they will be instantly rejected as insane and outrageous by all right-thinking men, and so apposite and sound that they will eventually conquer that instinctive opposition, and force themselves into the traditional wisdom of the race. I hope I need not confess that a large part of my stock in trade consists of platitudes rescued from the cobwebbed shelves of yesterday, with new labels stuck rakishly upon them. This borrowing and refurbishing of shop-worn goods is the invariable habit of traders in ideas, at all times and everywhere. It is not that all the conceivable human notions have been thought out; it is simply, to be quite honest, that the sort of men who volunteer to think out new ones seldom, if ever, have wind enough for a full day's work. The most they can ever accomplish in the way of genuine originality is an occasional spurt, and half a dozen such spurts, particularly if they come close together and show a certain coördination, are enough to make a practitioner celebrated, and even immortal.

Nature, indeed, conspires against all genuine originality in this department, and I have no doubt that God is against it on His heavenly throne, as His vicars and partisans unquestionably are on this earth. The dead hand pushes all of us into intellectual cages; there is in all of us a strange tendency to yield and have done. Thus the impertinent colleague of Aristotle is doubly beset, first by a public opinion that regards his enterprise as subversive and in bad taste, and secondly by an inner weakness that limits his capacity for it, and especially his capacity to throw off the prejudices and superstitions of his race, culture and time. The cell, said Haeckel, does not act, it *reacts*—and what is the instrument of reflection and speculation save a congeries of cells? At the moment of the contemporary metaphysician's loftiest flight, when he is most gratefully warmed to the feeling that he is far above all the ordinary air-lanes and has an absolutely novel concept by the tail, he is suddenly pulled up by the discovery that what is entertaining him is simply the ghost of some ancient idea that his schoolmaster forced into him in 1887, or the mouldering corpse of a doctrine that was made official in his country during some recent war, or a sort of fermentation-product, to mix the figure, of a banal heresy launched upon him recently by his wife. This is the penalty that the man of intellectual curiosity and vanity pays for his violation of the divine edict that what has been revealed from Sinai shall suffice for him, and for his resistance to the natural process which seeks to reduce him to the respectable level of a patriot and taxpayer.

To an American the business of pursuing ideas is especially difficult, for public opinion among us is not only passively but actively against it and the man who engages in it is lucky, indeed, if he escapes the secular arm. In the United States there is a right way to think and a wrong way to think in everything—not only in theology, or politics, or economics, but in the most trivial matters of everyday life. Thus, in the average American city the citizen who, in the face of an organized public clamor (usually fomented by parties with something to sell) for the erection of an equestrian statue of Susan B. Anthony in front of the chief railway station, or the purchase of a dozen leopards for the municipal zoo, or the dispatch of an invitation to the Structural Iron Workers' Union to hold its next annual convention in the town Symphony Hall—the citizen who, for any logical reason, opposes such a proposal—on the ground, say, that Miss Anthony never rode a horse in her life, or that a dozen leopards would be less useful than a gallows to hang the City Council, or that the Structural Iron Workers would spit all over the floor of Symphony Hall and knock down the busts of Bach, Beethoven and Brahms—this citizen is commonly denounced as an anarchist and a public enemy. It is not only erroneous to think thus; it has come to be immoral. And so on many other planes, high and low. For an American to question any of the articles of fundamental faith cherished by the majority is for him to run grave risks of social disaster. All such toyings with illicit ideas are construed as *attentats* against democracy, which, in a sense, perhaps they are. For democracy is grounded upon so childish a complex of fallacies that they must be protected by a rigid system of taboos, else even half-wits would argue it to pieces. Its first concern must thus be to penalize the free play of ideas. In the United States this is not only its first concern, but also its last concern.

The Cult of Hope

From PREJUDICES: SECOND SERIES, 1920, pp. 211–18

Of all the sentimental errors that reign and rage in this incomparable Republic, the worst is that which confuses the function of criticism, whether aesthetic, political or social, with the function of reform. Almost invariably it takes the form of a protest: "The fellow condemns without offering anything better. Why tear down without building up?" So snivel the sweet ones: so wags the national tongue. The messianic delusion becomes a sort of universal murrain. It is impossible to get an audience for an idea that is not "constructive"—*i.e.*, that is not glib, and uplifting, and full of hope, and hence capable of tickling the emotions by leaping the intermediate barrier of the intelligence.

In this protest and demand, of course, there is nothing but the babbling of men who mistake their feelings for thoughts. The truth is that criticism, if it were confined to the proposing of alternative schemes, would quickly cease to have any force or utility at all, for in the overwhelming majority of instances no alternative scheme of any intelligibility is imaginable, and the whole object of the critical process is to demonstrate it. The poet, if the victim is a poet, is simply one as bare of gifts as a herring is of fur: no conceivable suggestion will ever make him write actual poetry. And the plan of reform, in politics, sociology or what not, is simply beyond the pale of reason; no change in it or improvement of it will ever make it achieve the impossible. Here, precisely, is what is the matter with most of the notions that go floating about the country, particularly in the field of governmental reform. The trouble with them is not only that they won't and don't work; the trouble with them, more importantly, is that the thing they propose to accomplish is intrinsically, or at all events most probably, beyond accomplishment. That is to say, the problem they are ostensibly designed to solve is a problem that is insoluble. To tackle them with a proof of that insolubility, or even with a colorable argument of it, is sound criticism; to tackle them with another solution that is quite as bad, or even worse, is to pick the pocket of one knocked down by an automobile.

Unluckily, it is difficult for the American mind to grasp the concept of insolubility. Thousands of poor dolts keep on trying to square the circle; other thousands keep pegging away at perpetual motion. The number of persons so afflicted is far greater than the records of the Patent Office show, for beyond the circle of frankly insane enterprise there lie circles of more and more plausible enterprise, and finally we come to a circle which embraces the great majority of human beings. These are the optimists and chronic hopers of the world, the believers in men, ideas and things. It is the settled habit of such folk to give ear to whatever is comforting; it is their settled faith that whatever is desirable will come to pass. A caressing confidence—but one, unfortunately, that is not borne out by human experience. The fact is that some of the things that men and women have desired most ardently for thousands of years are not nearer realization today than they were in the time of Rameses, and that there is not the slightest reason for believing that they will lose their coyness on any near tomorrow. Plans for hurrying them on have been tried since the beginning; plans for forcing them overnight are in copious and antagonistic operation today; and yet they continue to hold off and elude us, and the chances are that they will keep on holding off and eluding us until the angels get tired of the show, and the whole earth is set off like a gigantic bomb, or drowned, like a sick cat, between two buckets.

Turn, for example, to the sex problem. There is no half-baked ecclesiastic, bawling in his galvanized-iron temple on a suburban lot, who doesn't know precisely how it ought to be dealt with. There is no fantoddish old suffragette, sworn to get her revenge on man, who hasn't a sovereign remedy for it. There is not a shyster of a district attorney, ambitious for higher office, who doesn't offer to dispose of it in a few weeks, given only enough help from the city editors. And yet, by the same token, there is not a man who has honestly studied it and pondered it, bringing sound information to the business, and understanding of its inner difficulties and a clean and analytical mind, who doesn't believe and hasn't stated publicly that it is intrinsically and eternally insoluble. For example, Havelock Ellis. His remedy is simply a denial of all remedies. He admits that the disease is bad, but he shows that the medicine is infinitely worse, and so he proposes going back to the plain disease, and advocates bearing it with philosophy, as we bear colds in the head, marriage, the noises of the city, bad cooking and the certainty of death. Man is inherently vile—but he is never so vile as when he is trying to disguise and deny his vileness. No prostitute was ever so costly to a community as a prowling and obscene vice crusader, or as the dubious legislator or prosecuting officer who jumps at such swine pipe.

Cassandra's Lament

From the Baltimore *Evening Sun*, Nov. 18, 1929

In all ages there arise protests from tender men against the bitterness of criticism, especially social criticism. They are the same men who, when they come down with malaria, patronize a doctor who prescribes, not quinine, but marshmallows.

Criticism of Criticism of Criticism

From PREJUDICES: FIRST SERIES, 1919, pp. 9–31. In a somewhat shorter form this essay first appeared in the New York *Evening Mail*, July 1, 1919. For a later, less romantic view of the critical process, see *A Mencken Chrestomathy*; New York, 1949, pp. 432–33

Every now and then, a sense of the futility of their daily endeavors falling suddenly upon them, the critics of Christendom turn to a somewhat sour and depressing consideration of the nature and objects of their own craft. That is to say, they turn to criticising criticism. What is it in plain words? What is its aim, exactly stated in legal terms? How far can it go? What good can it do? What is its normal effect upon the artist and the work of art?

The answers made by the brethren are quite as divergent as their views of the arts they deal with. One group argues, partly by direct statement and partly by attacking all other groups, that the one defensible purpose of the critic is to encourage the virtuous and oppose the sinful—in brief, to police the fine arts and so hold them in tune with the moral order of the world. Another group, repudiating this constabulary function, argues hotly that the arts have nothing to do with morality whatsoever—that their concern is solely with pure beauty. A third holds that the chief aspect of a work of art, particularly in the field of literature, is its aspect as psychological document—that if it doesn't help men to know themselves it is nothing. A fourth reduces the thing to an exact science, and sets up standards that resemble algebraic formulae—this is the group of the counters of strong and weak endings, the sleuths of sly stealings, the anatomists of tropes. And so, in order, follow groups five, six, seven, eight, nine, ten, each with its theory and its proofs.

Anon some extraordinary member of the faculty revolts against all this dogma, and nails it, so to speak, to his barn-door. This was the case, for example, with Dr. J. E. Spingarn, who made an uproar a generation ago with a revolutionary and contumacious tract, by title "Creative Criticism."[1] An example of his doctrine: "To say that poetry is moral or immoral is as meaningless as to say that an equilateral triangle is moral and an isosceles triangle immoral." Worse: "It is only conceivable in a world in which dinner-table conversation runs after this fashion: 'This cauliflower would be good if it had only been prepared in accordance with international law.' " It is easy to imagine the perturbation of the current stars of

---

[1] New York, 1917. Spingarn was born in 1875 and died in 1939. Educated at Columbia and bearing its Ph.D., he rose to be professor of comparative literature there. He was a man of large means and was one of the backers of the publishing firm of Harcourt, Brace & Co. He devoted most of his energies, in his later years, to succoring the colored folk from the Confederate *Kultur*.

academic criticism when they encountered such heresies, for example, Prof. Dr. W. C. Brownell, the Amherst Aristotle, with his eloquent pleas for standards as iron-clad (and withal as preposterous) as those of the Westminster Confession;[2] Prof. Dr. William Lyon Phelps, of Yale, with his discovery that Joseph Conrad preached "the axiom of the moral law,"[3] and Prof. Dr. Stuart Pratt Sherman, the Iowa patriot-critic, with his maxim that Puritanism is the official philosophy of America, and that all who dispute it are enemy aliens and should be deported.[4] Dr. Spingarn here performed a treason most horrible upon the reverend order he adorned, and having achieved it, he straightway performed another and then another. That is to say, he tackled all the antagonistic groups of orthodox critics seriatim, and knocked them about unanimously—first the aforesaid agents of the sweet and pious; then the advocates of unities, meters, all rigid formulae; then the experts in imaginary psychology; then the historical comparers, pigeon-holers and makers of categories; finally, the professors of pure aesthetic. One and all, they took their places upon his operating table, and one and all they were stripped and anatomized.

But what was the anarchistic ex-professor's own theory?—for a professor must have a theory, as a dog must have fleas. In brief, what he offered was a doctrine borrowed from the Italian, Benedetto Croce, and by Croce filched from Goethe—a doctrine anything but new in the world, even in Goethe's time, but never-

---

[2] Brownell printed his chief work, Standards, in 1917. He was born in 1851 and died in 1929. He was literary adviser to Charles Scribner's Sons for thirty-nine years.

[3] I think this was in his The Advance of the English Novel; New York, 1917, which I reviewed in the *Smart Set* in June of that year. Phelps was born in 1865 and died in 1943. After taking his Ph.D. at Yale, he spent a year at Harvard, and then returned to his alma mater for the rest of his life. Despite his Calvinist principles, he was a charming fellow, and in his later years I saw a good deal of him and liked him very much.

[4] Sherman was born in 1881 and died in 1927. His effort to dispose of Dreiser during World War I, on the ground that Dreiser was of German origin, was thoroughly disingenuous and dishonorable. In 1924 he moved to New York as literary editor of the *Herald Tribune* and presently yielded so far to the antinomianism of the town that he became a Dreiser partisan.

theless long buried in forgetfulness—to wit, the doctrine that it is the critic's first and only duty, as Carlyle once put it, to find out "what the poet's aim really and truly was, how the task he had to do stood before his eye, and how far, with such materials as were afforded him, he has fulfilled it." What is this generalized poet trying to do? asked Spingarn, and how has he done it? That, and no more, is the critic's quest. The morality of the work does not concern him. It is not his business to determine whether it heeds Aristotle or flouts Aristotle. He passes no judgment on its rhyme scheme, its length and breadth, its politics, its patriotism, its piety, its psychological exactness, its good taste. He may note these things, but he may not protest them—he may not complain if the thing criticised fails to fit into a pigeon-hole. Every sonnet, every drama, every novel is *sui generis*; it must stand on its own bottom; it must be judged by its own inherent intentions. "Poets," said Spingarn, "do not really write epics, pastorals, lyrics, however much they may be deceived by these false abstractions; they express *themselves, and this expression is their only form.* There are not, therefore, only three or ten or a hundred literary kinds; there are as many kinds as there are individual poets." Nor is there any valid appeal *ad hominem*. The character and background of the poet are beside the mark; the poem itself is the thing. Oscar Wilde, weak and swine-like, yet wrote beautiful prose. To reject that prose on the ground that Wilde had Byzantine habits is as absurd as to reject "What Is Man?" on the ground that its theology was beyond the intelligence of the editor of the *War-Cry*.

This Spingarn-Croce-Carlyle-Goethe theory, of course, throws a heavy burden upon the critic. It presupposes that he is a civilized and tolerant man, hospitable to all intelligible ideas and capable of reading them as he runs. This is a demand that at once rules out nine-tenths of the grown-up sophomores who commonly carry on the business of criticism in America. Their trouble is simply that they lack the intellectual resilience necessary for taking in ideas of any force and originality, and particularly new ideas. The only way they can ingest one is by transforming it into some one or another of current clichés—usually a harsh and devastating operation. They can get down what has been degraded to the mob level, and so brought into forms that they know and comprehend—but they exhibit alarm immediately they come into the presence of the extraordinary. Here we have an explanation of Brownell's loud appeal for a tightening of standards—*i.e.*, a larger respect for precedents, patterns, rubber-stamps—and here we have an explanation of Phelps's inability to comprehend the colossal phenomenon of Dreiser, and of Boynton's childish nonsense about realism, and of Sherman's efforts to apply the Espionage Act to the arts, and of Paul Elmer More's[5] querulous enmity to romanticism, and of all the fatuous pigeon-holing that passes for criticism in the more solemn literary periodicals.

As practised by such learned and diligent but essentially ignorant and unimaginative men, criticism is little more than a branch of homiletics. They judge a work of art, not by its clarity and sincerity, not by the force and charm of its ideas, not by the professional virtuosity of the artist, not by his originality and artistic courage, but simply and solely by what they conceive to be his correctness. If he devotes himself to advocating the transient platitudes, political, economic and aesthetic, in a sonorous manner, then he is worthy of respect. But if he lets fall the slightest hint that he is in doubt about any of them, or worse still, that he is indifferent to them, then he is a scoundrel, and hence, by their theory, a bad artist.

Against such idiotic notions American criticism makes but feeble headway. We are, in fact, a nation of evangelists; every third American devotes himself to improving and lifting up his fellow-citizens, usually by force; the messianic delusion is our national disease. Even the vicious are still in favor of crying vice down. "Here is a novel," says the artist. "Why didn't you write a tract?" roars the critic—and down the chute go novel and novelist. "This girl is pretty," says the painter. "But she has left off her brassière," comes the protest—and off goes the poor dauber's head. Genuine criticism is as impossible to such inordinately narrow and cocksure

---

[5] More, in his day, was extremely influential, and his eleven volumes of Shelburne Essays were accepted as gospel by all the young professors. Born in 1864, he died in 1937. He was editor of the *Nation* for the five years before Oswald Garrison Villard took it over, and its pages were filled with his lucubrations and those of his disciples.

men as music is to a man who is tone-deaf. The critic, to interpret his artist, even to understand his artist, must be able to get into the mind of his artist; he must feel and comprehend the vast pressure of the creative passion; as Spingarn says, "aesthetic judgment and artistic creation are instinct with the same vital life." This is why most of the best criticism of modern times has been written by men who have had within them, not only the reflective and analytical faculty of critics, but also the gusto of artists—Goethe, Carlyle, Lessing, Schlegel, Sainte-Beuve, and, to drop a story or two, Hazlitt, Georg Brandes and James Huneker. Huneker, tackling "Also sprach Zarathustra," revealed its content in illuminating flashes. But tackled by Paul Elmer More, it became no more than a dull student's exercise, ill-naturedly corrected. . . .

Such is the theory of Spingarn—now, alas, an angel in Heaven. It demands that the critic be a man of intelligence, of toleration, of wide information, of genuine hospitality to ideas. Unfortunately, the learned brother had been a professor in his day, and, professor-like, he began to take in too much territory. Having laid and hatched, so to speak, his somewhat stale but still highly nourishing egg, he began to argue fatuously that the resultant flamingo was the whole mustering of the critical Aves. The fact is, of course, that criticism, as humanly practised, must needs fall a good deal short of this intuitive re-creation of beauty, and what is more, it must go a good deal further. For one thing, it must be interpretation in terms that are not only exact but are also comprehensible to the reader, else it will leave the original mystery as dark as before— and once interpretation comes in, paraphrase and transliteration come in. What is recondite must be made plainer; the transcendental, to some extent at least, must be done into common modes of thinking. Well, what are morality, hexameters, movements, historical principles, psychological maxims, the dramatic unities— what are all these save common modes of thinking, short cuts, rubber-stamps, words of one syllable? Moreover, beauty as we know it in this world is by no means the apparition in vacuo that Spingarn seemed to see. It has its social, its political, even its moral implications. The finale of Beethoven's C Minor Symphony is not only colossal as music; it is also colossal as revolt; it says something against something. Yet more, the springs of beauty are not within itself alone, nor even in genius alone, but often in

things without. Brahms wrote his *Deutsches-Requiem*, not only because he was a great artist, but also because he was a good German. And in Nietzsche there are times when the divine afflatus
takes a back seat, and the *spirochaetae* have the floor.

Spingarn himself appeared to harbor some sense of this limitation on his doctrine. He gave warning that "the poet's intention
must be judged at the moment of the creative act"—which
opened the door wide enough for many an ancient to creep in.
But limited or not, he at least cleared off a lot of moldy rubbish,
and got further toward the truth than any of his former colleagues
of the birch. They wasted themselves upon theories that only concealed the poet's achievement the more, the more diligently they
were applied; he, at all events, grounded himself upon the sound
notion that there should be free speech in art, and no protective
tariffs, and no *a priori* assumptions, and no testing of ideas by
mere words. The safe ground probably lies between the two
camps, but nearer Spingarn. The critic who really illuminates
starts off much as he started off, but with a more careful regard for
the prejudices and imbecilities of the world. I think the best feasible practise is to be found in certain chapters of Huneker, a critic
of vastly more solid influence and of infinitely more value to the
arts than any prating pedagogue has ever been disposed to grant.
In his case, as in that of Poe, a sensitive and intelligent artist re-
created the work of other artists, but there also came to the ceremony a man of the world, and the things he had to say were
apposite and instructive too. To denounce moralizing out of hand
is to pronounce a moral judgment. To dispute the categories is to
set up a new anti-categorical category. And to admire the work of
Shakespeare is to be interested in his social aspirations, his shot-
gun marriage and his frequent concessions to the bombastic frenzy
of his actors, and to have some curiosity about Mr. W.H. The
really competent critic must be an empiricist. He must conduct
his exploration with whatever means lie within the bounds of his
personal limitation. He must produce his effects with whatever
tools will work. If pills fail, he gets out his saw. If the saw won't
cut, he seizes a club. . . .

Perhaps, after all, the chief burden that lies upon Spingarn's theory is to be found in its label. He called it "creative," which suggested, unhappily, the "constructive" of the Rotarians. It said what

he wanted to say, but it said a good deal more. In this emergency, I propose getting rid of his misleading label by pasting another over it. That is, I propose the substitution of "catalytic" for "creative," despite the fact that "catalytic" is an unfamiliar word, and suggests the dog-Latin of the seminaries. I borrow it from chemistry, and its meaning is really quite simple. A catalyzer, in chemistry, is a substance that helps two other substances to react. For example, consider the case of ordinary cane sugar and water. Dissolve the sugar in the water and nothing happens. But add a few drops of acid and the sugar changes into glucose and fructose. Meanwhile, the acid itself is unchanged. All it does is to stir up the reaction between the water and the sugar. The process is called catalysis. The acid is a catalyzer.

Well, this is almost exactly the function of a genuine critic of the arts. It is his business to provoke the reaction between the work of art and the spectator. The spectator, untutored, stands unmoved; he sees the work of art, but it fails to make any intelligible impression on him; if he were spontaneously sensitive to it, there would be no need for criticism. But now comes the critic with his catalysis. He makes the work of art live for the spectator; he makes the spectator live for the work of art. Out of the process comes understanding, appreciation, intelligent enjoyment—in brief, a close approximation to the effect that the artist tried to produce. That is the intent of criticism and that is also its function.

A Novel a Day

From the *Smart Set*, Sept., 1912, pp. 151–52. Fredric Weldin Splint, then the editor of the *Smart Set*, offered me the job of literary reviewer in 1908. Splint's proposal was that I should fill eight pages of his space every month, and should have $50 for my pains, with the review books thrown in as my perquisite. I did not look this gift horse in the mouth, but fell to gratefully and with great energy, and so began a connection with that magazine which ran on until the end of 1923

For four years I have averaged a novel a day. On many a rainy Sunday I have read two or three, and in one week, incommunicado and on my back, I actually got through twenty-four. But that, of course, was extraordinary, unparalleled, a unique collocation of bravura and bravado. I do not say I'll ever do it again. With one such exploit in a lifetime the average man must rest content. It is not given to mortals to work incessantly upon such high gears, to rise so stupendously above the common level of achievement. I look back upon the deed with undisguised pride, and even with a touch of wonder. It ranks me with astounding and inordinate fellows—Hobson the osculator, Holmes the homicide, Home-run Kelly, Butcher Weyler and Brigham Young the matrimoniac.

> *Say I'm weary, say I'm sad;*
> *Say that health and wealth have missed me;*
> *Say I'm growing old, but add—*

—that I once read twenty-four novels in a week—not, perhaps, from cover to cover, skipping not a word, cutting every page—but still diligently and even thoroughly, and to the end that the ensuing reviews, composed on my discharge from hospital, were pretty fair and comprehensive, as reviews go in this vale of crime, and so pleased half of the publishers and almost one of the novelists.

But what I started out to do was not to boast about my Gargantuan appetite for prose fiction—an appetite so insatiable that in the intervals between best-sellers it sends me back to "Huckleberry Finn" and "Germinal" and "Kim" and "Vanity Fair"—but to apologize to the dear publishers for occasionally overlooking a single novel, or even a whole flock of novels. I try to have a glance at every one they send me, and to go through at least thirty every thirty days, but after all I have only two hands, and thus it sometimes happens, when nine or ten come bouncing in together, that I muff three or four of them. And again it sometimes happens that I am utterly unable, with the best intentions in the world, to read far enough into a given volume to find out what it is about. And yet again it sometimes happens that, having found out, I am unable to describe the contents without violating the laws against the use of profane and indecent language. And finally it sometimes happens—more often, indeed, than merely sometimes—that my toilsome surmounting of all these difficulties is rendered null and vain by assassins in the *Smart Set* office, who reduce me from eight pages to six without warning, or pi a couple of galleys of my arduous type, or send their devil to me with orders to let novels alone for a month and give them something sapient and racy about the latest published dramas or the new treatises on psychotherapy. All this by way of explanation and apology, not only to the Barabbases who publish, but also to those kind readers who protest in courteous terms when I happen to neglect their favorites among the Indiana genii. The whole thing, I must admit, is rather a muddle. I do not review upon any systematic, symmetrical plan, with its roots in logic and the *jus gentium*, but haphazard and without a conscience, and so it may occur that a fourth-rate novel gets a page, or even two pages, while a work of high merit goes inequitably to my ash-barrel and is hauled away in the night, unwept, unhonored and unsung, along with my archaic lingerie and my vacant beer bottles.

Meditation at Vespers

From the Baltimore *Evening Sun*, Dec. 12, 1927

After long years of active and sometimes gaudy controversy, literary, political, ethical, legal and theological, I find myself, at the brim of senility, cherishing the following thoughts: (*a*) that I can't recall ever attacking an adversary who was not free to make a reply, and in tones as blistering as he liked, and (*b*) that I can't recall ever calling for quarter, or indulging in any maneuvers to get it. Such are the banal satisfactions that must content a rat-catcher in his declining years. Like all other satisfactions, they are probably largely delusory—in fine, Freudian phenomena. That is to say, I suspect that an impartial inquiry would show that I have hit below the belt more than once, and ducked more than once. Do I forget it grandly, and flap my wings? Then it is for the same reason that a Sunday-school superintendent forgets stealing 15 cents from his blind grandmother back in 1895.

But if I thus have to lie a little, if only unconsciously, to make my record clear, I can at least say with complete honesty that the uproars I have been engaged in from time to time have been very agreeable, and left me without any rancor. Speaking generally, I am of a sombre disposition and get very little happiness out of life, though I am often merry; but what little I have got has come mainly out of some form of combat. Why this should be so I don't know. Maybe it indicates that I am only half civilized. But if so, then Huxley was also only half civilized, and Voltaire before him, and St. Paul before Voltaire. Is controversy of any use? Obviously, it is the only device so far invented that actually spreads the enlightenment. Exposition, persuasion, homiletics, exegesis—these devices are all plainly inferior, for you must first get your crowd. How difficult that is every preacher knows. But a combat brings the crowd instanter, and if that combat is furious enough and over an issue of any importance at all, the crowd will stay to the end.

True enough, what it gets out of the immediate uproar is often only folly. It is, save in extreme circumstances, in favor of whoever takes and holds the offensive. The chief desideratum in practical controversy, indeed, is to do that, and the second is to make your opponent angry: the moment he begins to fume he is lost. But though the immediate victory may thus go simply to the better gladiator, I believe it is safe to say that he often ruins his cause, if it is intrinsically a bad one, by winning. The Prohibitionists scored a glorious triumph in 1920. They not only got their law; they also converted at least four-fifths of all the morons in America. But they began to go downhill from that moment. The history of controversy, in truth, is a long history of winners losing and losers winning. There is more to the thing than the concrete battle. Ideas are shot into the air, and some of them keep on flying. The first ecclesiastical rush in the '60s apparently overwhelmed Huxley— but it also gave him his chance. Voltaire had to flee from France in 1726, but he scattered seeds as he fled, and they are still sprouting and making fruit.

XIX. PRESENT AT THE CREATION

A Novel of the First Rank

From the *Smart Set*, Nov., 1911, pp. 153–55. A review of JENNIE GERHARDT, by Theodore Dreiser; New York, 1911. Ever since I began to find myself as a literary critic, I had been on the lookout for an author who would serve me as a sort of tank in my war upon the frauds and dolts who still reigned in American letters. What I needed was an author who was completely American in his themes and his point of view, who dealt with people and situations of wide and durable interest, who had something to say about his characters that was not too obvious, who was nevertheless simple enough to be understood by the vulgar, and who knew how to concoct and tell an engrossing story. When the gorgeous phenomenon of Jennie Gerhardt burst upon me, I was frankly enchanted. This flaming review was the first long one to be printed, and its positive tone undoubtedly influenced a good many of those that followed. Thereafter, for five or six years, Dreiser was the stick with which I principally flogged the dullards of my country, at least in the field of beautiful letters

IF YOU MISS reading "Jennie Gerhardt," by Theodore Dreiser, you will miss the best American novel, all things considered, that has reached the book counters in a dozen years. On second thought, change "a dozen" into "twenty-five." On third thought, strike out everything after "counters." On fourth thought, strike out everything after "novel." Why back and fill? Why evade and qualify? Hot from it, I am firmly convinced that "Jennie Gerhardt" is the best American novel I have ever read, with the lonesome but Himalayan exception of "Huckleberry Finn," and so I may as well say it aloud and at once and have done with it. Am I forgetting "The Scarlet Letter," "The Rise of Silas Lapham" and (to drag an exile unwillingly home) "What Maisie Knew"? I am not. Am I forgetting "McTeague" and "The Pit"? I am not. Am I forgetting the stupendous masterpieces of James Fenimore Cooper, beloved of the pedagogues, or those of James Lane Allen, Mrs. Wharton and Dr. S. Weir Mitchell, beloved of the women's clubs and literary monthlies? No. Or "Uncle Tom's Cabin" or "Rob o' the Bowl" or "Gates Ajar" or "Ben Hur" or "David Harum" or "Lewis Rand" or "Richard Carvel"? No. Or "The Hungry Heart" or Mr. Dreiser's own "Sister Carrie"? No. I have all these good and bad books in mind. I have read them and survived them and in many cases enjoyed them. And yet in the face of them, and in the face of all the high authority, constituted and self-constituted, behind them, it seems to me at this moment that "Jennie Gerhardt" stands apart from all of them, and a bit above them. It lacks the grace of this one, the humor of that one, the perfect form of some other one; but taking it as it stands, grim, gaunt, mirthless, shapeless, it remains, and by long odds, the most impressive work of art that we have yet to show in prose-fiction—a tale not unrelated, in its stark simplicity, its profound sincerity, to "Germinal" and "Anna Karenina" and "Lord Jim"—a tale assertively American in its scene and its human material, and yet so European in its method, its point of view, its almost reverential seriousness, that one can scarcely imagine an American writing it. Its personages are few in number, and their progress is along a path that seldom widens, but the effect of that progress is ever one of large movements and large masses. One senses constantly the group behind the individual, the natural law behind the human act. The result is an indefinable impression of bigness, of epic dignity. The thing is not a mere story, not a novel in the ordinary American meaning of the word, but a criticism of and interpretation of life—and that interpretation loses nothing in validity by the fact that its burden is that doctrine that life is meaningless, a tragedy without a moral, a joke without a point. What else have Moore and Conrad and Hardy been telling us these many years? What else does all the new knowledge of a century teach us? One by one the old, ready answers have been disposed of. Today the one intelligible answer to the riddle of aspiration and sacrifice is that there is no answer at all.

"The power to tell the same story in two forms," said George Moore not long ago, "is the sign of the true artist." You will think of this when you read "Jennie Gerhardt," for in its objective plan, and even in its scheme of subjective unfolding, it suggests "Sister Carrie" at every turn. Reduce it to a hundred words, and those same words would also describe that earlier study of a woman's soul, with scarcely the change of a syllable. Jennie Gerhardt, like Carrie Meeber, is a rose grown from turnip seed. Over each, at the start, hangs poverty, ignorance, the dumb helplessness of the Shudra—and yet in each there is that indescribable something, that element of essential gentleness, that innate, inward beauty which levels all caste barriers and makes Esther a fit queen for Ahasuerus. And the history of each, reduced to its elements, is the history of the other. Jennie, like Carrie, escapes from the physical miseries of the struggle for existence only to taste the worse miseries of the struggle for happiness. Not, of course, that we have in either case a moral, maudlin fable of virtue's fall; Mr. Dreiser, I need scarcely assure you, is too dignified an artist, too sane a man, for any such banality. Seduction, in point of fact, is not all tragedy for either Jennie or Carrie. The gain of each, until the actual event has been left behind and obliterated by experiences more salient and poignant, is rather greater than her loss, and that gain is to the soul as well as to the creature. With the rise from want to security, from fear to ease, comes an awakening of the finer perceptions, a widening of the sympathies, a gradual unfolding of the delicate flower called personality, an increased capacity for loving and living. But with all this, and as a part of it, there comes, too, an increased capacity for suffering—and so in the end, when love slips away and the empty years stretch before, it is the awakened and supersentient woman that pays for the folly of the groping, bewildered girl. The tragedy of Carrie and Jennie, in brief, is not that they are degraded but that they are lifted up, not that they go to the gutter but that they escape the gutter.

But if the two stories are thus variations upon the same sombre theme, if each starts from the same place and arrives at the same dark goal, if each shows a woman heartened by the same hopes and tortured by the same agonies, there is still a vast difference between them, and that difference is the measure of the author's

progress in his art. "Sister Carrie" was a first sketch, a rough
piling-up of observations and impressions, disordered and often in-
coherent. In the midst of the story of Carrie, Mr. Dreiser paused
to tell the story of Hurstwood—an astonishingly vivid and tragic
story, true enough, but still one that broke the back of the other.
In "Jennie Gerhardt" he falls into no such overelaboration of episode. His narrative goes forward steadily from beginning to end.
Episodes there are, of course, but they keep their proper place,
their proper bulk. It is always Jennie that holds the attention; it is
in Jennie's soul that every scene is ultimately played out. Her father and mother, Senator Brander the god of her first worship, her
daughter Vesta and Lester Kane, the man who makes and mars
her—all these are drawn with infinite painstaking, and in every
one of them there is the blood of life. But it is Jennie that dom-
inates the drama from curtain to curtain. Not an event is unrelated to her; not a climax fails to make clearer the struggles going
on in her mind and heart.

I have spoken of reducing "Jennie Gerhardt" to 100 words. The
thing, I fancy, might be actually done. The machinery of the tale
is not complex; it has no plot, as plots are understood in these days
of "mystery" stories; no puzzles madden the reader. It is dull, unromantic poverty that sends Jennie into the world. Brander finds
her there, lightly seduces her, and then discovers that, for some
strange gentleness within her, he loves her. Lunacy—but he is
willing to face it out. Death, however, steps in; Brander, stricken
down without warning, leaves Jennie homeless and a mother. Now
enters Lester Kane—not the villain of the book, but a normal, decent, cleanly American of the better class, well-to-do, level-headed,
not too introspective, eager for the sweets of life. He and Jennie
are drawn together; if love is not all of the spirit, then it is love that
binds them. For half a dozen years the world lets them alone. A
certain grave respectability settles over their relation; if they are
not actually married, then it is only because marriage is a mere
formality, to be put off until tomorrow. But bit by bit they are
dragged into the light. Kane's father, dying with millions, gives
him two years to put Jennie away. The penalty is poverty; the reward is wealth—and not only wealth itself, but all the pleasant and
well remembered things that will come with it; the lost friends of

other days, a sense of dignity and importance, an end of apologies and evasions, good society, the comradeship of decent women— particularly the comradeship of one decent woman. Kane hesitates, makes a brave defiance, thinks it over—and finally yields. Jennie does not flood him with tears. She has made progress in the world, has Jennie; the simple faith of the girl has given way to the pride and poise of the woman. Five years later Kane sends for her. He is dying. When it is over, Jennie goes back to her lonely home, and there, like Carrie Meeber before her, she faces the long years with dry eyes and an empty heart. "Days and days in endless reiteration, and then—"

A moral tale? Not at all. It has no more moral than a string quartette or the first book of Euclid. But a philosophy of life is in it, and that philosophy is the same profound pessimism which gives a dark color to the best that we have from Hardy, Moore, Zola and the great Russians—the pessimism of disillusion—not the jejune, Byronic thing, not the green sickness of youth, but that pessimism which comes with the discovery that the riddle of life, despite all the fine solutions offered by the learned doctors, is essentially insoluble. One can discern no intelligible sequence of cause and effect in the agonies of Jennie Gerhardt. She is, as human beings go, of the nobler, finer metal. There is within her a great capacity for service, a great capacity for love, a great capacity for happiness. And yet all that life has to offer her, in the end, is the mere license to live. The days stretch before her "in endless reiteration." She is a prisoner doomed to perpetual punishment for some fanciful, incomprehensible crime against the gods who make their mirthless sport of us all. And to me, at least, she is more tragic thus than Lear on his wild heath or Prometheus on his rock.

Nothing of the art of the literary lapidary is visible in this novel. Its form is the simple one of a panorama unrolled. Its style is unstudied to the verge of barrenness. There is no painful groping for the exquisite, inevitable word; Mr. Dreiser seems content to use the common, even the commonplace coin of speech. On the very first page one encounters "frank, open countenance," "diffident manner," "helpless poor," "untutored mind," "honest necessity" and half a dozen other such ancients. And yet in the long run it is this very *naïveté* which gives the story much of its impressiveness. The narrative, in places, has the effect of a series of unisons in music—an effect which, given a solemn theme, vastly exceeds that of the most ornate polyphony. One cannot imagine "Jennie Gerhardt" done in the gipsy phrases of Meredith, the fugal manner of James. One cannot imagine that stark, stenographic dialogue adorned with the brilliants of speech. The thing could have been done only in the way that it has been done. As it stands, it is a work of art from which I for one would not care to take anything away—not even its gross crudities, its incessant returns to C major. It is a novel that depicts the life we Americans are living with extreme accuracy and criticises that life with extraordinary sight. It is a novel, I am convinced, of the very first consideration.

Marginal Note

From the *Smart Set*, March, 1923, p. 51

The truth has a horrible sweat to survive in this world, but a piece of nonsense, however absurd on its face, always seems to prosper. I come at once to an example: the notion that I "discovered," as the phrase has it, Theodore Dreiser, the novelist. This imbecility is constantly cropping up in the newspapers; it costs me a large sum annually to buy it from the clipping bureaux. There is no more truth in it than in the notion that the botanical name of the whale is *blatta orientalis*. Dreiser wrote "Sister Carrie" in 1899, and it got into type in 1900. I first heard of it in 1902, when I was handed a copy of the suppressed and rare first edition by the late George Bronson-Howard, a man of very sound taste in letters. It was not until 1906 that I ever enjoyed the honor of witnessing Dreiser personally; it was not until 1907 that I ever had any traffic with him, and then it was as a contributor to the *Delineator*, of which he was editor; it was not until 1908 that I even wrote a line about him. Long before this he was a very well-known man. . . .

A trivial matter, to be sure. But why is it that such puerile nonsense always shows such tenacity of life? When "Sister Carrie" was published I was precisely 20 years old. In these days, of course, with the Foetal School in full flower, that is mature age for an American critic of the arts, but in my time it was generally believed, and I think with some show of plausibility, that a youth short of his majority was fit only for writing poetry. To that banal art, in fact, I then devoted myself, and connoisseurs of adolescent glycosuria are familiar with the result, "Ventures into Verse."[1] Nothing, I need not add, would give me greater joy than to be able to say truthfully that I had discovered Dreiser. He retains, after all these years, a rare and peculiar eminence. He has had a larger influence upon the development of the serious American novel than any other man, living or dead. He is a *Kopf* of the first rank among us. But long before I wrote my first dithyrambs upon him, he had been praised lavishly by various distinguished English critics, and even a few advanced American professors had heard of him.

So much for the simple facts. But will they dispose of the contrary nonsense? They will not. When Dreiser is hanged at last, at least three-fourths of the morons who write obituaries of him in the newspapers will say that I discovered him, and perhaps half of them will add that it is a good reason for hanging me with the same rope.

An American Novel

From the *Smart Set*, Jan., 1921, pp. 138–40. A review of MAIN STREET, by Sinclair Lewis; New York, 1920. One evening in the latter part of 1920 George Jean Nathan and I went to a party in New York where I met Lewis. He had published nothing, up to that time, save a few light novels that had been *Saturday Evening Post* serials, and I had never

---

[1] My first book, published in 1903. I am astonished, thumbing through that embarrassing volume, to observe how little critical sense I had in 1902, when it was put together. As incredible as it may seem, it got a number of friendly notices, but on the whole I gathered that it was not a success, and I was glad when it began to be forgotten, which was very soon. I made a resolution to write no more verse, and have kept it pretty well to this day, though with a few backslidings. (See, for example, p. 460.)

reviewed any of them, nor read them. He was, as always in society, far gone in liquor, and when he fastened upon me with a drunkard's zeal, declaring that he had lately finished a novel of vast and singular merits full worthy of my most careful and critical attention, I tried hard to shake him off. Long before the usual time for departing I got hold of Nathan and proposed to him that we clear out. The next day I returned to Baltimore, and before leaving the *Smart Set* office gathered up an armful of review books to examine on the train. I took up one as the train plunged into the Pennsylvania tunnel. By the time it got to Newark I was interested, and by the time it got to Trenton I was fascinated. At Philadelphia I called a Western Union boy and sent a telegram to Nathan. I forget the exact text, but it read substantially: "That idiot has written a masterpiece." The book was Main Street

After all, Munyon was probably right: there is yet hope. Perhaps Emerson and Whitman were right too; maybe even Sandburg is right. What ails us all is a weakness for rash over-generalization, leading to shooting pains in the psyche and delusions of divine persecution. Observing the steady and precipitate descent of promising postulants in beautiful letters down the steep, greasy chutes of the *Saturday Evening Post*, the *Metropolitan*, the *Cosmopolitan* and the rest of the Hearst and Hearstoid magazines, we are too prone, ass-like, to throw up our hands and bawl that all is lost, including honor. But all the while a contrary movement is in progress, far less noted than it ought to be. Authors with their pockets full of best-seller money are bitten by high ambition, and strive heroically to scramble out of the literary Cloaca Maxima. Now and then one of them succeeds, bursting suddenly into the light of the good red sun with the foul liquors of the depths still streaming from him, like a prisoner loosed from some obscene dungeon. Is it so soon forgotten that Willa Cather used to be one of the editors of *McClure's*? That Dreiser wrote editorials for the *Delineator* and was an editor of dime novels for Street & Smith? That Huneker worked for the *Musical Courier*? That Amy Lowell imitated George E. Woodberry and Felicia Hemans? That E. W. Howe was born a Methodist? That Sandburg was once a Chautauqua orator? That Cabell's first stories were printed in *Harper's Magazine*? . . . As I say, they occasionally break out, strange as it may seem. A few months ago I recorded the case of Zona Gale, emerging from her stew of glad books with "Miss Lulu Bett." Now comes another fugitive, his face blanched by years in the hulks, but his eyes alight with high purpose. His name is Sinclair Lewis, and the work he offers is a novel called "Main Street."

This "Main Street" I commend to your polite attention. It is, in brief, good stuff. It presents characters that are genuinely human, and not only genuinely human but also authentically American; it carries them through a series of transactions that are all interesting and plausible; it exhibits those transactions thoughtfully and acutely, in the light of the social and cultural forces underlying them; it is well written, and full of a sharp sense of comedy, and rich in observation, and competently designed. Superficially the story of a man and his wife in a small Minnesota town, it is actually the typical story of the American family—that is, of the family in its first stage, before husband and wife have become lost in father and mother. The average American wife, I daresay, does not come quite so close to downright revolt as Carol Kennicott, but that is the only exaggeration, and we may well overlook it. Otherwise, she and her Will are triumphs of the national normalcy—she with her vague stirrings, her unintelligible yearnings, her clumsy gropings, and he with his magnificent obtuseness, his childish belief in meaningless phrases, his intellectual deafness and near-sightedness, his pathetic inability to comprehend the turmoil that goes on within her. Here is the essential tragedy of American life, and if not the tragedy, then at least the sardonic farce; the disparate cultural development of male and female, the great strangeness that lies between husband and wife when they begin to function as members of society. The men, sweating at their sordid concerns, have given the women leisure, and out of that leisure the women have fashioned disquieting discontents. To Will Kennicott, as to most other normal American males, life remains simple; do your work, care for your family, buy your Liberty Bonds, root for your home team, help to build up your lodge, venerate the flag. But to Carol it is far more complex and challenging. She has become aware of forces that her husband is wholly unable to comprehend, and that she herself can comprehend only in a dim and muddled way. The ideas of the great world press upon her, confusing her and making her uneasy. She is flustered by strange heresies, by romantic personalities, by exotic images of beauty. To Kennicott she is flighty, illogical, ungrateful for the benefits that he and God have heaped upon her. To her he is dull, narrow, ignoble.

Mr. Lewis depicts the resultant struggle with great penetration. He is far too intelligent to take sides—to turn the thing into a mere harangue against one or the other. Above all, he is too intelligent to take the side of Carol, as nine novelists out of ten would have done. He sees clearly what is too often not seen—that her superior culture is, after all, chiefly bogus—that the oafish Kennicott, in more ways than one, is actually better than she is. Her war upon his Philistinism is carried on with essentially Philistine weapons. Her dream of converting a Minnesota prairie town into a sort of Long Island suburb, with overtones of Greenwich Village and the Harvard campus, is quite as absurd as his dream of converting it into a second Minneapolis, with overtones of Gary, Ind., and Paterson, N.J. When their conflict is made concrete and dramatic by the entrance of a *tertium quid*, the hollowness of her whole case is at once made apparent, for this *tertium quid* is a Swedish trousers-presser who becomes a moving-picture actor. It seems to me that the irony here is delicate and delicious. Needless to say, Carol lacks the courage to decamp with her Scandinavian. Instead, she descends to sheer banality. That is, she departs for Washington, becomes a war-worker, and rubs noses with the suffragettes. In the end, it goes without saying, she returns to Gopher Prairie and the hearth-stone of her Will. The fellow is at least honest. He offers her no ignominious compromise. She comes back under the old rules, and is presently nursing a baby. Thus the true idealism of the Republic, the idealism of its Chambers of Commerce, its Knights of Pythias, its Rotary Clubs and its National Defense Leagues, for which Washington froze at Valley Forge and Our Boys died at Chateau Thierry—thus this genuine and unpolluted article conquers the phony idealism of Nietzsche, Edward W. Bok, Dunsany, George Bernard Shaw, Margaret Anderson, Mrs. Margaret Sanger, Percy Mackaye and the I.W.W.

But the mere story, after all, is nothing; the virtue of the book lies in its packed and brilliant detail. It is an attempt, not to solve the American cultural problem, but simply to depict with great care a group of typical Americans. This attempt is extraordinarily successful. The figures often remain in the flat; the author is quite unable to get that poignancy into them which Dreiser manages so superbly; one seldom sees into them very deeply or feels with them very keenly. But in their externals, at all events, they are done with uncommon skill. In particular, Mr. Lewis represents their speech vividly and accurately. It would be hard to find a false note in the dialogue, and it would be impossible to exceed the verisimilitude of the various extracts from the Gopher Prairie paper, or of the sermon by a Methodist dervish in the Gopher Prairie Wesleyan cathedral, or of a speech boy by a boomer at a banquet of the Chamber of Commerce. Here Mr. Lewis lays on with obvious malice, but always he keeps within the bounds of probability, always his realism holds up. It is, as I have said, good stuff. I have read no more genuinely amusing novel for a long while. The man who did it deserves a hearty welcome. His apprenticeship in the cellars of the tabernacle was not wasted.

XX. CONSTRUCTIVE CRITICISM

The Uplift as a Trade

From the Baltimore *Evening Sun*, March 2, 1925

LITTLE DOES the public reck how much of the news it devours every day is manufactured by entrepreneurs. Not infrequently I have detected as much as a whole page of it in the eminent *Sunpaper*, a journal more suspicious than most: it is far worse in others. One reads that the representative of a national organization is before Congress demanding this or that radical change in the laws; the plain fact is that the national organization consists of its representative—that the rest of the members are simply dolts who have put up the money for his salary and expenses in order to bathe themselves in the glare of his publicity. One hears that a million children in Abyssinia are starving, that a fund of $5,000,000 is being raised to succor them, that Baltimore's quota is $216,000; the plain fact is that an accomplished drive manager has got a new job. One hears that "the women of the United States" are up in arms about this or that; the plain fact is that eight fat women, meeting in a hotel parlor, have decided to kick up some dust.

It is extraordinarily hard for newspapers to distinguish what is real from what is false in such movements. Those that are private enterprises are commonly run by very cunning fellows, male or female; they are always apparently backed by persons of the highest standing; the demands that they make, for money and support, are often based upon grounds that seem to be very virtuous. Their promoters do not simply beg for space; they make news—and news is news, whatever its origin. The eight fat women, meeting in their hotel parlor, find it easy to alarm the politicians, who are not only dreadful cowards but almost unbelievable asses. Something thus gets afoot. Governors jump; legislators rush through new laws; judges respond to "public sentiment." How is a newspaper to avoid reporting such stuff? Yet it is often as bogus, at bottom, as a theatrical press-agent's report that a Follies girl has lost a $100,000 diamond necklace or is engaged to a professor in Harvard University.

I believe, however, that something might be done, at least against the bolder and more flagrant performers. What comes over the wires, perhaps, is beyond careful investigation, but every newspaper might at least keep watch in its own town; if all did so, the daily stream of blather would lessen by at least eighty per cent. I am in a mood of constructive criticism, and offer concrete suggestions to the two *Sunpapers*.

1. Let a rule be set up that no appeal for public funds or subscriptions will be printed until there is filed, under oath, a complete list of all the persons engaged to collect them, with their compensation.

2. Let it be required that, after the collection has been made, a statement shall be filed, in detail, showing what was done with every cent of the money.

3. In case the money is for a continuing organization, let it be blacklisted unless it publishes annual statements of its receipts and expenditures in detail, with the name of every person on its payroll.

4. Whenever resolutions are presented for publication, setting forth any view about a public matter, let it be required that the exact number of persons at the meeting adopting them to be printed with them.

These rules are not unreasonable. No honest organization, devoted sincerely to good works, could plausibly object to them. But they would fetch many organizations which now prey upon the sentimentality and credulity of the public, and they would put a great many professional uplifters out of business in the community. My scheme is rough, and perhaps defective. I present it as it stands, not only to the two *Sunpapers* but also to the Society of American Newspaper Editors, which now labors with nonsensical codes of ethics—jewelry and fur coats for a profession which is just learning to wash behind the ears. Let learned counsel lay their heads together, and perfect the imperfect. The public deserves a rest from pious and highfalutin tosh. Until newspapers learn how to keep it out of their news columns, completely and permanently, they will fail to discharge one of their principal functions: the detection and exposure of frauds. Suppose a physician let a chiropractor and a Christian Scientist bark and catch in his waiting room?

A New Constitution for Maryland

From the Baltimore *Evening Sun*, April 12, 1937. The existing Constitution of Maryland was ratified on Sept. 18, 1867. It voices the resentment of the people of the State against military control during the Civil War, and some of its provisions are quite extraordinary. The Declaration of Rights, for example, provides that the rights to jury trial, to habeas corpus, and to free speech and free assembly shall prevail "in time of war as in time of peace," and Article VI provides that "whenever the ends of government are perverted" the people may overthrow the existing government and set up a new one, and that "the doctrine of non-resistance against arbitrary power and oppression is absurd, slavish and destructive of the good and happiness of mankind." Article XIV of the Constitution proper provides for calling a constitutional convention every twenty years after 1867. But there was no such convention in 1927 or 1947. In 1937 I proposed my new Constitution. Only a few of its provisions are given; the rest were less novel. It got some attention among judges and lawyers through the country, and I received some interesting commentaries on it, but in Maryland it went almost unnoticed and none of its innovations has been adopted since, or even discussed

Article I
The Elective Franchise

Section 1. The people of the Maryland Free State consist of all natural persons denizened within its confines, without regard to age, color, sex, race or national origin. All shall have the equal protection of its laws.

Sec. 2. Voting in the Maryland Free State shall be a privilege, and not a right. Every natural person denizened within the State who is a citizen of the United States and has reached the age of twenty-five years and can speak, read and write the American or English language, shall have the privilege of voting at elections . . . provided that he or she has been registered as a voter as provided by law, and provided further that no one shall vote who is under guardianship as a lunatic or as a person *non compos mentis*, or who has been convicted, either within the State or elsewhere, of felony or of bribery at any election, or who occupies any office of profit under the Maryland Free State or the United States, or who has been in receipt, during the five years next preceding an election, of any grant or benefit from the public treasury, or from any local treasury, or from the treasury of the United States, save for full value in goods or services. . . .

Article II
Bill of Rights

Section 1. No law shall be passed abridging the freedom of speech, or of the press, or of teaching, but everyone exercising such freedom shall be accountable at law and equity for any actual damage directly and beyond a reasonable doubt flowing therefrom, whether to the common welfare or to private persons.

Sec. 2. No law shall be passed establishing a religion, or favoring the tenets or practises of any faith or sect, or penalizing any discussion thereof as blasphemy, or impeding the conduct of religious exercises at any place or in any manner not imperiling the public peace or health, or appropriating public funds for any religious purpose, or for any institution controlled by a religious body; but the funds of any division or agency of the State may be paid out to such an institution by law to an amount not greater than the reasonable and actual value of its care for public charges.

Sec. 3. The right of the people openly to bear arms and to exercise themselves in the use thereof shall not be infringed, but the bearing of concealed weapons by any person or of any weapons by persons convicted of felony involving the use of arms may be prohibited. . . .

Sec. 5. No law shall be passed regulating the conduct of any person in his own house, save such conduct as may be directly invasive of his neighbors' peace or security, or imminently dangerous to the general health or safety. . . .

Sec. 11. In all cases wherein prosecutions shall have been initiated on the complaint of a private person, no conviction shall follow save that person appear against the accused in open court.

Sec. 12. In all criminal cases it shall be competent for the prosecution to produce evidence that the accused is an habitual and incorrigible criminal, and the judge and/or jury may take such evidence into account in estimating the degree of his guilt. . . .

Sec. 15. The writ of *habeas corpus* shall never be suspended, and no person, save members of the militia in actual service, shall be subject to or punishable by martial law.

Sec. 16. Justice shall be free to all, and no officer of any court or any other person employed in the administration of the laws shall be compensated by fees. . . .

Sec. 19. Large and onerous bail shall not be required save in case of manifest necessity, and in every such case the sitting judge or magistrate shall announce in full, in open court, his reasons for requiring it. . . .

Sec. 21. No person shall be charged with sedition who advocates the reform of the government by peaceful means, or the orderly substitution of another form of government for it. . . .

Sec. 24. Any person wrongfully imprisoned, whether by the unlawful act of a judge, jury or magistrate, or by any other failure of justice, may enter suit for compensation in any District Court, sitting without a jury, and the Governor and Legislative Council shall provide by a general law for the payment of any damages therein awarded. . . .

Sec. 25. The right to private property lawfully acquired shall not be destroyed or diminished by law, save as otherwise provided in this Constitution, but the Governor and Legislative Council may by law limit the value of money or goods devisable by will to any one natural person.

Article III
General Policies

Section 1. It shall be the policy of the Maryland Free State to repay and cancel its present public debt as soon as possible, and to avoid incurring onerous public debts hereafter. No debt shall be incurred save by authority of a majority of the registered voters of the State, ascertained by plebiscite, and no plebiscite or plebiscites shall be submitted in any one calendar year providing for the borrowing of a sum greater than ten per centum of the total revenue actually collected by the State from direct taxes, excluding licenses, during the calendar year preceding. No law providing for a loan shall be valid unless it also provides for the retirement of that loan within ten years, and levies a tax sufficient to meet the necessary amortization and interest. The provisions of this section shall apply *pari passu* to loans made by all divisions and agencies of the State authorized by law to borrow money, to the end that they may reduce their debts as soon as possible.

Sec. 2. No law shall be passed appropriating or authorizing the expenditure of money for the enjoyment or benefit of any person or persons that does not provide for the same or equal enjoyment and benefit to any other person, nor shall any such appropriation be made by any division or agency of the State.

Sec. 3. Divorce in the Maryland Free State shall be granted by a general law only, and no special bill of divorcement shall be passed by the Legislative Council. No divorce shall be granted until the marriage shall have endured at least three years. No testimony shall be taken in a divorce case, save only the testimony of one or both parties to the marriage that he, she or they desire it to end. In case both parties so testify a divorce may be granted forthwith. In case one party dissents no divorce shall be granted until at least two years have passed since the filing of the action. . . .

Sec. 5. No license to marry shall be granted to any female who has not reached the age of 18 years, nor to any male who has not reached the age of 21, nor to any person of either sex who has been married more than twice previously, or who has been divorced within the two years next preceding. . . .

Sec. 7. Laws may be passed providing for the sterilization of persons adjudged by due process, by law established, to be biologically unfit for reproduction, whether physically or mentally, and criminality involving violence to the person may be reckoned as an evidence of such unfitness.

Sec. 8. No person shall be paroled, pardoned or released on suspended sentence a second time.

Sec. 9. It shall be competent for any judge, in passing sentence for felony or other grave crimes, to make removal from the Maryland Free State a part of the punishment, whether for a definite time or for life, and to make imprisonment for the same time the alternative.

Sec. 10. All laws carrying punishment by fine shall provide that the fine be apportioned to the known or apparent income of the person fined, whether earned or unearned, to the end that the pains of punishment may be equalized and the equal protection of the laws better effected. . . .

Sec. 11. No law shall be passed licensing the practise of the healing art, or any part of it, to any person whose qualification is not at least equal to that of a graduate of the Medical School of the University of Maryland, and the Legislative Council, with the approval of the Governor, may pass laws forbidding the said practise to all other persons, on penalty of imprisonment. . . .

Sec. 15. The Legislative Council, with the approval of the Governor, may provide by law for the payment of old-age pensions to indigent persons beyond the age of 60 years, for the insurance of workers, including farm laborers and domestic servants, against unemployment, and for the humane care of the sick, disabled and indigent, but no person shall have any right to any benefit from such laws who has not been a *bona fide* resident of Maryland for the five years next preceding his application for such benefit.

Sec. 16. The Legislative Council, with the approval of the Governor, may provide by law for the investigation and adjudication of labor disputes, but no law shall be passed compelling any man to work against his will, or to employ another against his will.

Sec. 17. No law shall be passed relieving any corporation or non-corporate association from liability for damages inflicted on others by its officers and members as such, or by any of them.

Article IV
The Executive

Section 1. The executive power of the Maryland Free State shall be vested in a Governor, whose term of office shall be continued ten years, or, in case no successor lawfully qualifies at the end of his term, until such successor qualifies.

Sec. 2. No one shall be eligible to the office of Governor save one who is a natural-born citizen of the Maryland Free State, and has resided within its boundaries for the ten years immediately preceding his entrance into office.

Sec. 3. No one shall be eligible to the office of Governor who is less than 30 years of age, or more than 60 years, nor anyone who has held any office of profit under the Maryland Free State or the United States during the five years next preceding the beginning of the term for which he offers to serve, save only that of members of the Legislative Council; nor anyone who has received any fee or other reward during that time for advocating or opposing any legislation in the Maryland Free State.

Sec. 4. The Governor shall be the fount of mercy, and shall have the power to diminish or remit the penalties inflicted in all criminal cases, to issue reprieves of sentence, and to restore to citizenship persons disfranchised for crime, but in every case he shall file with the clerk of the High Court a memorandum setting forth at length his reasons for such action, and embodying a full and true list of the persons who have petitioned or advised him to take it, and in no case shall he pardon or reprieve or diminish the punishment of any person lawfully convicted of bribery at an election or of being an habitual and incorrigible criminal, or of any person impeached by the Grand Inquest. Nor shall he commute the death sentence of any person previously adjudged on true evidence to be an habitual and incorrigible criminal, or convicted of murder committed in the perpetration of a felony with arms. . . .

Sec. 9. The Executive Authority in each district . . . shall consist of a District Council of three persons,[1] to be elected by the voters

---

[1] Article IV, Section 8 provides that the State shall be divided into five districts and a Metropolitan district consisting of Baltimore. The present counties are abolished.

of the whole district, without regard to former county lines. No person shall be eligible to election who has not been a *bona fide* resident and taxpayer in the district for at least five years next preceding the election, or who does not meet the qualifications for the office of Governor set forth in Article IV, Section 3 of this Constitution.

Sec. 10. Of the three members of each District Council first elected, one shall be elected for three years, one for six years, and one for nine years, but thereafter all members shall serve for nine years, save as hereinafter provided, and shall be ineligible for reëlection.

Sec. 11. The term of any member of a District Council shall terminate forthwith if he shall remove from the district he serves, or if he shall be declared bankrupt, or if he shall be impeached as provided by this Constitution, or if he shall be convicted of bribery or felony, or if he shall come under guardianship as a lunatic or a person *non compos mentis*, or if he shall accept any other office of profit under the Maryland Free State or any of its divisions or agencies, or under the United States. . . .

Sec. 13. Every District Council shall hold a meeting for the transaction of business not less often than once in every calendar week, and every such meeting shall be open to the press and public.

Sec. 14. The Elective Authority for Baltimore city shall consist of a Mayor and City Council, and it shall be elected in such manner and vested with such powers as the Governor and Legislative Council may from time to time determine by charter, but the qualifications of its members shall be those for members of District Councils, and they may be disqualified when in office for the same reasons, and they shall be bound by all the provisions of this Constitution regarding the incurring of public debts.

Sec. 15. The City Council shall consist of a single chamber of nine members, to be elected for the Metropolitan District as a whole. It shall meet at least once in every calendar week, and the vote of five or more members shall be sufficient to validate its acts. All its meetings shall be open to the press and public. . . .

Sec. 18. The term of office of every officer and employé of the District Councils and of every officer and employé of the Mayor and City Council of Baltimore shall be for good behavior, save as otherwise provided in this Constitution, or until he shall have reached the age of 70 years, and every officer and employé, on his honorable retirement by law, shall receive for life an annual pension of sixty per centum of his average annual pay during his last five years in office.

Article V
The Legislature

Section 1. The Legislature of the Maryland Free State shall consist of a Legislative Council of fifteen members, to be elected at State-wide elections. . . .

Sec. 3. No person shall be eligible to election who is less than 30 years of age, or more than 60 years, nor anyone who has held any office of profit under the Maryland Free State or the United States during the five years next preceding the beginning of the first term for which he offers to serve.

Sec. 4. No person shall be eligible who is or has ever been a minister of the gospel, or who has ever been under guardianship as a lunatic, or as a person *non compos mentis*, or who has ever been convicted, either within the State or elsewhere, of felony or of bribery at any election, or who has received any fee or other reward during the five years next preceding the election at which he offers himself, for advocating or opposing any legislation in the State, or who has not been a registered voter in the State for at least five years next preceding the said election, or who is or has ever been declared bankrupt, or who has not been a taxpayer in the State for at least five years, or who has ever failed, within one year of the date they first became due, to pay in full the taxes lawfully levied against him by the State or any division or agency thereof. . . .

Sec. 7. The Legislative Council, with the approval of the Governor, shall establish all departments, bureaus and offices necessary to the government and security of the State, shall provide by law for the appointment of all officers and employés thereof, and shall determine their compensation and their pensions on retirement. It shall make all laws, levy all State taxes, make all appropriations of public money, determine the powers and prerogatives of all public officers and employés, including the members of District Councils, save as otherwise provided in this Constitution, determine the compensation of all judges and of all officers and employés of the judiciary, and in general have all the powers hitherto possessed by the General Assembly. . . .

Sec. 10. The Legislative Council shall meet at Annapolis and shall be in session for the consideration of public business at least ten days in every calendar month save July and August. Its meetings shall be open to the press and public, and there shall be no limitation upon its debates save by the vote of at least twelve members. It shall appoint committees for the expedition of its business, and its committees shall grant public hearings to all parties interested in legislation before it, or bringing complaints of grievances.

Sec. 11. The compensation of members of the Legislative Council shall be determined by law, but no member who votes for an increase in that compensation shall enjoy it during the term for which he was elected, or, if he be reëlected, for the term next succeeding. . . .

Sec. 14. The Legislative Council shall provide by law for the punishment of all persons who willfully violate the rights of people of the Maryland Free State under this Constitution, and all such punishment shall be by imprisonment, with no alternative of fine.

Article VI
The Judiciary

Section 1. The judicial power of the Maryland Free State shall be vested in a High Court, in District Courts, in an Administrative Court, and in justices of the peace.

Sec. 2. All judges and justices of the peace shall be appointed by the Governor, by and with the consent of the Legislative Council.

Sec. 3. The persons selected for appointment as judges shall be not less than 30 years old and not more than 50. . . . No one shall be eligible who has not been engaged in the practise of the law or in teaching the law, as his principal source of earned income, for at least seven years next preceding his appointment. Nor shall anyone be appointed who has held any office of profit under the Maryland Free State or the United States during the five years next preceding his appointment, or who has been a candidate for such office at any election.

Sec. 4. Every judge shall be appointed for life or during good behavior, but no judge shall serve beyond his seventy-fifth birthday. No judge shall be engaged, during his service, in the practise of the law, and no judge, after his retirement, whether by age, removal, or resignation, shall be eligible to appointment or election to any other office of profit under the Maryland Free State, or any of its districts or agencies.

Sec. 5. The compensation of judges ... shall continue for the lifetime of every judge, notwithstanding his retirement, provided that if he resign his office, or be removed for misconduct, or resume the practise of the law in his retirement, it shall terminate forthwith. The compensation of a judge may be increased but not diminished during his continuance in service or retirement. In case a judge, on the certificate of the chief judge and at least three other judges of the High Court to the Governor, shall be determined to be totally disabled but shall not resign his office, another shall be appointed in his place and his service shall terminate, but his compensation shall continue.

Sec. 6. The High Court shall consist of nine judges, of whom one shall be designated chief judge by the Governor, to continue as such while he remains a judge. In appointing judges to the High Court the Governor shall give the preference to District Court judges of at least five years diligent and competent service, and when he appoints some other person he shall publish his reasons for departing from this policy.

Sec. 7. In each of the four districts of the State and in Baltimore city there shall be a District Court composed of as many judges as the Legislative Council, with the approval of the Governor, shall from time to time determine. . . .

Sec. 14. To the end that the deliberations of the courts may be enlightened and just, they may appoint any number of assessors skilled in any art, science or mystery to advise them in cases involving matters within the said assessors' knowledge. Such assessors shall take the oath required by law of judges, and shall sit with the judges, and have the right to question witnesses, but they shall not vote on the decisions of the court. . . .

Sec. 15. The employment of expert witnesses by the State or by a defendant in a criminal case or by any other litigant is prohibited, but on the motion of any party to an action the trial judge or judges shall appoint competent assessors as provided in the preceding section. . . .

Sec. 18. There shall be a Court of Criminal Appeals, consisting of three members of the High Court, to be appointed for the purpose by the chief judge thereof, and serving for such times as he may determine. He may appoint himself to this court. It shall have jurisdiction of all criminal cases appealed from the District Courts, and its decision shall be the decision of the High Court. It may sit at any place within the State determined by the chief judge to be most convenient for the business in hand. It shall have power to review both the law and the facts, to examine the record in the court below, to hear the witnesses heard there, to hear other witnesses, to examine any papers or documents that it deems apposite, and to undertake any other inquiry that, in its judgment, is likely to throw light upon a case before it. It may, in its discretion, quash a conviction and direct that a verdict of not guilty be entered, or affirm, reduce or increase a sentence, or order a new trial. All appeals to it shall be filed within twenty days of the entering of judgment in the court below, and it shall announce its own decision within ten days of the termination of proceedings before it. It shall simplify as much as possible its rules of evidence and other procedure, to the end that the actual guilt or innocence of persons before it may be determined beyond doubt. . . .[2]

Sec. 22. In capital cases wherein no appeal is entered within twenty days by the convicted defendant, the Court of Criminal Appeals shall assume jurisdiction on its own motion, and shall conduct an inquiry into the law and the facts precisely as if an appeal had been entered. Whenever its judgment sustains the sentence in

---

[2] This was borrowed from the English Criminal Appeal Act of 1907, as amended in 1908.

a capital case, the sentence shall be executed within ten days thereafter. . . .

Sec. 24. There shall be an Administrative Court for hearing and determining complaints against officers and employés of the Maryland Free State and its divisions and agencies. It shall consist of three judges, appointed and compensated as judges of the District Courts are appointed and compensated, and possessing the same qualifications. . . .

Sec. 25. The Administrative Court shall have jurisdiction over all officers and employés of the State, and all officers and employés of the divisions and agencies thereof, save only the Governor, the Attorney-General, members of the Legislative Council, members of the District Councils, the Mayor of Baltimore, members of the City Council of Baltimore, judges, officers and employés of the courts, and officers of the militia.

Sec. 26. On the filing of information under oath by any group of not less than ten citizens, to the effect that any officer or employé within the jurisdiction of the Administrative Court is incapable of or unwilling to perform his duties, or has neglected them, or violated any of the laws of the State or any of the rights of the people under this Constitution, or administered the laws partially or unfairly, or engaged in partisan political activity, or accepted any favor, whether of monetary value or not and whether directly or indirectly, from any person having official business with him, the court shall summon him for a hearing within ten days, and if it appears at that hearing that a *prima facie* case against him has been established, it shall order him for trial within thirty days thereafter.

Sec. 27. The trial of any such officer or employé shall be either before the three judges of the Administrative Court without a jury or before one of them with a jury, as he may elect. On conviction he shall be removed from office forthwith. In addition in the discretion of the trial judge or judges, he may be fined or imprisoned according to law, and judgment may be entered against him for any damage he may have caused to any person or persons by his misconduct. No officer or employé thus removed shall ever be appointed to any other office of trust or profit under the Maryland Free State, or under any division or agency thereof. . . .

Sec. 31. The High Court, sitting *en banc*, shall have the power to determine the constitutionality of all laws of the State. Its decision shall be by a majority vote of all its members, and no dissenting opinion shall be entered upon the record or otherwise published. The decision shall specify all the particulars in which the law under consideration violates this Constitution, whether all parts of it shall be in question or not, and any decision may, in the discretion of the court, include recommendations to the Legislative Council for amendments.

Sec. 32. No person who has been a prosecuting officer in any court shall be eligible for any elective office under the State, or under any division or agency thereof, during the five years next following the termination of his service as prosecuting officer.

Article VII
The Grand Inquest

Section 1. There shall be a Grand Inquest of the State for the trial of impeachments, and for the investigation of other grave matters. It shall have all the powers of a court, and may summon any person to give evidence or produce documents before it, including judges. It shall have the power to punish summarily, by fine or imprisonment, any person who shall disobey its mandates, but it may not issue any mandate or inflict any punishment in violation of the inalienable rights of the people under this Constitution. . . .

Sec. 3. The Grand Inquest shall consist of the following persons:

(*a*) Two members of the Legislative Council, to be chosen by lot.

(*b*) Two judges of the High Court, to be chosen by lot.

(*c*) Three judges of the District Courts, to be chosen by lot.

(*d*) Two other persons notable for their intelligence, worldly experience and integrity, to be elected by a majority vote of the seven persons hitherto named. Neither of these two persons shall be a member or former member of the bar. . . .

Sec. 8. The Grand Inquest shall have jurisdiction in all proceedings for the impeachment of the Governor, members of the Legislative Council, members of the District Councils, the Mayor of

Baltimore, members of the City Council of Baltimore, and judges. Such proceedings may be instituted by a resolution of at least nine members of the Legislative Council, or by writ of the Governor, or by petition of not less than six judges, or by petition of not less than 5,000 registered voters. The parties complained of shall be informed of the charges against them, they shall have not less than one month to prepare their defense, they shall be confronted by their accusers, and they shall have the right to representation by counsel. . . .

Sec. 9. The Grand Inquest shall sustain no impeachment by the votes of less than seven of its members, including at least one of each category. In case an impeachment is not so sustained, it shall fail, and the party or parties accused shall go harmless. In case an impeachment is sustained, the Grand Inquest may order any punishment that it deems fitting, including removal from office and fine or imprisonment, and there shall be no appeal from its sentence. No person against whom an impeachment has been sustained shall ever occupy any office of trust or honor under the Maryland Free State, or any of its divisions or agencies, and no such person shall be permitted to vote at any election.

Sec. 10. The Grand Inquest may sustain an impeachment for any sort or degree of neglect, misconduct or incompetence in office, whether or not it involves moral turpitude. . . .

Article VIII
The Constitution

Sec. 2. The Legislative Council, by a vote of not less than ten members, and with the approval of the Governor, may propose amendments of this Constitution at any time. No such amendment shall become a part of this Constitution until it shall have been approved by a plebiscite of the registered voters of the State, on a day designated by the Legislative Council. Every such plebiscite shall be held by secret ballot, or by secret voting machine, and the full text of the amendment shall be posted in every polling place. No such plebiscite shall be held sooner than three months after the date of the proposal of an amendment by the Legislative

Council, nor more than six months thereafter. In order that a proposed amendment may become a part of this Constitution it must be approved either by a majority of all the registered voters of the State or by three-fourths of those actually voting; whichever may be the larger number.

Hooch for the Artist

From the New York *American*, Jan. 3, 1936

In Delaware, a few weeks ago, an author named Victor Thaddeus was thrown into jail. It seemed to me, when I heard of it, an excellent idea, and Mr. Thaddeus himself appears to have thought likewise, for when the magistrate gave him his choice between a moderate fine and a term behind the bars he chose the bars. My belief is that all authors should be benefited by a dose of the same elixir, and not only all authors, but also all other men who devote themselves to telling humanity what it is all about, and where to get off.

Every such man, soon or late, falls a victim to his professional technic. His very skill at publishing his notions degenerates inevitably into mere virtuosity, and so he becomes a sorry mountebank, juggling brilliantly a set of gaudy but increasingly hollow balls. It commonly takes his customers a long time to observe that they are hollow; sometimes, indeed, they never notice it at all. Worse, he is in the same situation himself, for artists are notoriously incompetent critics of their own performances. So he goes on with his show until some uncouth iconoclast raids it, or his years run out and he is translated to bliss eternal. What he needs, from time to time, is a renewal of first-hand observation, of illuminating personal experience, of the fundamental raw materials of his trade. He must return to the world for a rejuvenating sniff of humanity on the half shell, and another load of data. For, though the tower he works in may not be of ivory, it is still always a tower. The things that enter into a work of art are gathered in crowds, but the works themselves are concocted behind closed doors. The danger to the artist lies in the fact that he is very comfortable there, and prone to stay too long.

In order to avoid offending literary friends, I turn to music for an example. In 1865 Richard Wagner seemed about to settle down into the bovine lethargy of a court composer. King Ludwig of Bavaria had given him a pension and a house, he had mastered the trick of writing operas as no man had ever written them before, and it looked a safe bet that he would go on bringing out versions of "Lohengrin," each more diluted than the last, to the end of his days. But then came the dreadful shock of his meeting with Cosima Liszt-Bülow, and at once a new Wagner was born. In manner and aspect Cosima was far nearer a police sergeant than a sweetie, and life with her must have been comparable to going through an earthquake every day, or fleeing endlessly from a posse of lynchers, but the effect upon Wagner was superb. He dropped all his old tricks and took on a set of new and immensely better ones, and in a little while he had finished the "Ring," written "Die Meistersinger," and sketched out "Parsifal." In the ivory tower of King Ludwig he would have faded away into repetitious futility, but with Cosima chasing him around the stump he gathered in a host of novel, vivid and, indeed, nerve-shattering impressions, and when he got them into his music he was sure of immortality.

Wagner, of course, was a very tough fellow. Very few men could have survived Cosima as he did. Most of us, after a few months, would have dived headlong into Lake Starnberg. A brief term in jail is much safer. Jails are jammed with humanity on the half shell, and thus reek with supplies for the artist, but life in them is nevertheless reasonably safe and peaceful. I therefore applaud the wise choice of Mr. Thaddeus. He will write better stuff hereafter.

Notice to Neglected Geniuses

From the Baltimore *Evening Sun*, April 23, 1920. This offer apparently attracted a great deal of attention in the ante-chambers and subcellars of literary endeavor. It was reprinted by all the magazines devoted to the instruction and encouragement of bad authors, and enjoyed the honor of notice in many other periodicals. The result was a landslide of manuscripts. They came by express, by mail and by messenger. In all that mountain of writing I discovered but one printable effort, and the author of that one, far from being a neglected genius, was a man who had had a novel printed a year previous. This fact I somehow overlooked, but the publisher to whom I rushed with the manuscript had a better memory. He reminded me that I had praised the work extravagantly in the *Smart Set*

The gabble about neglected masterpieces is merely gabble; there is not the slightest shadow of truth in it. I believe that every piece of passable writing produced in America, if only it be intelligently offered in a reasonably probable market, is absolutely certain to be printed, and, what is more, to be paid for at a fair rate. In ten years I have not heard of a single exception. Time after time, when news has come to me of some great work lately achieved by a school teacher in Iowa or a newspaper reporter in Alabama, I have sent for it, read it with eyes a-pop—and found it to be a fabric of piffle, time-worn in plan and childish in execution. And every other editor in the United States goes through the same experience constantly. Every one of them spends half his time hunting for the extraordinary novelty, the pearl of great price—and the other half damning himself for wasting time upon a piece of balderdash.

The delusion of the contrary is hard to kill, but it is a delusion nonetheless. It seems impossible to convince the unsuccessful aspirant that his manuscript is actually read, and yet read it is, and by readers who live in the hope, from day to day, that the morrow will bring them an epoch-making discovery, then at least something printable. No other business of a magazine office is pursued with such relentless assiduity; every member of the staff takes a hack at it. To carry it on costs a great deal of money, and the return per annum is commonly next to nothing, but nevertheless there is always hope, and upon that hope is grounded a diligence that is truly amazing. And among publishers of books it is almost matched. No publisher is ever so disillusioned that he can bring himself to send back a strange manuscript without at least a peek into it, and no publisher is ever so close to bankruptcy that he can resist the temptation to take one more chance.

Two or three years ago, exposing notions of this general tendency in a popular magazine, I defied the whole college of literati of
the country to produce a single great work that was not already in
print. In case any such neglected masterpiece appeared I agreed to
make myself personally responsible for its instant publication on
fair terms—as a book if fat enough and in some reputable magazine if too thin. The response was a vast avalanche of manuscripts,
some of them written by hand, some of them tied with pink and
blue ribbons, many of them suffocatingly perfumed. By slow
stages, though it was in the midst of Summer, I got through them
all. There was not, in the whole lot, a single piece of work that
met the specifications of my offer. There was not, in fact, a single
piece of manuscript that was printable at all. One and all, the neglected manuscripts that reached me were dull, flatulent, imitative
and without merit.

Hope is hard to kill. I have had a lesson, but I have not learned
it. Perhaps that one trial was not enough. Well then, I make another. That is to say, I renew my offer, and make its terms the most
liberal conceivable to the human mind. Let any author in America
who thinks that he has produced a masterpiece and is convinced
that the publishers have entered into a conspiracy to prevent its
publication—let any and every such author, male or female, white
or black, native or alien, free or jailed, drunk or sober, virtuous or
sinful, college-bred or self-taught, send me his or her manuscript
before 6 P.M. of September 1, 1920 and, if it turns out on inspection
to be as stated, if it turns out to be an actual masterpiece or even
a fair piece of everyday writing, then I hereby promise and engage
to find a reputable publisher for it, to see that it is published
promptly, and to get a reasonable royalty for it without commissions, grafts or deductions of any kind whatsoever. And if I fail,
then I agree to eat it.

The strings to this offer are very few. First, I stipulate that the
manuscript shall not be accompanied by a letter of recommendation from the author's pastor, or from anyone else. Secondly, I stipulate that it reach me with the postage fully prepaid. Thirdly, I
stipulate that it be accompanied by a self-addressed and fully
stamped envelope for its return. Further than this I stipulate nothing. There are no entrance fees. I exact and shall look for no grat-

itude. I desire no presents of bad cigars, jewelry, gold pens, neckties, homemade preserves or bound sets of O. Henry and Bulwer-Lytton. My sole reward will come from the riotous appreciation of the publishers to whom I pass on the masterpieces unearthed—if any. They will deluge me with Havanas, first editions of George Moore, plug hats, diamonds, cases of contraband wine. They will invite me to banquets. It will be hard for me to prevent them kissing me.

XXI. UNFINISHED BUSINESS

Another Long-Awaited Book

From the Chicago *Tribune*, Sept. 12, 1926

SINCE Philip Dormer Stanhope, Earl of Chesterfield, published his celebrated letters to his morganatic son, in 1744, there has been no adequate book, in English, of advice to young men. I say adequate, and the adjective tells the whole story. There is not, of course, a college president or a boss Y.M.C.A. secretary, or an uplifting preacher in the United States who has not written such a book, but all of them are alike filled with bilge. They depict and advocate a life that no normal young man wants to live, or could live without ruin if he wanted to. They are full of Sunday-school platitudes and Boy Scout snuffling. If they were swallowed by the youth of today the Republic of tomorrow would be a nation of idiots.

I point to the obvious example of the volumes of so-called sex hygiene. If there is anything in them save pious balderdash then I have yet to encounter it—and in the pursuit of my dismal duties as a critic of letters and ideas I have read literally hundreds of them. All of them are devoted to promoting the absurd and immoral idea that the sexual instinct is somehow degrading and against God—that whenever a young man feels it welling within him it is time for him to send for a physician and perhaps even for a policeman. If he is moved to kiss his girl he is in grave peril. If he yields to the Devil and actually necks her he is already half-way to Hell.

What could be worse rubbish? The sole effect of it, assuming it to be believed, is to send the young reader into manhood full of preposterous fears and shames and to shut him off from one of the chief sources of human happiness. For life without sex might be safer, but it would be unbearably dull. There would be very little hazard in it and even less joy. It is the sex instinct that makes women seem beautiful, which they are only once in a blue moon, and men seem wise and brave, which they never are at all. Throttle it, denaturize it, take it away, and human existence would be reduced to the prosaic, laborious, boresome, imbecile level of life in an ant hill.

But it is not when they address young men as males, but when they address them as citizens that the current authors of such books achieve their worst nonsense. The absurd cult of service, invented by swindlers to conceal their knaveries, is hymned eloquently in all of them. The chief aim and purpose of civilized man in the world, it appears, is to do good. In other words, his chief duty is to harass and persecute his neighbors. If he shirks it, then he is a bad citizen, and will go to Hell along with the draft dodgers, tax evaders, atheists and bachelors.

It seems to me that this highly dubious doctrine is responsible for much of the uneasiness and unhappiness that are visible in the United States today, despite the growing wealth of the country. Accepting it gravely, the American people have converted themselves into a race of nuisances. It is no longer possible, making a new acquaintance, to put any reasonable trust in his common decency. If he is not a policeman in disguise he is very apt to be a propagandist without disguise, which is even worse. The country swarms with such bores, and the chief aim of the current instruction in the duties of the citizen seems to be to make more of them.

No argument, I take it, is needed to show that this is an evil tendency. The happiness of men in the world depends very largely upon their confidence in one another—in A's belief that B is well disposed toward him and will do nothing intentionally to make him uncomfortable. But the whole purpose of the uplift is to make other people uncomfortable. It searches relentlessly for men who are having a pleasant time according to their lights and tries to put them in jail, or, still worse, to stir up their conscience. In other words, it tries to make them unhappy. It is an engine for the dissemination of the disagreeable. Seeking ostensibly to increase the number of good citizens, it only increases the number of bad ones.

But the young, it is argued, must be schooled in public spirit, else they will all become highwaymen, just as they must be schooled in virtue, else they will all become debauchees. That argument, in various mellifluous forms, is constantly heard. It constitutes the fundamental postulate of such organizations as the Y.M.C.A. and the Boy Scouts. To question it becomes a sort of indecorum and is commonly represented as a questioning of public spirit and virtue themselves. Nevertheless, it remains nonsensical. There is not the slightest evidence that the normal young American, deprived of his books of civics, would take to the highroad, or that, deprived of his books of sex hygiene, he would set up practise as a roué.

The young come into the world, indeed, with a great deal of innate decency. It is their inheritance from the immemorial dead who fashioned and gave a direction to the delicate and complicated organism known as human society. That organism arose out of mutual good will, out of tolerance and charity, out of the civilizing tendency to live and let live. It emerged from the level of savagery by yielding to that tendency. The savage is preëminently his brother's keeper. He knows precisely what his brother ought to do in every situation and is full of indignation when it is not done. But the civilized man has doubts, and life under civilization is thus more comfortable than it is in a Tennessee village or an African *kraal*.

If the young are to be instructed at all, it seems to me that they ought to be instructed in the high human value of this toleration. They should be taught what they learn by experience in the school yard: that human beings differ enormously, one from the other, and that it is stupid and imprudent for A to try to change B. They should be taught that mutual confidence and good will are worth all the laws ever heard of, ghostly or secular, and that one man who minds his own business is more valuable to the world than 10,000 cocksure moralists. This teaching, I fear, is being neglected in the United States. We are hearing—and especially the young are hearing—far too much about brummagem utopias and far too little about the actual workings of the confusing but not unpleasant world we live in.

I know of no course in honor in any American Sunday-school, yet it must be plain that human relations, when they are profitable and agreeable, are based upon honor much oftener than they are based upon morals. It is immoral, in every rational meaning of the word, to violate the Volstead Act, and it is moral to give the *Polizei* aid against anyone who does so. But what is the practical answer of decent men to those facts? Their practical answer is that such giving of aid is dishonorable. The law does not punish it; it rewards it. But it is punished swiftly and relentlessly by civilized public opinion.

My contention, in brief, is that there is room for a book showing why this is so—for a book of advice to young men setting forth, not what some ancient hypocrite of a college president or Y.M.C.A. secretary thinks would be nice, but what is regarded as nice by the overwhelming majority of intelligent and reputable men. In other words, there is room for a book of inductive ethics, based upon the actual practises of civilized society. Such a book, in the department of sexual conduct, would differ enormously from the present banal manuals. It would denounce as ignoble many of the acts they advocate and it would give its approval to others that they ban. And in the wider field of the relations between man and man it would differ from them even more radically. It would have little to say about ideals, but a great deal about realities.

Most boys admire their fathers and take their notions from them in this department. The boy who has a father who is a genuinely civilized man needs no advice from outside experts. Common decency will be in him when he grows up. He will not be afraid of women and he will not try to make over men. But vast herds of American fathers, succumbing to the Service buncombe, have ceased to be safe guides for their sons. Their practise is misleading and their counsel is dangerous. Thus the way opens for a counselor less credulous and more sagacious. Thus a vast market shows itself for the sort of book I have been trying to describe.

Advice to Young Men

From PREJUDICES: THIRD SERIES, 1922, pp. 310–19. These notes were to have been part of a book of the same title, long planned and never done. I began to toy with the idea of it in 1914 or thereabout, and made notes for it, off and on, for the next thirty years, but it never got itself finished. From 1920 onward I also played with the notion of a book to be called Homo Sapiens—a wholly objective treatise on the human species, following the lines of Thomas Henry Huxley's treatise on the crayfish, but with plenty of attention, of course, to mental processes and institutions, including government and religion. I accumulated a great deal of material from the literature of biology and psychology, and in 1936 or thereabout my old friend Raymond Pearl, professor of biology at the Johns Hopkins, confided to me that he was contemplating a book on the same subject, so I gave up mine, for Pearl's competence for the job was plainly and enormously superior. He presently fell to work, and the first fruits of his labors appeared in five lectures of the Patten Foundation at Indiana University in October, 1938. Unhappily, his sudden death on November 17, 1940, left his book unfinished. But by that time I had abandoned mine and dispersed most of my notes, and I never resumed. Pearl's lectures were published by Indiana University under the title of Man the Animal in 1946. They represent but a small fragment of what he had in mind

1
The Venerable Examined

The older I grow the more I distrust the familiar doctrine that age brings wisdom. It is my honest belief that I am no wiser today than I was years ago; in fact, I often suspect that I am appreciably *less* wise. Every man goes uphill in sagacity to a certain point, and then begins sliding down again. Theoretically, the old fellows should be much wiser than younger men, if only because of their greater experience, but actually they seem to take on folly faster than they take on wisdom. Certainly it would be difficult to imagine any committee of relatively young men, of thirty-five, showing the unbroken childishness, ignorance, and lack of humor of the Supreme Court of the United States. The average age of the learned justices must be well beyond sixty, and all of them are supposed to be of finished and mellowed sagacity. Yet their grasp of the most ordinary principles of justice often turns out to be extremely feeble, and when they spread themselves grandly upon a great case their reasoning powers are usually found to be precisely equal to those of a respectable Pullman conductor.

2

Duty

First printed in the *Smart Set*, May, 1919, p. 51

Some of the loosest thinking in ethics has duty for its theme. Practically all writers on the subject agree that the individual owes certain unescapable duties to the race—for example, the duty of engaging in productive labor, and that of marrying and begetting offspring. In support of this position it is almost always argued that if *all* men neglected such duties the race would perish. The logic is hollow enough to be worthy of the college professors who are guilty of it. It simply confuses the conventionality, the pusillanimity, the lack of imagination of the majority of men with the duty of *all* men. There is not the slightest ground for assuming, even as a matter of mere argumentation, that *all* men will ever neglect these alleged duties. There will always remain a safe majority that is willing to do whatever is ordained—that accepts docilely the government it is born under, obeys its laws, and supports its theory. But that majority does not comprise the men who render the highest and most intelligent services to the race; it comprises those who render nothing save their obedience.

For the man who differs from this inert and well-regimented mass, however slightly, there are no duties *per se*. What he is spontaneously inclined to do is of vastly more value to all of us than what the majority is willing to do. There is, indeed, no such thing as duty-in-itself; it is a mere chimera of ethical theorists. Human progress is furthered, not by conformity, but by aberration. The very concept of duty is thus a function of inferiority; it belongs naturally only to timorous and incompetent men. Even on such levels it remains largely a self-delusion, a soothing apparition, a euphemism for necessity. When a man succumbs to duty he merely succumbs to the habit and inclination of other men.

3
Martyrs

First printed in the *Smart Set*, April, 1922, pp. 45–46

"History," says Henry Ford, "is bunk." I inscribe myself among those who dissent from this doctrine; nevertheless, I am often hauled up, in reading history, by a feeling that I am among unrealities. In particular, that feeling comes over me when I read about the religious wars of the past—wars in which thousands of men, women and children were butchered on account of puerile and unintelligible disputes over transubstantiation, the atonement, and other such metaphysical banshees. It does not surprise me that the majority murdered the minority; the majority, even today, does it whenever it is possible. What I can't understand is that the minority went voluntarily to the slaughter. Even in the worst persecutions known to history—say, for example, those of the Jews of Spain—it was always possible for a given member of the minority to save his hide by giving public assent to the religious notions of the majority. A Jew who was willing to be baptized, in the reign of Ferdinand and Isabella, was practically unmolested; his descendants today are 100% Spaniards. Well, then, why did so many Jews refuse? Why did so many prefer to be robbed, exiled, and sometimes murdered?

The answer given by philosophical historians is that they were a noble people, and preferred death to heresy. But this merely begs the question. Is it actually noble to cling to a religious idea so tenaciously? Certainly it doesn't seem so to me. After all, no human being really *knows* anything about the exalted matters with which all religions deal. The most he can do is to match his private guess against the guesses of his fellow-men. For any man to say absolutely, in such a field, that this or that is wholly and irrefragably true and this or that is utterly false is simply to talk nonsense. Personally, I have never encountered a religious idea—and I do not except even the idea of the existence of God—that was instantly and unchallengeably convincing, as, say, the Copernican astronomy is instantly and unchallengeably convincing. But neither have

I ever encountered a religious idea that could be dismissed off-hand as palpably and indubitably false. In even the worst nonsense of such theological mountebanks as Brigham Young and Mrs. Eddy there is always enough lingering plausibility, or, at all events, possibility, to give the judicious pause. Whatever the weight of the probabilities against it, it nevertheless *may* be true that man, on his decease, turns into a gaseous vertebrate, and that this vertebrate, if its human larva has engaged in embezzlement, bootlegging, profanity or adultery on this earth, will be boiled for a million years in a cauldron of pitch. My private inclination, due to my defective upbringing, is to doubt it, and to set down any one who believes it as an ass, but it must be plain that I have no means of disproving it.

In view of this uncertainty it seems to me sheer vanity for any man to hold his religious views too firmly, or to submit to any inconvenience on account of them. It is far better, if they happen to offend, to conceal them discreetly, or to change them amiably as the delusions of the majority change. My own views in this department, being wholly skeptical and tolerant, are obnoxious to the subscribers to practically all other views; even atheists sometimes denounce me. At the moment, by an accident of American political history, these dissenters from my theology are forbidden to punish me for not agreeing with them. But at any succeeding moment some group or other among them may seize such power and proceed against me in the immemorial manner. If it ever happens, I give notice here and now that I shall get converted to their nonsense instantly, and so retire to safety with my right thumb laid against my nose and my fingers waving like wheat in the wind. I'd do it even today, if there were any practical advantage in it. Offer me a box of good Havana cigars, and I engage to submit to baptism by any rite ever heard of, provided it does not expose my gothic nakedness. Make it ten boxes, and I'll agree to be both baptized and confirmed.

4
The Disabled Veteran

The science of psychological pathology is still in its infancy. In all its literature in nine languages, I can't find a line about the permanent ill effects of acute emotional diseases—say, for example, love affairs. The common assumption of the world is that when a love affair is over it is over—that nothing remains behind. This is probably grossly untrue. It is my belief that every such experience leaves scars upon the psyche, and that they are quite as plain as the scars left on the neck by a carbuncle. A man who has passed through a love affair, even though he may eventually forget the lady's very name, is never quite the same thereafter. The sentimentalist, exposed incessantly, ends as a psychic cripple; he is as badly off as the man who has come home from the wars with shell-shock.

5
Patriotism

Patriotism is conceivable to a civilized man in time of stress and storm, when his country is wobbling and sore beset. His country then appeals to him as any victim of misfortune appeals to him—say, a street-walker pursued by the police. But when it is safe, happy and prosperous it can only excite his loathing. The things that make countries safe and happy are all intrinsically corrupting and disgusting. It is as impossible for a civilized man to love his country in good times as it would be for him to respect a politician.

XXII. THE PUBLIC PRINTS

The End of the Line

From Essay in Pedagogy,
Prejudices: Fifth Series, 1926, pp. 218–36

Most American novelists, before they challenge Dostoievski, put
in an apprenticeship on the public prints, and thus have a chance
to study and grasp the peculiarities of the journalistic mind; nevertheless, the fact remains that there is not a single genuine newspaper man, done in the grand manner, in the whole range of
American fiction. There are some excellent brief sketches, but
there is no adequate portrait of the journalist as a whole, from his
beginnings as a romantic young reporter to his finish as a Leader
of Opinion, correct in every idea and as hollow as a jug. Here,
I believe, is genuine tragedy. Here is human character in dis-
integration—the primary theme of every sound novelist ever heard
of, from Fielding to Zola and from Turgeniev to Joseph Conrad.
I know of no American who starts from a higher level of aspiration
than the journalist. He is, in his first phase, genuinely romantic.
He plans to be both an artist and a moralist—a master of lovely
words and a merchant of sound ideas. He ends, commonly, as the
most depressing jackass in his community—that is, if his career
goes on to what is called success. He becomes the repository of all
its worst delusions and superstitions. He becomes the darling of
all its frauds and idiots, and the despair of all its honest men.

Here I speak by the book, for I was in active practise as a journalist for more than forty years, and have an immense acquaintance in the craft. I do not say that all journalists go that route. Far
from it. Many escape by failing; some even escape by succeeding.
But the majority who get into the upper brackets succumb. They

begin with high hopes. They end with safe jobs. In the career of any such man, it seems to me, there are materials for fiction of the highest order. He is interesting intrinsically, for his early ambition is at least not ignoble—he is not born an earthworm. And he is interesting as a figure in drama, for he falls gradually, resisting all the while, to forces that are beyond his strength. Here is tragedy—and here is America. For the curse of this country, as of all democracies, is precisely the fact that it treats its best men as enemies. The aim of our society, if it may be said to have an aim, is to iron them out. The ideal American, in every public sense, is a respectable vacuum.

The Professional Man

From JOURNALISM IN AMERICA,
PREJUDICES: SIXTH SERIES, 1927, pp. 13–14

The essence of a professional man is that he is answerable for his professional conduct only to his professional peers. A physician cannot be fired by any one, save when he has voluntarily converted himself into a job-holder; he is secure in his livelihood so long as he keeps his health, and can render service, or what they regard as service, to his patients. A lawyer is in the same boat. So is a dentist. So, even, is a horse-doctor. But a journalist still lingers in the twilight zone, along with the trained nurse, the rev. clergy and the great majority of engineers. He cannot sell his services directly to the consumer, but only to entrepreneurs and so those entrepreneurs have the power of veto over all his soaring fancies. Nor has he the same freedom that the lawyers and the physicians have when it comes to fixing his own compensation; what he faces is not a client but a boss.

Reflections on Journalism

From the Baltimore *Evening Sun*, Dec. 29, 1924

The rapid multiplication of penny tabloid papers, which now spring up all over the United States, is probably not an indication that the standards of journalism are falling, as certain sour brethren appear to believe, but rather an indication that they have been rising, of late, too fast. In other words, the newspapers have gone ahead too swiftly for their readers. The latter have, as yet, but small taste for what is offered them: extensive and accurate news reports, editorials more or less sober and thoughtful, some approach to refinement in typography. What they want is cheap, trashy and senseless stuff, in bad English and with plenty of pictures. This is provided by the tabloids, or, at all events, by most of them. Their primary assumption is that the average reader of the folk is literate only in the most modest sense—that his public school education, if it has taught him to read, has still failed to teach him to read with ease. He has to spell out all "hard" words—*i.e.*, all words of more than two syllables. His vocabulary is extremely limited. He finds any reading whatever, even if there are no "hard" words, very slow work. The tabloid paper fetches him by reducing his agony to a minimum. Its news is couched in vulgar English, and brought into a small space. Whenever possible, a picture is added. Sometimes the only text is a line under this picture. Reading it thus becomes almost as simple as watching the movies.

The low average of literacy that prevails in the big American cities is kept down, not only by the incompetence and futility of the public-schools, but also by the large number of foreigners. These foreigners sometimes, though not often, read their own languages fluently, but English is difficult for them, and they thus prefer it in small doses. All of us, going abroad, are in the same boat. Like most literary gents, I have picked up some sort of crude acquaintance with most of the modern civilized languages—enough, at least, to read street signs and make out the principal contents of the newspapers. But if I am in Holland, say, I do not turn to the long editorials in the *Amsterdamsche Courant* or *Haagsche Post*. I content myself with the headlines and pictures in the lesser journals.

The general improvement in American newspapers that has been witnessed since the beginning of the present century—that is, in the larger and more serious newspapers—has not been due to any lofty moral purpose, but simply to the improvement of their financial position. They are richer than they used to be, and hence able to be more intelligent and virtuous. They got richer by first becoming poorer. In the year 1899, when I began newspaper work, two-thirds of the more eminent journals of the United States were in difficulties, or, at all events, suffering diminishing profits. What had brought them to this pass was, first, the devastating impact of yellow journalism, and secondly, an excess of competition in their own class. In most American cities there were four or five morning papers and as many evening papers, all struggling desperately for circulation and advertising. Even the paper that got both found the getting enormously expensive, and so profits diminished. In the end some of the most famous journals of the country began to lose heavily, and came upon the market. Their old owners, having, as a rule, no other resources, simply could not carry them on.

The men who bought them, in the main, were not professional journalists, but rich men who believed that it would be pleasant to play at molding public opinion. It was found to be pleasant, true enough, but it quickly turned out to be also very expensive, and the new owners accordingly began to sweat. The issue of their sweating was a series of consolidations. Two weak papers were combined to make one stronger one, and then a third and sometimes a fourth weak one was sucked in. As competition was thus reduced, prosperity began to return. Finally came the war boom in advertising, and the goose was run to the top of the pole. The principal newspapers of the United States are sounder financially today than they have ever been before. They are fewer than they used to be, but I know of none that is hard up. Some of them make annual profits that run into the millions. Money has given them dignity, as it gives dignity to individuals. They are no longer terrorized by advertisers. They show an increasing independence in politics. They are far more outspoken and untrammeled than they used to be in discussing such things as business and religion. More, they have got over their old fear of the yellow journals, and have thus abandoned all attempts to be yellow themselves. Must of them look decent, and most of them, I believe, are decent, as decency goes in this world. They are not for sale. They cannot be intimidated. They try to report the news as they understand it, and to promote the truth as they see it.

It is a curious fact, but it is nevertheless a fact, that this change, which raised newspaper salaries by at least 200 per cent. and greatly augmented the dignity of the newspaper profession, was bitterly resisted by the majority of working newspaper men. That resistance, at the start, was not hard to understand. The entrance of new owners and new methods imperiled jobs, and especially it imperiled the jobs of those journalists who were most secure under the old order—the ancient, picturesque class of happy, incompetent Bohemians—the "born" newspaper men of tradition, with the intellectual and cultural equipment of City Councilmen or police lieutenants. The fact that it simultaneously benefited all men of a greater professional competence was forgotten, even by such men themselves. They all resisted the new discipline, and longed for their old irresponsible freedom.

But resistance, of course, was futile. Expensive properties, potentially worth millions a year, could not be intrusted to amiable ignoramuses. The growing salaries attracted better men, and they quickly made their way. Today the chief problem before newspaper executives is that of making these better men better still—of getting rid of the old tradition altogether and lifting journalism to genuine professional dignity. The attempts to set up schools of journalism all have that end. So far, these schools have accomplished little, but that, I believe, is chiefly because they have been manned by fifth-rate instructors—largely old-time journalists out of jobs. This, of course, is simply saying what might have been said of most medical colleges thirty years ago. The medical men have solved the problem of professional education, the lawyers are about to solve it, and soon or late the newspaper men will solve it too.

The more decorous and decent newspapers, in striving for more civilized manners, have dragged the yellows with them. They themselves have ceased to be yellow, and so there is no longer any need for the yellows to be super-yellow. More, the yellows have learned the value of outward respectability in dollars and cents. Advertisers long ago discovered that an inch of space in a newspaper read at home was worth a foot in one read only on the street cars. Thus the yellows, when the advertising boom began, found that their quieter rivals were getting all the pickings. So they began to be quieter themselves. Today most of them seem somber indeed, if one recalls their aspect twenty years ago.

This cleaning up has not altogether pleased their public. On its lower levels it longs with a great longing for the old circus-poster headlines, the old scares and hoaxes, the old sentimentalities and imbecilities. It wants thrills, not news; pictures, not text. To meet its yearning the penny tabloids have come into being. They are cheaply produced and require little capital; they invariably attain to large circulations. But I doubt that many of them are making money. The difficulty they face is the difficulty the old-time yellows faced: advertisers are doubtful, and with sound reason, about the value of their space. They are thus forced to depend largely upon their circulation revenues for existence, and in that direction, even with a half size paper, there is little hope of profit. I believe that they'd all be better off if they raised their prices to the level maintained by the other newspapers. The boobs, in all probability, would still buy them, and with careful management they might show an actual profit on circulation.

The New York Sun

From the *American Mercury*, Dec., 1924, pp. 505–07.
A review of MEMOIRS OF AN EDITOR,
by Edward P. Mitchell; New York, 1924

Permit me, gents, an exultation and a sentimentality. Reading, the other evening, Mr. Mitchell's charming volume, I came, on page 381, to a few words that sent a thrill through me from glabella to astragalus. The editor of the New York *Tribune* is thrilled no more when he gets a picture postcard from H.M. King George, nor King George when he beats the chaplain of Windsor at parcheesi. And what caused all this uproar in my recesses? Simply the bald mention of my name—a line and a half of pleasant politeness—by the editor of the old New York *Sun*. I doubt that I can make you understand it. For you were not, I take it, a hopeful young newspaper reporter in the year '99, and so your daily food and drink, your dream and your despair, was not the *Sun*. Dana was dead then, but Munsey had not yet come in to make a stable of the shrine. The reigning editor was Edward P. Mitchell— scarcely a name to the barbarians without the gates, but almost a god to every young journalist. I would not have swapped a word from him, in those days, for three cheers from the Twelve Apostles. He was to me the superlative journalist of this great, heroic land, as the *Sun* itself was the grandest, gaudiest newspaper that ever went to press. I have suffered much from heartache and heartburn in the years that have passed since then, and in consequence my store of wisdom has increased so vastly that my knees begin to buckle under it, but I still believe that my judgment of Mitchell and the *Sun* was sound, and I herewith ratify and reiterate it in the solemnest tones I can muster. The one is retired now, and puts in his mornings communing with Habakkuk, his prize turkey-gobbler, and in watching the deer come out of his woods; the other is a corpse hideously daubed to make it look like a respectable groceryman with fashionable aspirations. This Republic will be luckier than it deserves if it ever looks upon their like again.

The dull professors who write literary histories never mention the New York *Sun*. It is not even listed in the index to the Cambridge History of American Literature, though the Baltimore *American* and the New York *Staats-Zeitung* are both there. Nevertheless, I presume to believe that its influence upon the development of American literature, and particularly upon the liberation of the younger writers of its time from the so-called American tradition, was incomparably greater than that of any of the magnificos hymned in the books. What Charles Dana and his aiders taught these youngsters was double: to see and savor the life that swarmed under their noses, and to depict it vividly and with good humor. Nothing could have been at greater odds with the American tradi-

tion. The heroes of the Stone Age were all headed in other directions. The life of their place and time interested them very little,
especially the common, the ordinary life, and depicting things vividly was always far less their purpose than discussing them profoundly. Even Holmes and Walt Whitman, despite their superficial
revolts, ran true to type: they were philosophers long before they
were artists. The only exceptions were the humorists, and all the
humorists were below the salt: even Mark Twain had to wait until
1910, when death was upon him, before the first American of any
academic authority accepted him ungrudgingly. It was the great
service of Dana that he stood against all this mumbo-jumbo. From
its first issue under his hands the *Sun* showed a keen and unflagging interest in the everyday life of the American people—in the
lowly traffic of the streets and tenements, in the tricks and devices
of politicians and other zanies, in all the writings and cavortings of
the national spirit. And it depicted these things, not in a remote
and superior manner, but intimately and sympathetically, and with
good humor and sound understanding. To Dana such a man as
Big Tim Sullivan was not a mere monster, to be put in a barrel of
alcohol and labeled "Criminal"; he was, above all, a human
being—imperfect, perhaps, but still not without his perfections.
And so, at the other end, were the communal heroes and demi-
gods. Dana saw through all the Roosevelts, Wilsons and Coolidges
of his time; they never deceived him for an instant. But neither
did they outrage him and set him to spluttering; he had at them,
not with the crude clubs and cleavers of his fellows, but with the
rapier of wit and the bladder of humor. Long before "Main Street"
he had discovered the street itself, and peopled it with a rich stock
company of comedians. And long before "Babbitt" he had paved
the way for all the "Babbitts" that remain to be written.

Mr. Mitchell notes with some surprise that the *Sun*, at least in
its earlier days, was not read by the Best People—that it was
barred, for example, from the reading-room of the Century Club.
I see nothing surprising in that. The Century Club, at that time,
was a sarcophagus of petrified brains; its typical member was a
man of immense dignity and no intelligence. The *Sun*, to the end
of the Dana-Mitchell-Laffan dynasty, was never popular among
such dull pedants; not until Dr. Munsey added it to his chain of

journalistic grocery-stores did they begin to read it. To this moment, in fact, the paper it once was seems to be but little esteemed by the decayed editorial writers and unsuccessful reporters who teach in schools of journalism. Such stupid fellows, when they were in practise, did not admire the *Sun*; they admired the New York *Times*, the Cincinnati *Enquirer* and the Washington *Post*. But the *Sun* had plenty of other customers, and many of them were converted into disciples. It was at the hands of these men, I believe, that American literature was delivered from its old formalism and hollowness. They were the young reporters who made the movement of the '90s. They became the novelists, the dramatists and the critics of the new century. The *Sun* showed them their own country, and gave them eyes to see it clearly. It created among them a sophisticated and highly civilized point of view. It rid them of the national fear of ideas, the national dread of being natural.

How Dana accomplished all this remains a bit dim, even in Mr. Mitchell's chronicle. There was apparently no formal instruction in the *Sun* office, and certainly none of the harsh discipline which makes the modern city-room like a school-room or a bank. Dana did his own work casually and easily, and seems to have let his men run on in the same way. He was extremely tolerant of drunkards, as he was, in his reception-room, of cranks. He gathered recruits wherever he could, and without too much care. But the massive fact remains that, once he had gathered them, he converted them quickly into journalists of a new and superior kind, never matched since. The commonest treadmill work on his paper was done in a lively and excellent manner; its very sporting news, on most papers frankly idiotic, was distinguished. All his men wrote good English; all of them gathered something of his shrewd wisdom. Many of them, graduating from his staff, went in for literature in the grand manner, and did work of importance. But more important still were the men who were taught their trade by the *Sun* without ever having worked for it. Think of all those who were influenced by the criticism of James Huneker, a thorough *Sun* man to the end of his days, never happy on any other paper. When the record is written at last, if it is ever written honestly, he will stand among the genuine makers of American literature, though his own books be forgotten. What Huneker had to teach was precisely what the *Sun* in general had to teach: the stupidity of pedantry and all formal knowledge, the charm and virtue of fresh observation and hearty joy in life.

The Baltimore Sunpaper

From the Baltimore *Sun*, Jan. 26, 1941. This was the last article, save two, that I wrote for the *Sun* until 1948. Early in February the paper began supporting Roosevelt II's effort to horn into World War II in a frantic and highly unintelligent manner, and I withdrew from its editorial pages, after having cavorted there more or less regularly for thirty-five years. The *Sun* is always called the *Sunpaper* in Baltimore, and its evening edition, founded in 1910, is usually the *Evening Sunpaper*. The elder morning sheet was founded in 1837

When I hung up my hat in the *Sun* office, on July 30, 1906, the grandsons of Arunah S. Abell, the Founder, were in active control of the paper. They were Walter W. Abell, who died last Monday; Arunah S. Abell II, who died on July 26, 1914; and their cousin, Charles S. Abell, who is now living in Washington. I came to the paper to edit the Sunday edition, which was then but five years old and still more or less vague in contents and aim, and in that capacity I naturally had constant business with the three Abells. They were all young men in that remote era, the oldest, Arunah, being barely past forty. They differed enormously in character and mien, and especially the two brothers, Walter and Arunah. Arunah, the treasurer of the A. S. Abell Company, was one of the most jovial men I have ever known, and I can't recall ever seeing him in bad humor—not even when he caught an office boy stealing books from the *Sun* library. Charles S., the secretary, seemed almost austere by comparison, but he too was extremely amiable, and he got much closer to the members of the staff than the other two. But Walter, the president, was genuinely on the formal side, and there were not a few *Sun* men, including several of the older ones, who regarded him as unapproachable, and even forbidding.

He was, in fact, nothing of the sort, as I soon found by almost daily palavers with him. What gave him his false appearance of aloofness was simply a sort of boyish shyness—a charming weakness, if weakness it be called, that seemed to have been born in him, but got encouragement from the circumstances of his situation. He was in command over men who, in many cases, were much his elders in years and experience, and some of them had been trained under his grandfather. He was thus very diffident about pitting his judgment against theirs, but nevertheless he had to do it constantly, and so there was conflict between his native courtesy, which was marked, and his responsibility as captain of the ship. He solved the problem by concealing his authority beneath a grave reserve, and the impression got about that it was difficult to penetrate. There was another conflict, too, and that was between his filial devotion to the *Sun* tradition and his intelligent appreciation that when times change traditions must be modified. It was a day of revolution in journalism, largely due to the increasing efficiency of the linotype, and he had before him in Charles H. Grasty, of the Baltimore *Evening News*, a competitor who became more formidable every day. Mr. Abell never allowed that competition to hurry him, but he was acutely aware of it, and if he met it quietly he also met it boldly. Some of his reforms were so radical that, to the oldsters of the staff, they seemed almost catastrophic, but he put them through resolutely, and it is apparent today, looking back over a generation, that all of them were sound.

In this business he had the eager support of his cousin Charles, who was always for any novelty that was actually improvement, and the ready acquiescence of his brother, who preferred administration to grand strategy, and so kept rather to the sidelines. But there was active opposition in other quarters, and not infrequently it impeded the flow of events. Some of the old-timers, bred in hand-set days, were constitutionally unable to go along, and they had the zealous reënforcement of a large body of old subscribers, many of whom held as a cardinal article of faith that the *Sun* of 1887 could never be surpassed on this or any earth, and that any attempt to change it was a sin against the Holy Ghost. I well remember the uproar when the first large illustrations began to appear in the Sunday edition. It was not illustrations *qua* illustrations that outraged the guardians of tradition, for a few had been printed even in the Founder's time; it was their size. One column—yes; and maybe even two. But four, five, six—God help us all! When, on a fateful Sunday, Mr. Abell gave me *pratique* for one running the full width of the page, and dropping down to half its depth, there was a moan that reverberated throughout the *Sun* Building, and next morning the president's office was jammed with complainants and objurgators.

But it was not only in the editorial rooms that the old *Sunpaper* suffered a face-lifting at the hands of that quiet and determined man; in the business office (then called the counting room) there were operations of even more serious nature and import. What Baltimore thought when the paper put its first advertising solicitor on the street should have been taken down in shorthand and embalmed in history, for it was surely aplenty. And when this revolution was followed by the publication of circulation figures (at first, to be sure, only confidentially, and to a select few) the whole town was aghast. It was almost as if the Johns Hopkins University had sent out sandwich-men whooping up courses in meat-cutting and chiropractic. But Abell, if he was deliberate, was also sure-footed, and I can recall none of his innovations that turned out, on trial, to be a mistake. Nor were any mistakes made during the administration of his cousin and successor, Charles S. The whole *Sun* organization was renovated from top to bottom, and not only renovated but also reoriented. When these youngsters took the paper in hand at the death of Edwin F. Abell in 1904, just after the great Baltimore fire, it still looked back toward the days of the Founder. When they handed it over to a new management in 1910 it was headed for the future, and well prepared for the notable advances, both in editorial enterprise and in business prosperity, which followed the World War.

Life in the *Sun* office in the era of the Abells was comfortable and leisurely, and I once described the atmosphere as that of a good club. There was a stately courtesy that is uncommon in the dens of journalism, and indeed in any other working place of busy men. All hands save the office boys were mistered by the proprietors, and no one was ever upbraided for a dereliction of duty, however inconvenient. The worst a culprit ever encountered was a mild expostulation, usually couched in very general terms. I recall with blushes a day when my own carelessness admitted to the *Sunday Sun* an unhappy sentence which made the issue a collector's item in the barrooms of Baltimore the next day, with the price approaching $1. When I got to the office Monday morning a note was on my desk saying that Walter Abell wanted to see me. There was no defense imaginable, so I entered his office as jauntily as possible, saying, "I am not here for trial, but for sentence." But there was no sentence, nor even any trial. Mr. Abell, in fact, referred to the matter in hand only obliquely, and with great politeness. All his talk was about the paramount necessity, on a paper as ancient and honorable as the *Sun*, for the utmost care in copyreading. He discoursed on that theme at length, but always in broad philosophical terms. Finding his argument unanswerable, I offered no caveat, and withdrew quietly at the first chance.

The Pulitzer Prizes

From the Baltimore *Evening Sun*, May 20, 1926. Sinclair Lewis refused the award of the Pulitzer Prize for his Arrowsmith at my instigation. I believed and had often advised him that he should resolutely refuse all prizes, college degrees and other such empty honors, heaving them to the muckers who pulled wires for them. But the ambitious and go-getting Dorothy Thompson, his second wife, was avid for honors and attention, no matter how cheap, and when in 1930 they took the lordly form of the Nobel Prize, she naturally grabbed for it with loud hosannahs. If I had heard of this award in time I'd certainly have made some effort to induce Lewis to decline it, for I had long been convinced that the Stockholm Academy, which chose the recipients of the prizes for literature, was a diligent player of politics. Besides, Lewis knew very well that, if any American deserved to be chosen, it was Dreiser

Sinclair Lewis's refusal to accept the $1,000 Pulitzer Prize, awarded to him for his novel, "Arrowsmith," was a gallant and excellent gesture, and deserves all the cheers that it is getting. It is shocking to find Ralph Pulitzer, editor of the New York *World* and a member of the committee, hinting that the refusal was ground upon a desire for "self-exploitation." This is preposterous, and Mr.

Pulitzer should know it. Mr. Lewis stands in no need of "exploitation" of that sort. His position among American novelists is high and secure—so high and secure that it cannot be damaged, even, by an ill-advised and ridiculous effort to put him among the Pollyannas.

The Pulitzer committee, during the eight years of its existence, has shown a complete incapacity to distinguish between work that is sound and honest in the novel and work that is cheap and false. In 1918 it gave its first award to "His Family," by Ernest Poole, a fourth-rate story, already long forgotten. That same year Miss Willa Cather published "My Antonia," perhaps the finest novel ever written by an American woman. In 1922 it gave the award to Miss Cather's "One of Ours," her worst book—a thing of blowsy sentimentalities all compact, and disconcerting, to say the least, to her admirers. The same year Lewis published "Babbitt." So in other years. In 1919, the year of Cabell's "Jurgen" and Hergesheimer's "Java Head," it gave the award to a novel by Booth Tarkington. In 1920, the year of "Main Street," it withheld the award altogether, on the ground that no work of sufficient importance to receive it had been published! Such imbecilities, repeated annually, cannot be accidental. Either the committee is bound by rules that prevent it making intelligent awards, or its members are incompetent. In either case a novelist of Lewis's rank is certainly justified in spurning its highly dubious accolade, and in protesting against the damage that its approval does to his reputation.

The difficulties confronting such a committee are, of course, obvious. It is confronted by an immense mass of candidates, many of them vigorously supported by their publishers and other interested persons, and it faces the physical impossibility of reading all the books nominated. Thus its decision is bound to be more or less casual and arbitrary. When it seeks counsel, it apparently turns to men of conventional mind, not likely to be sound judges of works of genuine originality. The prize-winner is finally chosen, I daresay, as candidates for the Presidency are chosen—by gradually eliminating all those whose deviation from normalcy has made them enemies. So "Arrowsmith," a work avoiding controversy, was selected, after "Main Street" and "Babbitt," both of them far more important, had been rejected.

The chief stumbling-block is the word "best" in the terms of the award. If it could be eliminated, the committee would have a freer hand and be less often absurd. Some of the novels that it has honored have been works of serious merit—not masterpieces, surely, but at least respectable. There was plenty of good writing, for example, in Miss Cather's "One of Ours," especially in the first half. It would be impossible, indeed, for her to do a book wholly bad. But when "One of Ours" was solemnly determined to be better than "Babbitt," there could be but one answer from persons of anything properly describable as decent taste. That answer was a shout of derision.

Confronted by the word "best," the committee is bound, at the least, to remember that it has an intelligible meaning. No award could conceivably meet the notions of all competent judges, but it should certainly be possible to avoid awards that provoke their unanimous protest. That protest was justly made when Miss Cather's "My Antonia" was passed over in favor of Mr. Poole's "His Family," and it was justly made again when "Babbitt," perhaps the best novel ever written in America, was passed over in favor of Miss Cather's "One of Ours."

In its award of the other prizes within its gift the committee sometimes shows a better discretion. The fact that this year's gold medal for "the most disinterested and meritorious public service rendered by an American newspaper" goes to Julian and Julia Harris, of the Columbus (Ga.) *Enquirer-Sun*, will be applauded by all American journalists who respect their profession. More than once, in the past, I have called attention to the work of Mr. and Mrs. Harris in this place, and it has been frequently praised by the *Sunpaper*, the New York *World*, the *Nation* and other eminent journals. When they returned to their native Georgia from Europe, half a dozen years ago, the State was wallowing in the intellectual depths of Tennessee and Mississippi. Its principal newspapers were quaking before the Ku Klux Klan; Fundamentalism was spreading like a pestilence; its politics had reached the very nadir of degradation. With little money, but with stout hearts and the finest sort of journalistic skill, Mr. Harris and his extraordinary wife began a battle for the restoration of decency. It seemed, at the start, quite hopeless. All the politicians of the State were against them; the Klan was violently against them; they were opposed with ferocity by the whole pack of evangelical clergy. Nevertheless, they kept on bravely, and in the course of time they began to show progress. Here and there a little country paper joined them; individual supporters popped up in all parts of the State. Now Georgia has turned the corner. Some hard sledding is still ahead, but, led by the *Enquirer-Sun*, it is headed in the right direction.

The principal dailies of the State gave the Harrises little if any support. Most of them are still covertly on the other side. Thus the whole credit for whatever has been accomplished belongs to the *Enquirer-Sun*. The award honors the Pulitzer Foundation far more than it honors the Harrises. That the fact is not lost upon the committee is shown by its election of Mr. Harris to membership. In so far as his voice determines future awards, it will determine them in a way satisfactory to every friend of honest and courageous journalism.

In other fields the committee occasionally shows sound discretion. Few will quarrel, for example, with its award of the $1,000 prize for "the best American biography teaching patriotic and unselfish service" to Dr. Harvey Cushing's "William Osler," albeit the work is less a formal biography than a collection of materials for one. And few, I daresay, will quarrel with its award of $500 to Edward M. Kingsbury, of the New York *Times*, for the best editorial of the year. I have not seen this editorial, but I have been familiar with Mr. Kingsbury's work for twenty-six years, first for the New York *Sun* and more recently for the *Times*, and if he has ever written anything downright bad I have yet to hear of it. Within the limits of his peculiar interests and his highly individual manner, Mr. Kingsbury is undoubtedly the best editorial writer now living.

Unfortunately, the record shows that such sound and just awards are not common. In 1924, as all newspaper men will recall, the committee astounded the whole journalistic fraternity by awarding the prize for the best editorial to a mawkish and absurd composition called "Who Made Coolidge?", printed in the Boston *Herald*. The motives behind this award remain mysterious, and of the piece itself the least said the better. I only wonder what the late Joseph Pulitzer, summoned back from the tomb, would have said of it. He was a man of sound journalistic judgment, and his language, when he was annoyed, was certainly not that of a Sunday-school superintendent.

There have been other awards of equal absurdity, mingled with a few of manifest soundness. On the whole, it is doubtful that the prizes have accomplished any good. In the field of the novel they have unquestionably exalted puerile mush at the cost of honest work, and in the field of journalism they have seldom accentuated the qualities of originality and genuine courage. Newspapers have been rewarded, in the main, for "crusades" of the conventional cut, requiring only plenty of money to make them effective. The Harrises are the first editors to be honored for a public service involving grave risks of failure and disaster, and made in the face of a hostile public sentiment. Now that Mr. Harris himself has been appointed to the advisory board, there is reason for hoping that such awards will be more common hereafter—that is, that the money of the Foundation will be withheld from editorial writers who lack professional dignity and newspapers which simply do again what has been done before, and given to editorial writers who have something to say and know how to say it, and to papers which actually contribute something to the advancement of decent journalism.

The Muck-Rakers

From THE AMERICAN MAGAZINE,
PREJUDICES: FIRST SERIES, 1919, pp. 177–79.
Reprinted in part from the *Smart Set*, Dec., 1916, pp. 138–40

The muck-raking magazines of the Roosevelt I era came to grief, not because the public tired of muck-raking, but because the muck-raking that they began with succeeded. That is to say, the villains so long belabored by the Steffenses, the Tarbells and the Lawsons were either driven from the national scene or forced (at least temporarily) into rectitude. Worse, their places in public life were largely taken by nominees whose chemical purity was guaranteed by these same magazines, and so the latter found their occupation gone and their following with it. The great masses of the plain people, eager to swallow denunciation in horse-doctor doses, gagged at the first spoonful of praise. They chortled and read on when Aldrich, Boss Cox, John D. Rockefeller and the other bugaboos of the time were belabored every month, but they promptly sickened and went elsewhere when Judge Ben B. Lindsey, Francis J. Heney, Governor Folk, Jane Addams, and the rest of the saints of the day began to be hymned.

The same phenomenon is constantly witnessed upon the lower level of daily journalism. Let a vociferous "reform" newspaper overthrow the old gang and elect its own candidate, and at once it is in a perilous condition. Its stock in trade is gone. It can no longer give a good show—within the popular meaning of a good show. For what the public wants eternally—at least the American public—is rough stuff. It delights in vituperation. It wallows in scandal. It is always on the side of the man or journal making the charges, no matter how slight the probability that the accused is guilty. Roosevelt I, one of the greatest rabble-rousers the world has ever seen, was privy to this fact, and made it the corner-stone of his singularly cynical and effective politics. He was forever calling names, making accusations, unearthing and denouncing demons. Woodrow Wilson, also a demagogue of talent, sought to pursue the same plan, with varying fidelity and success. He was a popular hero so long as he confined himself to reviling men and things— the Hell Hounds of Plutocracy, the Socialists, the Kaiser, the Irish, the Senate minority. But the moment he found himself counsel for the defense, he began to wobble, just as Roosevelt before him had begun to wobble when he found himself burdened with the intricate and unintelligible programme of the Progressives. Roosevelt shook himself free by deserting the Progressives, but Wilson found it impossible to get rid of his League of Nations, and so came to present a quite typical picture of a muck-raker hamstrung by blows from the wrong end of the rake.

Acres of Babble

From the Baltimore *Evening Sun*, Aug. 11, 1923.
A review of THE EDITORIALS OF HENRY WATTERSON,
compiled with an Introduction and notes
by Arthur Krock; New York, 1923

This is an extremely depressing book. For forty years or more Watterson was the most distinguished editorial writer on the American press, quoted endlessly and known everywhere, and yet in this large volume of his best editorials, very intelligently and fairly selected by his chief-of-staff, Mr. Krock, there is scarcely a line that is worth reading today. What ailed Watterson, of course, was that he was preëminently the professional editorial writer, engaged endlessly upon a laborious and furious discussion of transient futilities. During all the while that he wrote upon politics—and no man ever wrote more copiously or to greater immediate applause—he was apparently wholly unconscious of the underlying political currents of the country. The things he discussed were simply the puerile combats of parties and candidates; politics, to him, was scarcely to be distinguished from a mere combat for jobs. On all other subjects he was equally hollow and superficial—for example, on Prohibition, which he attacked violently without understanding it, and without the slightest apparent realization of its certainty of triumph. His editorials on foreign politics are empty mouthings of an unintelligent chauvinism. His occasional ventures into economics are pathetic.

Why editorial writing in the United States should be in such low estate is hard to understand. It enlists a great deal of excellent writing ability—Watterson himself, indeed, was an extremely charming writer—and whatever it was in the past, it is now relatively free. Nevertheless, the massed editorial writers of the United States seldom produce a new idea, and are almost unheard of when the problems of the country are soberly discussed. Of all the writers who have published important and influential books upon public affairs during the past decade, not one, so far as I can recall, was a newspaper editorial writer, and not one owed anything to editorial writers for either his facts or his arguments. One might naturally suppose that men devoted professionally to the daily discussion of public questions would frequently achieve novel and persuasive ideas about them, and be tempted to set forth those ideas in connected and effective form, but the fact remains that nothing of the sort ever happens. What is printed in the newspapers of the United States, acres and acres of it every day, is dead the day after it is printed. Nine-tenths of it is mere babble and buncombe, and the rest seems to lack, somehow, the elements that make for conviction and permanence. The newspapers do not lead in the formation of public opinion; they either follow the mob or feebly imitate a small group of leaders. In Watterson's book I can't recall reading a single sensible thing that had not been said, before he said it, by some one else.

Perhaps the anonymity of editorial writing is largely to blame for its flaccidity. The lay view is that anonymity makes for a sort of brutal vigor—that the unsigned editorial is likely to be more frank and scathing than the signed article. But the truth is quite the opposite. The man who has to take personal responsibility for what he writes is far more apt than the anonymous man to be frank. He cannot hedge and evade the facts as he sees them without exposing himself to attack and ridicule. He must be wary and alert at all times, and that very circumstance gradually strengthens him in his opinions, and causes him to maintain them tenaciously and with vigor. Under the cover of anonymity it is fatally easy to be facile and lazy—to take refuge behind the prevailing platitudes. The anonymous writer gets no personal credit for it when he is intelligent, fair and eloquent; there is thus a constant temptation upon him to lighten his labors by employing formulae. Even Watterson, who was known by name to all of his readers, often succumbed to this temptation, for his actual editorials were unsigned, and when he was idiotic his admirers charitably blamed it upon his subordinates. Writing steadily over his own name, I am convinced that he would have done far better work. As it is, Mr. Krock's collection can be regarded only as an appalling proof of the general vacuity of American journalism.

XXIII. PROFESSORS

The Public-School

From the *Smart Set*, March, 1921, pp. 140–41

EDUCATION in the highest (and rarest) sense—education directed toward awaking a capacity to differentiate between fact and appearance—is and always will be a more or less furtive and illicit thing, for its chief purpose is the controversion and destruction of the very ideas that the majority of men—and particularly the majority of official and powerful men—regard as incontrovertibly true. To the extent that I am genuinely educated, I am suspicious of all the things that the average citizen believes and the average pedagogue teaches. Progress consists precisely in attacking and disposing of these ordinary beliefs. It is thus opposed to education as the thing is now managed, and so there should be no surprise in the fact that the generality of pedagogues in the public-schools, like the generality of policemen and saloon-keepers, are bitter enemies to all new ideas.

Think of what the average American schoolboy is taught today, say of history or economics. Examine the specific orders to teachers issued from time to time by the School Board of New York City—a body fairly representative of the forces that must always control education at the cost of the state. Surely no sane man would argue that the assimilation of such a mess of evasions and mendacities will make the boy of today a well-informed and quick-minded citizen tomorrow, alert to error and wary of propaganda. This plain fact is that education is itself a form of propaganda—a deliberate scheme to outfit the pupil, not with the capacity to weigh ideas, but with a simple appetite for gulping ideas ready-made. The aim is to make "good" citizens, which is to say, docile and uninquisitive citizens. Let a teacher let fall the slightest hint to his pupils that there is a body of doctrine opposed to the doctrine he is officially ordered to teach, and at once he is robbed of his livelihood and exposed to slander and persecution. The tendency grows wider as the field of education is widened. The pedagogue of Emerson's day was more or less a free agent, at all events in everything save theology; today his successor is a rubber-stamp, with all the talent for trembling of his constituent gutta-percha. In the lower schools the thing goes even further. Here the teachers are not only compelled to stick to their text-books, but also to pledge their professional honor to a vast and shifting mass of transient doctrines. Any teacher who sought to give his pupils a rational view of the late Woodrow Wilson at the time Woodrow was stalking the land in the purloined chemise of Moses would have been dismissed from his pulpit, and probably jailed. The effects of such education are already distressingly visible in the Republic. Americans in the days when their education stopped with the three R's, were a self-reliant, cynical, liberty-loving and extremely rambunctious people. Today, with pedagogy standardized and school-houses everywhere, they are the herd of sheep (*Ovis aries*).

The War upon Intelligence

From the Baltimore *Evening Sun*, Dec. 31, 1928

The American public-schools inculcate far more nonsense than sense, and the great majority of American colleges are so incompetent and vicious that, in any really civilized country, they would be closed by the police. In all American States save a few anyone who has the yearning may start a college and, with the full consent and authority of the State, grant degrees. There is no official machinery for testing the competence of the professors and none for scrutinizing what they teach. Thousands of such burlesque colleges are scattered over the country, and in some States they are the only kind that exist. Their graduates, armed with formidable diplomas, go out into the world in the character of educated men and

women. What they really know is less than the average bright policeman knows.

The public-schools are even worse. In the typical American
State they are staffed by quacks and hag-ridden by fanatics. Everywhere they tend to become, not centers of enlightenment, but
simply reservoirs of idiocy. Not one professional pedagogue out of
twenty is a man of any genuine intelligence. The profession
mainly attracts, not young men of quick minds and force of character, but flabby, feeble fellows who yearn for easy jobs. The childish mumbo-jumbo that passes for technique among them scarcely
goes beyond the capacities of a moron. To take a Ph.D. in education, at most American seminaries, is an enterprise that requires no
more real acumen or information than taking a degree in window-
dressing.

Most pedagogues male, and the overwhelming majority of the
female ones, are not even Ph.D.'s. They are simply dull persons
who have found it easy to get along by dancing to whatever tune
happens to be lined out. At this dancing they have trained themselves to swallow any imaginable fad or folly, and always with enthusiasm. The schools reek with this puerile nonsense. Their
programmes of study sound like the fantastic inventions of comedians gone insane. The teaching of the elements is abandoned for
a dreadful mass of useless fol-de-rols, by quack psychology out of
the uplift. No one ever hears of a pedagogue protesting against this
bilge. The profession is almost completely lacking in professional
conscience. If physicians, by some fiat of Demos, were ordered to
dose all of their patients with Swamp Root, most of them would
object and a great many of them would refuse. Even lawyers, I
daresay, have a limit of endurance: there are things that they
would decline to do, even at the cost of their incomes. But the
pedagogues, as a class, seem to have no such qualms. They are
perfectly willing, on the one hand, to teach the nonsense prescribed for them by frauds, and they are immensely fertile, on the
other hand, in inventing nonsense of their own. Anything that will
make their jobs secure seems good enough to inflict upon their
pupils.

If you think I exaggerate, then all I ask is that you read a couple
of issues of any high-toned educational journal, say, the *Journal of*

the National Education Association. Or examine a dozen or two
of the dissertations, chosen at random, turned out by candidates
for the doctorate at any eminent penitentiary for pedagogues, say
Teachers College, Columbia. What you will find is a state of mind
that will shock you. It is so feeble that it is scarcely a state of
mind at all. The pedagogues harangue one another in the precise
terms of visiting Odd Fellows, and when they discuss a technical subject they commonly do it so witlessly that one is almost
tempted to suspect them of irony. It is an appalling experience to
read such stuff. But, save in a few fortunate places, the men and
women who perpetuate it run the public-schools of America, and
have upon them the burden of making the youth of the land fit for
citizenship. How badly they achieve that business is made manifest
every time there is a fair test. After more than a century of free education at least two out of three Americans, here as elsewhere, remain completely ignorant of the veriest fundamentals of human
knowledge, and are aroused to fury against them on hearing them
stated.

Katzenjammer

From the Baltimore *Evening Sun,* Aug. 24, 1931

There was a time when teaching school was a relatively simple
and easy job, and any young woman who had no talent for house-
work was deemed fit for it. But that time is no more. The pedagogue of today, whether male or female, must not only undergo a
long and arduous course of preliminary training; he (or she) must
also keep on studying after getting an appointment. The science of
pedagogy has become enormously complicated, and it changes
constantly. Its principles of today are never its principles of tomorrow: they are incessantly modified, improved, revised, adorned.
They borrow from psychology, metaphysics, sociology, pathology,
physical culture, chemistry, meteorology, political economy, psychiatry and sex hygiene. And through them, day and night, blows
the hot wind of moral endeavor. Thus the poor gogue (or goguess)
has to sweat incessantly. In Summer, when the rest of us are loll-

ing in the cool speakeasies, he suffers a living death in Summer school, trying to puzzle out the latest arcana from Columbia University. Has he a normal school diploma in his pocket? Then it is waste paper in two years. Is he *artium baccalaureus?* Then an M.A. is set to prodding and shaming him. Is he himself an M.A.? Then two Ph.D.s are on his tail. It is a dreadful life.

The Golden Age of Pedagogy

From the Baltimore *Evening Sun,* June 6, 1927

The stray student of genuine intelligence must find life in the great rolling-mills of learning very unpleasant, and I suppose that he seldom stays until the end of his course. He must see very quickly that the learning on tap in them is mainly formal and bogus—that it consists almost wholly of feeble nonsense out of text-books, put together by men who are unable either to write or to think. And he must discover anon that its embellishment by the faculty is almost as bad—that very few college instructors, as he encounters them in practise, actually know anything worth knowing about the subject they presume to teach. Has the college its stars—great whales of learning, eminent in the land? Well, it is not often that an undergraduate so much as sees those whales, and seldom indeed that he has any communion with them. The teaching is done almost exclusively by understrappers, and the distinguishing marks of those understrappers is that they are primarily pedagogues, not scholars. The fact that one of them teaches English instead of mathematics and another mathematics instead of English is trivial and largely accidental. Of a thousand head of such dull drudges not ten, with their doctors' dissertations behind them, ever contribute so much as a flyspeck to the sum of human knowledge.

Here, of course, I speak of the common run of colleges and the common run of pedagogues. The list of such colleges, in the World Almanac, runs to six pages of very fine print. They are scattered all over the land, but they are especially thick in the Cow States, where the peasants have long cherished a superstitious veneration for education, and credit it with powers almost equal to those of a United Brethren bishop or Lydia Pinkham's Vegetable Compound. The theory is that a plow hand, taught the binomial theorem and forced to read Washington Irving, a crib to Caesar's "De Bello Gallico," and some obscure Ph.D.'s summary of "The Wealth of Nations," with idiotic review questions, becomes the peer of Aristotle, Abraham Lincoln, and B. J. Palmer, the Mr. Eddy of chiropractic. It is, I fear, a false theory; he becomes simply a bad plow hand—perhaps with overtones, if Mendel is kind to him, of a good Rotarian. In the more pretentious vats of learning, I suppose there is an atmosphere more favorable to human husbandry, but even there it is probably far less favorable than popular legend makes it out. I can't imagine a genuinely intelligent boy getting much out of college, even out of a good college, save it be a cynical habit of mind. For even the good ones are manned chiefly by third-rate men, and any boy of sharp wits is sure to penetrate to their inferiority almost instantly. Men can fool other men, but they can seldom fool boys. The campus view of professors is notoriously highly critical, and even cruel. Well, the view is formulated by the whole body of students—the normal, half-simian majority as well as the intelligent minority. What must the really bright boys think!

Such bright boys, I believe, get little out of college, aside from the salubrious cynicism that I have mentioned. If they learn anything there, it is not by the aid of their instructors, but in spite of them. They read. They weigh ideas. They come into contact, perhaps, with two or three genuinely learned men. They react sharply against the general imbecility of their fellows. Such is the process of education.

The half-wits get even less, but what they get is obviously more valuable to them. Though they emerge with their heads quite empty of anything rationally describable as knowledge, they have at least gained something in prestige: the hinds back at home, still chained to the plow, admire and envy them. So they go into politics and begin the weary trudge to Congress, or they enter upon one of the learned professions and help to raise it to the level of the realtor's art and mystery, or they become mortgage sharks, or perhaps they proceed to the lofty rank and dignity of *Artium*

Magister or *Doctor Philosophiae*, and consecrate themselves to ironing out the rabble following after them. In addition to the prestige, they carry home certain cultural (as opposed to intellectual) gains. They have learned the rules of basket-ball, football, high-jumping, pole-vaulting and maybe lawn tennis. They have become privy to the facts that a dress coat is not worn in the morning or with plus-fours, that an Episcopalian has something on a Baptist and even on a Presbyterian, that smoking cigarettes is not immediately followed by general paralysis, and that a girl may both believe in the literal accuracy of Genesis, and neck. They have become, in a sense, house-broken, and learned how to trip over a rug gracefully, without upsetting the piano. They have read "Mlle. de Maupin," "Night Life in Chicago," and the complete files of *Hot Dog*. They have tasted gin. Above all, they have acquired heroes: the aurochs who broke the Ohio Wesleyan line, the swellest dresser on the campus, the master politician, the cheer leader, the senior who eloped with the ingénue of the No. 8 "Two Orphans" company, the junior caught in the raid on the roadhouse, the sophomore who made $3,000 letting out "Ulysses" at $1 a crack, the baseball captain, the champion shot-putter, the winner of the intercollegiate golf tourney. In other words, they have become normal, healthy-minded Americanos, potential Prominent Citizens, the larvae of sound Coolidge men; they have learned how to meanly admire mean things.

If I had a son and he seemed middling dull, I'd send him to Harvard, for Harvard is obviously the best of all American universities. It not only inculcates the sublime principles of Americanism as well as any other; it also inoculates all its customers with a superior air, and that superior air, in a democratic country, is a possession of the utmost value, socially and economically. The great masses of men never question it: they accept it at once, as they accept a loud voice. These masses of men are uneasy in their theoretical equality: their quest is ever for superiors to defer to and venerate. Such superiors are provided for them by Harvard. Its graduates have a haughty manner. Moreover, they are entitled to it, for Harvard is plainly the first among American universities, and not only historically. I believe that a bright boy, sent to its halls, is damaged less than he would be damaged anywhere else, and that a dull boy enjoys immensely greater benefits. Its very professors show a swagger; there is about them nothing of the hang-dog look that characterizes their colleagues nearly everywhere else. The tradition of the place is independent and contumacious. It was the first American university to throw out the theologians. It encourages odd fish. It cares nothing for public opinion. But all the while it insists upon plausible table manners, and has no truck with orators.

A Harvard man feels at ease in Zion, and with sound reason. A Yale man, however he may snort and roar, can never get rid of the scarlet fact that, while he was being fattened for the investment securities business, he was herded into chapel every morning. It rides him through life like a Freudian suppression; he recalls it in the forlorn blackness of the night as a Y.M.C.A. secretary recalls a wicked glass of beer, or the smooth, demoralizing, horrible whiteness of a charwoman's neck. A Princeton man remembers the Fundamentalists at commencement—flies in amber, spectres at memory's feast. In all the other great universities there are co-eds. In the lesser colleges there are rules against smoking, beadles, courses in Americanization, praying bands. The Harvard man, looking back, sees only a pink glow. His college has not turned out a wowser in 150 years. His accent and necktie are correct. His classmates continue to be worth knowing. No wonder he regards the Republic as his oyster.

A Liberal Education

From the *Smart Set*, May, 1921, pp. 140–42

On the first page of "American Writers of the Present Day, 1890 to 1920," by the learned Dr. T. E. Rankin, professor of rhetoric in the University of Michigan, I find the following sentence: "Precisely the same situation *pertains* now."

Somehow this use of the word interests me. Obviously, a professor of rhetoric in a great university should be an authority on such matters—but just how can a situation *pertain*? I go to the Standard Dictionary for light, and find that the synonyms of *pertain* are *appertain, concern, belong, regard, relate.* I substitute them and obtain:

> Precisely the same situation *appertains* now.
> Precisely the same situation *concerns* now.
> Precisely the same situation *belongs* now.
> Precisely the same situation *regards* now.
> Precisely the same situation *relates* now.

I turn to page 52 of the same great work, and find the following:

On the basis of such a distinction as that of length or brevity, one might as well speak of the two or three act play as a dramalette or dramolet, which no one appears *anxious* to do.

Anxious? Does the professor mean *eager?* Again, on page 56, what does he mean by the word *pseudo-hallucination?* Pseudo is from the Greek word, *pseudes,* meaning false. Well, how can an hallucination be true? Is it not, by its very nature, a falsity? If so, then we have here a double falsity, a false falsehood. I procced to page 60. I find: "*One* is 'playing safe' when *he. . . .*" On page 109 it occurs again: "If *one* will turn to page 239, . . . *he* will find . . ." And on page 126: "*One* cannot refrain from quoting when *he* thinks. . . ." And so on.

Obviously, the science of rhetoric is developing rapidly at the University of Michigan. Here is a professor who has already thrown overboard the dictionaries and is fast preparing himself to do the same with the grammar-books. Ring Lardner himself is scarcely more disdainful of Harvey and Webster. But that is as far as his rebellious spirit goes. When it comes to moral and aesthetic matters, as opposed to purely lexicographical and grammatical matters, he shows all of the conservatism that befits an awakener of the souls and intellects of youth. His book, indeed, is an almost perfect model of professorial critical theory. It praises Coningsby Dawson's "Carry On" as the work of "a master of literary style," it puts Cale Young Rice "high among those who belong to the really tuneful throng," it hails F. Marion Crawford as "beyond a doubt a man of genius"—and it groups James Huneker with Christopher

Morley and Robert Cortes Holliday, dismisses Dreiser on the ground that he is "uncreative," calls Hamlin Garland's "A Son of the Middle Border" a novel, and elaborately avoids any mention whatsoever of James Branch Cabell and Willa Cather. I find myself, indeed, so fascinated by this work that I am unable to put it down; I have already read it three times. Almost every page introduces me to literati of whose existence I have been hitherto unaware: Mrs. Sherwood Bonner MacDowell, Mrs. Louise Clarke Prynelle, Miss Martha Young, Mrs. Annie C. Allinson, Miss Sara Jeannette Duncan, Eric Mackay Yoeman, Hugh J. Maclean, Dr. J. B. Dollard, Prof. J. D. Logan, Arthur S. Bourinot, and so on. And everywhere I find judgments that offer me light and leading. Of all the "young men of America who are now writing novels, Ernest Poole perhaps gives the greatest promise." Edward Lucas White, it appears, is a man of such talent that "we should have more abiding books" if more of our writers imitated him. Huneker was a laborious fellow, but his style was "jerky, unpleasantly so," and his "diction often not so much erudite as so far-fetched as to be strained to misapplication." William Allen White's "A Certain Rich Man" is a "great novel": "few books are more persuasive—partly because the author devoted three years to the writing of it." Charles D. Stewart's "Partners of Providence" is "such a book as the world has waited for ever since Mark Twain's stories of river life came to the end of their writing." Edwin Markham and Cale Young Rice are first-rate poets, but Carl Sandburg and Amy Lowell are frauds. Richard Hovey spoiled his verse by imitation of "the vagrom spirit of Walt Whitman." But best of all are the professor's reticences. Mark Twain, it appears, wrote "Tom Sawyer Abroad" after 1890, but not "The Mysterious Stranger" or "What Is Man?" As for such writers as Montague Glass, Charles G. Norris, Henry B. Fuller, Joseph Medill Patterson, George Ade, Abraham Cahan, E. W. Howe, Vincent O'Sullivan, Frank Norris, Sinclair Lewis and Zona Gale, they simply do not exist. Sherwood Anderson is condemned to Coventry along with Cabell and Miss Cather. Ezra Pound, John McClure and Eunice Tietjens are unheard of among the poets. The salient American critics of life are Paul Elmer More and Agnes Repplier. There is no mention whatever of any critic of music or painting or the drama (save only the "unpleasant" Huneker), or of any of the young Liberals, or of any such fellow as Upton Sinclair, Norman Hapgood, Brooks Adams, Ralph Adams Cram, or Brand Whitlock. Among the dramatists there is praise for Charles Rann Kennedy, Charles Kenyon, Marguerite Merington and Percy Mackaye, but not a word either for or against Zoë Akins and Eugene O'Neill.

A curious work, indeed. A perfect specimen of the depths of banality to which the teaching of "English" and "literature" has descended in some of our public seminaries. I do not offer it as the worst that I know of, but as something fairly typical; I have on my desk a book from the University of Nebraska that is ten times as nonsensical. Nor do I expose it to the gaze of the nobility and gentry simply to poke fun at a poor professor—one who, according to "Who's Who in America," has pursued the humanities for twenty-four years, and holds two learned degrees, and is a favorite lecturer, and contributes to such gazettes as *Poet-Lore* and the *Homiletic Review*, and has taught rhetoric at the University of Michigan since 1905, and is, moreover, an unyielding patriot and a sound Christian. What interests me is the effect upon the poor yokels who strive heroically for a "liberal" education at such universities as Michigan, and are then belabored and stupefied with such balderdash. Can you imagine the thirst for enlightenment that must be in some of those candidates for the arts degree, and the vast sacrifices that must stand behind their candidacy—remote farmers sweating like slaves for year after year that their sons and daughters may be "educated," farmwives wearing out their lives in miserable drudgery and loneliness, pennies saved one by one, thousands of little deprivations, hopes cherished through whole generations? And then the result—a bath of bosh. If a professor writes a textbook, I assume that it is for his students: who else would want to read it? Well, imagine a young man or woman outfitted with such a notion of the literature of the country as one finds in the tome of Prof. Rankin. Think of raising chickens and milking cows for twenty years to pay for such an education. I am surely not one to laugh at the spectacle. To me it seems to be tragic.

The Lower Depths

From the *American Mercury*, March, 1925, pp. 380–81.
A review of THE SOCIAL OBJECTIVES OF SCHOOL ENGLISH,
by Charles S. Pendleton; Nashville, 1924

Here, in the form of a large flat book, eight and a half inches wide and eleven inches tall, is a sight-seeing bus touring the slums of pedagogy. The author, Dr. Pendleton, professes the teaching of English (not English, remember, but the teaching of English) at the George Peabody College for Teachers, an eminent seminary at Nashville, in the Baptist Holy Land, and his object in the investigation he describes was to find out what the teachers who teach English hope to accomplish by teaching it. In other words, what, precisely, is the improvement that they propose to achieve in the pupils exposed to their art and mystery? Do they believe that the aim of teaching English is to increase the exact and beautiful use of the language? Or that it is to inculcate and augment patriotism? Or that it is to diminish sorrow in the home? Or that it has some other end, cultural, economic or military?

In order to find out, Pendleton, with true pedagogical diligence, proceeded to list all the reasons for teaching English that he could find. Some he got by cross-examining teachers. Others came from educators of a higher degree and puissance. Yet others he dug out of the text-books of pedagogy in common use, and the dreadful professional journals read by teachers. Finally, he threw in some from miscellaneous sources, including his own inner consciousness. In all, he accumulated 1,581 such reasons, or, as he calls them, objectives, and then he sat down and laboriously copied them upon 1,581 very thin 3×5 cards, one to a card. Some of these cards were buff in color, some were blue, some were yellow, some were pink, and some were green. On the blue cards he copied all the objectives relating to the employment of English in conversation, on the yellow cards all those dealing with its use in literary composition, on the green cards all those having to do with speech-making, and so on. Then he shook up the cards, summoned eighty professional teachers of English, and asked them to sort out the objectives in the order of appositeness and merit. The results of this laborious sorting he now sets before the learned.

Here is the objective that got the most votes—the champion of the whole 1,581:

The ability to spell correctly without hesitation all the ordinary words of one's writing vocabulary.

Here is the runner-up:

The ability to speak, in conversation, in complete sentences, not in broken phrases.

And here is No. 7:

The ability to capitalize speedily and accurately in one's writing.

And here is No. 9:

The ability to think quickly in an emergency.

And here are some more, all within the first hundred:

The ability to refrain from marking or marring in any way a borrowed book.

An attitude of democracy rather than snobbishness within a conversation.

Familiarity with the essential stories and persons of the Bible.

And some from the second hundred:

The ability to sing through—words and music—the national anthem.

The ability courteously and effectively to receive orders from a superior.

The avoidance of vulgarity and profanity in one's public speaking.

The ability to read silently without lip movements.

The habit of placing the page one is reading so that there will not be shadows upon it.

The ability to refrain from conversation under conditions where it is annoying or disagreeable to others.

The ability to converse intelligently about municipal and district civic matters.

The ability to comprehend accurately the meaning of all common abbreviations and signs one meets with in reading.

The ability, during one's reading, to distinguish between an author's central theme and his incidental remarks.

I refrain from any more: all these got enough votes to put them among the first 200 objectives—200 out of 1,581. Nor do I choose them unfairly; most of those that I have not listed were quite as bad as those I have. But, you may protest, the good professor handed his cards to a jury of little girls of eight or nine years, or to the inmates of a home for the feeble-minded. He did, in fact, nothing of the kind. His jury was very carefully selected. It consisted of eighty teachers of such professional heft and consequence that they were assembled at the University of Chicago for postgraduate study. Every one of them had been through either a college or a normal school; forty-seven of them held learned degrees; all of them had been engaged professionally in teaching English, some for years. They came from Michigan, Nebraska, Iowa, Missouri, Wisconsin, Toronto, Leland Stanford, Chicago and Northwestern Universities; from Oberlin, De Pauw, Goucher, Beloit and Drake Colleges; from a dozen lesser seminaries of the higher learning. They represented, not the lowest level of teachers of English in the Republic, but the highest level. And yet it was their verdict by a solemn referendum that the principal objective in teaching English was to make good spellers, and that after that came the breeding of good capitalizers.

I present Pendleton's laborious work as overwhelming proof of a thesis that I have maintained for years, perhaps sometimes with undue heat: that pedagogy in the United States is fast descending to the estate of a childish necromancy, and that the worst idiots, even among pedagogues, are the teachers of English. It is positively dreadful to think that the young of the American species are exposed day in and day out to the contamination of such dark minds. What can be expected of education that is carried on in the very sewers of the intellect? How can morons teach anything that is worth knowing? Here and there, true enough, a competent teacher of English is encountered. I could name at least twenty in the whole country. But it does not appear that Dr. Pendleton, among his eighty, found even one. There is not the slightest glimmer of intelligence in all the appalling tables of statistics and black, zig-zag graphs that he has so painfully amassed. Nor any apparent capacity for learning. The sound thing, the sane thing and the humane thing to do with his pathetic herd of A.B.'s would be to take them out in the alley and knock them in the head.

Pedagogues A-flutter

From the *American Mercury*, May, 1930, pp. 125–27.
A review of HUMANISM & AMERICA:
ESSAYS ON THE OUTLOOK
OF MODERN CIVILIZATION,
edited by Norman Foerster; New York, 1930

This collection of essays is a manifesto for a movement called, by its proponents, Humanism, which, so Dr. Foerster says in his preface, "is rapidly becoming a word to conjure with."[1] It is not, it appears, a new movement, but goes back, like Freemasonry, to a remote and hoary antiquity, and has been supported, at one time or another, "by persons as various as Homer, Phidias, Plato, Aristotle, Confucius, Buddha, Jesus, Paul, Virgil, Horace, Dante, Shakespeare, Milton, Goethe; more recently, by Matthew Arnold in England and Emerson and Lowell in America." But at the moment, lacking any such whales, it is in the hands of a group of American pedagogues, of whom the imperial wizard is Prof. Irving

---

[1] Unhappily, it blew up a few years afterward.

Babbitt of Harvard, the grand goblin Prof. Paul Elmer More of Princeton, and the supreme sinister kligraph Prof. Foerster himself. The present pronunciamento embraces fifteen essays, three of them by the learned men I have just named and the rest by various lesser initiates, including eight more professors, an advanced poet, two college boys, and the author of "Waldo Frank: A Study."

In so large a collection there is necessarily some difference of opinion, both as to what is wrong with the world and what ought to be done about it. Prof. More seems to be most disturbed by Dr. A. F. Whitehead's somewhat ribald speculations about the nature of God and by the transcendental prose printed in the magazine called *transition*. His brother, Prof. Louis Trenchard More, denounces Whitehead too, but is also against Einstein and Planck, not to mention John B. Watson. Prof. G. R. Elliott of Amherst rages against "softening God's laws" and pleads for "a rediscovery of their severity": he believes that "the two most potent and distinguished personalities . . . that have so far appeared in the English literature of the Twentieth Century" are the late Baron Friedrich von Hügel and Prof. Babbitt. Prof. Thompson prints an earnest essay on the nature of tragedy: it would get him an A in any course in Freshman English. Prof. Robert Shafer of the University of Cincinnati compares Dreiser to Aeschylus and proves that Aeschylus was the better when it came to asserting "his faith that Moral Law uncompromisingly governs the life of man." Prof. Harry H. Clark of Wisconsin shows that the only recent American novel worth a hoot is Dorothy Canfield's "The Brimming Cup," and argues that the only way to get better ones is for "our interpreters of literature in college and university" to put their heads together, and show the boys "the unerring congruency to human nature demanded of great art." And so on down to Mr. Gorham B. Munson, author of the monograph on Waldo Frank, who first shows that criticism is in a sad state in America, and then "takes the risk"—his own words—"of nominating Matthew Arnold as having the build of a great critic." Alas, Mr. Munson is modest.

All this, I fear, will strike the reader of these lines as mainly rubbish, and that, in truth, is what it is. The only contributors to the volume who go to the trouble of stating plainly what Humanism is are Dr. Foerster and Prof. Babbitt. Dr. Babbitt, who has been in the movement for years, says that it represents an effort to set up a criterion of values which "the phenomenal world does not supply"—in other words, to add intuition to experience. The trouble with such a fellow, say, as Dreiser, is that he simply describes the world as he sees it, and lets it go at that. Ask him what meaning there is in the story of Jennie Gerhardt and he tells you that he doesn't know. Dr. Babbitt believes that, at least for many men, this is insufficient. They want some assurance, some certainty, some answer to the riddle. As for Dr. Babbitt himself, he believes that it is to be found in "religious insight." "For my own part," he says, "I range myself unhesitatingly on the side of the supernatural." And he believes that it would be a good thing to round up all persons who think the same way, that they may "move toward a communion" and become "an element of social order and stability." Dr. Foerster inclines the same way. He believes that man lives "on three planes, the natural, the human and the religious," and that Humanism "should be confined to a working philosophy seeking to make a resolute distinction between man and nature and between man and the divine."

In all this, of course, there is nothing new, though I fear Dr. Foerster is going beyond the facts when he says that Homer, Shakespeare and Goethe believe it. The same thing precisely has been preached in all the Little Bethels of the world since the invention of original sin, and is even today the theme of nine evangelical sermons out of ten—that is, when they deal with religion at all. More, it is at the bottom of all the secular schemes for getting rid of uncomfortable realities by conjuring up something grander and gaudier—for example, Rotarianism. George F. Babbitt, in fact, was quite as sound a Humanist as Dr. Foerster: he too yearned and panted for a sweet and simple arcanum and could see something divine in a bank cashier, or even a lawyer. Nor is it hard to understand why the Humanist theology should appeal powerfully to young college instructors, and to the colicky sophomores who admire them. It is the natural and inevitable refuge of all timorous and third-rate men—of all weaklings for whom the struggle with hard facts is unendurable—of all the nay-sayers of Nietzsche's immortal scorn. The hot sun is too much for them; they want an asylum that is reassuringly dark and damp, with incense burning and the organ playing soft and delicate hymns.

The demand for that asylum is couched in mellifluous terms, but it remains nonsense. The progress of the human race is not forwarded by any such vague and witless blather. It is forwarded by extending the range of man's positive knowledge, by grappling resolutely with facts, by facing life, not like a school-ma'am, but like a man. With that business the finishers of bond salesmen have no more to do today than their melancholy predecessors had to do in the past. It is the enterprise of far better men—most of them, though they may not always know it, creative artists. It is an enterprise demanding the highest capacities of mankind, and so it is naturally not comprehensible to campus Pollyannas.

Prima Facie

From the Baltimore *Evening Sun*, July 25, 1931

Ever and anon another so-called radical professor is heaved out of a State university, always to the tune of bitter protests in the liberal weeklies. The usual defense of the trustees is that the doctrines he teaches are dangerous to the young. This puts him on all fours with Socrates—surely a somewhat large order. The real objection to his ideas, nine times out of ten, is that only idiots believe such things. But that objection has to be kept quiet, for it is saying nothing apposite against a professor in the average State university to prove that he is an idiot.

The Philosopher

From PREJUDICES: FOURTH SERIES, 1924, p. 198

Between a speech by a Salvation Army convert, a Southern Congressman, or a Grand Goblin of the Rotary Club and a treatise by an American professor of philosophy there is no more to choose than between the puling of an infant and the puling of an ancient veteran of the wars. Both show the human cerebrum loaded far beyond its Plimsoll mark; both, strictly speaking, are idiotic.

The Saving Grace

From DAMN! A BOOK OF CALUMNY, 1918, p. 13

Let us not burn the universities—yet. After all, the damage they do might be worse. . . . Suppose Oxford had snared and disemboweled Shakespeare. Suppose Harvard had set its rubber-stamp upon Mark Twain.

XXIV. MUSIC

The Tone Art

From DAMN! A BOOK OF CALUMNY, 1918, pp. 75–79

THE NOTION that the aim of art is to fix the shifting aspects of nature, that all art is primarily representative—this notion is as unsound as the theory that Friday is an unlucky day, and is dying as hard. The true function of art is to criticise, embellish and edit nature—particularly to edit it, and so make it coherent and lovely. The artist is a sort of impassioned proof-reader, blue-pencilling the *lapsus calami* of God. The sounds in a Beethoven symphony, even the Pastoral, are infinitely more orderly, varied and beautiful than those of the woods. The worst flute is never as bad as the worst soprano. The best violoncello is immeasurably better than the best tenor.

All first-rate music suffers by the fact that it has to be performed by human beings—that is, that nature must be permitted to corrupt it. The performance one hears in a concert hall or opera house is no more than a baroque parody upon the thing the composer imagined. In an orchestra of eighty men there is inevitably at least one man with a sore thumb, or bad kidneys, or a brutal wife, or *katzenjammer*—and one is enough. Some day the natural clumsiness and imperfection of fingers, lips and larynxes will be overcome by mechanical devices, and we shall have Beethoven and Mozart and Schubert in such wonderful and perfect beauty that it will be almost unbearable. If half as much ingenuity had been lavished upon music machines as has been lavished upon the telephone and the steam engine, we would have had mechanical orchestras long ago.

When the human performer of music thus goes the way of the galley-slave, the charm of personality, of course, will be pumped out of the performance of music. But the charm of personality does not help music; it hinders it. It is not a reënforcement; it is a rival. When a beautiful singer comes upon the stage, two shows, as it were, go on at once; first the music show, and then the arms, shoulders, neck, nose, ankles, eyes, hips, calves and ruby lips—in brief, the sex-show. The second of these shows, to the majority of persons present, is more interesting than the first—to the men because of the sex interest, and to the women because of the professional or technical interest—and so music is forced into the background. What it becomes, indeed, is no more than a half-heard accompaniment to an imagined anecdote.

The purified and dephlogisticated music of the future, to be sure, will never appeal to the mob, which will keep on demanding its chance to gloat over gaudy, voluptuous women, and fat, scandalous tenors. The mob, even disregarding its insatiable appetite for the improper, is a natural hero worshiper. It loves, not the beautiful, but the strange, the unprecedented, the astounding; it suffers from an incurable *héliogabalisme*. A soprano who can gargle her way up to G sharp in altissimo interests it almost as much as a contralto who has slept publicly with a grand duke. If it cannot get the tenor who receives $3,000 a night, it will take the tenor who fought the manager with bung-starters last Tuesday. But this is merely saying that the tastes and desires of the mob have nothing to do with music as an art. For its ears, as for its eyes, it demands anecdotes—on the one hand the Suicide symphony, "The Forge in the Forest," and the general run of Italian opera, and on the other hand such things as "The Angelus," "Playing Grandpa" and the so-called "Mona Lisa." It cannot imagine art as devoid of moral content, as beauty pure and simple. It always demands something to edify it, or, failing that, to shock it.

These concepts, of the edifying and the shocking, are closer together in the psyche than most persons imagine. The one, in fact, depends upon the other: without some definite notion of the improving it is almost impossible to conjure up an active notion of the improper. All salacious art is addressed, not to the damned, but to the consciously saved; it is Sunday-school superintendents, not bartenders, who chiefly patronize peep-shows, and know the dirty books, and have a high artistic admiration for sopranos of superior gluteal development. But all art, to the yahoo, must have a certain bawdiness in it, or he cannot abide it. His favorite soprano in the opera house, is not the fat and middle-aged lady who can actually sing, but the girl with the bare back and translucent drawers. Condescending to the concert hall, he is bored by the posse of aliens in funereal black, and so demands a vocal soloist—that is, a gaudy creature of such advanced corsetting that she can make him forget Bach for a while, and turn his thoughts pleasantly to amorous intrigue.

In all this, of course, there is nothing new. Other and better men have noted the damage that the personal equation does to music, and some of them have even sought ways out. For example, Richard Strauss. His so-called ballet, "Josefslegende," is an attempt to write an opera without singers. All of the music is in the orchestra; the folks on the stage merely go through a pointless pantomime; their main function is to entertain the eye with shifting colors. Thus, the romantic sentiments of Joseph are announced, not by some eye-rolling tenor, but by the first, second, third, fourth, fifth, sixth, seventh and eighth violins (it is a Strauss score!), with the incidental aid of the wood-wind, the brass, the percussion and the rest of the strings. And the heroine's reply is made, not by a soprano with a cold, but by an honest man playing a flute. The next step will be the substitution of marionettes for actors. The removal of the orchestra to a sort of trench, out of sight of the audience, is already an accomplished fact. The end, perhaps, will be music purged of its current ptomaines. In brief, music.

The Joyless Master

From the same, pp. 73–74

Romain Rolland's "Beethoven" is based upon a thesis that is of almost inconceivable inaccuracy, to wit, the thesis that old Ludwig was an apostle of joy, and that his music reveals his determination to experience and utter it in spite of all the slings and arrows of outrageous fortune. Nothing could be more absurd. Joy, in truth, was precisely the emotion that Beethoven could never conjure up; it simply was not in him. Turn to the *scherzi* of any of his trios, quartettes, sonatas or symphonies. A sardonic waggishness is there, and sometimes even a wistful sort of merriment, but joy in the real sense—a kicking up of legs, a light-heartedness, a complete freedom from care—is not to be found. It is in Haydn, it is in Schubert and it is often in Mozart, but it is no more in Beethoven than it is in Tschaikowsky. Even the hymn to joy at the end of the Ninth Symphony narrowly escapes being a parody on the thing itself; a conscious effort is in every note of it; it is almost as lacking in spontaneity as (if it were imaginable at all) a limerick by Augustus Montague Toplady.

Nay; Ludwig was no leaping buck. Nor was it his deafness, nor poverty, nor the crimes of his rascally nephew that pumped joy out of him. The truth is that he lacked it from birth; he was born a Puritan—and though a Puritan, by a miracle, may also become a great man (as witness Herbert Spencer and Beelzebub), he can never throw off being one. Beethoven stemmed from the Low Countries, and the Low Countries, in those days, were full of blue-nosed refugees from England; the very name, in its first incarnation, may have been Barebones. If you want to comprehend the authentic man don't linger over Rolland's fancies but go to his own philosophizing, as garnered in "Beethoven, the Man and the Artist," by Friedrich Kerst. There you will find a collection of moral banalities that would have delighted Jonathan Edwards—a collection that might well be emblazoned on gilt cards and hung in Sunday-schools. He begins with a naïve anthropomorphism that is now almost perished from the world; he ends with solemn repudiation of adultery. . . . But a great man, my masters, a great man! We have enough biographies of him, and talmuds upon his works. Who will do a full-length psychological study of him?

De Profundis

From the Baltimore *Evening Sun*, Nov. 19, 1928

A hundred years ago today, in Vienna, Franz Schubert died. He was one of the greatest geniuses the world has ever seen, but he was a poor man, and so his funeral was very modest. At first his father, who was a schoolmaster, planned to bury him under the floor of a parish church, but some one suggested that a more suitable place would be somewhere near Beethoven, who had died the year before. So a grave was found in the Währing cemetery, and there he was planted, and still rests. His funeral cost 70 florins. When, a week or so later, his estate was listed for the public records, it was found to be worth 60 florins. Thus he died bankrupt.

But it is not to be assumed from this that Schubert, in life, had been unknown, or neglected. Far from it. His immense talent was recognized when he was a boy of 15, and by the time he was 25 he was already something of a celebrity. The Viennese certainly had ears: they could hear his music, and hearing it was enough to convince anyone that it was good. But Schubert himself was the sort of man who, in all societies and at all times, finds it hard to get along. He was so modest that it was simply impossible for him to push himself; he even shrank from meeting Beethoven, who needed only a glance at his songs to see his genius. Worse, he wrote so much that he constantly broke his own market. There were always stacks of Schubert manuscripts in waiting, and so the publishers paid very little for what they took. This fecundity ran to almost incredible lengths. In fifteen years Schubert wrote more than 1,200 compositions, some of them full-length symphonies. His songs run to at least 600, and he wrote the astonishing number of 146 in a single year, 1815. In the August of that year he wrote 29, and on one day he wrote 8. It seems unbelievable, but it is a fact. Some of these songs were better than others, but not one of them was downright bad. The best are among the imperishable glories of the human race. They are wholly and overwhelmingly lovely. No one has ever written lovelier.

Schubert was poor, but he had what must have been, at least in its externals, a pleasant life. A bachelor at large in the most charming of cities, with a father and brothers who appreciated him and plenty of amiable friends, he had a daily round that was quite devoid of hardship. All morning he would work at his desk, as steadily and busily as a bookkeeper. When he finished one composition he would start another, sometimes on the same page. Most men, completing so formidable a thing as a string quartette, are exhausted, and have to resort to drink, travel, politics or religion for recuperation. But not Schubert. He simply began an opera or a

mass. At 1 o'clock or thereabout he would knock off for the day
and go to dinner at a restaurant, usually the one called "Zum
roten Kreuz"—the Red Cross. It was a cheap place, but the food
was good and the beer was better. Like most bachelors, Schubert
never dined alone. There were always agreeable companions,
mainly young musicians like himself. They would remain at table
for hours, and then Schubert would take a walk. In the evening he
and his brothers and their friends made music. They started with
a little family orchestra, but it grew so large that the family home
could not contain it, and it moved to the larger house of an acquaintance. It played almost every night. Schubert usually played
the viola, but sometimes he was the pianist.

This was his routine from October to June. In summer he wandered about the Danubian countryside, usually with a friend or
two. They were always welcome, and had many more invitations
than they could accept. They would go to this or that country
house, stay a week, and enchant the family and other guests with
their music. Schubert would often write something for the occasion. It was thus that he produced his superb setting to Shakespeare's "Who Is Sylvia?" It was thus that he wrote most of his
German dances—waltzes and *Ländler*. He composed a great many
more of these dances than he ever put upon paper. He would sit
at the piano and they would flow from his fingers by the hour.
Those that survive are all very beautiful.

Schubert thus had little need for money, and hence made an
easy mark for the music publishers. He sold some of his songs to
them for as little as 20 cents. Now and then, pulling himself together, he resolved to make a stake, and usually, on such occasions, he wrote an opera. But his operas were always failures, and
most of them never got to the stage. A successful opera composer
is half musician and half clown; sometimes the clown part of him
is two-thirds, or even nine-tenths. Schubert had no talent in that
direction. He was an artist, not a showman. Much of his best music he never heard played, save by the family orchestra. This was
true even of his Unfinished Symphony, one of the noblest works
in the whole range of music. He wrote the two movements that we
have six years before his death, but then abandoned it, and it did
not become generally known until long afterward. His great C Ma-

jor fared even more badly. In 1844 the London Philharmonic put it into rehearsal, but the members of the orchestra, for some unknown reason, laughed at it, and it was shelved until 1856. After Schubert's death so many of his unpublished songs began to appear that many persons suspected his brother Ferdinand of forging them.

But Schubert, in life, wasted little time worrying about the fate of his music. He wrote it, not to entertain concert audiences, but to please himself, and out of that fact flowed a great deal of its magnificent merit. It is, in large part, so familiar to the musicians of today that they often overlook its astounding originality. Not infrequently one finds anticipations in it—even of Wagner!—but it is almost wholly bare of reminiscence. Schubert's harmonies were unlike the harmonies of any composer who had gone before him. They were not only different; they were better. His melodies differed enormously from those of his forerunners. He did not look back to Mozart and Haydn: he looked forward to Brahms. Maybe Beethoven influenced him. There are, indeed, indications that way in the Tragic Symphony, written in 1816, and especially in the slow movement. But Beethoven would have been proud of that slow movement if he had written it himself—and it remains, in the last analysis, pure Schubert. No one else, before or since, could have done it.

As I have said, Schubert led a placid and care-free life. Now and then he was on short commons, and had to double up in lodgings with a friend or two, but that was no hardship for a young bachelor. He knew a great many pleasant people, male and female, and they admired him and made much of him. The gals were not unappreciative of him, though he was surely no beauty. He loved good wine, and got down many a carboy of it in his time. Vienna was gay and charming, even when there was war—and the war was over before he was nineteen. Nevertheless, such stray confidences as we have from him indicate that he was given to melancholy and often fell into cruel depressions. His music, he once wrote in a diary, came out of the depths of his sorrow. The fact is written all over it. It is sometimes sparkling, but it is very seldom merry. Schubert wrote some of the most dark and sombre music ever written—for example, the "Winterreise" cycle, the last movement of the Unfinished, the slow movement of the Tragic, the first movement of the quintette with the two 'cellos, and such songs as the familiar Serenade. Even his *scherzi* tend to be gloomy, as witness the two in the octette.

Love? Heartache? A haughty wench? Hardly. Schubert's contemporaries heard of nothing of the sort. To them he was simply Schwammerl, a care-free and charming fellow, handy with the girls and a capital companion at the *Biertisch*. They forgot, seeing him every day, that he was also an artist—one of the greatest, indeed, ever known in the world. They forgot that an artist forges his work out of his inner substance by a process almost cannibalistic— that the price of beauty is heavy striving and cruel pain—that all artists, at bottom, are forlorn and melancholy men. They had Beethoven before them, wracked and consumed by his own vapors, but they were too close to Schubert to see into him.

Thus artists pay for what they give us. Schubert got off easily. He was dead at 32, and behind him trailed a series of almost incomparable masterpieces. His genius was of the first caliber. Dead a hundred years, he remains as alive as the child born yesterday. Out of his dark moods came treasures that belong to all of us. He increased the stature and dignity of man. He was one of the truly great ones.

Dvořák

From the *Smart Set*, July 1914, p. 160

My earnest advice to all those who dismiss "From the New World" as no more than a piece of musical journalism, is that they get the score of it and give it prayerful study. They will find writing of the highest quality in it—the music of a man who had something to say, and who knew how to say it. And if they will then turn to Dvořák's "Dumky" trio, they will get a lesson in musical clarity, dignity and economy of means. Here the composer runs the whole gamut of moods, and yet he never finds it necessary to yell like a Comanche Indian, or to weep like Marguerite Gautier, or to pile up senseless technical difficulties, to assault the ear with bizarre dissonances, or to depart from the keys and scales of "The Well-Tempered Clavier."

Tschaikowsky

From the same, p. 159

Turn from Tschaikowsky's "Manfred" or his "Pathétique" to Mozart's "Jupiter," or to Schubert's "Unfinished," or Beethoven's Eighth: it is like coming out of a *kaffeeklatsch* into the open air, almost like escaping from a lunatic asylum. The one unmistakable emotion that much of this modern music arouses is a hot longing for form, clarity, coherence, a tune. The snorts and moans of these pothouse Werthers are as irritating, in the long run, as the bawling of a child, the rage of a disappointed job seeker, the squeak of a pig under a gate. One yearns unspeakably for a composer who gives out his pair of honest themes, and then develops them with both ears open, and then recapitulates them unashamed, and then hangs a brisk coda to them, and then shuts up.

Russian Music

From the *American Mercury*, Jan., 1924, pp. 120–21.
A review of My Musical Life, by Nikolay Andreyevich
Rimsky-Korsakoff, with an introduction
by Carl Van Vechten; New York, 1923

This is the full story—meticulous, humorless, full of expository passion—of the Immortal Five: Balakireff, Cui, Musorgski, Borodin and Rimsky-Korsakoff himself. The book is enormous, and details are piled on without the slightest regard for the reader's time and patience. One plows through exhaustive criticism, often highly waspish, of concerts given fifty and sixty years ago; one attends to minute discussions of forgotten musical politics. Nevertheless, the general effect of the tome is surely not that of boredom.

It somehow holds the attention as securely as Thayer's monumental "Beethoven" or the memoirs of William Hickey. And no wonder, for the world that the good Nikolay Andreyevich describes is a world that must always appear charming and more than half fabulous to Western eyes—a world in which unfathomable causes constantly produced unimaginable effects—a world of occult motives, exotic emotions and bizarre personalities—in brief, the old Russia that went down to tragic ruin in 1917. Read about it in the memoirs of the late Count Witte, and one feels oneself magically set down—still with one's shoes shined, still neatly shaved with a Gillette!—at the court of Charlemagne, William the Conqueror, Genghis Khan. Read about it in Rimsky-Korsakoff's book, and one gets glimpses of Bagdad, Samarkand and points East.

The whole story of the Five, in fact, belongs to the grotesque and arabesque. Not one of them had more than the most superficial grasp of the complex and highly scientific art that they came so near to revolutionizing. Balakireff, the leader, was a mathematician turned religious mystic and musical iconoclast; he believed until middle age that writing a fugue was, in some incomprehensible manner, as discreditable an act as robbing a blind man. Cui was a military engineer who died a lieutenant general. Borodin was a chemist with a weakness for what is now called Service; he wasted half his life spoiling charming Russian girls by turning them into lady doctors. Musorgski was a Guards officer brought down by drink to a job in a railway freight-station. Rimsky-Korsakoff himself was a naval officer. All of them, he says, were as ignorant of the elements of music as so many union musicians. They didn't even know the names of the common chords. Of instrumentation they knew only what was in Berlioz's "Traité d'Instrumentation"—most of it archaic. When Rimsky-Korsakoff, on being appointed professor of composition in the St. Petersburg Conservatory—a typically Russian idea!—bought a *Harmonielehre* and began to experiment with canons, his fellow revolutionists repudiated him, and to the end of his life Balakireff despised him.

Nevertheless, these astounding ignoramuses actually made very lovely music, and if some of it, such as Musorgski's "Boris Godunoff," had to be translated into playable terms afterward, it at least had enough fundamental merit to make the translation feasible.

Musorgski, in fact, though he was the most ignorant of them all, probably wrote the best music of them all. Until delirium tremens put an end to him, he believed fondly that successive fourths were just as good as successive thirds, that modulations required no preparation, and that no such thing as a French horn with keys existed. More, he regarded all hints to the contrary as gross insults. Rimsky-Korsakoff, alone among them, was genuinely hospitable to the orthodox enlightenment. He learned instrumentation by the primitive process of buying all the orchestral and band instruments, and blowing into them to find out what sort of sounds they would make. The German *Harmonielehre* filled him with a suspicion that Bach, after all, must have known something, and after a while it became a certainty. He then sat down and wrote fifty fugues in succession! Later he got tired of polyphony and devoted himself chiefly to instrumentation. He became, next to Richard Strauss, the most skillful master of that inordinately difficult art in Europe. Incidentally, he and his friends taught Debussy and Schoenberg how to get rid of the diatonic scale, and so paved the way for all the cacophony that now delights advanced musical thinkers.

A curious tale, unfolded by Rimsky-Korsakoff with the greatest earnestness and even indignation. A clumsy writer, he yet writes brilliantly on occasion—for example, about the low-comedy household of the Borodins, with dinner at 11 P.M. and half a dozen strange guests always snoring on the sofas. Is there a lesson in the chronicle, say for American composers? I half suspect that there is. What ails these worthy men and makes their music, in general, so dreary is not that they are incompetent technicians, as is often alleged, but that they are far too competent. They are, in other words, so magnificently trained in the standard tricks, both orthodox and heterodox, that they can no longer leap and prance as true artists should. The stuff they write is correct, respectable, highly learned—but most of it remains *Kapellmeistermusik*, nay, only too often mere *Augenmusik*. Let them give hard study to this history of the five untutored Slavs who wrote full-length symphonies without ever having heard, as Rimsky-Korsakoff says, that the seventh tends to progress downward. Let them throw away their harmony-books, loose their collars, and proceed to write music.

The Bryan of Bayreuth

From the *American Mercury*, Nov., 1933, pp. 382–83

Wagner's merits, I believe, were mainly on the technical side. Though he was always, judged by conservatory standards, an amateur with only the most sketchy training in the elements of his craft, he became in the end the most stupendous musical technician who ever lived. There is in his scores an almost appalling virtuosity. So great, indeed, was his skill that he disdained most of the tricks that other composers resort to. His harmony was colorful and pungent but essentially orthodox, and there is no sign in it of the sensational cacophony that has since become the rage. His melody was almost as undistinguished, and he seems to have picked up from Beethoven the notion that very little of it was enough for an ingenious man. As for his instrumentation, though there was a considerable boldness in it, and it made extraordinarily heavy demands upon the performers, it still fell short of the bizarre inventions of Berlioz, the one composer among his contemporaries, save Johann Strauss, whom he seems to have respected. But with these meagre, and often downright austere materials, he yet managed to achieve astounding effects. Consider, for example, the prelude to "Lohengrin." It sounds banal enough today, and in melody and harmony there was surely nothing very novel about it, even in 1850, but when it was first heard even the retired *Hofräte* of Weimar must have gathered that something extraordinary was before them. Its virtue lies in its sheer virtuosity; it is the work of a man who is the complete master of his materials, and can do things with them, naturally and easily, that are quite impossible to other men. To compare it to the first movement of Beethoven's Fifth Symphony would be, of course, to flatter it, but nevertheless the two works belong roughly to the same class; both are the products of musicians who were so superbly competent that they could throw the ordinary devices of their craft overboard, and perform miracles in a sort of vacuum. The leap from Weber to "Lohengrin" was enormous, and yet there was nothing in "Lohengrin" that was not implicit in Weber—nothing, that is, save the hard, ever-ready, overwhelming brilliance of a man who was as far beyond Weber, technically speaking, as Weber was beyond a rustic *Stadtpfeiffer*.

This brilliance, of course, carried its own penalties. Wagner, an egoist undiluted, was intensely aware of it, and trusted it to get him round every difficulty. In fact, he trusted it so fully that it led him to disdain all the more homely and less exhilarating devices of a practising composer—for example, the laborious polishing of melodies à *la* Beethoven. Wagner's melodies, only too often, are obvious and ineffective, and sometimes they are almost idiotic; he knew that he could erect gorgeous structures upon them, however bad they were to begin with, and so he did not bother to perfect them. This over-confidence, for all his skill, sometimes got him into difficulties, as anyone may discover by sitting through the Ring. It is magnificent, but there are times when it leaves the hearer cold and bored. The ear longs for simple beauty, for honest, innocent emotion, such as one finds in all of Schubert, and in most of Brahms. The thing sounds more like oratory than like music, and the fact that the orchestra is meanwhile giving a fine show only makes one wish that the so-called singers would shut down altogether and let the fiddlers and horn-players have their way.

The music of the master is being played more than ever before, but not in the opera-house: even in Germany there has been a flight toward the simpler lyricism of Verdi. It may be childish, but it is a relief from the rhetoric of sopranos and tenors who are seldom permitted to sing, even when they *can* sing, which is surely not always. To be sure, some incomparable moments remain, and the second act of "Tristan und Isolde" suggests itself at once. But even the second act of "Tristan und Isolde" would probably be surer of life if it were a double concerto for violin and cello, as, indeed, it may be become on some near tomorrow. In the concert-hall Wagner's music is still immensely effective; none other, new or old, can match its brilliance at its high points, which may be isolated there very conveniently and effectively. But in the opera-house it has to carry a heavy burden of puerile folk-lore, brummagem patriotism, and bilge-water Christianity, and another and even heavier burden of choppy and gargling singing. No wonder it begins to stagger.

Debussy and Wagner

From the *Smart Set*, March, 1909, pp. 156–57

Lawrence Gilman maintains that Debussy's "Pelleas and Melisande" is a music drama which carries out the plans of Richard Wagner better than Wagner was ever able to carry them out himself. The Sage of Bayreuth, says Mr. Gilman, made a gallant and constant effort to subordinate his music to his drama, but ever and anon a luscious tune began to buzz in his ears, and, for all his struggles, he couldn't keep it off his music paper. In Debussy there is no such amiable weakness. With him the play is the thing from curtain to curtain, and he never stops the action to tickle our ears with high C's. At critical moments, indeed, he silences his orchestra altogether, and irons out the melodic line in his voice parts so resolutely that it recalls the haunting pedal point of an auctioneer.

There is a good deal of truth in Mr. Gilman's argument, but far from proving that Debussy is Wagner's superior, it may merely prove that Wagner's art theories were and are impracticable. It is all well enough to talk of reducing the music to the level of the scenery and the strophes, but, all the same, people go to opera houses, not to look at backdrops and gestures, but to hear singing—to hear the soaring, super-delicious wolf tones of the tenor, the sweet shrieks of the soprano and the genial grunts of the gentlemen of Brabant. In those melodramas which have an accompaniment of shiver music for every foul stab and sigh of love the art theories of Wagner are put into execution with absolute and unmerciful literalness, and yet civilized folks cannot be induced to enjoy such plays, despite their vast superiority in sentiment, logic and morals to the ordinary run of grand opera librettos.

XXV. THE PURSUIT OF HAPPINESS

Alcohol

From DAMN! A BOOK OF CALUMNY, 1918, pp. 64–66

THE SOLEMN proofs, so laboriously deduced from life insurance statistics, that the man who uses alcohol dies slightly sooner than the teetotaler—these proofs merely show that this man is one who leads an active and vigorous life, and so faces hazards and uses himself up—in brief, one who lives at high tempo and with full joy, what Nietzsche used to call the *ja-sager*, or yes-sayer. He may, in fact, die slightly sooner than the teetotaler, but he lives infinitely longer. Moreover, his life, humanly speaking, is much more worth while, to himself and to the race. He does the hard and dangerous work of the world, he takes the chances, he makes the experiments. He is the soldier, the artist, the innovator, the lover. All the great works of man have been done by men who thus lived joyously, strenuously, and perhaps a bit dangerously. They have never been concerned about stretching life for two or three more years; they have been concerned about making life engrossing and stimulating and a high adventure while it lasts. Teetotalism is as impossible to such men as any other manifestation of cowardice, and, if it were possible, it would destroy their utility and significance just as certainly.

A man who shrinks from a couple of cocktails before dinner on the ground that they may flabbergast his hormones, and so make him die at 69 years, ten months and five days instead of 69 years, eleven months and seven days—such a man is as absurd a poltroon as the fellow who shrinks from kissing a woman on the ground that she may floor him with a chair leg. Each flees from a purely theoretical risk. Each is a useless encumberer of the earth, and the sooner dead the better. Each is a discredit to the human race, already discreditable enough, God knows.

Teetotalism does not make for human happiness; it makes for the dull, idiotic happiness of the barnyard. The men who do things in the world, the men worthy of admiration and imitation, are men constitutionally incapable of any such pecksniffian stupidity. Their ideal is not a safe life, but a full life; they do not try to follow the canary bird in a cage, but the eagle in the air. And in particular they do not flee from shadows and bugaboos. The alcohol myth is such a bugaboo. The sort of man it scares is the sort of man whose chief mark is that he is scared all the time.

The Great American Art

From the *Smart Set*, March, 1916, pp. 304–07.
A review of THIRTY-FIVE YEARS OF PUBLIC LIFE,
by Alfred Jefferson; New York, 1915

Let the bibliographical psychologist explain why it is that the first serious work upon bartending ever to reach the Library of Congress is this small volume. One would think that a science so widely practised in Christendom and of such intimate and constant interest and value to so many men would have long ago brought forth a copious literature, but as a matter of fact the only books on bartending put into type before Dr. Jefferson's volume were absurd pamphlets of the "Every Man His Own Bartender" type. I myself, while still a high school student, compiled such a pamphlet, receiving for it the sum of $12.50 from a Boston publisher. Most of them (and at one time they were greatly in evidence on the bookstalls) were put together by hacks employed at weekly wages. My youthful introduction to the business brought me into contact with several such literati and I found them to be, in the main, gentlemen whose literary daring was only equalled by their lack of information. One of them, still a vivid memory, told me that he had written no less than twelve books in one week, ranging in character from a hymnal for the use of colored Methodists in Virginia to a text-book of legerdemain for county fair gamblers and Chautauqua magicians.

Dr. Jefferson's volume has nothing in common with the confections of such eighth-rate virtuosi. The learned doctor (whose title, though espoused only by custom and courtesy, is nevertheless as well deserved as that of any surgeon, evangelist or college professor in the land) is a man of long and profound experience, and of unquestioned professional dignity. He learned the principles of his invaluable art under the late Prof. Dr. Martin Dalrymple, for many years head bartender at the old Astor House. After serving for five years under this incomparable mentor, young Jefferson spent a *wanderjahr* or two in the West, and among other adventures saw service at the Palmer House in Chicago and at the old Planters' Hotel in St. Louis. At the latter hostelry, then in the heyday of its eminence, he became intimately acquainted with Col. Lucius W. Beauregard, of Jackson, Miss., perhaps the greatest authority upon corn whiskey and its allied carbohydrates that the world has ever seen. Col. Beauregard took a warm interest in the young man, and one finds the marks of his influence, after all these years, in the latter's book.

After his service in the Middle West, Dr. Jefferson became head bartender at the old Shoreham Hotel in Washington, from which he was translated, in the middle eighties, to the post of head bartender and chief of the wine cellar at the Rennert Hotel in Baltimore, that last surviving bulwark of the palmy days of American epicureanism and conviviality. The so-called wine cellar at the Rennert, of course, was chiefly stocked, not with the juices of the grape, but with the rarer and more potent essences that come from the still. Here, when Dr. Jefferson took charge, were ten barrels of rye whiskey that had been released from bond in 1844. Here was a whole vat of Kentucky corn that registered no less than 166 proof. The greatest of America's connoisseurs visited the majestic vaults and dungeons of the old *gasthaus* as pilgrims might visit some holy shrine. Down in those aromatic depths Dr. Jefferson reigned a benevolent despot, and there he acquired his enormous knowledge of the history, etiology, chemical constitution, surface tension, specific gravity, flash point, muzzle velocity, trajectory and psychiatrical effects of each and every member of the standard répertoire of alcoholic drinks.

In one of his most interesting chapters he discusses the place that alcohol occupies in pharmacology, and shows clearly that the common notion that it is a stimulant is ill-founded. As a matter of fact it is not a stimulant at all, but a depressant. The civilized man does not drink alcoholic beverages to speed himself up, but to let himself down. This explains the extremely agreeable sensation produced by a cocktail or two before dinner. One cocktail, if it be skillfully prepared, is sufficient to put a man into a mellow and comfortable frame of mind. It quiets his nerves by anaesthetizing the delicate nerve ends; it dulls his reactions to external stimuli by shrinking and blocking up the cutaneous follicles; it makes him less sensitive to all distracting ideas and impressions, whether of a financial, domestic or theological character; and so, by the combination of all these processes, it puts him into that placid and caressing mood which should always accompany the ingestion of food.

I speak here, of course, of its general effects—that is, of its effects upon the nervous and vascular systems, and through them, upon the mind. Its local effect upon the esophagus and the stomach walls is probably stimulating, at least momentarily. For one thing, it increases the secretion of most of the constituent elements of the gastric juices, particularly hydrofluoric acid and citrate of manganese, and thus must necessarily make digesting more facile. But even here it operates as a depressant eventually, for it is obvious to anyone familiar with elementary physiology that a rise in the activity of the stomach is invariably accompanied by a compensatory fall in the buzzing and bubbling of the cerebrum and cerebellum. Our mental reactions are always a bit dull after a hearty meal; hence the feeling of peace which overtakes us at that time. The same feeling is produced by a few ounces of diluted alcohol.

Of even more interest than his discussing of such scientific aspects of his art is Dr. Jefferson's account of what may be called its social or spectacular evolution. He has an interesting chapter, for example, upon the garb affected by bartenders in various ages of the Christian era. At one time, it appears, it was the custom for the bartenders in the chief American hotels to wear full dress when on duty, like head waiters, professional dancers and Pinero actors. (This same uniform, by the way, was worn by surgeons in England

before the days of asepsis. It was considered a gross insult for a surgeon to operate on a paying patient in other habiliments. The
sleeves of the dress-coat were provided with buttons like those on
shirt-sleeves, and the surgeon turned them back and fastened them
with rubber bands before spitting on his hands and beginning his
ministrations.) However, the claw-hammer disappeared from behind the bar during the Civil War and has not been seen since. Its
departure was succeeded by an era of grave looseness in dress, and
Dr. Jefferson says that there was a corresponding fall in the dignity
of the bartender. In the shirt-sleeve days of the seventies, he was a
nobody. It was a common custom indeed to address him indis-
criminately as John, or even as Jack, much as one might address
a waiter in a fourth-rate eating-house or a fellow convert at a revival. But once he got into his now familiar white coat, along
about 1886, the gulf separating him from the public on one hand
and from the caste of servants on the other began to widen rapidly,
and in first-class barrooms he now occupies a position comparable
to that of the druggist or the dentist, or even to that of the clergyman. He is no longer a mere pot-slinger, but a clean and self-
respecting craftsman, whose pride in his subtle and indispensable
art is signified by his professional accoutrements. This change
in the public attitude toward him has naturally reacted upon the
bartender himself. In the old days he took his swig from every
jug and it was common for him to end his career in the gutter.
But today he is a sober and a decent man and, unless fate has
borne very harshly upon him, he has money in the bank against
a rainy day, and dresses his wife and daughters as well as any
other honest man.

Dr. Jefferson (whose aesthetic taste seems to be very advanced,
for he quotes James Huneker's books and W. H. Wright's "Modern
Painting," and is satirical at the expense of the impressionists) believes that the modern barroom is one of the most marked triumphs of American design. He says there are at least twenty
barrooms in the United States that deserve to be ranked, in their
separate way, with St. Thomas's Church in New York and the Boston Public Library. In his early days, he says, the present movement toward quiet refinement in barroom design was unheard of
and the whole tendency of architects was toward an infantile gaud-

iness. The famous barroom of the Palmer House in Chicago—
paved with silver dollars!—was its extremist manifestation. But for
a half-dozen years past the architects have been putting away their
old onyx pillars and rococo carvings and substituting plain hardwood and simple lines. The improvement is too obvious to need
praise. The typical hotel barroom of today is not only a hospitable
and a comfortable place, but also and more especially, a notice-
ably beautiful place, and its effect upon those who visit it cannot
fail to be inspiring. Even the ordinary saloon bar shows a certain
forward movement. It is still, true enough, too flashily lighted, but
its design is a good deal less delirious than it used to be. In particular, there is a benign passing away of its old intricate spirals and
curlycues, and of its old harsh combination of mottled marble and
red mahogany, and of its old display of mirrors, so reminiscent of
the Paris bordello. One still fails, perhaps, to be soothed by it, but
at all events one is no longer so grossly assaulted and tortured by
it as one used to be.

Dr. Jefferson is an implacable antagonist of the American mixed
drink, and all his references to it are unmistakably hostile, but nevertheless he is interested in it sufficiently to inquire into its history.
Here, however, his diligence shows but meager reward. For example, he finds it quite impossible to determine the origin of the
cocktail, or even the origin of its name. Its first mention in polite
literature is in Nathaniel Hawthorne's "Blithedale Romance," published in 1852. But it seems to have been a familiar American
drink a good while further back, for there is a legend in Boston
that John Adams was very fond of it, and that he once caused
a scandal by trying it upon the then rector of the Old South
Church, the reverend gentleman quickly succumbing and taking
the count. But this legend, of course, is merely a legend. All that
one may safely say of the drink itself is that it was known in the
first half of the Nineteenth Century, and all that one may safely
say of its name is that it seems to be American. Even here, however, the pedant may be disposed to file a caveat, for the word
"cock" passed out of usage in this country at a very early date,
"rooster" taking its place, and so the primeval inventor of the
drink, supposing him to have been American, would have been inclined to call it a roostertail rather than a cocktail. The explana-

tion may be that the thing was invented on American soil, but by an Englishman.

A similar mystery surrounds the origin of "highball," despite the fact that the word goes back not more than twenty-five years. Why high? And why ball? In England, where the thing itself originated and where it has been familiar for many years, it is called a whiskey-and-soda. "Julep" presents equal difficulties. The etymologists say that it is an Americanized form of the Spanish word *julepe* (pronounced hoo-*lay*-pay), and derive the latter from the Persian *gul*, rose, and *ab*, water. But this derivation, as Dr. Jefferson justly points out, seems to be chiefly fanciful, and perhaps may be ascribed to some fantoddish journalist or college professor, either drunk or sober. It is highly improbable that the mint julep was known to the Spanish explorers of America, for they were not spirits drinkers but wine drinkers. Moreover, there is no mention of it in history until years after the last Spaniard had departed from these shores. Still more, it was first heard of, not in the Spanish parts of the country, but in the wholly English parts.

This scant and casual notice of Dr. Jefferson's book scarcely does justice to one of the most interesting of recent volumes. The common notion that a bartender is an ignorant man is here set at rest forever. The author reveals himself not only as a gentleman of sound information but also as one of cultured habits of reflection. His book is written in excellent English from cover to cover, and the arrangement of its materials certifies to his possession of a trained and orderly mind. It is sincerely to be hoped that he will not allow it to be his last essay in the philosophy of his ancient (and perhaps now dying) art. Bartending has suffered greatly from the ignorant and cynical attitude of mind of the general public. When the average man thinks of barrooms, his mind quickly turns to memories of some of his own worst stupidities and follies, and so he comes unconsciously to the notion that the man on the other side of the bar is an ass also. Nothing can be more grotesquely unjust and untrue. The typical American bartender in this year of grace 1916 is a man of education, intelligence and refinement. He must be able to meet all classes and conditions of men in a dignified and self-respecting manner; he must understand human vanity; he must keep himself steadfast in the midst of manifold temptations. Obviously, such a man can be no slouch. The boob, the osseocaput, the fat- or bonehead may get along very well in the pulpit, in business or at the bar, but it is quite impossible for him to survive *behind* the bar.

Night Club

From the Baltimore *Evening Sun*, Sept. 3, 1934

I hadn't been in one for three or four years, but save in the wine-list there was no visible change. The same side-show murals on the walls, and the same cacochromatic play of lights. The same sad youths laboring the same jazz. The same middle-aged couples bumping and grunting over the dance floor like dying hogs in a miasmatic pen. The same interludes of dismal professional entertainment, with the same decayed vaudevillians. The same crooners, male and female, bawling maudlin jingles into the same mikes. The same shuffling and forgetful waiters. The same commonplace food. The same poky service.

The wine-list showed some cuts in price. Highballs had come down from the 75 cents of Prohibition days to half a dollar, and some of the simpler kinds of cocktails were but 40 cents. There were champagnes as low as $5 a quart, and still wines at $2.25, $2, and even, in a few cases, $1.75. But the transcripts of the labels (often misspelled) were empty of temptation: they all seemed to be third-rate trade-goods. Every beer listed was, to my unhappy personal knowledge, bad. Of the good beers now on the market there was no mention. It was a task to make up one's mind what to drink. I chose an almost anonymous white wine, and regretted it heartily.

What the mark-up is in such places I don't know, but it can't be much less than 100 per cent. For the overhead is heavy, and the flow of business is not swift. While the clients are performing the lethargic obscenity that they call dancing they are not drinking, and most of them seem to dance every number. I observed one crème de menthe frappé that lasted, by my watch, more than an hour, and one bottle of indeterminate red wine that sufficed for four people all evening. There was nowhere in the place, so far as I could see, any high-pressure boozing, and certainly no one was tight, save maybe my waiter—an habitual heel-drainer, or I am no criminologist. The dancers, with few exceptions, looked very silly, but they were all sober. No carcasses of the stewed, whether male or female, hung along the bar.

Why do people go to such places? It is hard to make out. To lose themselves in the color and gayety? I could discern no more gayety than is usual in a Bible class, and the standard color scheme is far more exhilarating to bulls than to human beings. To be soothed and carried away by the music? There is no music, but only an idiotic beating of tom-toms, with occasionally a few measures of a banal tune. To seek grace and exercise in the dance? There is no grace in such stupid wriggling, and no exercise in doing it over a few square yards of floor. To dally with amour? But surely the place for amour is not under 5,000 candle-power of red, yellow, green and blue lights, with strangers ricocheting from the cabooses of the high contracting parties, and catapulting them hither and yon.

The music interested me most, for one often hears, even from good musicians, that jazz is not to be sniffed at—that there is really something in it. But what, precisely? I can find nothing in what is currently offered. Its melodies all run to a pattern, and that pattern is crude and childish. Its rhythms are almost as bad; what is amusing in them is as old as Johann Sebastian Bach, and what is new is simply an elephantine hop, skip and jump. Nor is there anything charming in jazz harmony, once it has been heard a couple of times. The discords, three times out of four, seems to be due to ignorance far more than to craft, and the modulations, in the main, are simply those of a church organist far gone in liquor. As for the instrumentation, it appears to be based frankly on the theory that unpleasant sounds are somehow more pleasant, at least to certain ears, than pleasant ones. That theory is sound, and it has many corollaries: indeed, the love of ugliness is quite as widespread, and hence quite as human, as the love of beauty. But it still remains a scientific fact that a thin and obvious tune played badly on an imperfect reed instrument, is hideous, and no metaphysics, however artful, can ever reduce that fact to fancy. And it is likewise a fact that a single fiddle, if it be pitted against three or four saxophones, a trumpet, a bull-fiddle and a battery of drums, gives a very bad account of itself, and can make little more actual music than a pig under a fence.

My guess is that jazz remains popular, not because of any virtue (even to anthropoid ears) in its melodies, harmonies and instrumentation, nor even to any novelty in its rhythm, but simply to its monotonous beat. No matter what syncopations may be attempted in the upper parts, the drums and bull-fiddle bang along like metronomes, and that is the thing that apparently soothes and delights the customers. It is music reduced to its baldest elementals, and hence music that they can follow. It might be made just as well by a machine, and some day, I suppose, the experiment of so making it will be tried.

That there are artistic possibilities in it may be granted, for on rare occasions some unusually competent composer develops and reveals them. But they are certainly not apparent in the sorry trash that loads the radio every night. It is simply undifferentiated musical protoplasm, dying of its own effluvia. There is no more ingenuity in it than you will find in the design of a series of fence-posts. One tune is so much like another that it is hard to tell them apart, and the cheap harmonies that support the first also support all the rest. Every squeal of the clarinets is an old and familiar squeal, and there is seldom any effort to break the monotony by introducing new instruments, or by working out new ways of using the old ones. The muted trumpet is still offered gravely as something novel and saucy.

The dancing that goes with this noise is, if anything, even worse. It is the complete negation of graceful and charming motion. In its primeval form I used to watch it in the Negro dives of Hawk street thirty-five years ago. There would be a dance-floor packed to the walls, and on it the colored brethren and their ladies, policed by Round Sergeant Charles M. Cole and his storm troopers, would stamp and wriggle, each sticking to a space of a few square feet. In those days the proud Aryan pursued the waltz and two-step, and ballroom dancing had sweeping linear patterns, and went to tripping and amusing tunes. But now the patterns are gone, and dancing everywhere degenerates to what it was in Hawk street—a puerile writhing on a narrow spot.

It is a feeble and silly art at best, and so its decay need not be lamented. It comes naturally to the young, whose excess of energy demands violent motion, but when it is practised by the mature it can never escape a kind of biological impropriety, verging upon the indecent. The real damage that the new mode has done is to music, the cleanest and noblest of all the arts. There is in the repertory a vast amount of dance music, and in it are some of the loveliest tunes ever written. But now they are forgotten as if they had never been, and people heave and pant to rubbish fit only for tin whistles.

That we owe the change to Prohibition is certainly arguable. By putting all social intercourse in America on an alcoholic basis, it forced people to dance when they were not quite themselves, and in consequence they had to avoid the complications of the waltz and its congeners, and to seek safety in more primitive measures. The simple beat of the tomtom was the safest of all, so it came in. Simultaneously, ears and brains were dulled, and it became painful to follow the complicated and exciting tunes of Johann Strauss, so the crude banalities of jazz were substituted. Thus we have music purged of everything that makes it music, and dancing reduced to a duck-like wabbling, requiring hardly more skill than spitting at a mark.

This is not my hypothesis: I have heard it from authorities worth attending to. They seem to agree that the gradual deboozification of the country, following upon Repeal, will eventually restore decent music to the ballroom and with it a more seemly kind of dancing. As I have noted, the people that I saw in that night club the other evening all seemed to be soberer than was common in Anti-Saloon League days. I should add that most of them looked a bit sad, and that many even looked a bit shamefaced. They had little applause for the music, and were plainly not having anything properly describable as a high old time. In the main, they were old enough to have the pattern of the waltz packed in their knapsacks. What if the professor had choked his horrible saxophones and burst into "Wiener Blut"? My guess is that a wave of genuine joy would have rolled over that dismal hall.

The Peaceable Kingdom

From the Baltimore *Evening Sun*, Aug. 28, 1931

The professional wets continue in the folly of representing and libeling the saloon. It is not only a folly; it is also a thumping hypocrisy, for all of them know very well that the saloon was never as bad as the drys painted it. There were, of course, saloons of a low character, but they were never as low in character as the neighborhoods in which they flourished. Every saloon was measurably cleaner, more cheerful and more orderly than the street in which it stood. Not uncommonly it was a school of manners for the whole vicinity. The bombast and ill-nature that marks family life among the proletariat was strictly forbidden. A visitor who spoke to the bartender or to another visitor in the tones he was free to use to his wife had his skull nicked with a bung-starter, and learned a salutary lesson in decorum. A saloon free-lunch was always composed of better food than could be had at home by those who consumed it. The art on saloon walls, though it may have been of the fleshly school, was better than the art on the walls of American parlors. The most humble man, if he had a nickel to put upon the bar, was free to stand before it for an hour and listen to the discourse of his betters. If no great dignitary ever came in, then at least the police sergeant came in, and what he had to say after a few beers was always instructive and sometimes astonishing. Moreover, the brewery's collector, or *Todsäufer*, dropped in regularly—if not daily, then certainly once a week. He was a man of wide information and polished manners, and not infrequently he was a member of the City Council. His talk echoed the thoughts and projects, the hopes and despairs, of the great world. His Shriner's button was of solid gold, and the claws, teeth and wishbones of elks, moose, lions, tigers and eagles upon his watch-chain were set in the same noble metal. Many a Baltimorean, now a rich banker or manufacturer, owes his start in life to the friendly interest of a *Todsäufer*, met in a saloon.

The Home of the Crab

From the Baltimore *Evening Sun*, June 13, 1927

That Baltimore is a center of gastronomical debauchery is a delusion still cherished by thousands of Americans who have never been there. It is remarkable how long such notions last. This one, I daresay, was true at some time in the past, but certainly it has not been true since the great fire of 1904. That catastrophe left indelible scars upon the town. It not only changed it physically, and for the worse; it also dethroned the old ruling caste of easy-going, good-living gentry, and turned loose a mob of go-getters, most of them not natives. Baltimore used to run to shady, red-bricked streets, gorgeous victuals and sound liquors; its white marble front steps were almost as famous as its soft crabs, its oysters, its terrapin and its seven-year-old rye. But now it runs to long rows of hideous homes in all the horrible shades of yellow, with front porches fit for railway terminals—and with them have come boulevards and stadiums, and with the boulevards and stadiums, soda water and hot dogs. I remember myself when there were at least twoscore first-rate eating houses in the city: now there are not half a dozen. Two of the best are run by Italians, or at all events, on the Italian plan. The food they offer is, in many ways, the most appetizing in town, but it is Italian, not Baltimorean. When a visitor of civilized tastes honors the town with his presence he doesn't want to eat Italian dishes; he wants to try the Maryland dishes he has heard of all his life—the chicken *à la Maryland*, the planked shad, the Maryland beaten biscuit, the steamed hard crabs, the jowl and sprouts, the soft crabs and so on. Where is he to get them? Maybe, by accident, in some lunchroom. The rest of the eating-houses of the town, ignoring all such local delicacies, serve only the dull, uninspired victuals that are now the standard everywhere in America, from Boston to Los Angeles. Year by year their cuisine comes closer and closer to that of the Pennsylvania Railroad dining-car.

This decay, of course, is not peculiar to Baltimore. It is to be observed all over the United States, and the local causes, when they are discernible at all, are perhaps less potent than the increasing standardization and devitalization that now mark all American life. The American people have become the dullest and least happy race in Christendom. When they seek amusement it is in huge herds, like wild animals. There was a time when even the poorest man, in such a place as Baltimore, at least ate decent food. It was cheap and his wife knew how to cook it, and took pride in the fact. But now the movie parlor engulfs her every afternoon, and what he eats comes mainly out of cans. His midday lunch was once her handiwork, and he washed it down with honest beer. Now he devours hot dogs.

Hot Dogs

From the Baltimore *Evening Sun*, Nov. 4, 1929

The hot dog, as the phrase runs, seems to have come to stay. Even the gastroenterologists have given up damning it, as they have given up damning synthetic gin. I am informed by reliable spies that at their convention in Atlantic City last May they consumed huge quantities of both, and with no apparent damages to their pylorus. In such matters popular instinct is often ahead of scientific knowledge, as the history of liver eating shows so beautifully. It may be that, on some near tomorrow, the hot dog will turn out to be a prophylactic against some malady that now slays its thousands. That this will be the case with respect to gin I am willing to prophesy formally. Meanwhile, hot dog stands multiply, and millions of young Americans grow up who will cherish the same veneration for them that we, their elders, were taught to give to the saloon.

My own tastes in eating run in another direction, and so it is very rarely that I consume a hot dog. But I believe that I'd fall in line if the artists who confect and vend it only showed a bit more professional daring. What I mean may be best explained by referring to the parallel case of the sandwich. When I was a boy there were only three kinds of sandwiches in common use—the ham, the chicken and the Swiss cheese. Others, to be sure, existed, but it was only as oddities. Even the club sandwich was a rarity, and in most eating-houses it was unobtainable. The great majority of people stuck to the ham and the Swiss cheese, with the chicken for feast days and the anniversaries of historic battles. Then came the invasion of the delicatessen business by Jews, and a complete reform of the sandwich. The Jewish mind was too restless and enterprising to be content with the old repertoire. It reached out for the novel, the dramatic, the unprecedented, as it does in all the arts. First it combined the ham sandwich and the cheese sandwich—and converted America to the combination instanter. Then it added lettuce, and after that, mayonnaise—both borrowed from the club sandwich. Then it boldly struck out into the highest fields of fancy, and presently the lowly sandwich had been completely transformed and exalted. It became, as the announcements said, "a meal in itself." It took on complicated and astonishing forms. It drew on the whole market for materials. And it leaped in price from a nickel to a dime, to a quarter, to fifty cents, even to a dollar. I have seen sandwiches, indeed, marked as much as a dollar and a half.

The rise in price, far from hurting business, helped it vastly. The delicatessen business, once monopolized by gloomy Germans who barely made livings at it, became, in the hands of the Jewish reformers, one of the great American industries, and began to throw off millionaires. Today it is on a sound and high-toned basis, with a national association, a high-pressure executive secretary, a trade journal, and a staff of lobbyists in Washington. There are sandwich shops in New York which offer the nobility and gentry a choice of no less than 100 different sandwiches, all of them alluring and some of them downright masterpieces. And even on the lowly level of the drug-store sandwich counter the sandwich has taken on a new variety and a new dignity. No one eats plain ham and cole-slaw to set it off. At its best it is hidden between turkey, Camembert and sprigs of endive, with anchovies and Russian dressing to dress it.

What I have to suggest is that the hot dog *entrepreneurs* borrow a leaf from the book of the sandwich men. Let them throw off the chains of the frankfurter, for a generation or more their only stay, and go seeking novelty in the vast and brilliant domain of the German sausage. They will be astonished and enchanted, I believe, by what they find there, and their clients will be astonished and enchanted even more. For there are more different sausages in Germany than there are breakfast foods in America, and if there is a bad one among them then I have never heard of it. They run in size from little fellows so small and pale and fragile that it seems a crime to eat them to vast and formidable pieces that look like shells for heavy artillery. And they run in flavor from the most delicate to the most raucous, and in texture from that of feathers caught in a cobweb to that of linoleum, and in shape from straight cylinders to lovely kinks and curlycues. In place of the single hot dog of today there should be a variety as great as that which has come to prevail among sandwiches. There should be dogs for all appetites, all tastes, all occasions. They should come in rolls of every imaginable kind and accompanied by every sort of relish from Worcestershire sauce to chutney. The common frankfurter, with its tough roll and its smear of mustard, should be abandoned as crude and hopeless, as the old-time ham sandwich has been abandoned. The hot dog should be elevated to the level of an art form.

I call upon the Jews to work this revolution, and promise them confidently even greater success than they have found in the field of the sandwich. It is a safe and glorious business, lying wide open to anyone who chooses to venture into it. It offers immense opportunities to men of genuine imagination—opportunities not only for making money but also for Service in its best Rotarian sense. For he who improves the eating of a great people is quite as worthy of honor as he who improves their roads, their piety, their sex life or their safety. He does something that benefits every one, and the fruits of his benefaction live on long after he has passed from this life.

I believe that a chain of hot dog stands offering the novelties I suggest would pay dividends in Baltimore from the first day, and that it would soon extend from end to end of the United States. The butchers and bakers would quickly arise to the chance it offered, and in six months the American repertoire of sausages would overtake and leap ahead of the German, and more new rolls would be invented than you may now find in France. In such matters American ingenuity may be trusted completely. It is infinitely resourceful, venturesome and audacious. I myself am acquainted with sausage-makers in this town who, if the demand arose, would produce sausages of hexagonal or octagonal section, sausages with springs or music boxes in them, sausages flavored with malt and hops, sausages dyed any color in the spectrum, sausages loaded with insulin, ergosterol, anti-tetanus vaccine or green chartreuse.

Nor is there any reason to believe that the bakers would lag behind. For years their ancient art has been degenerating in America, and today the bread that they ordinarily offer is almost uneatable. But when the reformers of the sandwich went to them for aid they responded instantly with both wheat and rye breads of the highest merit. Such breads, to be sure, are not used in the manufacture of drug-store sandwiches, but they are to be found in every delicatessen store and in all of the more respectable sandwich shops. The same bakeries that produce them could produce an immense variety of first-rate rolls, once a demand for them was heard.

I believe in my scheme so thoroughly that I throw it overboard freely, eager only to make life in the United States more endurable. *Soli Deo gloria!* What we need in this country is a general improvement in eating. We have the best raw materials in the world, both quantitatively and qualitatively, but most of them are ruined in the process of preparing them for the table. I have wandered about for weeks without encountering a single decent meal. With precious few exceptions, the hotels of America all cook alike — and what they offer is hard to distinguish from what is offered on railway dining-cars.

Reminiscence in the Present Tense

From MINORITY REPORT, 1956, pp. 102–03.
First printed in the *Smart Set*, Feb., 1920, p. 47

One of the fellows I can't understand is the man with violent likes and dislikes in his drams — the man who dotes on highballs but can't abide malt liquor, or who drinks white wine but not red or who holds that Scotch whiskey benefits his kidneys whereas rye whiskey corrodes his liver. As for me, I am prepared to admit some merit in every alcoholic beverage ever devised by the incomparable brain of man, and drink them all when the occasions are suitable — wine with meat, the hard liquors when my so-called soul languishes, beer to let me down gently of an evening. In other words, I am omnibibulous, or, more simply, ombibulous.

XXVI. LESSER EMINENTOES

Portrait of an Immortal Soul

From Prejudices: First Series, 1919, pp. 224–35. First printed in the *Smart Set*, June, 1915, pp. 290–93. After the book herein discussed came out I heard nothing more from the author until 1935, when he wrote to me from Wisconsin and then from Chicago. It appeared that he had married, had nine children, and was out of work, and that the whole family was trying to live on a dole of $17.28 a week. He said that he had written another book—not the one mentioned herein—, but I never heard any more about it

ONE DAY long ago I received a letter from a man somewhere beyond the Wabash announcing that he had lately completed a very powerful novel and hinting that my critical judgment upon it would give him great comfort. Such notifications, at that time, reached me far too often to be agreeable, and so I sent him a form-response telling him that I was ill with pleurisy, had just been forbidden by my oculist to use my eyes, and was about to become a father. The aim of this form-response was to shunt all that sort of trade off to other reviewers, but for once it failed. That is to say, the unknown kept on writing to me, and finally offered to pay me an honorarium for my labor. This offer was so unusual that it quite demoralized me, and before I could recover I had received, cashed and dissipated a modest check, and was confronted by an accusing manuscript, perhaps four inches thick, but growing thicker every time I glanced at it.

One night, tortured by conscience and by the inquiries and reminders arriving from the author by every post, I took up the sheets and settled down for a depressing hour or two of it. . . . No, I did *not* read all night. No, it was *not* a masterpiece. No, it has *not* made the stranger famous. Let me tell the story quite honestly. I am, in fact, far too rapid a reader to waste a whole night on a novel; I had got through this one by midnight and was sound asleep at my usual time. And it was by no means a masterpiece; on the contrary, it was inchoate, clumsy, and, in part, artificial, insincere and preposterous. And to this day the author remains unknown. . . . But underneath all the amateurish writing, the striving for effects that failed to come off, the absurd literary self-consciousness, the recurrent falsity and banality—underneath all these stigmata of a neophyte's book there was yet a capital story, unusual in content, naïve in manner and enormously engrossing. What is more, the faults that it showed in execution were, most of them, not ineradicable. On page after page, as I read on, I saw chances to improve it—to get rid of its intermittent bathos, to hasten its action, to eliminate its spells of fine writing, to purge it of its imitations of all the bad novels ever written—in brief, to tighten it, organize it, and, as the painters say, tease it up.

The result was that I spent the next morning writing the author a long letter of advice. It went to him with the manuscript, and for weeks I heard nothing from him. Then the manuscript returned, and I read it again. This time I had a genuine surprise. Not only had the unknown followed my suggestions with much intelligence; in addition, once set up on the right track, he had devised a great many improvements of his own. In its new form, in fact, the thing was a very competent and even dexterous piece of writing, and after re-reading it from the first word to the last with even keener interest than before, I sent it to Mitchell Kennerley, then an active publisher in New York, and asked him to look through it. Kennerley made an offer for it at once, and eight or nine months later it was published with his imprint. The author chose to conceal himself behind the *nom de plume* of Robert Steele; I myself gave the book the title of "One Man." It came from the press—and straightway died the death. The only favorable review it received was mine. No one gabbled about it. No one, so far as I could make out, even read it. The sale was small from the start, and quickly stopped altogether. To this day the fact fills me with wonder. To this day I marvel that so dramatic, so penetrating and so curiously moving a story should have failed so overwhelmingly. . . .

For I have never been able to convince myself that I was wrong about it. On the contrary, I am more certain than ever that I was right—that it was and is one of the most honest and absorbing human documents ever printed in America. I have called it, following the author, a novel. It is, in fact, nothing of the sort; it is autobiography. More, it is autobiography unadorned and shameless, autobiography almost unbelievably cruel and betraying, autobiography that is as devoid of artistic sophistication as an operation for gall-stones. This so-called Steele was simply too stupid, too ingenuous, too moral to lie. He was the very reverse of an artist; he was a born and incurable Puritan—and in his alleged novel he drew the most faithful and merciless picture of an American Puritan that has ever got upon paper. There was never the slightest effort at amelioration; he never evaded the ghastly horror of it; he never tried to palm off himself as a good fellow, a hero. Instead, he simply took his stand in the center of the platform, where all the spotlights met, and there calmly stripped off his raiment of reticence—first his long-tailed coat, then his boiled shirt, then his shoes and socks, and finally his very B.V.D.s. The closing scene showed the authentic *Mensch-an-sich*, the eternal blue-nose in the nude, with every wart and pimple glittering and every warped bone and flabby muscle telling its abhorrent tale. There stood the Puritan stripped of every artifice and concealment.

Searching my memory, I can drag up no recollection of another such self-opener of secret chambers and skeletonic closets. Set beside this pious babbler, the late Giovanni Jacopo Casanova de Seingalt shrinks to the puny proportions of a mere barroom boaster, a smoking-car Don Juan, an Eighteenth Century movie actor or whiskey drummer. So, too, Benvenuto Cellini: a fellow vastly entertaining, true enough, but after all, not so much a psychological historian as a liar, a yellow journalist. One always feels, in reading Benvenuto, that the man who is telling the story is quite distinct from the man about whom it is being told. The fellow, indeed, was too noble an artist to do a mere portrait with fidelity; he could not resist the temptation to repair a cauliflower ear here, to paint out a tell-tale scar there, to shine up the eyes a bit, to straighten the legs down below. But this Steele—or whatever his name was—never stepped out of himself. He never described the gaudy one he would *like* to have been, but always the commonplace, the weak, the emotional, the ignorant, the third-rate Christian male he actually was. He deplored himself, he distrusted himself, he plainly wished heartily that he was not himself, but he never made the slightest attempt to disguise and bedizen himself. Such as he was, cheap, mawkish, unaesthetic, conscience-stricken, he depicted himself with fierce and unrelenting honesty.

Superficially, the man that he set before us seemed to be a felonious fellow, for he confessed frankly to a long series of youthful larcenies, to a somewhat banal adventure in forgery (leading to a term in jail), to sundry petty deceits and breaches of trust, and to an almost endless chain of exploits in amour, most of them sordid and unrelieved by anything approaching romance. But the inner truth about him, of course, was that he was really a moralist of the moralists—that his one fundamental and all-embracing virtue was what he himself regarded as his viciousness—that he was never genuinely human and likable save in those moments which led swiftly to his most florid self-accusing. In brief, the history was that of a good young man, the child of God-fearing parents, and its moral, if it had one, was that a strictly moral upbringing injects poisons into the system that even the most steadfast morality cannot resist. One saw an apparently sound and normal youngster converted into a sneak and rogue by the intolerable pressure of his father's abominable Puritanism. And once a rogue, one saw him make himself into a scoundrel by the very force of his horror of his roguery. Every step downward was helped from above. It was not until he resigned himself frankly to the fact of his incurable degradation, and so ceased to struggle against it, that he ever stepped out of it.

The external facts of the chronicle were simple enough. The son of a school-teacher turned petty lawyer and politician, the hero depicts himself as brought up under such barbaric rigors that he has already become a fluent and ingenious liar, in sheer self-protection, at the age of five or six. From lying he proceeds quite naturally to stealing: he lifts a few dollars from a neighbor, and then rifles a tin bank, and then takes to filching all sorts of small articles from the storekeepers of the vicinage. His harsh, stupid, Christian father, getting wind of these peccadilloes, has at him in the manner of a mad bull, beating him, screaming at him, half killing him. The boy, for all the indecent cruelty of it, is convinced of the justice of it. He sees himself as one lost; he accepts the fact that he is a disgrace to his family; in the end, he embraces the parental theory that there is something strange and sinister in his soul, that he couldn't be good if he tried. Finally, filled with some vague notion of taking his abhorrent self out of sight, he runs away from home. Brought back in the character of a felon, he runs away again. Soon he is a felon in fact, and his father allows him to go to prison.

The prison term gives the youngster a chance to think things out for himself, without the constant intrusion of his father's Presbyterian notions of right and wrong. The result is a measurably saner philosophy than that he absorbed at home, but there is still enough left of the old moral obsession to cripple him in all his thinking, and especially in his thinking about himself. His attitude toward women, for example, is constantly conditioned by puritanical misgivings and superstitions. He can never view them innocently, joyously, unmorally, as a young fellow of twenty or twenty-one should, but is always oppressed by Sunday-schoolish notions of his duty to them, and to society in general. On the one hand, he is appalled by his ready yielding to those hussies who have at him unofficially, and on the other hand he is filled with the idea that it would be immoral for him, an ex-convict, to go to the altar with a virgin. The result of these doubts is that he gives a good deal more earnest thought to the woman question than is good for him. The second result is that he proves an easy victim to the discarded mistress of his employer. This worthy working girl craftily snares him and marries him—and then breaks down on their wedding night, unwomaned, so to speak, by the pathetic innocence of the ass, and confesses to a choice roll of her past doings, ending with the news that she is suffering from what crusaders of the day called a social disease.

Naturally enough, the blow almost kills the poor boy—he is still, in fact, scarcely out of his nonage—and the problems that grow out of the confession engage him for the better part of the next two years. Always he approaches them and wrestles with them morally; always his search is for the way that the copy-book maxims approve, not for the way that self-preservation demands. Even when a brilliant chance for revenge presents itself, and he is forced to embrace it by the sheer magnetic pull of it, he does so hesitatingly, doubtingly, ashamedly. His whole attitude to this affair, indeed, is that of an Early Christian Father. He hates himself for gathering buds while he may; he hates the woman with a double hatred for strewing them so temptingly in his path. And in the end, like the moral and upright fellow that he is, he sells out the temptress for cash in hand, and salves his conscience by handing over the money to an orphan asylum!

So in episode after episode. The praying brother of yesterday is the roisterer of today; is the snuffling penitent and pledge-taker of tomorrow. Finally, he is pulled both ways at once and suffers the greatest of all his tortures. Again, of course, a woman is at the center of it. He has no delusions about her virtue—she admits herself, in fact, that it is extinct—but all the same he falls head over heels in love with her, and is filled with an inordinate yearning to marry her and settle down with her. Why not, indeed? She is pretty and a nice girl; she seems to reciprocate his affection; she is naturally eager for the obliterating gold band; she will undoubtedly make him an excellent wife. But he has forgotten his conscience—and it rises up in revenge and floors him. What! Marry a girl with such a Past! Take a fancy woman to his bosom! Jealousy quickly comes to the aid of conscience. Will he be able to forget? Contemplating the damsel in the years to come at breakfast, at dinner, across the domestic hearth, in the cold, blue dawn, will he ever rid his mind of those abhorrent images, those phantasms of men?

Here, at the very end, we come to the most engrossing chapter in this extraordinary book. The duellist of sex, thrust through the gizzard at last, goes off to a lonely hunting camp to wrestle with his intolerable problem. He describes his vacillations faithfully, elaborately, cruelly. On the one side he sets his honest yearning, his desire to have done with light loves, the girl herself. On the other hand he ranges his moral qualms, his sneaking distrusts, the sinister shadows of those nameless ones, his morganatic brothers-in-law. The struggle within his soul is gigantic. He suffers as Prometheus suffered on the rock; his very vitals are devoured; he emerges battered and exhausted. He decides, in the end, that he will marry the girl. She has wasted the shining dowry of her sex; she comes to him spotted and at second-hand; snickers will appear in the polyphony of the wedding music—but he will marry her nevertheless. It will be a marriage unblessed by Holy Writ; it will be a flying in the face of Moses; luck and the archangels will be against it—but he will marry her all the same, Moses or no Moses. And so, with his face made bright by first genuine revolt against the archaic, barbaric morality that has dragged him down, and his heart pulsing to his first display of authentic, unpolluted charity, generosity and nobility, he takes his departure from us.

I daresay any second-hand bookseller will be able to find a copy of the book for you. There is some raciness in the detail of it. Perhaps, despite its public failure, it enjoys a measure of *pizzicato* esteem behind the door. The author, having achieved its colossal self-revelation, became intrigued by the notion that he was a literary man of sorts, and informed me that he was undertaking the story of the girl last-named—the spotted virgin. But he apparently never finished it. Such a writer, once he has told the one big story, is done for.

A Texas Schoolma'am

From the *American Mercury*, June, 1926, pp. 123–25.
A review of MY FIRST THIRTY YEARS,
by Gertrude Beasley; Paris, 1926

This book, I suspect, comes out with a Paris imprint because no American publisher would risk printing it. I offer the very first paragraph as a specimen of its manner:

Thirty years ago I lay in the womb of a woman, conceived in an act of rape, being carried through the pre-natal period by an unwilling and rebellious mother, finally bursting forth only to be tormented in a family whose members I despised or pitied, and brought into association with people whom I should never have chosen. Sometimes I wish that, as I lay in the womb, a pink soft embryo, I had somehow thought, breathed or moved and wrought destruction to the woman who bore me, and her eight miserable children who preceded me, and the four round-faced mediocrities who came after me, and her husband, a monstrously cruel, Christ-like, and handsome man with an animal's appetite for begetting children.

This is free speaking, surely, but only a Comstock, reading it, would mistake it for an attempt at pornography. There is, in fact, not the slightest sign of conscious naughtiness in the book; it is the profoundly serious and even indignant story of a none too intelligent woman, lifted out of the lowest levels of the Caucasian race by her own desperate efforts, and now moved to ease her fatigue by telling how she did it. She is far too earnest to sophisticate her narrative; there is absolutely nothing in it that suggests the artful grimacing of the other Americanos printed by the philanthropic Three Mountains Press. When, looking back over her harsh and feverish life, she recalls an episode in the mire, she describes it simply and baldly, and in the words that clothed it in her own mind when she lived through it. Some of these words are ancient monosyllables, and very shocking. But they somehow belong in the story. If they were taken out, it would become, to that extent, unreal. As it is, it is as overwhelmingly real as a tax-bill.

La Beasley, it appears, came into the world on the Texas steppes, the ninth child of migratory and low-down parents. Her father was an unsuccessful farmer who practised blacksmithing on the side. During her first half dozen years the family moved three or four times. Always prosperity was beckoning in the next township, the next county. Children were born at every stop, and as the household increased it gradually disintegrated. Finally, the mother heaved the father out, took her brood to Abilene, and there set up a boarding-house. The sons quickly drifted away; one of the daughters became a lady of joy; the others struggled pathetically with piddling jobs. Gertrude was the flower of the flock. She worked her way through a preposterous "Christian college," got a third-rate teacher's certificate, and took a rural school. The country parents liked her; she kept their barbarous progeny in order, often by beating them. After a while she took other examinations, and was transferred to better schools. In the end, she went to Chicago, and there tackled pedagogy on a still higher level. For all I know, she may be teaching in that great city yet. She closes her record arbitrarily at the end of her thirtieth year. We see her, with money saved, setting off for Japan. Her mother has prospered and is fat and happy. Her excommunicated father is dead. Her brothers and sisters are scattered all over the Southwest.

The book is full of sharp and tremendously effective character sketches, and the best of them all is that of Ma Beasley. How many of our novelists could beat it? I think of Dreiser and Anderson, and no other. The old woman is done unsparingly and almost appallingly. We are made privy to her profound and bellicose ignorance, her incurable frowsiness, her banal pride in her obscure and ignoble family, her relatives, her lascivious delight in witless and malicious scandal-mongering. But there is something heroic in her, too. Her struggle to cadge a living for her squirming litter takes on a quality that is almost dignity. She is shrewd, unscrupulous, full of oblique resource. Her battles with her husband, and particularly with him in his capacity of chronic father, often have gaudy drama in them. Consider her final and only effective device for birth control: a loaded shot-gun beside her bed! One longs to meet the old gal, and shake her red hand. She is obscene, but she is also curiously admirable.

The book is a social document of the utmost interest. It presents the first genuinely realistic picture of the Southern poor white trash ever heard of. The author has emancipated herself from her native wallow, but she does not view it with superior sniffs. Instead, she frankly takes us back to it, and tells us all she knows about its fauna, simply and honestly. There is frequent indignation in her chronicle, but never any derision. Her story interests her immensely, and she is obviously convinced that it should be interesting to others. I think she is right.

For Rotary and God

From the *American Mercury*, Dec., 1930, pp. 509–10.
A review of A BIOGRAPHY OF EVERETT WENTWORTH HILL,
by Rex Harlow; Oklahoma City, 1930

One thinks of Oklahoma as a wilderness swarming with oil men daffy on golf, gin and women, but in truth it has begun to hatch idealists, and even to nourish a literature. Of the latter the author of the present work is a talented ornament, and of the former its subject is a shining star. When I say that Mr. Hill has been president of Rotary International I have said enough to indicate his measure. It is an honor that could go only to a great dreamer— one inflamed and even tortured by a vision of human perfection, with peace reigning in the world, every radical behind the bars, and the Boy Scouts as ecumenical as the Universal Church—, but he must be a dreamer with a gift, also, for practical affairs. Mr. Hill is precisely such a man. He is, on the one hand, the Ice King of Oklahoma, with vast and growing interests, not only in a great chain of colytic ice-plants but also in a multitude of other humane industries, and he is, on the other hand, an impassioned and relentless laborer, in season and out of season, for the good of his fellow-men. It is instructive to read about such a character, for in his career there is inspiration for all of us.

The rising town of Russell, Kansas, nurtured him, and he came into the world on "a cold, bleak day" in 1884. His father, John Harris Hill, affectionately known as Harry, was a man of substance, and what is more, a man of exemplary habits.

> Observing that both his father and mother were always careful of their persons, dress and home, [Everett] too learned to keep his clothes clean, his teeth brushed and his hair combed. . . . Following their example in financial matters as well, he saved his pennies, nickels and dimes, and the broad sweep of the rapidly increasing acres he saw his father acquire developed in him, small though he was, an intense desire to become a landowner himself.

The chance came soon enough: as a boy still in knee-pants he bought a farm, and by the time he got to high-school he was already on his way to fortune. His career there was a brilliant one, and among other things he learned the subtle art of resisting temptation. Says Mr. Harlow:

> He and a classmate, a girl whom he admired very much, became engaged in a heated contest for first honors of their class. Toward the close of the term the girl, counting on his generosity and chivalry, came to him and frankly asked that

he let down enough in his work that she could win. A scholarship in some college or university went as a prize to the winner, and as she was a poor girl winning meant that she could get a chance to attend college, while loss would ring a death-knell to her hope for a higher education. "Everett, it means everything to me to win—an education, a broader life, greater happiness," she pleaded. "To you it means only the pleasure of being first in your class. You can go to college whether you win or lose. Please help me by letting me win."

St. Anthony himself never faced a more dreadful temptation. Here was a chance to reach, at one stroke, a dizzy and singular eminence: in brief, to go down into the history of mankind as the first (and perhaps only) gentleman ever born on Kansan soil. But young Everett's irresolution was only momentary. Almost at once his baser nature yielded to his higher. "There were certain principles that he must uphold in his life, regardless of how they affected other people." So he stepped on the gas of his intellect and got the prize, and the wicked temptress thereupon disappears from the chronicle.

His career at the Cascadilla prep-school at Ithaca need not detain us, nor his brilliant years at the Wharton School of Finance and Commerce in Philadelphia. He is, to date, its most distinguished graduate, but his distinction does not rest upon his feats as an undergraduate, but upon his services to humanity in later years. From Wharton he proceeded to the post-graduate seminary of the Standard Oil Company, and was presently performing prodigies of salesmanship in Georgia, but his heart was in the Middle West, and after looking about a bit he decided to settle in Oklahoma and grow up with the country. How, with two young confederates, W. T. Leahy and John Bowman, he established the Western Ice and Cold Storage Company at Shawnee; how he met and conquered the wicked R. L. Witherspoon, manager of an ice-plant belonging to the Anheuser-Busch Brewery in the same town; how Leahy and Bowman gradually faded from the picture, and Hill reigned alone; and how, from Shawnee, he extended his operations from town to town, until now he is the undisputed Ice King of that whole rich empire—for this thrilling story you must turn to

Mr. Harlow's narrative. There, too, you will find the romantic story of his three marriages — one of which came to such wreck that "the newspapers of the world carried streamer headlines" about it, and he himself was impelled to "cancel all speaking engagements" and forced to "call upon all the philosophy at his command to keep from sinking into cynicism and losing faith in friendship." And there, finally, you will find a detailed account of his services to Rotary, and hence to the Republic, to humanity, and to God.

The book has savor. It is a pity that there are not more like it. We have too many biographies of politicians and literati, and too few of really great men.

Flamingo in Blue Stockings

From the *Smart Set*, Dec., 1920, pp. 142–44.
A review of MARGARET FULLER,
by Katharine Anthony; New York, 1920

Here, for the first time, is an attempt at a comprehensive and intelligent study of one of the strangest fish that ever disported in our pond of letters. The more one thinks of Margaret, indeed, the more fabulous she seems. On the one hand a bluestocking of the bluestockings, she was on the other hand a sombre and melodramatic adventuress, full of dark conspiracies and illicit longings. Imagine Agnes Repplier and the Theda Bara of the films rolled into one, with overtones of Margot Asquith and Mrs. Carrie Chapman Catt, and you have a rough image of her. Such diverse men as Hawthorne, Emerson, Horace Greeley, Channing, Carlyle and Mazzini were all more or less mashed on her, and mistook the fluttering of their hearts for intellectual homage. Tall, imperious, romantic, over-sexed, she queened it over the literati of two continents for twenty years, but it was not until she was nearly forty that she managed to bag a concrete husband, and even then she had to be satisfied with an out-at-elbows Italian nobleman, little more than half her age. This scarecrow enjoyed the curious honor of being seduced by the woman who had palsied Hawthorne by the mere flash of her eye. He reciprocated by marrying her, thus making her a *marquesa* and her imminent offspring legitimate. A few years later they died together in a shipwreck within a few miles of New York. Margaret had a chance to save herself, but preferred to die. The Dorcas Clubs were all busy with the scandal; she knew what was ahead of her in the land of the free. Thus she passed from the scene like Conrad's Lord Jim, "inscrutable at heart, unforgiven, and excessively romantic."

Emerson undertook a biography of her, aided by Channing and James Freeman Clarke, and Mazzini and Robert Browning promised to contribute to it, but never actually did so. There are other studies by Thomas Wentworth Higginson, Julia Ward Howe and Andrew Macphail, all bad. Miss Anthony undertakes to clear away the accumulated rubbish of speculation, and to get at the probable facts about this most mysterious of learned ladies. What she finds, as might be expected, is an elaborate outfit of Freudian suppressions. Margaret's history, in brief, was the history of a war between vigorous passions and equally vigorous Puritan inhibitions. Starting out, like every other sentimental girl, with an exaggerated affection for her own father, she went down the years craving love and romance, and never, until she nabbed the poor wop, gaining either. Men were flustered by her, but two things always scared them off: one being her amazing homeliness and the other her great reputation for learning. They admired this learning, but it made them wary. Thus Margaret was forced to work off her emotions in literature, politics and other such great affairs. It was not until she found the young Italian, a man too ignorant to know that she was learned, that she had her woman's chance. She seized it so eagerly that all of her New England prejudices vanished instanter, and with them her common sense. It was a ridiculous affair, but also somehow pathetic. Marrying Ossoli was an imbecility almost indistinguishable from that of marrying a chauffeur. He was a handsome fellow and of noble blood, and he apparently admired his wife vastly, but it is safe to guess that he bored her dreadfully; and that she saw disaster ahead and more fuel for the gossips. Margaret was wise to die at forty. At fifty she would have been a wreck.

Miss Anthony's book is well planned and entertainingly written. When her story is done she shuts down; there is none of the empty word-spinning so common in literary biography. It would be interesting to see her tackle Poe and Hawthorne in the same way—two very mysterious fellows, hitherto left as dim by their biographers as Lincoln has been by his. She evades, however, the chief problem: how did so gaudy a flamingo come to be hatched in drab New England? The Fullers seem to have been Puritans of the utmost respectability, over-educated and wholly lacking in imagination. Perhaps there was a concealed scandal in an earlier generation. A thin vein of scarlet runs down many an American family tree. . . .

Another defect: I think she over-estimates Margaret's stature as a writer. The fact is that the men who chiefly admired her were unconscious predecessors of Ossoli—preliminary studies for her shocking masterpiece. Bemused by the woman, they thought that they were intrigued by the sage. Her books are very dull stuff, indeed. She wrote, to the end, like a talented high-school girl. Poe himself was never more highfalutin. The fact that she recognized the genius of Goethe and the shallowness of Longfellow is surely no proof of genius. Would one call a man a competent critic of music on the simple ground that he venerated Bach and sniffed at Massenet?

The Incomparable Bok

From the *Smart Set*, Jan., 1921, pp. 140–42.
A review of THE AMERICANIZATION OF EDWARD BOK,
by Edward Bok; New York, 1920

Dr. Henrik Willem van Loon, in his acute and entertaining history, "The Fall of the Dutch Republic," more than once describes (sometimes, alas, with a scarcely concealed sniff) the salient trait of his fellow Netherlanders. It is an abnormal capacity for respecting respectability. Their ideal, it appears, is not the dashing military gent, gallantly leaping for glory down red-hot lanes of fire, nor is it the lofty and ineffable artist, drunk with beauty. No, the man they most admire is the virtuous citizen and householder, sound in politics and theology, happily devoid of all orgiastic tendencies, and with money in the bank. In other words, the ideal of Holland is the ideal of Kansas, as set forth with great ingenuousness by E. W. Howe. One thinks of that identity on reading "The Americanization of Edward Bok," an autobiographical monograph by the late editor of the *Ladies' Home Journal*. Edward was born in Holland and his parents did not bring him to America until he was already in breeches, but he had not been here a year before he was an absolutely typical American boy of the '70s. Nay, he was more: he was the typical American boy of the Sunday-school books of the '70s. By day he labored with inconceivable diligence at ten or twenty diverse jobs. By night he cultivated the acquaintance of all the moral magnificoes of the time, from Ralph Waldo Emerson to Henry Ward Beecher, laboring with what remained of his steam to penetrate to the secret of their high and singular excellence, that he, too, might some day shine as they shined, and be pointed out to good little boys on their way to the catechetical class and to bad little boys on their way to the gallows. Well, he got both wishes. At thirty he was sound in theology and politics, happily free from all orgiastic tendencies, and with money in the bank. At forty he was a millionaire and the foremost American soothsayer. At fifty he was a national institute.

It was anything but a dull boyhood, but I doubt that it was a very merry one. Bok was not only sorely beset by economic necessity; he was also held to a harsh and relentless industry by his peculiar enthusiasms. Now and then, of course, a bit of romance wormed into it; particularly toward the end of it. Once, for example, he got some hot tips from Jay Gould, and he and his Sunday-school teacher at Plymouth Church, a stock-broker outside the sacred house (this, to me, is a lovely touch) played them in Wall Street, and made a good deal of money. But soon his conscience revolted against the character of Gould, who was certainly very far from the Christian usurer standard accepted at Plymouth, and so he gave up the chance of tips in order to stay its gnawings. No other strayings are recounted. It is not recorded that young Edward ever played hookey, or that he ever tied a tin can to the tail of a cat, or that he ever blew a spitball at his school-teacher or at Henry Ward Beecher. Above all, there is no mention of a calf love. Deponent saith, in fact, that when he took charge of the *Ladies' Home Journal*, at twenty-six, he was almost absolutely innocent of the ways and means of the fair. He had, it appeared, never hugged a sweet creature behind the door, or kissed her neck in the privacy of an 1889 four-wheeler. He did not know that the girls like to be kissed on the eyes better than they liked to be kissed on the nose; he was unaware of their curious theory, after two cocktails, that every man who speaks to them politely is making love to them; he was densely innocent of the most elemental secrets of their *toilette*. This sublime ignoramus now undertook to be father confessor to all the women of America. More, he made a gigantic success of the business. Why? How? He himself offers no answer, and I am far too diffident to attempt one. Maybe his very normality was what fetched them—his startling resemblance, as of a huge portrait in exaggerated colors, to their fathers, their brothers, their husbands, their pastors, their family doctors. His point of view was the standard point of view of the respectable American man. When he shocked them, it was pleasantly and harmlessly, in the immemorial fashion of the clumsy male. He never violated their fundamental pruderies. He never really surprised them.

Nevertheless, this plu-normal Mr. Bok failed in his supreme enterprise; he never became quite a 100% American, and in his book he plainly says so. The trouble was that he could never wholly cure himself of being a European. Even a Hollander, though nearer the American than any other, is still a European. In Bok's case the taint showed itself in an irrepressible interest in things that had no place in the mind of a truly respectable man— chiefly in things artistic. When he looked at the houses in which his subscribers lived, their drab hideousness made him sick. When he went inside and contemplated the lambrequins, the gilded cattails, the Rogers groups, the wax fruit under glass domes, the emblazoned seashells from Asbury Park, the family Bible on the marble-topped center-table, the crayon enlargement of Uncle Richard and Aunt Sue, the square pianos, the Brussels carpets, the grained woodwork—when his eyes alighted upon such things, his soul revolted, and at once his moral enthusiasm incited him to attempt a reform. The result was the long series of *Ladies' Home Journal* crusades against the hideousness of the national scene—in domestic architecture, in house furnishing, in dress, in town buildings, in advertising. Bok flung himself headlong into his campaigns, and practically every one of them succeeded. He was opposed furiously by all right-thinking American men, even by such extraordinary men as the late Stanford White. Nevertheless, he fought on, and in the long run he drew blood. He is almost alone responsible for the improvement in taste that has shown it-self in America during the past thirty years. No other man or woman deserves a tenth of the credit that should go to him. He carried on his fight with the utmost diligence and intelligence, wearing down all opposition, proceeding triumphantly from suc-cess to success. If there were gratitude in the land, there would be a monument to him in every town in the Republic. He has been, aesthetically, probably the most useful citizen that ever breathed its muggy air.

But here I come upon an inconvenient moral, to the effect, to wit, that his chief human value lay in his failure to become wholly Americanized, that he was a man of mark in direct proportion as he was not a 100% American. This moral I refrain from plainly stating on patriotic grounds. . . .

Dr. Townsend and His Plan

From the Baltimore *Sun*, July 2, 1939

Dr. Francis E. Townsend, the originator, organizer and sole pro-prietor of the $200-a-month old-age pension movement bearing his name, was 72 years old last January 13. Few men in American his-tory, or indeed in any history, have leaped from obscurity to celeb-rity so late in life. Up to the time he was seized by the one and only idea to his credit on the scrolls of time, and the bush burst into flame under his nose, he was a family doctor in a poor way of practice, and his fame, such as it was, was circumferenced by a few streets. For more than thirty years he had been looking at the tongues of what he himself describes as "the indigent"—first in the little town of Belle Fourche, S.D. (population, 2,000), and then in Long Beach, the waterfront annex of Los Angeles.

How he hit upon the notion that made him known from coast to coast, and got him a following of a million or more cocksure and howling disciples, with another million or two hanging about the side-lines and brought him to such puissance that more than 100 head of Congressmen, Democrats and Republicans alike, now take his orders and eat from his hand—how this miracle was set in train will probably never be known. The doctor himself says that he was inspired by seeing a couple of poor people, in the depths of the depression, searching garbage cans for scraps of food, but that, of course, is only half the story, and not the more important half. Many other persons of tender heart had been shocked by the same spectacle, and not a few of them had resolved mightily that something had to be done about it. But. Dr. Townsend was the only one who hatched a simple, completely preposterous and hence irresistibly convincing scheme. It had three parts, all of them easily comprehensible to the meanest understanding. The first consists in paying every American more than 60 years old a pension of $200 cash a month. The second consisted in requiring every recipient to spend every cent of it before the month's end. And the third consisted in raising the money by laying a sales tax of two per cent. upon each and every transaction involving the exchange of money, of whatever shape or sort.

That all this was original with the doctor is, of course, hard to believe. Parts of it, in fact, had been adumbrated by other wizards, and long before the depression. But the chances are at least even that he had never heard of these other wizards, even at second hand, and the fact remains indisputable that he was the first to put the various elements together, and the first to sign on customers for the whole. He began in a small way in the purlieus of Los Angeles, but in a strangely little while he was roving all of California, and before a year had come and gone his anything but clarion voice was being heard as far east as Ohio, as far south as Florida, and as far north as Maine.

At the start, obviously, he had the advantages of a singularly favorable terrain. In Southern California the density of people thirsting for novel and unprecedented gospels is greater than anywhere else on earth. All the messiahs of new religions, new diets, new schemes of healing, new economic theories, new systems of logic, new values for *pi* and new technics in amour gravitate thither as surely as pickpockets gravitate toward a Shriners' Convention. It is the chosen seat of hundreds of advanced thinkers of the highest eminence, ranging from Aimée Semple McPherson to Upton Sinclair. It is the Holy Land alike of the Rosicrucians and the mental telepathists, the yogis and the New Thoughters, the vegetarians and the anti-vivisectionists. One of the largest hospitals in Los Angeles is operated by the osteopaths, and the Christian Scientists have a voice in all matters of public health. Thus the soil was ready for Dr. Townsend's evangel—but so was it ready for the tilling of the thousand and one other messiahs who worked it when he did. Why did he succeed so much better than any of the others? Why did he bulge out of Southern California so quickly, and begin to roll up converts in all parts of the United States? Why was he riding herd on Congressmen and United States Senators at a stage when all his rivals were still cadging nickels in Los Angeles gospel-tents and public parks?

The answer, it seems to me, must be divided into two parts. The first is that his scheme, from the standpoint of the customers, was enormously simpler, cheaper and juicier than what any of the other messiahs had to offer. He did not promise the underprivileged a vague Utopia in some indefinite future on this earth or another; he promised them the exact sum of $200 a month, here and now. And he didn't demand that they build a vast and expensive tabernacle or elect him to some high and glittering public office, or buy unintelligible text-books of his new arcanum, or clownish uniforms or even badges; he told them he wanted nothing for himself, and convinced them that he meant it, and the most he ever asked them to chip in for expenses was 25 cents a year.

That was half of his advantage over his rivals. He offered poor and hopeless people quick and cheap relief, and he offered it to them in amounts that, to them, seemed almost unlimited. How many of them, in the days of their youth, had ever earned so much as $200 a month? Probably not two per cent. But now all of them were to get it regularly—and not only get it, but be free (and even obliged) to spend every cent of it. No wonder they rushed up to sign their names. Here at last, so to speak, was Utopia with teeth in it. Here was salvation in hard coin, payable on the nail. No more painful figuring! No more longing and waiting! No more ifs or buts! The thing was magnificently specific, detailed, concrete, categorical.

The other half of the doctor's advantage lay in his transparent honesty. The poor fish had been listening for years to evangelists of a wholly different sort. All the theologians they patronized were made up like chorus girls in a Biblical play, all the medical revolutionaries were duplicates of the corn doctors they had encountered at county fairs, and all the politicians were patently porch climbers. But here was an elderly man who looked and talked like themselves—a soft-spoken and decent-appearing fellow in a neat gray suit, who expounded his gospel without heat and yet without the faintest shadow of a doubt—a man so earnest, so calm and confident, so lacking in all the familiar hocus-pocus, so curiously and astoundingly respectable that they fell for him as easily as a delirium tremens patient falls for a kindly nurse who sponges his red-hot head and sneaks him a jug.

Does Dr. Townsend, after five or six years of heavy campaigning, still believe in the Townsend Plan? I am convinced that he does. He is no longer, to be sure, the innocent that he must have been when he began. Hard experience with chiselers and worse has revealed to him the dangers of too much trustfulness. He has ceased to be willing, as he once was, to listen to racketeers with oily tongues, full of intelligent self-interest. His subordinates today are all subordinates, and not partners. He keeps a tight rein upon them and punishes contumacy without mercy. But he still believes.

Two lessons that he has learned serve to keep his movement alive today, and will probably keep it alive for a good while to come, despite the rise of formidable imitators and competitors, and a series of crushing legislative reverses. The first is that his followers are *his* followers, and no other's. When they meet in convention they never debate anything; they simply wait for him to make his will known, and then sustain it unanimously. Let him give the word and they are for it; let him shake his head and they are agin it. The other thing he has learned is the danger of compromise. Three years ago he nearly came to grief by an imprudent alliance with Father Coughlin, William Leimke, and a large assortment of other such sorcerers; today he will have nothing to do with any of them. It is not sufficient that a Congressman in his pen holler vaguely for old-age pensions; he must holler specifically for the Townsend Plan, and for nothing else. John L. Lewis, it is announced, is planning to collar him by offering to support him; it will be as easy as collaring Tom Girdler, and no easier.

How long will he last? I refuse to guess. In the long run, the plain people always turn upon and butcher their messiahs. But of one thing I am certain: that the Townsend movement is not dead yet, nor even seriously sick. The old folks still hope, trust and believe.

One Who Will Be Missed

From the *American Mercury*, Sept., 1931, pp. 35–36

As soon as Congress reassembles a gang of shabby politicians will arise upon their hind legs in the hall of the House and heap encomiums upon the late Nicholas Longworth, LL.D. Not one of them, I suppose, will think to mention that his chief distinction among American statesmen lay in this: that he regarded nearly all men of their order as rogues and asses, and dealt with them habitually as such.

Here, of course, I do not accuse the deceased of entertaining moral ideas: they were, indeed, completely foreign to his nature. To understand him one must always remember that a rogue, to him, was not a sinner to be scorned but a clown to be enjoyed, and that above all other varieties of clowns he loved and cherished the ass political. In Washington, given such tastes, he was in Paradise, and so he stayed there as much as he could. From his pulpit in the House he could look up at any moment and see a dozen of the most talented mountebanks in Christendom. Moreover, his official powers were such that he could set them to performing whenever he chose, and in a curious and stupendous manner. No wonder he stuck to politics. It gave him, I believe, one of the pleasantest lives ever led by mortal man. Existence, to him, was an endless and ever charming circus, with clowns five deep in the ring. Nor was he above slipping on a piebald nightshirt on occasion, and reddening his nose, and grabbing a slapstick, and leaping into the ring to do some amiable clowning himself.

When he died (alas, before his time) some of the Washington

correspondents hinted delicately that his cynicism was a blot upon his patriotism, and ill became a Speaker of the House. What nonsense! It was precisely his cynicism that *made* him Speaker of the House, and it was the same that made him a good one—the best, perhaps, since Tom Reed. He was always clearly superior to the quacks he enjoyed so vastly, and knew so well how to lead, and they were all well aware of it. There was nothing mysterious about his influence over them, and, above all, there was nothing ignominious. He was anything but a back-slapper. What they sensed in him was simply a kind of intellectual security that they themselves longed for but could never attain—the easy and safe confidence of a man who has sized up his world with great accuracy and knows his way about in it. They called him Nick, and cherished the privilege with naïve exultation, but in their secret hearts, I am convinced, they always thought of him as Mr. Longworth. He was not as they were, and they knew it.

So far as I have heard, there is no Longworth Act in the lawbooks; the hon. gentleman, in fact, was against most of the more salient laws of his country, and violated some of them without apology. That attitude, I believe, was not the least of his contributions to current statecraft. He knew that the American belief in laws was a superstition too profound to be dissipated, and so he went along with it when he had to, but there is no record that he ever sought to reënforce it. Plainly enough, he'd have been happy if he could have blown it up altogether. But that was impossible, and so he contented himself with keeping its operations within bounds. That is to say, he hampered and crippled the mountebanks in front of him as much as he could, all the while taking his delight in their gyrations. The ideal House of his dreams was one in which a few realistic men made a few inescapable laws, and the rest of the brethren gave a bawdy and harmless show. That ideal was never realized, but I think it came nearer realization than most. The Longworth House, at its worst, was at least innocent of the grosser sort of false pretenses. In the hands of its realistic Speaker it came to be presented to the country as precisely what it was: a conglomeration of puerile political hacks, most of them asses and many of them rogues. Even the Washington correspondents, perhaps the most romantic men on earth, ceased to be fooled by it. Turning from it in horror they sought their world-savers in the Senate.

It seems to me that this achievement was a public service of a high order, though it will get no notice in the history books. If we had a dozen Longworths in Washington we'd have a far more sensible grappling with the difficulties which now beset the country. If there were two or three in the Cabinet, to police the Doaks, Hydes, Andy Mellons and other such zanies, even the Hoover administration would take on a certain intellectual dignity, not to say integrity. It is silly to call the Longworth attitude cynicism, and to assume that giving it that evil name has disposed of it. There was a great deal more to it than mere shirking. It did not seek to evade the facts; it sought, rather, to expose them and make them plain. It was the philosophy of a man who revolted instinctively against the blather that is wisdom to ordinary politicians. He knew, on occasion, how to use that blather too, but not even his worst enemy—if he left an enemy—will argue that he ever believed in it. His point of view, first and last, was that of a thoroughly civilized man. His values, whether at work or at play, were at once more subtle and more solid than those of the general, whether in or out of office. He was one of the few men of any genuine culture to succeed in politics in our time. He will be missed.

The End of a Happy Life

From the Baltimore *Evening Sun*, Nov. 21, 1932

The late Albert Hildebrandt, who died last Thursday, had barely turned sixty, but he really belonged to an elder Baltimore, and it was far more charming than the Rotarian Gehenna we endure today. He was one of its genuine notables, though he got into the newspapers very seldom. What kept him out was mainly his own surpassing amiability: he was completely innocent of that yearning to harass the neighbors which commonly passes among us as public spirit. If he ever made a speech it must have been before I met him, which was more than thirty years ago. When the Babbitts of the town held a banquet and afflicted one another sadly he stayed at home, playing the violoncello, or went to a beerhouse for a decent evening with his friends. When a public committee was appointed to improve mankind and solve the insoluble he was not on it.

Nevertheless, there were few Baltimoreans of his time who were better worth knowing, for he stood in the first rank of a very difficult profession, he practised it all his life with unfailing devotion and complete honesty, and that practise not only engrossed him but also pleasantly entertained him, and made him content. He enjoyed violins as other men enjoyed pictures or books. When he encountered a good one he would strip off his coat and have at it with the enthusiasm of a Schliemann unearthing a new Troy, and when a bad one came into his hands he would demolish its pretensions with a gusto but little less. If his judgment was ever questioned, it was not by sensible men. He was so obviously the master of his subject that, once he had exposed his views and offered his reasons, there was no answer short of complaining to the police. There were chances in his business for considerable killings, but he seldom took advantage of them. His attitude toward the violins that passed through his hands was commonly far more sentimental than commercial, and he spent a lot of time and energy upon labors that brought him little profit, and sometimes not even thanks. It always seemed to me that a sort of professional delicacy stayed him—that he was too sensitive about the honor of his distinguished house, and had too much respect for violins themselves, to traffic in them too brutally. When the impulse to pile up money came upon him he always turned to some other enterprise, usually highly speculative. That other enterprise was never a shining success, but while it lasted it at least gave him the feeling that, within the bounds of his vocation, he could remain the free artist, and suffer no compulsion to approach the unseemly, which was to him the impossible.

His instrument, as I have said, was the cello, which he mastered in early youth, and stuck to faithfully all his life. Violins were always in his hands, but he never ventured to play them, and in fact had no talent for the business. But as a cellist he had great skill, and in the Baltimore of his day there was no amateur to match him. He was a big fellow, tall, muscular, handsome and imposing, and he had a tone to go with his size. When he would get a good grip upon his bow and fall upon a passage to his taste the sounds that came out of his cello were like an army with banners. Moreover, they were always the precise sounds in the score, for he had a fine ear and he played in tune all the way up the scale, even to the treacherous peaks of the A string.

He remained strictly an amateur to the end. He was often besought to play professionally, but he always refused. Years ago he was a member of the Haydn and Garland Orchestras and other such amateur organizations, and often appeared in public, sometimes as a soloist, but as he grew older he withdrew from this activity, and confined himself to playing with his family and his friends. So long as St. Mary's Seminary was in operation in Paca street, he played there at the midnight mass every Christmas Eve. He was completely empty of piety, but he got on very well with the clergy, and one of his close friends was the late Dr. Theodore C. Foote, of St. David's, Roland Park, another amateur cellist. More than once I have done accompaniments to their duets, with each exhorting the other to lay on, and the evening ending with the whole band exhausted.

On the secular side he had got through almost everything written for the cello. For twenty-five years he went to the late Frederick H. Gottlieb's house every Sunday night to engage in chamber music, and for even longer he played with the Saturday Night Club, of which he was a charter member. Nor was this all, for he put in many evenings playing with his wife, his daughter and his sister-in-law, and in his earlier days there were weeks when he made music every night. He was always ready to drop everything for a session with his cello. Once, years ago, I happened into his place one afternoon when a German exchange student was calling on him. The German allowed that he was a fiddler, and Al suggested a couple of trios. We played from 4 to 6:30, went out to dinner, returned at 7:30, and kept on until 11. Another time he was a party to a desperate scheme to play the first eight Beethoven symphonies *seriatim*. We began late one afternoon, and figured that, allowing for three suppers, one breakfast, one lunch, and five pauses for wind and beer, the job would take 24 hours. But we blew up before we got to the end of the Eroica.

The headline that I have put on these lines indicates that this was a happy man. I believe that, in all my days, I have never known a happier. There were some people he disliked, and in discussing them he was capable of a blistering invective, but on the whole he was too good-humored to have enemies, and he got on well even with musicians, who are sometimes very difficult. He was a bachelor for many years, but was always quartered with friends, and so had a comfortable home. He made a good living, spent his money freely, had a civilized taste for sound eating and drinking, and never tired of music for an instant. When he married, relatively late in life, his luck remained with him, and he was presently the center of a charming family circle, with a little daughter whose precocious talent gave him great delight. He had a long and trying illness, but he was nursed with singular devotion and his doctor was an old and valued friend—and, I hope I need not add, a fiddler too. He faced death calmly, and slipped into oblivion at last with simple courage and no foolish regrets.

Such a man, it seems to me, comes very close to the Aristotelian ideal of the good citizen and the high-minded man. There was no pretension in him, but his merits were solid and enduring. He possessed a kind of knowledge that was not common, and it was very useful. He treated his clients with great scrupulosity, and his professional reputation, unchallenged for many years, went far beyond the bounds of Baltimore. He was so unfailingly kindly, so thoroughly square and decent, so completely lovable that the whole world that he knew was filled with his friends. Most of his leisure, in his later days, was spent with men he had played with, musically and otherwise, for twenty, thirty and even forty years. The old-timers all stuck to him, and there were always youngsters coming in, to learn him and to love him. Save when illness made a prisoner of him he saw them constantly, and even as he lay dying he knew that he was in their daily thoughts, and would never pass out of their memories.

They drop off one by one—Sam Hamburger, Phil Green, John Wade, Carl Schon, Henry Flood, Fred Colston, Charlie Bochau, and now Al Hildebrandt. These were pleasant fellows, one and all. The common bond between them was their love of music, and I suppose there is no better to be found. Certainly there can be none that makes life more genuinely cheerful and contented. Most of the men I have named were amateurs, and some were only listeners, but they had in common that amiable weakness for the squeaks of the fiddle and the burbles of the flute, and it kept them together for long years. They clustered around Al Hildebrandt. He was, in his way, the best friend of every one of them, and he remains the best friend of many who still live.

Mourning him would be rather silly. He died too soon, but so do we all. The universe is run idiotically, and its only certain product is sorrow. But there are yet men who, by their generally pleasant spirits, by their intense and enlightened interest in what they have to do, by their simple dignity and decency, by their extraordinary capacity for making and keeping friends, yet manage to cheat, in some measure, the common destiny of mankind, doomed like the beasts to perish. Such a man was Albert Hildebrandt. It was a great privilege to be among his intimates; he radiated a sound and stimulating philosophy, and it was contagious. In all my days I have known no other who might have taken to himself with more reason the words of the ancient poet: "The lines are fallen unto me in pleasant places; yea, I have a goodly heritage."

XXVII. IRONIES

Wild Shots

From Damn! A Book of Calumny, 1918, pp. 71–72.
First printed in the Smart Set, Jan., 1917, pp. 271–72

If I had the time, and there were no sweeter follies offering, I should like to write an essay on the books that have quite failed of achieving their original purposes, and are yet of respectable use and potency for other purposes. For example, the Book of Revelation. The obvious aim of the learned author of this work was to bring the early Christians into accord by telling them authoritatively what to expect and hope for; its actual effect during nineteen hundred years has been to split them into a multitude of camps, and so set them to denouncing, damning, jailing and murdering one another. Again, consider the autobiography of Benvenuto Cellini. Ben wrote it to prove that he was an honest man, a mirror of all the virtues, an injured innocent; the world, reading it, hails him respectfully as the noblest, the boldest, the gaudiest liar that ever lived. Again, turn to "Gulliver's Travels." The thing was planned by its rev. author as a devastating satire, a terrible piece of cynicism; it survives as a story-book for sucklings. Yet again, there is "Hamlet." Shakespeare wrote it frankly to make money for a theatrical manager; it has lost money for theatrical managers ever since. Yet again, there is Caesar's "De Bello Gallico." Julius composed it to thrill and arouse the Romans; its sole use today is to stupefy and sicken schoolboys. The list might be lengthened almost *ad infinitum*. When a man writes a book he fires a machine-gun into a wood. The game he brings down often astonishes him, and sometimes horrifies him. Consider the case of Ibsen. . . . After my book on Nietzsche I was actually invited to lecture at Princeton.

Between the Lines

From PREJUDICES: FOURTH SERIES, 1924, pp. 106–07

The world has very little sense of humor. It is always wagging its ears solemnly over elaborate jocosities. For 600 years it has gurgled over the "Divine Comedy" of Dante, despite the plain fact that the work is a flaming satire upon the whole Christian hocus-pocus of Heaven, Purgatory and Hell. To have tackled such nonsense head-on, in Dante's time, would have been to flout the hangman; hence the poet clothed his attack in an irony so delicate that the ecclesiastical police were baffled. Why is the poem called a comedy? I have read at least a dozen discussions of the question by modern pedants, all of them labored and unconvincing. The same problem obviously engaged the scholars of the poet's own time. He called the thing simply "comedy"; they added the adjective "divine" in order to ameliorate what seemed to them to be an intolerable ribaldry. Well, here is a "comedy" in which human beings are torn limb from limb, boiled in sulphur, cut up with red-hot knives, and filled with molten lead. Can one imagine a man capable of such a magnificent poem regarding such fiendish imbecilities seriously? Certainly not. They appeared just as idiotic to him as they appear to you or me.

The Fat Man

From the Baltimore Evening Sun, Feb. 11, 1910

Many vain tears are wasted upon the fat man. He is supposed to suffer from an appalling shortness of breath, and his florid complexion is ascribed to painful disorders of the circulation. The cartoonists picture him as being reduced to a sort of oily lava in Summer and as coming down upon the lee in Winter with sickening thuds and to the accompaniment of world-wide seismic disturbances. In plays he is always the target of slap-stick and seltzer siphon, but a note of pity appears in every laugh he raises. People are sincerely sorry for him, and are prone to dwell, with maudlin sentimentality, upon the fact that no sane woman ever falls in love with a fat man.

Squandered sympathy! Wasted tears! The fat man, far from asking for them, cannot even understand them. To him the most beautiful thing in nature—the one thing, indeed, that convinces him of the essential benignity of the cosmic process—is the fact that he is fat. The fatter he gets the happier he grows. With every increase in his diameter there comes an access of comfort, of ease, of geniality, of contentment. Forced by a kind nature to give over violent physical exercise, he devotes himself to poetry, piano-playing, mathematics, philosophy, and other elevating divertissements. He is a hearty and discriminating eater and has time to make acquaintance with all the more rare and delightful victuals. He sleeps soundly and snores in the safe and sane key of C major. Excused, by public opinion, from all sartorial display, he is able to clothe himself in loose and comfortable garments. A happy man, taking his ease in his inn!

The fact that sentimental women abhor the man of bulk is not a curse laid upon him, but a stroke of good fortune. As he fares through the world, radiating joy like some soothing emanation, his footsteps are not dogged by matchmaking mammas and debutantes of prehistoric vintages. No one lures him into dim-lit parlors. No one would think of inviting him to sit in a hammock or to row a boat. He is not a dancing man; he does not excel at tennis; long walks down Lovers' Lane fatigue his feet. So the girls leave him to his exquisite reveries and sublime contemplations, and he goes through life unhunted, unharassed and unwed, growing fatter day by day and gaining happiness with every ounce, pound and ton.

Thus he lives and dies, a being to be envied. To beauty, true enough, he cannot pretend, but in that virtue which proceeds from high thinking and that peace of mind which grows out of independence, public respect and efficiency—in these things he leads all other sentient creatures.

Sunday Afternoon

From the Baltimore *Evening Sun*, April 1, 1929

In the decaying neighborhood where I live Sunday afternoon is ordinarily very quiet. Such of the people as are pious seem to take religion very heavily. Thus their morning devotions exhaust them, and after the midday meal they are fit only for snoozing. The rest, I suspect, give over Sunday afternoons to home brewing: there is a pleasant smell of malt and hops in the air, and now and then a whiff of something stronger. Not many seem to have automobiles, and I am glad to be able to add that phonographs, automatic pianos, radio loud-speakers, and other such abominations are not common. Thus the second semester of the Sabbath is generally quiet, and I devote it to work.

But last Sunday this work got itself interrupted, for there was a great commotion in the square opposite my house. The first sign of it was a series of bugle blasts, followed by vague shouts and murmurs. Going to the window, I found that the Salvation Army had taken possession of the square. Apparently it had come in force, for I counted at least fifty brothers and sisters in uniform, and with them they had a band. They also had a photographer with a huge camera, a dozen or more little girls in a sort of scout uniform, and an odd brother who wore what appeared to be the war-time livery of the Y.M.C.A. In front of the square, and directly before my house, were three Salvation Army trucks. Presently half a dozen of the brethren stripped off their coats and began unloading the trucks. First they threw out five or six contraptions not unlike carpenters' trestles, but larger. There followed as many heavy boards cut in zigzags, like the risers of cellar steps. And then came fifteen or twenty long planks of pine, planed but not otherwise cut. It took a great deal of whooping and gesticulating to get these things out of the trucks. At least four brothers grabbed every plank, and by the time they had hoisted it over the side of the truck and dropped it on the sidewalk they had muffed it two or three times and one or another of them had got a clout from it. It was a warm day, and they sweated freely. For each one who actually touched a plank there were three or four to boss him.

Meanwhile, a big crowd had begun to collect, mainly children from the nearby streets, and my neighbors forsook their bottling to hang out of their windows and watch. It soon appeared that the planks and trestles constituted the flesh and bones of a sort of grandstand that was to be erected on the lawn of the square, under two big trees. First the trestles were set up fifty or sixty feet from the sidewalk, and then a dignitary in uniform rushed up and ordered them taken nearer. Then it appeared that they were too far apart, and he ordered them put closer. Then they were too close, and he ordered them spread a bit. All this was done to the tune of a vast chattering and whooping. The members of the band, lolling under the trees, their instruments under their arms, took no part in putting up the grandstand: apparently they were excused, as artists, from such labor. But all the other Salvationists, at least those who were male, gave aid, and every one of them shouted orders to the others. Finally the trestles were got in place, the zigzag boards were laid against them, and the long planks were deposited upon the zigzags. The grandstand now began to reveal itself, and a couple of small boys were swinging their legs from the top plank before the lowermost one was in place. All the while the shouting and scurrying about went on, and now and then a cornetist in the band tooted an encouraging blast.

The job still needed perfecting. At one end, on the top row, the planks ran out for four or five feet beyond the last trestle. If anyone happened to be sitting out there and the folks further in got up, it was obvious that the laws of gravitation would come into play. Half a dozen majors and colonels noticed the fact at once and sounded warnings. A dozen lesser warriors leaped at their call, and after a few minutes of heaving, tugging and shoving the planks were thrust back, so that they no longer ran out into space. The grandstand looked fragile, but it was ready for occupancy. The business of filling it began. First the small boys who had climbed it were chased off, and then the little girls in scout uniforms were lined up and ordered to get themselves to the top. They seemed reluctant to venture up, for the highest plank was at least seven feet above the lawn, but in a little while, with much urging by a dozen officers in uniform, two braved the climb, and then the others swarmed after them. They stood on the top plank and completely filled it. Between the trestles it sagged under them, and they held on to one another in plain fear, but the majors and colonels, aided by the Y.M.C.A. brother, assured them that it was all right, and so they stuck.

Then began the business of filling the lower levels. This took even more shouting and running about than had gone before. Lady Salvationists had to be summoned from clear across the square. They came slowly, and the majors and colonels puffed and showed choler, but in the end, with the aid of a bugler, enough of them were got upon the scene. They clambered up the stand and sat in rows, and below them and between them crowded dozens of children—whether converts or mere spectators I could not make out. Soon the stand was packed to its capacity. Every plank was bowed with the weight upon it, and the trestles began to settle into the soft earth of the lawn. A final hullabaloo, with the shirt-sleeved officers sweating more than ever, chased away unwanted volunteers and the photographer brought up his camera and began to focus it.

This business took some time, for saucy boys were always leaping into the field of the lens, and having to be run out again. The Girl Scouts on the top plank did a lot of squealing, and every few seconds one of them began to wobble and there was an alarm, and more shouting and scurrying about, but none actually fell off, and so the photographer proceeded. Finally, he was ready, and twenty officers joined in cautioning everyone to be still. And then, just as he was about to expose his plate, the whole grandstand began to sway gently from side to side, and an instant later, to go over. The legs of the trestle at one end had sunk into the ground. Over she went!—and up rose a yell that must have been heard for three blocks. Fortunately, there were no serious casualties. The whole squad of majors and colonels, with the Y.M.C.A. brother for good measure, piled upon the wreck in one frantic leap, and the sisters in the background prepared to faint, but there was no sign of blood, and only one of the victims seemed to need aid. She was one of the older girls, and she came out with a bruised shoulder. Forty Samaritans fought to carry her to a nearby automobile, but she made it under her own steam.

At once the work of cleaning up the debris began. It took almost as long as erecting the stand. Every plank was seized by four brothers, each with three or four more to boss him. The trestles and zigzags took six or eight. Several generals emerged from the mass, planning the grand strategy of the removal. The truck was moved down the street six feet, and then moved back again. Orders came roaring from all points of the compass. Gaping small boys were knocked over. The sod was hoofed and gouged up for yards around. Two brothers leaped into the truck to receive the planks. One was knocked over and went sprawling. Finally the truck was loaded and rolled away, and a general went about shouting "Go to the hall!" Then the band ambled off, the sisters followed, the children dispersed, and the show was over.

I present the record as a small contribution to the literature of human imbecility. Seen in retrospect, the episode seems quite fantastic. Imagine setting up those slim trestles on a soft lawn, and then loading them with a couple of tons of women and children! The planks sagged from the first moment. The trestles wobbled and dug in. But not a man in that whole gang of saved and polished souls had wit enough to see what was bound to follow. With the energy of beavers and the devotion of holy martyrs they erected their crazy machine, loaded it with children and then stood by in amazement as it slid from under their noses. The facts belong to any psychologist who cares to anatomize them. As for me, I confess that I got a considerable pleasure out of the spectacle. It was harmless in its effects, and it was perfect in its essence.

Interlude Sentimentale

From the *Smart Set*, Sept., 1919, p. 42

Ah, those far-off, half-forgotten days, when there was yet enough alcohol in malt to make a vase of it romantic, and the girls were not afraid of shocking a man of my years, and I roamed the great world, sipping beauty like a bee. . . . I'll never forget one flaming Spring morning at Versailles, perhaps between 10 A.M. and 10:15. Ed Moffett and I stood on the little bridge near the Petit Trianon watching the famous carp leap into the tiny stream below. "Those carp," said Ed, "are happy. They never get sore feet hoofing through these wet woods. They are never thirsty. They have no religion. They don't know that Marie Antoinette is dead. They have never heard of Socialism."

To make conversation I disputed. "They can't be wholly happy," I argued. "They haven't any vices."

Ed considered the point a moment and then hauled out a large plug of Gravely's Choice, the Corona-Corona of chewing tobaccos. "It is," he said, "possible." Then he broke off three inches of the plug and dropped it with great precision into the gaping mouth of the largest carp.

"Come," said Ed. "Let us get away before he discovers how happy he is."

Elegy in C Minor

From a hitherto unpublished manuscript

What has become of Brigham Young,
    That mastodon of lust?
Alas, his withers they are wrung,
    His gonads turned to dust.

And what's the news of Honest Abe,
    That paladin of truth?
Alas, but he was polished off
    By Wendell Willkie Booth.

And can you tell of U. S. Grant,
    Oh, have you any news?
Alas, he undermined his health
    By licking up the booze.

Jeff Davis, what's become of him?
    Where, tell me, does he dwell?
Alas, I hear by radio
    He's forty foot in Hell.

And what's become of R. E. Lee,
　Who fought with General Grant?
Alas, what little's left of him
　Is food for worm and ant.

And Calvin Coolidge, wonder man,
　How is he now, and where?
Alas, he's laid away for keeps
　In Yahweh's frigidaire.

And Harding, have you heard of him?
　Alas, he is no more;
The Nazis slit his weazand on
　The lone Pacific shore.

And Herbert Hoover, LL.D.,
　What news, if any, pray?
Alas, he waits the coming of
　A Brighter, Better Day.

And what, my friends, of old John D. —
　Has he been seen of late?
Alas, he's wearing out his fists
　Upon the Pearly Gate.

And John the Baptist—goodness me!
　Don't ask me where he's at;
The Scriptures say that he struck out
　His first time at the bat.

Of Moses I can tell you naught
　And know no one who can;
He vanished when he changed his name
　To Franklin D. Moran.

And what of Noah? Where could one
　Expect to find his clay?
Alas, the books say only that
　He's laid away to stay.

And what of Mary Magdalen?
　I'd tell you if I could,

But all that I can gather is,
She went to Hollywood.

And Adam, father of us all?
Alas, the myst'ry mounts;
The one thing sure is that he was
Still dead at last accounts.

The Jocose Gods

From DAMN!: A BOOK OF CALUMNY, 1918, p. 37

What humor could be more cruel than that of life itself? Franz Schubert, on his deathbed, read the complete works of J. Fenimore Cooper. John Millington Synge wrote "Riders to the Sea" on a second-hand typewriter, and wore a celluloid collar. Richard Wagner made a living, during four years, arranging Italian opera arias for the cornet. Herbert Spencer sang bass in a barber-shop quartette and was in love with George Eliot. One of the greatest soldiers in Hungarian history was named Hunjadi Janos.

XXVIII. NIETZSCHE

The Bugaboo

From the *Smart Set*, Jan., 1920, pp. 55–56

MUCH OF the current blabber against the late Friedrich Wilhelm Nietzsche is grounded upon the doctrine that his capacity for consecutive thought was clearly limited. In support of the doctrine his critics cite the fact that most of his books are no more than strings of apothegms, with the subject changing on every second page. All this, it must be obvious, is fundamentally nonsensical. What deceives the professors is the traditional garrulity and prolixity of philosophers. Because the average philosophical writer, when he essays to expose his ideas, makes such copious drafts upon the parts of speech that the dictionary is almost emptied, these defective observers jump to the conclusion that his intrinsic notions are of corresponding elaborateness. This is not true. I have read Kant, Hegel, Spencer, Spinoza, Descartes, Leibnitz, Fichte, Locke, Schleiermacher, James and Bergson, not to mention the Greeks and the Romans; the more I read, the more I am convinced that it is not true.

What makes philosophy hard to read is not the complexity of the ideas set forth, but the complexity of the language in which they are concealed. The typical philosopher, having, say, four new notions, drowns them in a sea of words—all borrowed from other philosophers. One must wade through endless chapters of old stuff to get at the minute kernels of the new stuff. . . . This process Nietzsche avoided. He always assumed that his readers knew the books, and that it was thus unnecessary to rewrite them. Having an idea that seemed to him to be novel and original, he stated it in as few words as possible, and then shut down. Sometimes he got it into a hundred words; sometimes it took a thousand. But he never wrote a word too many; he never pumped up an idea to make it appear bigger than it actually was. . . . The professors are not used to that sort of writing. Nietzsche employed too few words for them—and he had too many ideas.

Nietzsche on Christianity

From my translation of THE ANTICHRIST, 1920. This translation, like the first edition of The American Language, was undertaken as a recreation during World War I, when the prevailing spy-hunt made it impossible to do any rational writing on public questions. There had been two previous translations, but it seemed to me that they were somewhat stiff. What I tried to do was get into mine some reflection of the extraordinary dramatic quality and verbal coruscation of the original. It came out with the approbation of Dr. Oscar Levy, editor of the English edition of Nietzsche and owner of the rights thereto

What is good?—Whatever augments the feeling of power, the will to power, power itself, in man.

What is evil?—Whatever springs from weakness.

What is happiness?—The feeling that power *increases*—that resistance is overcome.

Not contentment, but more power; *not* peace at any price, but war; *not* virtue, but efficiency (virtue in the Renaissance sense, *virtu*, virtue free of moral acid).

The weak and the botched shall perish: first principle of *our* charity. And one should help them to it.

What is more harmful than any vice?—Practical sympathy for the botched and the weak—Christianity. . . .

The problem that I set here is not what shall replace mankind in the order of living creatures (—man is an end—): but what type of man must be *bred*, must be *willed*, as being the most valuable, the most worthy of life, the most secure guarantee of the future.

This more valuable type has appeared often enough in the past: but always as a happy accident, as an exception, never as deliberately *willed*. Very often it has been precisely the most feared; hitherto it has been almost *the* terror of terrors;—and out of that terror the contrary type has been willed, cultivated and *attained*: the domestic animal, the herd animal, the sick brute-man—the Christian. . . .

Christianity has waged a war to the death against this *higher* type of man, it has put all the deepest instincts of this type under its ban, it has developed its concept of evil, of the Evil One himself, out of these instincts—the strong man as the typical reprobate, the "outcast among men." Christianity has taken the part of all the weak, the low, the botched; it has made an ideal out of *antagonism* to all the self-preservative instincts of sound life; it has corrupted even the faculties of those natures that are intellectually most vigorous, by representing the highest intellectual values as sinful, as misleading, as full of temptation. . . .

I call an animal, a species, an individual corrupt, when it loses its instincts, when it chooses, when it *prefers*, what is injurious to it. A history of the "higher feelings," the "ideals of humanity" would almost explain why man is so degenerate. Life itself appears to me as an instinct for growth, for survival, for the accumulation of forces, for *power*: whenever the will to power fails there is disaster. My contention is that all the highest values of humanity have been emptied of this will—that the values of *décadence*, of *nihilism*, now prevail under the holiest names.

Christianity is called the religion of *pity*.—Pity stands in opposition to all the tonic passions that augment the energy of the feeling of aliveness: it is a depressant. Suffering is made contagious by pity; under certain circumstances it may lead to a total sacrifice of life and living energy—a loss out of all proportion to the magnitude of the cause (—the case of the death of the Nazarene). This is the first view of it; there is, however, a still more important one. If one measures the effects of pity by the gravity of the reactions it sets up, its character as a menace to life appears in a much clearer light. Pity thwarts the whole law of evolution, which is the law of natural selection. It preserves whatever is ripe for destruction; it fights on the side of those disinherited and condemned by life; by maintaining life in so many of the botched of all kinds, it gives life itself a gloomy and dubious aspect. This depressing and contagious instinct stands against all those instincts which work for the preservation and enhancement of life: in the rôle of *protector* of the miserable, it is a prime agent in the promotion of *déca-dence*—pity persuades to extinction. . . . Of course, one doesn't say "extinction," one says "the other world," or "God," or "the *true* life," or Nirvana, salvation, blessedness. . . . This innocent rhetoric, from the realm of religious-ethical balderdash, appears *a good deal less innocent* when one reflects upon the tendency that it conceals beneath sublime words: the tendency to *destroy life.* . . . Nothing is more unhealthy, amid all our unhealthy modernism, than Christian pity. To be the doctors *here*, to be unmerciful *here*, to wield the knife *here*—all this is *our* business, all this is *our* sort of humanity, by this sign we are philosophers.

The poisoning goes a great deal further than most people think: I find the arrogant habit of the theologian among all who regard themselves as "idealists"—among all who, by virtue of a higher point of departure, claim a right to rise above reality, and to look upon it with suspicion. . . . The idealist, like the ecclesiastic, carries all sorts of lofty concepts in his hand (—and not only in his hand!); he launches them with benevolent contempt against "understanding," "the senses," "honor," "good living," "science"; he sees such things as *beneath* him, as pernicious and seductive forces, on which "the soul" soars as a pure thing-in-itself—as if humility, chastity, poverty, in a word, *holiness*, had not already done much more damage to life than all imaginable horrors and vices. . . . The pure soul is a pure lie. . . . So long as the priest, that *professional* denier, calumniator and poisoner of life, is accepted as a *higher* variety of man, there can be no answer to the question, What *is* truth? Truth has already been stood on its head when the obvious attorney of mere emptiness is mistaken for its representative. . . .

The Christian concept of a god—the god as the patron of the sick, the god as a spinner of cobwebs, the god as a spirit—is one of the most corrupt concepts that has ever been set up in the world: it probably touches low-water mark in the ebbing evolution of the god-type. God degenerated into the *contradiction of life.* Instead of being its transfiguration and eternal Yea! In him war is declared on life, on nature, on the will to live! God becomes the formula for every slander upon the "here and now," and for every lie about the "beyond"! In him nothingness is deified, and the will to nothingness is made holy! . . .

When the centre of gravity of life is placed, *not* in life itself, but in "the beyond"—in *nothingness*—then one has taken away its centre of gravity altogether. The vast lie of personal immortality destroys all reason, all natural instinct—henceforth, everything in the instincts that is beneficial, that fosters life and that safeguards the future, is a cause of suspicion. So to live that life no longer has any meaning: *this* is now the "meaning" of life.

Christianity also stands in opposition to all *intellectual* well-being,—sick reasoning is the only sort that it *can* use as Christian reasoning; it takes the side of everything that is idiotic; it pronounces a curse upon "intellect," upon the *superbia* of the healthy intellect. Since sickness is inherent in Christianity, it follows that the typically Christian state of "faith" *must* be a form of sickness too, and that all straight, straightforward and scientific paths to knowledge *must* be banned by the church as *forbidden* ways. Doubt is thus a sin from the start. . . . "Faith" means the will to avoid knowing what is true. The pietist, the priest of either sex, is a fraud *because* he is sick: his instinct *demands* that the truth shall never be allowed its rights on any point. "Whatever makes for illness is *good*; whatever issues from abundance, from superabundance, from power, is *evil*": so argues the believer.

The whole labor of the ancient world gone for naught. To what end the Greeks? to what end the Romans?—All the prerequisites to a learned culture, all the *methods* of science, were already there; man had already perfected the great and incomparable art of reading profitably—that first necessity to the tradition of culture, the unity of the sciences; the natural sciences, in alliance with mathematics and mechanics, were on the right road—*the sense of fact*, the last and more valuable of all the senses, had its schools, and its traditions were already centuries old! Every *essential* to the beginning of the work was ready—and the *most* essential, it cannot be said too often, are methods, and also the most difficult to develop, and the longest opposed by habit and laziness. What we have to-day reconquered, with unspeakable self-discipline, for ourselves—for certain bad instincts, certain Christian instincts, still lurk in our bodies—that is to say, the keen eye for reality, the cautious hand, patience and seriousness in the smallest things, the whole *integrity* of knowledge—all these things were already there, and had been there for 2,000 years! *All gone for naught!* Overnight it became merely a memory!

Here it becomes necessary to call up a memory that must be a hundred times more painful to Germans. The Germans have destroyed for Europe the last great harvest of civilization that Europe was ever to reap—the *Renaissance*. Is it understood at last, *will* it ever be understood, *what* the Renaissance was? *The transvaluation of Christian values,*—an attempt with all available means, all instincts and all the resources of genius to bring about a triumph of the *opposite* values, the more *noble* values.... This has been the one great war of the past; there has never been a more critical question than that of the Renaissance; there has never been a form of *attack* more fundamental, more direct, or more violently delivered by a whole front upon the center of the enemy! To attack at the critical place, at the very seat of Christianity, and there enthrone the more noble values—that is to say, to *insinuate* them into the instincts, into the most fundamental needs and appetites of those sitting there.... I see before me the *possibility* of a perfectly heavenly enchantment and spectacle:—it seems to me to scintillate with all the vibrations of a fine and delicate beauty, and within it there is an art so divine, so infernally divine, that one might search in vain for thousands of years for another such possibility; I see a spectacle so rich in significance and at the same time so wonderfully full of paradox that it should arouse all the gods on Olympus to immortal laughter—*Caesar Borgia as pope!* ... Am I understood? ... Well then, *that* would have been the sort of triumph that *I* alone am longing for today—: by it Christianity would have been *swept away!*

What happened? A German monk, Luther, came to Rome. This monk, with all the vengeful instincts of an unsuccessful priest in him, raised a rebellion *against* the Renaissance in Rome.... Instead of grasping, with profound thanksgiving, the miracle that had taken place: the conquest of Christianity at its *capital*—instead of this, his hatred was stimulated by the spectacle. A religious man thinks only of himself.—Luther saw only the *depravity* of the papacy at the very moment when the opposite was becoming apparent: the old corruption, the *peccatum originale*, Christianity itself, no longer occupied the papal chair! Instead there was life! Instead there was the triumph of life! Instead there was a great yea to all lofty, beautiful and daring things! ... And Luther *restored the church*: he attacked it. ... The Renaissance—an event without meaning, a great futility!

—With this I come to a conclusion and pronounce my judgment. I *condemn* Christianity; I bring against the Christian church the most terrible of all the accusations that an accuser has ever had in his mouth. It is, to me, the greatest of all imaginable corruptions; it seeks to work the ultimate corruption, the worst possible corruption. The Christian church has left nothing untouched by its depravity; it has turned every value into worthlessness, and every truth into a lie, and every integrity into baseness of soul. Let anyone dare to speak to me of its "humanitarian" blessings! Its deepest necessities range it against any effort to abolish distress; it lives by distress; it *creates* distress to make *itself* immortal. ... For example, the worm of sin; it was the church that first enriched mankind with this misery!—The "equality of souls before God"— this fraud, this *pretext* for the *rancunes* of all the base-minded— this explosive concept, ending in revolution, the modern idea, and the notion of overthrowing the whole social order—this is *Christian* dynamite. ... The "humanitarian" blessings of Christianity forsooth! To breed out of *humanitas* a self-contradiction, an art of self-pollution, a will to lie at any price, an aversion and contempt for all good and honest instincts! All this, to me, is the "humanitarianism" of Christianity! Parasitism as the *only* practise of the church; with its anaemic and "holy" ideals, sucking all the blood, all the love, all the hope out of life; the beyond as the will to deny all reality; the cross as the distinguishing mark of the most subterranean conspiracy ever heard of—against health, beauty, well-being, intellect, *kindness* of soul—*against life itself*. ...

This eternal accusation against Christianity I shall write upon all walls, wherever walls are to be found—I have letters that even the blind will be able to see. ... I call Christianity the one great curse, the one great intrinsic depravity, the one great instinct of revenge, for which no means are venomous enough, or secret, subterranean and *small* enough,—I call it the one immortal blemish upon the human race.

XXIX. CREDOS

H. L. Mencken, by Himself

From the *Nation*, Dec. 5, 1923, pp. 647–48

ASK A professional critic to write about himself and you simply ask him to do what he does every day in the practise of his art and mystery. There is, indeed, no criticism that is not a confidence, and there is no confidence that is not self-revelation. When I denounce a book with mocking and contumely, and fall upon the poor author in the brutal, Asiatic manner of a drunken longshoreman, a Ku Kluxer, or a midshipman at Annapolis, I am only saying, in the trade cant, that the fellow disgusts me—that his ideas and his manner are somehow obnoxious to me, as those of a Methodist, a golf player, or a clog dancer are obnoxious to me—in brief, that I hold myself to be a great deal better than he is and am eager to say so. And when, on the other hand, I praise a book in high, astounding terms, and speak of the author as if his life and sufferings were of capital importance to the world, then I am merely saying that I detect something in him, of prejudice, tradition, habit of mind, that is much like something within myself, and that my own life and sufferings are of the utmost importance to me. That is all there ever is in criticism, once it gets beyond cataloguing. No matter how artfully the critic may try to be impersonal and scientific, he is bound to give himself away.

With criticism thus so transparent, so unescapably revelatory, I often marvel that the gentlemen who concern themselves with my own books, often very indignantly, do not penetrate more competently to my essence. Even for a critic I am excessively garrulous and confidential; nevertheless, it is rare for me to encounter a criticism that hits me where I live and have my being. A great deal of ink is wasted trying to discover and denounce my motive in being a critic at all. I am, by one theory, a German spy told off to flay, terrorize and stampede the Anglo-Saxon. By another I am a secret radical, while professing to admire Coolidge and Genghis Khan. By a third, I am a fanatical American chauvinist, bent upon defaming and ruining the motherland. All thse notions are nonsense; only the first has even the slightest plausibility. The plain truth is—and how could it be plainer?—that I practise criticism for precisely the same reason that every other critic practises it: because I am a vain fellow, and have a great many ideas on all sorts of subjects, and like to put them into words and harass the human race with them. If I could confine this flow of ideas to one subject I'd be a professor and get some respect. If I could reduce it, say, to one idea a year, I'd be a novelist, a dramatist, or a newspaper editorial writer. But being unable to stanch the flux, and having, as I say, a vast and exigent vanity, I am a critic of books, and through books of *Homo sapiens*, and through *Homo sapiens* of God.

So much for the motive. What, now, of the substance? What is the fundamental faith beneath all the spurting and coruscating the ideas that I have just mentioned? What do I primarily and immovably believe in, as a Puritan believes in Hell? I believe in liberty. And when I say liberty I mean the thing in its widest imaginable sense—liberty up to the extreme limits of the feasible and tolerable. I am against forbidding anybody to do anything, or say anything, or think anything, so long as it is at all possible to imagine a habitable world in which he would be free to do, say and think it. The burden of proof, as I see it, is always upon the policeman, which is to say upon the lawmaker, the theologian, the right-thinker. He must prove his case doubly, triply, quadruply, and then he must start all over and prove it again. The eye through which I view him is watery and jaundiced. I do not pretend to be "just" to him—any more than a Christian pretends to be just to the Devil. He is the enemy of everything I admire and respect in this world—of everything that makes it various and amusing and charming. He impedes every honest search for the truth. He stands against every sort of good will and common decency. His ideal is that of an animal trainer, an archbishop, a major-general in the Army. I am against him until the last galoot's ashore.

This simple and childlike faith in the freedom and dignity of man—here, perhaps, stated with undue rhetoric—should be obvious, I should think, to every critic above the mental backwardness of a Federal judge. Nevertheless, very few of them, anatomizing my books, have ever showed any sign of detecting it. But all the same even the dullest of them has, in his fashion, sensed it; it colors unconsciously all the diatribes about myself that I have ever read. It is responsible for the fact that in England and Germany (and, to the extent that I have ever been heard of at all there, in France and Italy) I am regarded as a highly typical American—in truth, as almost the archetype of the American. And it is responsible equally for the fact that here at home I am often denounced as the worst American unhung. The paradox is only apparent. The explanation of it lies in this: that to most Europeans the United States is still regarded naïvely as the land of liberty *par excellence*, whereas to most Americans the thing itself has long since ceased to have any significance, and to large numbers of them, indeed, it has of late taken on an extreme obnoxiousness. I know of no civilized country, indeed, in which liberty is less esteemed than it is in the United States today; certainly there is none in which more persistent efforts are made to limit it and put it down. I am thus, to Americans, a bad American, but to Europeans, still unaware of the practical effects of the idealism of Wilson and the saloon-bouncer ethic of Roosevelt I, I seem to be an eloquent spokesman of the true American tradition. It is a joke, but the joke is not on me.

Liberty, of course, is not for slaves; I do not advocate inflicting it on men against their conscience. On the contrary, I an strongly in favor of letting them crawl and grovel all they please—before the Supreme Court of the United States, Samuel Gompers, J. P. Morgan, Henry Cabot Lodge, the Anti-Saloon League, or whatever other fraud or combination of frauds they choose to venerate. I am thus unable to make the grade as a Liberal, for Liberalism always involves freeing human beings against their will—often, indeed, to their obvious damage, as in the cases of the majority of Negroes and women. But all human beings are not congenital slaves, even in America. Here and there one finds a man or a woman with a great natural passion for liberty—and a hard job getting it. It is, to me at least, a vast pleasure to go to the rescue of such a victim of the herd, to give him some aid and comfort in his struggle against the forces that seek to regiment and throttle him. It is a double pleasure to succor him when the sort of liberty he strives for is apparently unintelligible and valueless—for example, liberty to address conventions of the I.W.W., to read the books of such bad authors as D. H. Lawrence and Petronius Arbiter, to work twelve hours a day, to rush the can, to carry red flags in parades, to patronize osteopaths and Christian Science healers, to belong to the best clubs. Such nonsensical varieties of liberty are especially sweet to me. I have wrecked my health and dissipated a fortune defending them—never, so far as I know, successfully. Why, then, go on? Ask yourself why a grasshopper goes on jumping.

But what has liberty to do with the art of literary criticism, my principal business in this vale? Nothing—or everything. It seems to me that it is perfectly possible to write profound and valuable literary criticism without entering on the question of freedom at all, either directly or indirectly. Aesthetic judgment may be isolated from all other kinds of judgments, and yet remain interesting and important. But this isolation must be performed by other hands; to me it is as sheer a psychological impossibility as believing that God condemned forty-two little children to death for poking fun at Elisha's bald head. When I encounter a new idea, whether aesthetic, political, theological or epistemological, I ask myself, instantly and automatically, what would happen to its proponent if he should state its exact antithesis. If nothing would happen to him, then I am willing and eager to listen to him. But if he would lose anything valuable by a *volte face*—if stating his idea is profitable to him, if the act secures his roof, butters his parsnips, gets him a tip—then I hear him with one ear only. He is not a free man. *Ergo*, he is not a man.

For liberty, when one ascends to the levels where ideas swish by and men pursue Truth to grab her by the tail, is the first thing and the last thing. So long as it prevails the show is thrilling and stupendous; the moment it fails the show is a dull and dirty farce.

Salutatory

From the *American Mercury*, Vol. I, No. 1, Jan., 1924, pp. 27–30

The aim of the *American Mercury* is precisely that of every other monthly review the world has ever seen: to ascertain and tell the truth. So far, nothing new. But the Editors cherish the hope that it may be possible, after all, to introduce some element of novelty into the execution of an enterprise so old, and upon that hope they found the magazine. It comes into being with at least one advantage over all its predecessors in the field of public affairs: it is entirely devoid of messianic passion. The Editors have heard no Voice from the burning bush. They will not cry up and offer for sale any sovereign balm, whether political, economic or aesthetic, for all the sorrows of the world. The fact is, indeed, that they doubt that any such sovereign balm exists, or that it will ever exist hereafter. The world, as they see it, is down with at least a score of painful diseases, all of them chronic and incurable; nevertheless, they cling to the notion that human existence remains predominantly charming. Especially is it charming in this unparalleled Republic of the West, where men are earnest and women are intelligent, and all the historic virtues of Christendom are now concentrated. The Editors propose, before jurisprudence develops to the point of prohibiting skepticism altogether, to give a realistic consideration to certain of these virtues, and to try to save what is exhilarating in them, even when all that is divine must be abandoned. They engage to undertake the business in a polished and aseptic manner, without indignation on the one hand and without too much regard for tender feelings on the other. They have no set programme, either destructive or constructive. Sufficient unto each day will be the performance thereof.

As has been hinted, the Editors are not fond enough to believe in their own varieties of truth too violently, or to assume that the truth is ascertainable in all cases, or even in most cases. If they are convinced of anything beyond peradventure, it is, indeed, that many of the great problems of man, and particularly of man as a member of society—are intrinsically insoluble—that insolubility is as much a part of their essence as it is of the essence of squaring the circle. But demonstrating this insolubility thus takes on something of the quality of establishing a truth, and even merely arguing it gathers a sort of austere virtue. For human progress is achieved, it must be manifest, not by wasting effort upon hopeless and exhausting enigmas, but by concentrating effort upon inquiries that are within the poor talents of man. In the field of politics, for example, utopianism is not only useless; it is also dangerous, for it centers attention upon what ought to be at the expense of what might be. The *American Mercury* will devote itself pleasantly to exposing the nonsensicality of all such hallucinations, particularly when they show a certain apparent plausibility. Its own pet hallucination will take the form of an hypothesis that the progress of knowledge is less a matter of accumulating facts than a matter of destroying "facts." It will assume constantly that the more ignorant a man is the more he knows, positively and indignantly. Among the great leeches and barber-surgeons who profess to medicate the body politic, it will give its suffrage to those who admit frankly that all the basic diseases are beyond cure, and who consecrate themselves to making the patient as comfortable as possible.

In some of the preliminary notices of the *American Mercury*, kindly published in the newspapers, apprehension has been expressed that the Editors are what is called Radicals, *i.e.*, that they harbor designs upon the Republic, and are bound by a secret oath to put down 100% Americanism. The notion is herewith denounced. The Radical proposals to destroy the capitalistic system at one blow seem to them to be as full of folly as the Liberal proposals to denaturize it by arousing its better nature. They believe that it is destined to endure in the United States, perhaps long after it has broken up everywhere else, if only because the illusion that any bright boy can make himself a part of it remains a cardinal article of the American national religion—and no sentient man will ever confess himself doomed to life imprisonment in the proletariat so long as the slightest hope remains, in fact or in fancy, of getting out of it. Thus class consciousness is not one of our national diseases; we suffer, indeed, from its opposite—the delusion that class barriers are not real. That delusion reveals itself in many forms, some of them as beautiful as a glass eye. One is the Liberal doctrine that a prairie demagogue promoted to the United States Senate will instantly show all the sagacity of a Metternich and all the high rectitude of a Pierre Bayard. Another is the doctrine that a moron run through a university and decorated with a Ph.D. will cease thereby to be a moron. Another is the doctrine that J. P. Morgan's press-agents and dish-washers make competent Cabinet Ministers and Ambassadors. Yet another, a step further, is the doctrine that the interests of capital and labor are identical — which is to say, that the interests of landlord and tenant, hangman and condemned, cat and rat are identical. Such notions, alas, seem to permeate all American thinking, the shallowness of which has been frequently remarked by foreign observers, particularly in the motherland. It will be an agreeable duty to track down some of the worst nonsense prevailing and to do execution upon it — not indignantly, of course, but nevertheless with a sufficient play of malice to give the business a Christian and philanthropic air.

In the field of the fine arts the *American Mercury* will pursue the course that the Editors have followed for fifteen years past in another place. They are asking various other critics to share their work and they will thus be able to cover a wider area than heretofore, but they will not deviate from their old programme — to welcome sound and honest work, whatever its form or lack of form, and to carry on steady artillery practise against every variety of artistic pedant and mountebank. They belong to no coterie and have no aesthetic theory to propagate. They do not believe that a work of art has any purpose beyond that of being charming and stimulating, and they do not believe that there is much difficulty, taking one day with another, about distinguishing clearly between the good and the not good. It is only when theories begin to enter into the matter that counsels are corrupted — and between the transcendental, gibberishy theory of a Greenwich village aesthete and the harsh, moral, patriotic theory of a university pedagogue there is not much to choose. Good work is always done in the middle ground, between the theories. That middle ground now lies wide open; the young American artist is quite as free as he needs to be. The Editors do not believe that he is helped by nursing and coddling him. If the obscure, inner necessity which moves him is not powerful enough to make him function unassisted, then it is not powerful enough to make a genuine artist of him. All he deserves to have is aid against the obscurantists who occasionally beset him — men' whose interest in the fine arts, by some occult Freudian means, seems to be grounded upon an implacable hatred of everything that is free, and honest, and beautiful. It will be a pleasure to pursue such obscurantists to their fastnesses, and to work the *lex talionis* upon them. The business is amusing and now and then it may achieve some by-product of good.

In general, the *American Mercury* will live up to the adjective in its name. It will lay chief stress at all times upon American ideas, American problems and American personalities because it assumes that nine-tenths of its readers will be Americans and that they will be more interested in their own country than in any other. A number of excellent magazines are already devoted to making known the notions of the major and minor seers of Europe; at least half a dozen specialize in the ideas emanating from England alone. This leaves the United States rather neglected. It is, as the judicious have frequently observed, an immense country, and full of people. These people entertain themselves with a vast number of ideas and enterprises, many of them of an unprecedented and astounding nature. There are more political theories on tap in the Republic than anywhere else on earth, and more doctrines in aesthetics, and more religions, and more other schemes for regimenting, harrowing and saving human beings. Our annual production of messiahs is greater than that of all Asia. A single session of Congress produces more utopian legislation than Europe has seen since the first meeting of the English Witenagemot. To explore this great complex of inspirations, to isolate the individual prophets from the herd and examine their proposals, to follow the ponderous revolutions of the mass mind — in brief, to attempt a realistic presentation of the whole gaudy, gorgeous American scene — this will be the principal enterprise of the *American Mercury*.

Further Exposition

From the *American Mercury*, May, 1924, pp. 25–26

The *American Mercury* does not pretend to any austere judicial spirit in its dealings with charlatans. It is frankly against fortune-tellers, osteopaths, communists, New Thoughters, Wilsonian idealists, dowsers, Kiwanians, Christian Scientists, Ku Kluxers, Prohibitionists and all other such dolts and swindlers. Its columns are no more open to their rantings against sense than they are open to the political drivel of Mr. Coolidge, the prospectuses of the sellers of Texas oil stock, or the advertisements of Peruna. This magazine, in brief, is not dedicated to such debates as go on in country barber-shops, Epworth League meeting-rooms, and the smoking-cars of slow trains. It does not pretend to compete with the *Congressional Record*. It assumes that its readers are civilized, and that they are thus not partisans of any of the bizarre gospels which now engage 100% Americans, in all fields from aesthetics to obstetrics. It proposes, from time to time, to give them glimpses into these gospels, but not, certainly, with any notion that they are in danger of being converted. Its aim is to amuse them, not to insult them.

Thus the pussyfoots of the new evangels may as well take warning forthwith that no conceivable bombardment of protests and demands, however cunningly disguised as neutral and virtuous, will ever penetrate to these chaste pages. But to be anaesthetic to their lascivious approaches is one thing; to cherish the doctrine that they ought to be put down is quite another thing. Too much of that doctrine has been heard in the United States in late years. Until they grew strong enough to exert political power, the osteopaths, for example, were harassed in State after State, and even now, if I do not err, they are denied certain rights that all orthodox physicians, however incompetent, freely exercise. The Christian Scientists, before they perfected their press department, went through the same bedevilment, and elsewhere there are constant attacks upon fortune-tellers, layers-on of hands, communists,

Ku Kluxers, Holy Rollers, Negrophiles, heroin addicts, cancer quacks, and a hundred and one other varieties of imbeciles and mountebanks. Here the strange American ardor for passing laws, the insane belief in regulation and punishment, plays into the hands of the reformers, most of them quacks themselves. Their efforts, even when honest, seldom accomplish any appreciable good. The Harrison Act, despite its cruel provisions, has not diminished drug addiction in the slightest. The Mormons, after years of persecution, are still Mormons, and one of them is now a power in the Senate. Socialism in the United States was not laid by the Espionage Act, nor was the stately progress of osteopathy and chiropractic halted by the early efforts to put them down. Oppressive laws do not destroy minorities; they simply make bootleggers.

An American Mercury Circular

The following, which bore no headline, was printed on an *American Mercury* letter-head, signed by me, and stuffed into the office mail. Its date I do not know, but it must have been 1930 or thereabout, at which time many innocents were looking to the magazine for leadership in the current war upon the Philistines

So far as I know—and I'd certainly have got news of it if it were a fact,—the *American Mercury* is wholly without moral purpose or what is called public spirit. It harbors no yearning to make the world better, and least of all the American world. It rejoices in this great Republic as in something rich and racy, and strives only to depict its life realistically and in good humor. What a show! What leapers through hoops! What clowns! I only hope that the readers of the magazine get half as much fun out of looking on as I get out of shifting the scenes.

Starting Point

From the *American Mercury*, June, 1925, pp. 215–16

I believe unreservedly only in what may be demonstrated scientifically. All the rest is pure speculation, and, only too often, pure bosh. It may, at times, be beautiful, but it is never important. That Shakespeare was a great poet is not a fact; it is only an opinion. It may be abandoned during the next century, as the doctrine that the Bible was written by God has been abandoned since 1850. But the fact that the blood circulates in the arteries and veins will never be abandoned. It is true now, and it will be true forever.

Petition

From the *Smart Set*, April, 1912, p. 157

From pale parsons with translucent ears and from little girls who speak pieces; from the scent of tuberoses and from medicated lingerie; from dinner invitations from friends who have wives who have sisters who have no living husbands; from tight collars and from "No Smoking" signs; from elderly ladies who have sure cures for toothache, and from barbers with perfumed fingers; from the nocturnes of Chopin, and from the New Thought; from persons who pasture their children in the hallways of hotels, and from postage-due stamps; from the harsh cacophony of liquorish snoring, and from imitation mahogany furniture; from adult males who wear diamonds, and from all high functionaries in fraternal orders; from *bier-fisch*, and from loose rugs on hardwood floors; from obscene novels by lady novelists, and from eczema; from grass butter, and from detachable cuffs; from fat women who loll grotesquely in automobiles, and from theater orchestras; from female bachelors of arts and from drizzly Sundays; from Fletcherism and from actors who speak of their "art"; from transcendentalism and from delirium tremens; from the Declaration of Independence and from cold dinner plates; from the key of B flat minor and from the struggle for existence; from pedants who denounce split infinitives, and from chemical purity; from canned book reviews and from German adverbs; from basso-profundos with prominent Adam's apples, and from platitudes; from Asiatic cholera and from the Harvardocentric theory of the universe — good Lord, deliver us!

XXX. SELF-PORTRAIT

The Man and His Shadow

From Prejudices: Fourth Series, pp. 120–23.
First printed in the *Smart Set*, Oct., 1921, pp. 41–42

Every man, whatever his actual qualities, is credited with and judged by certain general qualities that are supposed to appertain to his sex, particularly by women. Thus man the individual is related to Man the species, often to his damage and dismay. Consider my own case. I am by nature one of the most orderly of mortals. I have a place for every article of my personal property, whether a Bible or a machete, an undershirt or an eye-dropper, and I always keep it where it belongs. I never drop cigar-ashes on the floor. I never upset a waste-basket. I am never late for trains. I never go out with a purple necktie on a blue shirt. I never fail to appear in time for dinner without telephoning or telegraphing. Yet the women who have been cursed by God with the care of me have always maintained and cherished the fiction that I am an extremely careless and even hoggish fellow—that I have to be elaborately nursed, supervised and policed—that the slightest relaxation of vigilance over my everyday conduct would reduce me to a state of helplessness and chaos, with all my clothes mislaid, half my books in the ash-can, my mail unanswered, and my weasand unshaven. I make no protest; I merely record the facts. On my death-bed, I daresay, I shall try to make up for my life-long cantankerousness by doing what is expected of me. That is to say, I shall swallow a clinical thermometer or two, upset my clam-broth over my counterpane, keep a Ouija board and a set of dice under my pillow, and maybe, at the end, fall clumsily out of bed.

Personal Record

From the *Smart Set*, March, 1920, p. 48

To one ineradicable prejudice I freely confess, and that is a prejudice against poverty. I never have anything to do, if it is possible to avoid it, with anyone who is in financial difficulties, and I particularly avoid all persons who are in that state habitually, or who tremble hazardously on the edge of it. Such persons do not excite my compassion; they excite my aversion. I do not pity them, and do not believe in their common plaint that they are the victims of cruel and inexplicable circumstance. I have yet to meet one who did not show plain evidence that external circumstance had little, if anything, to do with his condition. The blame, so far as my experience runs, always lies within. The poor man is a stupid man, and usually a lazy and sentimental man. His poverty, nine times out of ten, is not due to a lack of opportunity, but to a shirking of opportunity. He is one who has turned aside from what he could do, sometimes in ignorance, more often in hollow vanity, and attempted futilely to do something beyond his capacity. In brief, he is an egoist brought down by his own egoism—and that is a figure, not in tragedy, but in farce. But I can't laugh at him. It would cause a scandal, and get me an evil name. So I simply avoid him.

The Tight-Rope

From the Baltimore *Evening Sun*, May 9, 1927

In this department, by God's grace, my own conscience is perfectly clear—perhaps my one plausible boast as a moral agent: I have never consciously tried to convert anyone to anything. Like any other man bawling from a public stamp I have occasionally made a convert; in fact, in seasons when my embouchure has been good I have made a great many. But not deliberately, not with any satisfaction. Next to a missionary, a convert is the most abhorrent shape I can imagine. I dislike persons who change their basic ideas, and I dislike them when they change them for good reasons quite as much as when they change them for bad ones. A convert to a good idea is simply a man who confesses that he was formerly an ass—and is probably one still. When such a man favors me with a certificate that my eloquence has shaken him I feel about him precisely as I'd feel if he told me that he had started (or stopped) beating his wife on my recommendation. No: it is not pleasant to come into contact with such flabby souls, so lacking in character and self-respect. Their existence embitters the life of every man who deals in ideas. The hard-boiled fellows are far more agreeable, no matter what their concrete notions. Some of those who appear to depart the farthest from the elements of sense are the most charming, for example, certain varieties of evangelical pastors. I have known many such pastors, and esteemed not a few of them. But only, I should add, the relatively unsuccessful, who seldom if ever achieved the public nuisance known as saving a soul. They believed their depressing rubbish firmly, but they did not press it upon either their inferiors or their superiors. They were not wowsers.

Unluckily, there are very few such pastors in the average Christian community, especially in the United States. The great majority, forgetting their office of conducting worship, devote themselves mainly to harassing persons who do not care to join them. This harassing is bad enough when it fails of its purpose; when it succeeds its consequence is simply an increase in the sum of human degradation, publicly displayed. It is well known that natural believers are always suspicious of converts. No wonder. For precisely the same reason sober automobilists are suspicious of drunken drivers, and Prohibition agents of Prohibitionists.

Is the skeptic ever happy, in the sense that a man who believes that God is watching over him is happy? Privately, I often doubt it. Here the pious seem to have a certain bulge on the doubters. Immersed in their faith, they enjoy a quiet contentment that is certainly never apparent to a man of restless, inquisitive, questioning mind. The happiest people in the world, accepting this definition of happiness, are probably Christian Scientists—that is, until they come down with appendicitis or gall-stones. But there is a kind of satisfaction that is quite as attractive, to certain rugged types of men, as this somewhat cow-like form of contentment. It is related to the latter just as the satisfaction of a soldier on active duty is related to the satisfaction of a man securely at home. The man at home is quite safe, and the soldier runs a considerable risk of being killed or wounded. But who will argue that the man at home, on the whole, is happier than the soldier—that is, assuming that the soldier is a volunteer? The one is tightly comfortable, and hence happy. But the other, though in grave peril, is happy too—and I am inclined to think that his happiness is often of a palpably superior variety.

So with the skeptic. His doubts, if they are real, undoubtedly tend to make him uneasy, and hence unhappy, for they play upon themselves quite as much as upon the certainties of the other fellow. What comforts him, in the long run, I suppose, is his pride in his capacity to face them. He is not wobbled and alarmed, like my correspondent; he gets a positive thrill out of being uneasy, as the soldier gets a thrill out of being in danger. Is this thrill equal, as a maker of anything rationally describable as happiness, to the comfort and security of the man of faith? Ask me an easier question! Is a blonde lovelier than a brunette? Is *Dunkles* better than *Helles*? Is Los Angeles the worst town in America, or only next to the worst? The skeptic, asked the original question, will say yes: the believer will say no. There you have it.

Categorical Imperatives

1

On Health

From the *Smart Set*, Oct., 1919, p. 83

What we mean by health is a state or condition in which the organism finds itself so delicately adapted to its environment that it is unconscious of irritation. Such a state, in any organism above the simplest, is necessarily transient; the life of such an organism is so tremendously complex a series of reactions that it is almost impossible to imagine all of them going on without friction. The earthworm has few diseases and is seldom ill; when he gets out of order at all it is usually a serious matter, and he dies forthwith. But man, being well-nigh infinitely complicated, gets out of order in a hundred thousand minor ways, and is always ailing more or less.

Perfect health, indeed, might almost be called a function of inferiority. Within the fold of the human race it is possible only to the lowest orders. A professionally healthy man, *e.g.*, an acrobat, an athlete or an ice-wagon driver, is invariably an ass. In the Greece of the great days the athletes we hear so much about were very few in number, and most of them were imported barbarians. Not one of the eminent philosophers, poets or statesmen of Greece was a good high-jumper. Nearly all of them, in fact, had flabby muscles and bad stomachs, as you will quickly discern by examining their writings. The aesthetic impulse, like the thirst for truth, might almost be called a disease. It never appears in a perfectly healthy man.

2

On Honesty

From the Baltimore *Evening Sun*, March 5, 1923

The most dangerous of citizens to a democracy is the man who is honest—I do not mean honest, of course, in the mere policeman's sense, but in the intellectual sense. The Emersonian counsel, "Be true to your nature, and follow its teachings," is inevitably offensive to democrats; to put it into practice is to sin against the Holy Ghost. The history of the American Republic is simply a history of successive efforts to force successive minorities to be *un*true to their nature, and not only to their nature, but also to all ordinary honor and self-respect. Whenever success has rewarded such an effort it has been depicted as a triumph for the good, the true and the beautiful.

3
On *Truth*

From DAMN! A BOOK OF CALUMNY, 1918, p. 53

The final test of truth is ridicule. Very few dogmas have ever faced it and survived. Huxley laughed the devils out of the Gadarene swine. Not the laws of the United States but the mother-in-law joke brought the Mormons to surrender. Not the horror of it but the absurdity of it killed the doctrine of infant damnation. But the razor edge of ridicule is turned by the tough hide of truth. How loudly the barber-surgeons laughed at Harvey—and how vainly! What clown ever brought down the house like Galileo? Or Columbus? Or Darwin? ... They are laughing at Nietzsche yet. . . .

Behind the Mask

A hitherto unpublished note

Perhaps the most enviable form of command is that of a young city editor of a daily newspaper of some size, with a staff large enough to make him a real commander, not simply *primus inter pares.* The emergencies and exigencies of the place give him a kind of authority that is almost military, yet he does not exercise it over obvious inferiors, but over men who were but lately his colleagues and in many cases his seniors. I well remember how I was thrilled when I was made city editor of the old Baltimore *Morning Herald* in 1903. All save a few of the reporters put under me were as old as I was, and a few were old enough to be my father. This, of course, was very caressing to my ego, but it also filled me with concern, for I well knew that any error I made would be detected instantly. When all save one or two of the men began following me loyally I began to feel that I was genuinely somebody in that small world, though I knew very well that the dog-like obedience that is in most men was responsible more than professional respect in many cases.

A young city editor enjoys the great advantage of keeping nearly all his subordinates directly under his eye. He can thus judge them accurately, and is sensitive to their every reaction to his orders. The democracy common in newspaper offices helps here, for they are not slow to show it when they disapprove his orders. Thus he is doubly rewarded when they obey willingly, and especially when they show that they think he is right. By the time I became a magazine editor, a couple of years later, the satisfactions of command had begun to wear thin, and I was chiefly conscious of my responsibility. Moreover, a managing editor is in less intimate contact with his men, and some of them he hardly knows at all, for most of his orders are transmitted through lesser editors. By this time my taste for dignity and authority had pretty well vanished, and I had already begun, in fact, to esteem all such things very lightly, and was eager to avoid them in future. This feeling, I suppose, was at least partly responsible for my resolve to see authors as little as possible. I greatly disliked listening to their plans, and hearing their difficulties. I had too much business of my own in hand to be really interested in them. Also, I soon learned by experience that very few of them were persons of any charm, or worth knowing otherwise. Indeed, the only professional author I ever became genuinely intimate with was Joseph Hergesheimer, and I, in turn, was his only close friend. More than once, he told me sadly that he found other authors bores, and many of them downright obnoxious. Hergesheimer had many other friends, and so did I, but we avoided men of our own craft.

I sometimes wonder what satisfaction there can be for a man of mature age and experience, say a colonel in the Army, in commanding such youngsters as those who predominate in American wars, which have all been fought by boys. He can certainly have but little professional respect for them, for they can know, at best, much less than he has already forgotten, and even when they follow him gallantly and effectively their loyalty is always suggestive of that of schoolboys to their teacher. The same thing, of course, is true of the relations between a city editor and the recruits to his staff. As for me, I took but little interest in them, though I tried my

best to guide them: my preference was always for the older jour-
neymen, for they understood better what I had to say, and carried
out my orders with much greater competence, even when they
were third-raters. Perhaps a professional military officer is unaware
of this difference, for he is at best a rather elemental sort of man,
and closely resembles a pedagogue in many of his characters. His
subordinates, for one thing, cannot answer back: they are required
to obey his orders instantly, however unwise, and their dissent, if
any, must be indicated very discreetly. The effect of all this on the
man himself must be generally deleterious. An aging military big-
wig, in fact, usually deteriorates into a pedant and a bully. Unless,
like Sherman, he is a man of extraordinary intelligence, he must
inevitably mistake his official consequence and authority for real
superiority, forgetting that it may be only a product of the statisti-
cal fact that *some*one has to command.

The Popinjay

From MINORITY REPORT, 1956, p. 249.
First published in the *Smart Set*, Sept., 1922, p. 44

The vanity of man is quite illimitable. In every act of his life,
however trivial, and particularly in every act which pertains to his
profession, he takes all the pride of a baby learning to walk. It may
seem incredible but it is nevertheless a fact that I myself get great
delight out of writing such banal paragraphs as this one. The physical business of writing is extremely unpleasant to me, as it is to
most other human beings, but the psychic satisfaction of discharg-
ing bad ideas in worse English is enough to make me forget it entirely. I am almost as happy, writing, as a judge is on his bench,
listening with one ear to the obscene wrangles of two scoundrelly
attorneys, or a bishop in his *cathedra*, proving nonsensically that
God loves the assembled idiots.

Note for an Honest Autobiography

From the Baltimore *Evening Sun*, June 12, 1922

On blue, hyperacid days the suspicion often seizes me that most of my favorite notions are nonsensical—worse, that some of them are probably downright insane. It is a sad pleasure to examine them thus at leisure, and pick out the flaws in them. What is left is little save a pile of platitudes—the apple-cores of meditation. Well, who is better off? I know of no one, though neither do I know of anyone who admits it. A few propositions, perhaps, are immutably true, *e.g.*, that no man can hold his head under water half an hour and live, that the average Congressman is a moron, that Jonah swallowed the whale. The rest is mere illusion, folly, egomania.

Nevertheless, it comforts me to think that, in one respect at least, I am superior to my chief opponents. That is in the respect that, in the main, my ideas are unpopular, and hence not profitable. No one can reasonably allege that I emit them in order to gain political office, or to get an honorary degree from the Ohio Wesleyan University, or to acquire the *Légion d'honneur*. This may seem a small thing, but it is at least something, especially in an American. Practically all the other men that I know try to capitalize their doctrines in some way or other. Who ever heard of an up-lifter who was not looking for a job? Or, at all events, some one to finance his crusade? No one finances mine, such as it is. No one ever will.

For the Defense

Written for the Associated Press, for use in my obituary, Nov. 20, 1940

Having lived all my life in a country swarming with messiahs, I have been mistaken, perhaps quite naturally, for one myself, especially by the others. It would be hard to imagine anything more preposterous. I am, in fact, the complete anti-Messiah, and detest converts almost as much as I detest missionaries. My writings, such as they are, have had only one purpose: to attain for H. L. Mencken that feeling of tension relieved and function achieved which a cow enjoys on giving milk. Further than that, I have had no interest in the matter whatsoever. It has never given me any satisfaction to encounter one who said my notions had pleased him. My preference has always been for people with notions of their own. I have believed all my life in free thought and free speech—up to and including the utmost limits of the endurable.

Coda

From the Baltimore *Evening Sun*, June 12, 1922

When I mount the scaffold at last these will be my farewell words to the sheriff: Say what you will against me when I am gone, but don't forget to add, in common justice, that I was never converted to anything.

A NOTE ABOUT THE AUTHOR

Henry Louis Mencken was born in Baltimore, Maryland, in 1880 and died there in 1956. A son of August and Anna (Abhau) Mencken, he was educated privately and at Baltimore Polytechnic. In 1930 he married Sara Powell Haardt, who died in 1935.

Mencken began his long career as journalist, critic and philologist as a reporter for the Baltimore *Morning Herald* in 1899. In 1906 he joined the staff of the Baltimore *Sun*, thus initiating an association with the *Sunpapers* that would last until a few years before his death. He was coeditor of the *Smart Set* with George Jean Nathan from 1914 to 1923, and with Nathan he founded the *American Mercury*, of which he was sole editor from 1925 to 1933.

Terry Teachout is arts columnist for the New York *Daily News*. He is the author of *City Limits: Memories of a Small-Town Boy*, and the editor of *Beyond the Boom: New Voices on American Life, Culture and Politics* and *Ghosts on the Roof: Selected Journalism of Whittaker Chambers, 1931–1959*. An associate editor of *The New Dance Review*, Teachout also writes about literature and music for *The American Scholar, Commentary, National Review, The New Criterion, The New York Times Book Review, Washington Post Book World*, and other journals. He was a senior editor of *Harper's* magazine from 1985 to 1987 and an editorial writer for the New York *Daily News* from 1987 to 1993. He is currently writing *H. L. Mencken: A Life*.

A NOTE ON THE TYPE

The text of this book was set in Electra, a type face designed by W(il-liam) A(ddison) Dwiggins (1880–1956) for the Mergenthaler Linotype Company and first made available in 1935. Electra cannot be classified as either "modern" or "old style." It is not based on any historical model, and hence does not echo any particular period or style of type design. It avoids the extreme contrast between thick and thin elements that marks most modern faces, and it is without eccentricities that catch the eye and interfere with reading. In general, Electra is a sim-ple, readable type face that attempts to give a feeling of fluidity, power, and speed.

W. A. Dwiggins began an association with the Mergenthaler Lino-type Company in 1929 and over the next 27 years designed a number of book types, including Metro, Electra, Caledonia, Eldorado, and Falcon.

Composed by Creative Graphics, Allentown, Pennsylvania
Printed and bound by R. R. Donnelley & Sons, Harrisonburg, Virginia